Ecological Hermeneutics

Ecological Hermeneutics

Biblical, Historical and Theological Perspectives

Edited by

David G. Horrell
Cherryl Hunt
Christopher Southgate
and
Francesca Stavrakopoulou

t&t clark

Published by T&T Clark International,
A Continuum Imprint,
The Tower Building, 11 York Road, London SE1 7NX
80 Maiden Lane, Suite 704, New York, NY 10038

www.continuumbooks.com

All rights reserved. No part of this publication may be reproduced or transmitted in any form or by any means, electronic or mechanical, including photocopying, recording or any information storage or retrieval system, without permission in writing from the publishers.

Copyright © David G. Horrell, Cherryl Hunt, Christopher Southgate, Francesca Stavrakopoulou and contributors, 2010

David G. Horrell, Cherryl Hunt, Christopher Southgate, Francesca Stavrakopoulou and contributors have asserted their right under the Copyright, Designs and Patents Act, 1988, to be identified as the Author of this work.

British Library Cataloguing-in-Publication Data
A catalogue record for this book is available from the British Library

ISBN: 978-0-567-03303-1 (Hardback)
       978-0-567-03304-8 (Paperback)

Typeset by Pindar NZ, Auckland, New Zealand
Printed and bound in Great Britain by CPI Antony Rowe Ltd, Chippenham, Wiltshire

Contents

Preface	vii
Contributors	ix
Abbreviations	xi
Introduction – *David G. Horrell*	1
PART I: BIBLICAL PERSPECTIVES	13
Introduction to Part I – *Francesca Stavrakopoulou*	15
Chapter 1. THE CREATION STORIES: THEIR ECOLOGICAL POTENTIAL AND PROBLEMS – *John W. Rogerson*	21
Chapter 2. SACRIFICE IN LEVITICUS: ECO-FRIENDLY RITUAL OR UNHOLY WASTE? – *Jonathan Morgan*	32
Chapter 3. READING THE PROPHETS FROM AN ENVIRONMENTAL PERSPECTIVE – *John Barton*	46
Chapter 4. THE SIGNIFICANCE OF THE WISDOM TRADITION IN THE ECOLOGICAL DEBATE – *Katharine J. Dell*	56
Chapter 5. READING THE SYNOPTIC GOSPELS ECOLOGICALLY – *Richard Bauckham*	70
Chapter 6. AN ECOLOGICAL READING OF ROM. 8.19-22: POSSIBILITIES AND HESITATIONS – *Brendan Byrne, SJ*	83
Chapter 7. HELLENISTIC COSMOLOGY AND THE LETTER TO THE COLOSSIANS: TOWARDS AN ECOLOGICAL HERMENEUTIC – *Vicky S. Balabanski*	94
Chapter 8. RETRIEVING THE EARTH FROM THE CONFLAGRATION: 2 PETER 3.5-13 AND THE ENVIRONMENT – *Edward Adams*	108
PART II: INSIGHTS FROM THE HISTORY OF INTERPRETATION	121
Introduction to Part II – *Cherryl Hunt*	123

Chapter 9. IN THE BEGINNING: IRENAEUS, CREATION AND THE
    ENVIRONMENT – *Francis Watson*   127

Chapter 10. POWER AND DOMINION: PATRISTIC INTERPRETATIONS
    OF GENESIS 1 – *Morwenna Ludlow*   140

Chapter 11. THOMAS AQUINAS: READING THE IDEA OF DOMINION
    IN THE LIGHT OF THE DOCTRINE OF CREATION – *Mark Wynn*   154

Chapter 12. MARTIN LUTHER, THE WORD OF GOD AND NATURE:
    REFORMATION HERMENEUTICS IN CONTEXT – *H. Paul Santmire*   166

Chapter 13. 'REMAINING LOYAL TO THE EARTH': HUMANITY, GOD'S
    OTHER CREATURES AND THE BIBLE IN KARL BARTH
    – *Geoff Thompson*   181

Chapter 14. HANS URS VON BALTHASAR: BEGINNING WITH BEAUTY
    – *David Moss*   196

Chapter 15. BETWEEN CREATION AND TRANSFIGURATION: THE
    ENVIRONMENT IN THE EASTERN ORTHODOX TRADITION
    – *Andrew Louth*   211

Chapter 16. JÜRGEN MOLTMANN'S ECOLOGICAL HERMENEUTICS
    – *Jeremy Law*   223

PART III: CONTEMPORARY HERMENEUTICAL POSSIBILITIES   241

Introduction to Part III – *Christopher Southgate*   243

Chapter 17. GREEN MILLENNIALISM: AMERICAN EVANGELICALS,
    ENVIRONMENTALISM AND THE BOOK OF REVELATION
    – *Harry O. Maier*   246

Chapter 18. NEW TESTAMENT ESCHATOLOGY AND THE ECOLOGICAL
    CRISIS IN THEOLOGICAL AND ECCLESIAL PERSPECTIVE
    – *Stephen C. Barton*   266

Chapter 19. KEEPING THE COMMANDMENTS: THE MEANING OF
    SUSTAINABLE COUNTRYSIDE – *Tim Gorringe*   283

Chapter 20. WHAT ON EARTH IS AN ECOLOGICAL HERMENEUTICS?
    SOME BROAD PARAMETERS – *Ernst M. Conradie*   295

Index of Biblical References   315

Index of Names   323

Index of Subjects   329

Preface

This collection of essays is among the outputs from a collaborative research project at the University of Exeter, UK, on 'Uses of the Bible in Environmental Ethics' (for details and other publications, see http://www.huss.ex.ac.uk/theology/research/projects/uses). The project was funded by the Arts and Humanities Research Council of the UK (AHRC), and we would like to thank the Council most warmly for their generous support (Grant No. AH D001188/1). The project has sought to foster collaboration and interaction between biblical scholars and theologians, and the attempt to cross the boundaries of (sub)disciplinary specialisms is evident in the structure and contents of this volume. With the AHRC's support, we have been able to invite a number of speakers to address our research seminar over the past three years. Conscious of the need to minimize the carbon footprint of the project, especially given its subject, we invited to the seminar only scholars based in or otherwise visiting the UK. We did however invite two international scholars, Ernst Conradie and Harry Maier, to spend a month with us in Exeter as visiting professors; this seemed a more justifiable reason for long-distance air travel. We derived great benefit from these two visits, and express our sincere thanks to Ernst and Harry for their willingness to come and discuss our work over an extended period. These various speakers and visitors presented papers which, following revision in the light of discussion, are included here. Others, too, kindly agreed to write for the volume. In many cases, and quite deliberately, we invited contributors known for their expertise in some area of biblical studies or theology, but who have not previously worked in the area of ecotheology or ecological hermeneutics. In our view, this has helped to generate much fresh and stimulating thinking. We would like to express our thanks to all the contributors for their willingness to accept our invitation and to reflect on the kinds of issues central to the volume.

We also thank the members of the project's advisory group, most of whom are also among the contributors to the volume, for their very valuable support and advice through the course of the project: Edward Adams, John Barton, Stephen Barton, Esther Reed and John Rogerson. We are grateful to the two doctoral students who have worked under the auspices of the project, Dominic Coad and Jonathan Morgan, for their contribution to our work, and for many stimulating and helpful conversations. We would also like to record our thanks to our colleagues in the Department of Theology and Religion at Exeter, particularly those who kindly agreed to contribute to the volume. Much of the labour of checking and standardizing the essays has been undertaken by Cherryl Hunt, and the other editors would like to express their appreciation for her cheerful efficiency and hard work.

It may be pertinent to note here that the focus of this volume is the Christian Bible and its historical and theological interpretation in various Christian churches and traditions. We have not attempted to consider, for example, how Jewish interpreters, past and present, have reflected on some of the same texts, nor have we engaged other religious traditions and their possible responses to the contemporary ecological crisis. Even our coverage of the diverse Christian traditions is necessarily limited and illustrative only.

After a general introductory essay, the book is divided into three parts, each of which is introduced by one of the editors. The boundaries between the parts, especially between Parts II and III, are, however, somewhat blurry. Since each chapter is intended as a self-contained contribution we decided that it would be most helpful to readers to have a list of references at the end of each chapter, rather than a final compiled bibliography. Our chosen title, ecological hermeneutics, does not represent an established or widely recognized label or method, except in the work of the Earth Bible project and the Society of Biblical Literature Consultation led by members of that project (on which see the Introduction). Nor have we sought in any way to invite adherence to any particular method on the part of our contributors. The phrase does, however, seem most apposite to encapsulate the nature of the task in which the contributors to this volume are collectively engaged. Our hope is that the various essays will prove individually stimulating and, more importantly, that the collection as a whole will not only provide a rich resource for those with an interest in this field but also foster future work which will draw further connections between biblical studies, the history of interpretation and contemporary theological and ethical reflection in this vital area of global concern.

The Editors
Exeter, September 2009.

Each year the AHRC provides funding from the government to support research and postgraduate study in the arts and humanities, from archaeology and English literature to design and dance. Only applications of the highest quality and excellence are funded and the range of research supported by this investment of public funds not only provides social and cultural benefits but also contributes to the economic success of the UK. For further information on the AHRC, please see our website www.ahrc.ac.uk

CONTRIBUTORS

1. **Edward Adams** is Senior Lecturer in New Testament Studies at King's College London, UK.
2. **Vicky S. Balabanski** is Senior Lecturer in New Testament at Adelaide College of Divinity, Flinders University of South Australia, Adelaide, Australia.
3. **John Barton** is Oriel and Laing Professor of the Interpretation of Holy Scripture at Oriel College, University of Oxford, UK.
4. **Stephen C. Barton** is Reader in New Testament in the Department of Theology and Religion, University of Durham, UK.
5. **Richard Bauckham** is Emeritus Professor of New Testament Studies at the University of St Andrews, Scotland, and Senior Scholar at Ridley Hall, Cambridge, UK.
6. **Brendan Byrne, SJ** is Professor of New Testament, Jesuit Theological College, Melbourne College of Divinity, Victoria, Australia.
7. **Ernst M. Conradie** is Professor in the Department of Religion and Theology, University of the Western Cape, South Africa.
8. **Katharine J. Dell** is Senior Lecturer in Old Testament at the Faculty of Divinity, University of Cambridge, and Fellow of St Catharine's College, Cambridge, UK.
9. **Tim Gorringe** is St Luke's Foundation Professor of Theological Studies, Department of Theology and Religion, University of Exeter, UK.
10. **Jeremy Law** is Dean of Chapel at Canterbury Christ Church University, Canterbury, UK.
11. **Andrew Louth** is Professor of Patristic and Byzantine Studies in the Department of Theology and Religion, University of Durham, UK.
12. **Morwenna Ludlow** is Lecturer in Patristics, Department of Theology and Religion, University of Exeter, UK.
13. **Harry O. Maier** is Professor of New Testament Studies at Vancouver School of Theology, Vancouver, Canada.
14. **Jonathan Morgan** is a PhD Student in the Department of Theology and Religion, University of Exeter, UK.
15. **David Moss** is Principal of the South West Ministry Training Course and Honorary Fellow in Theology, University of Exeter, UK.

16. **John W. Rogerson** is Professor Emeritus of Biblical Studies, University of Sheffield, UK.
17. **H. Paul Santmire** is now retired having previously taught at Wellesley College, Wellesley, Massachusetts, USA.
18. **Geoff Thompson** is Director of Studies in Systematic Theology, Trinity Theological College, Brisbane, Australia.
19. **Francis Watson** is Professor of Biblical Interpretation in the Department of Theology and Religion, University of Durham, UK.
20. **Mark Wynn** is Senior Lecturer in the Philosophy of Religion, Department of Theology and Religion, University of Exeter, UK.

Abbreviations

References to biblical books follow standard and easily recognizable abbreviations. References in individual essays to other primary sources, and specific abbreviations thereof, are explained in the relevant list of references or in the essay itself. The following bibliographical abbreviations are used throughout the volume.

AB	Anchor Bible
ANRW	*Aufstieg und Niedergang der römischen Welt*, H. Temporini and W. Haase (eds), (Berlin and New York: De Gruyter, 1972–)
ANTC	Abingdon New Testament Commentaries
AOTC	Abingdon Old Testament Commentaries
BBR	*Bulletin for Biblical Research*
BDAG	*A Greek-English Lexicon of the New Testament and Other Early Christian Literature*, W. Bauer, F.W. Danker et al., (3rd edn, Chicago and London: University of Chicago Press, 2000).
BHT	Beiträge zur historischen Theologie
BJRL	*Bulletin of the John Rylands University Library of Manchester*
BNTC	Black's New Testament Commentaries
CBQ	*Catholic Biblical Quarterly*
CRINT	Compendia rerum iudaicarum ad Novum Testamentum
EDNT	*Exegetical Dictionary of the New Testament*, H. Balz and G. Schneider (eds), (Edinburgh: T&T Clark, 1990–1993)
ESV	English Standard Version
ICC	International Critical Commentary
ITC	International Theological Commentary
JBL	*Journal of Biblical Literature*
JECS	*Journal of Early Christian Studies*
JETS	*Journal of the Evangelical Theological Society*
JSJSup	Journal for the Study of Judaism Supplement Series

JSOT	*Journal for the Study of the Old Testament*
JSOTSup	Journal for the Study of the Old Testament Supplement Series
JSSR	*Journal for the Scientific Study of Religion*
JTS	*Journal of Theological Studies*
KJV	King James Version
LNTS	Library of New Testament Studies
NIGTC	New International Greek Testament Commentary
NRSV	New Revised Standard Version
NTS	*New Testament Studies*
OTG	Old Testament Guides
PG	*Patrologia Graeca*, J.-P. Migne (ed.), (Paris: Migne/Turnhout: Brepols).
PSCF	*Perspectives on Science and Christian Faith*
RRR	*Review of Religious Research*
SBL	Society of Biblical Literature
SBLSS	Society of Biblical Literature Symposium Series
SCE	*Studies in Christian Ethics*
SJT	*Scottish Journal of Theology*
SNTW	Studies of the New Testament and Its World
SP	Sacra Pagina
WBC	Word Biblical Commentary
WMANT	Wissenschaftliche Monographien zum Alten und Neuen Testament
WUNT	Wissenschaftliche Untersuchungen zum Neuen Testament
ZAW	*Zeitschrift für die alttestamentliche Wissenschaft*

Introduction

David G. Horrell

Environmental concerns are now widely recognized as among the most pressing issues facing the global community. The modern environmental movement has of course been active for some decades, spurred on by the early and provocative stimulus of Rachel Carson's 1962 classic *Silent Spring* – which detailed the impact of chemical pesticides in particular – and sustained by pressure groups such as Greenpeace and Friends of the Earth, both formed in 1971. But it is in recent years, and especially with the increasingly clear scientific consensus about the reality and wide-ranging impacts of anthropogenic global warming, that the environment has emerged as a central issue for international political concern. The level of public and political concern is reason enough to make the environment, or ecology,[1] a topic for reflection by theologians, ethicists and biblical scholars, whose agendas are to some extent set by contemporary issues and priorities. Indeed, given the status of the Christian Bible as holy scripture for members of the Christian churches, it is an established and obvious strategy, as part of theological and ethical reflection, to consider what the Bible might have to 'say' on a given topic, whether that consideration is done with a certain naivety (as if answers could simply be found by reading out the right verses) or with more hermeneutical and critical sophistication. This applies both to issues which are explicitly within the purview of the biblical writers, such as divorce, and also to issues which are clearly beyond their experience, such as nuclear weapons or genetic engineering.

There have also been more specific provocations to consider the ecological implications, positive or negative, of the biblical material. In a now famous article, published in 1967, the medieval historian Lynn White Jr argued that the (Western) Christian worldview, rooted in the creation stories and the notion of humanity made in God's image, introduced a dualism between humanity and nature, and established the notion that it was God's will that humanity exploit nature to serve human interests; this Christian worldview thus legitimated and encouraged humanity's aggressive

---

1 Ecology is a preferable term in many ways, since it suggests the sense that we are talking about the communities of living things in which we find our home (*oikos*), rather than about things which happen to surround us (our *environs*).

project to dominate and exploit nature (1967). From this perspective, White suggests, everything that exists in the natural world was 'planned' by God 'explicitly for man's benefit and rule; no item in the physical creation had any purpose save to serve man's purposes'. Humanity is seen as uniquely made in the image of God, and as having been given 'dominion' over all the creatures of the earth (Gen. 1.26-30). Sweeping aside other ancient mythologies, with their cyclical views of time and their animistic sacralization of nature, Christianity thus 'not only established a dualism of man and nature but also insisted that it is God's will that man exploit nature for his proper ends'. 'Man's effective monopoly . . . was confirmed and the old inhibitions to the exploitation of nature crumbled.' Thus, 'Christianity made it possible to exploit nature in a mood of indifference to the feelings of natural objects' (White 1967: 1205). White concludes that the active conquest of nature that characterizes the modern technological project and has led to the 'ecologic crisis' has in large part been made possible by the dominance in the West of this Christian worldview. Christianity therefore 'bears a huge burden of guilt' (1206).

Interestingly, as James Barr (1972) points out, White's argument is essentially a critical version of the earlier view that effectively credited the Judeo-Christian tradition with fostering and enabling the emergence of modern science – depicted as a positive achievement. For White, writing from an ecological perspective, the scientific and technological ideologies that emerged as the Christian worldview came to prominence have had a disastrous impact on the ways in which the relationship between humanity and 'nature' is conceived. White does not however call for the abandonment of the Christian tradition, but rather for its renewal and reorientation, appealing to St Francis as a potential 'patron saint for ecologists' (1207). Nonetheless, his provocative argument suggested that the biblical texts and their interpretation in the Western Christian tradition had had an essentially negative impact on humanity's interaction with the non-human creation.

Despite many telling criticisms of 'the Lynn White thesis', not least from biblical scholars who contest his (implicit) interpretation of the crucial text in Gen. 1.26-28 (e.g. Barr 1972), White's essay remains probably the most cited contribution to eco-theological debate.[2] Indeed, many of the writers in the present volume take White's article as something of a point of reference in the debate, even if they swiftly move beyond his particular perspective and analysis.

While White's critique has led to a focus on the meaning and impact of the Bible's creation stories, especially the mandate given to humanity to subdue and have dominion over the earth (Gen. 1.26-28), questions have also been raised about the impact of biblical eschatology. A number of biblical texts present images of cosmic destruction, depicting what will happen on 'the day of the Lord', the coming day of God's judgement and salvation (e.g. Joel 1.15; Amos 5.18-20; 1 Thess. 5.2).[3]

---

2   Cf. Baranzke and Lamberty-Zielinski 1995: 56. Blenkinsopp's comments on White are thus overly dismissive (Blenkinsopp 2004: 37–38).
3   For a comprehensive survey of such material, see Adams 2007.

Some texts suggest that catastrophes on the earth must precede this final day of salvation (e.g. Mk 13.8, 24-25); others depict Christians being 'caught up' to meet the returning Lord in the air (1 Thess. 4.16-17). Such texts, along with the enigmatic apocalyptic scenarios depicted in the book of Revelation, have, of course, shaped the development of contemporary Christian eschatologies. The critical question is whether such eschatological views foster a view of the earth as merely a temporary and soon-to-be destroyed habitation, from which the elect will be rescued (cf. Dyer 2002, esp. 45–49). The implication would be that preserving the earth is hardly a priority and may even represent opposition to the progress of God's eschatological purposes. Indeed, some writers have argued that such views make evangelical Christians disinclined to care for the earth. David Orr, for example, suggests that 'belief in the imminence of the end times tends to make evangelicals careless stewards of our forests, soils, wildlife, air, water, seas and climate' (Orr 2005: 291). Just as White's seminal article raised critical questions about the impact of the biblical creation stories, so the arguments of Orr and others raise critical questions about the impact of biblical eschatology on Christian attitudes towards the environment, particularly among some US fundamentalist and evangelical groups (see Harry Maier's essay).

Ecological Engagement with the Bible

Such critical arguments have clearly posed a challenge to theologians and biblical scholars concerned to draw on the Bible to foster a positive Christian response to the challenge of environmental care.[4] Unsurprisingly, considerable energy has gone into attempts to demonstrate that the Bible does not promote such a negative attitude to the non-human creation as writers such as White have implied. Positively, attempts have been made to show how an ecologically valuable message can be derived from scripture, rightly interpreted. Often, especially in the case of evangelical environmental writers, these efforts have been consciously directed against those who, either explicitly or implicitly, hold views antithetical to the environmental agenda on biblical grounds. For example, there have been fundamentalists who have opposed the environmental cause, regarding it as part of a satanic 'new age' deception, or as encouraging nature-worship. Some evangelicals have insisted that the Bible calls Christians to evangelism to save individuals from the coming judgement, not to action to sustain the material earth, while others argue that the biblical view does indeed give humanity a rightful dominion over the earth, and a God-given vocation to transform nature from wilderness to garden, in order for it best to serve human needs (Beisner 1997; see further Maier's essay).

Some treatments of the problematic 'dominion' text (Gen. 1.26-28), for example,

---

4   For a critical survey of such engagements with the Bible, see Horrell *et al.* 2008; 2010: chs 1–2.

have been primarily concerned to defend Genesis 1 by placing it in its ancient historical context (see further John Rogerson's essay). Norbert Lohfink argues that the 'blessing' of Gen. 1.28 refers to the divine plan for each nation to 'take possession of their own regions', and for humans to domesticate animals in a way which establishes a form of peaceful co-existence. Since the text has this kind of expansion of human civilization and domestication of animals in view, it is inappropriate in Lohfink's view to use it 'to legitimate what humanity has inaugurated in modern times . . . The Jewish-Christian doctrine of humanity . . . regards human beings very highly, but it would never designate them as absolute rulers of the universe' (Lohfink 1994: 8, 12–13, 17). Similar points have been made by Barr (1972), Bernhard Anderson (1984) and others.

A particularly significant and influential approach, which attempts to recover from biblical texts such as Gen. 1.28 a message of positive value to the ecological agenda, reinterprets the notion of human dominion as a model of *stewardship*. This approach picks up the use of kingly language in Gen. 1.26-28, and also the notion of tending the garden in Gen. 2.15, and interprets these within the broader treatment of kingship in the Hebrew Bible. Kingly rule, it is argued, was not about domination and exploitation, at least in terms of the biblical 'ideal'. The language of dominion can thus be read as giving a responsibility to humanity, to care for and tend the earth (see e.g. De Vos *et al.* 1980; Granberg-Michaelson 1987; Hall 1990 [1982]). Indeed, a focus on stewardship as a biblical image of humanity's role in creation is central to the realignment of major evangelical leaders and bodies behind a more environmentally conscious vision of Christian responsibility (e.g. The Evangelical Climate Initiative 2006).[5]

A similar tendency can be seen in relation to the equally difficult eschatological texts. A good deal of energy has gone into the attempt to demonstrate that such texts, or most of them at least, do not imply the destruction of the earth but rather its transformation (e.g. Russell 1996; Moo 2006). In an essay entitled 'New Testament Teaching on the Environment', for example, Ernest Lucas confronts the apparent difficulties of what is widely regarded as the most 'difficult' eschatological text in relation to environmental issues: 2 Peter 3 (see Edward Adams' essay). First, Lucas notes that the most likely reading of 3.10 is not that the earth will be 'burned up', as some manuscripts and English translations have it, but that it will be 'found', or exposed for judgement (cf. NRSV, ESV; Lucas 1999: 97). Secondly, he argues that the 'elements' (Gk *stoicheia*) in 3.10 refers not to the physical universe, but to spiritual powers or heavenly beings. More generally, he argues that the author is likely using 'figurative' language about cosmic events: 'Hence we should be wary of reading it as a literal account of the end of the physical cosmos'. The primary focus is on God's judgement, for which the metaphor of fire is used in the Old Testament (97). And since the author uses the Greek word *kainos* (new in quality) rather than *neos*

---

5   Available at http://christiansandclimate.org/learn/call-to-action/ (accessed 23 Sept 2009).

(new in the sense of previously non-existent), Lucas argues that 'although 2 Peter 3 is speaking of a radical transformation of the heaven and the earth, it is a renewal through transformation, not a total destruction of the old and its replacement by something quite different'. Thus, Lucas argues, '[i]t is certainly not a basis for arguing against Christian concern for, and involvement in, ecological issues' (97). Similar defences of 2 Peter 3 have been mounted by Thomas Finger (1998: 3–6) and Steven Bouma-Prediger (2001: 76–78).

In a discussion of Revelation 21–22, another famous and influential depiction of the apparent replacement of the 'old' heaven and earth with a 'new' creation, Bouma-Prediger argues that a positive ecological vision emerges (2001: 114–16). The 'new heaven and new earth' does not, he argues, imply the destruction of the old cosmos and the emergence of a new one, but rather 'connotes new in quality' (114). Furthermore, the separation between heaven and earth is overcome and evil and its consequences are no more. The holy city is an eloquent vision of 'the all-embracing scope of God's redemptive work' (115, quoting George Caird). So, Bouma-Prediger proposes, this is 'an earthly vision of life made good and whole and right, because of God's grace. Heaven and earth are renewed and are one. God dwells with us, at home in creation . . . In short, a world of shalom' (115–16).

As well as attempting to rescue the 'difficult' texts from the charge that they legitimate the unsustainable exploitation of the earth, such engagements with the Bible also draw attention to the ecological potential of texts that have often been neglected, or whose ecological relevance has generally been missed. Texts coming under consideration here include Gen. 9.9-17, with its references to the covenant with all the earth; various Psalms (e.g. chs 104, 148), with their references to the whole creation as displaying God's greatness and as joining in praise of its creator; the latter chapters of Job (38–41), with their apparent 'decentring' of humanity (see esp. McKibben 1994; Patrick 2001); and, in the New Testament, the Pauline texts which depict the whole creation as caught up in the redeeming and reconciling work of God in Christ (esp. Rom. 8.19-23; Col. 1.15-20).[6]

This kind of approach to the Bible, attempting to show how it contains a positive message of environmental care, is epitomized in the recently published *Green Bible* (2008). By highlighting in green texts that are deemed relevant to concerns about the earth, the editors of this new edition of the NRSV intend to reveal the 'clear' message of the Bible concerning care for creation. As the preface puts it:

> Our role in creation's care may be a new question unique to our place in history, but the Bible turns out to be amazingly relevant. In fact, it is almost as if it were waiting for this moment to speak to us. With over a thousand references to the earth and caring for creation in the Bible, the message is clear: all in God's creation – nature, animals, humanity – are inextricably linked

---

6   See, e.g. Bouma-Prediger 2001. For a critical survey of interpretations from ecological perspectives of these texts and others, see Horrell 2010b.

to one another. As God cares for all of creation, so we cannot love one dimension without caring for the others. We are called to care for all God has made.[7] (I–15)

In relation to 'difficult' texts like Gen. 1.26-28, the assumption of *The Green Bible* is clearly that this text does not legitimate aggressive human domination of the earth (*contra* White), but instead teaches a human responsibility to care for the earth as stewards (and hence can be highlighted in green). Indeed, the conviction that stewardship is central to the Bible's teaching about humanity's relationship to the earth runs through many of the essays in *The Green Bible*. Calvin DeWitt, for example, asserts that the Bible 'shows that dominion means responsible stewardship. God gave humans a special role and responsibility as stewards of his creation' (I–26). One of the themes picked out in the 'Trail Guide' Bible studies near the end of the volume is that we 'are meant to live . . . as stewards of creation', and the questions for reflection indicate that the image of dominion has been liable to be 'misunderstood'. Indeed, '[t]his stewardship role', we are told, 'is important enough that it is mentioned several times in the creation narrative' (1226).

Yet *The Green Bible* illustrates well some of the profound problems with such attempts to show that the Bible 'really' teaches humanity to love and care for creation (for a critique, see Horrell 2010a). For example, the notion of 'stewardship', so central to many attempts to construct a 'biblical' environmental ethic, does not appear as such in Genesis 1, nor indeed is it a major biblical theme, certainly not in relation to humanity's responsibility for creation: nowhere does the Bible *say* that humans are appointed stewards of creation. There are questions too about whether the language of Gen. 1.26-28 can so easily be softened and reclaimed, and about whether 'stewardship' is an adequate or valuable basis for an environmental ethic (see esp. Palmer 1992).[8] It may be argued that stewardship can usefully function as a key concept in an ecological interpretation of the Bible, but it should be clear, as Ernst Conradie suggests (see his essay in this volume), that this is a product of *interpretation*, not something somehow 'contained' within the Bible, waiting to be discovered. Moreover, it seems that the Bible's diverse material remains more ambivalent in relation to ecological issues and environmental responsibilities than many positive presentations of its 'green' message allow. The difficult texts cannot so easily be reclaimed (see further, e.g. the essays in this volume by Rogerson and Adams), and the positive ecological contribution of the Bible to theological and ethical discussion needs nuanced and critical interpretation.[9]

Indeed, one of the concerns at the heart of the Earth Bible project is, in the words

---

7   Pages in the introductory section of the book are prefaced with I–, distinguishing them from pages in the main section of the volume, which contains the biblical text (and additional end materials).
8   For an overview of such discussions, see Southgate 2006, and the range of materials collected in Berry 2006.
9   For further articulation of such critical points, see Horrell, Hunt and Southgate 2008: 231–38; 2010: ch. 2.

of its general editor, Norman Habel, to confront what Habel sees as the naïve use of the Bible in many works of ecotheology: 'The vast majority of these works assume that the Bible is environmentally friendly and quote biblical passages uncritically to support the contention that an ecological thrust is inherent in the text' (Habel 2000a: 30). The Earth Bible project, described briefly by one of its members, Vicky Balabanski, in her essay in this volume, and discussed also by Conradie, has been concerned to read biblical texts 'from the perspective of Earth' (cf. Habel 2000b), and to develop a critical ecojustice hermeneutic.[10] This approach, as Habel describes it, involves both suspicion and retrieval; there is critical suspicion concerning the anthropocentrism of the biblical writers (as well as their later interpreters) and a corresponding attempt to recover the voice of Earth (capitalized as a character) even where this is silenced or opposed by the explicit perspective of the text.

Fundamental to the approach taken in the five volumes of the Earth Bible series is a set of six ecojustice principles (these are listed in full in Conradie's essay, p. 307): the principle of intrinsic worth; the principle of interconnectedness; the principle of voice; the principle of purpose; the principle of mutual custodianship; and the principle of resistance (Habel 2000b: 24). These principles, deliberately formulated in non-theological and non-biblical terms (see The Earth Bible Team 2000a: 38), encapsulate the (ethical) commitments of the project team, and function as a standard against which the biblical texts are measured: the key task is to discern whether 'the text is consistent, or in conflict, with whichever of the six ecojustice principles may be considered relevant' in any particular case (The Earth Bible Team 2002: 2).[11]

More recently, the project's work has continued through a Society of Biblical Literature Consultation on Ecological Hermeneutics. In the introduction to a volume of essays based on papers presented at the seminar, Habel further outlines the hermeneutical method. Building on the earlier articulation of ecojustice principles, three key steps are outlined: suspicion (of the texts' anthropocentrism), identification (with non-human characters) and retrieval (of the perspective or voice of Earth) (Habel 2008).

The Earth Bible project has been ground-breaking and important in offering ecologically orientated readings of a variety of biblical texts, and in moving attention beyond a few 'key' texts. Also significant, not least in relation to approaches which imply that a green message can simply be found in the Bible once the right texts are highlighted, is the project's insistence that ecological interpretation of the Bible will require a critical and self-conscious hermeneutical strategy. Nonetheless, one difficulty with this approach, at least in terms of an approach to doing Christian theology, is that authority effectively lies not with the Bible or the Christian tradition,

---

10   The most important publications from the project are the five-volume Earth Bible series, and a recent volume of essays presented at the SBL Ecological Hermeneutics Consultation, led by members of the project. See Habel and Wurst (eds) 2000; 2001; Habel (ed.) 2000b; 2001; Habel and Balabanski (eds) 2002; Habel and Trudinger (eds) 2008.

11   For further discussion of these principles, see The Earth Bible Team 2000b.

but with the ecojustice principles, principles deliberately formulated in ways which are general and non-theological, not reflective of the specifically biblical and Christian tradition; it is these principles that present a set of norms and commitments to inspire and instruct human belief and action. But why, for Christians, should these principles be found *persuasive*, persuasive enough to serve as a basis for ethical commitment and critical evaluation of the Bible? The hermeneutical approach outlined in the most recent volume of essays (Habel and Trudinger 2008) invites the retrieval of perspectives and voices that may go against the content or grain of the text: many of the essays in that volume focus on voicing the perspective of Earth (as character), in some cases exercising suspicion against the chosen text and creating a new text, the product of the reader's imagination. Such reconstructions, needless to say, do not carry the same kind of potential theological significance as new interpretations of the biblical texts themselves. It is unclear how such readings might contribute to the reconfiguration *of the Christian tradition*, a reconfiguration in which constructive and critical readings of the Bible will certainly play a crucial part. Put differently, to be potentially persuasive as an attempt to reshape Christian theology and ethics, an ecological reading of the Bible will need to demonstrate that it offers an authentic rearticulation of the Christian tradition, albeit one that treads the delicate (and hotly contested) line between faithfulness and creativity.

The critical remarks here and earlier should help to indicate how, and why, much of the work undertaken by those of us involved in the Exeter project has explored ways to develop a position somewhere between the stance of 'recovery' represented in some evangelical writing and in *The Green Bible* on the one hand, and the critical ecojustice hermeneutic developed by The Earth Bible Team on the other (see esp. Horrell, Hunt and Southgate 2008, 2010). The former approach too easily gives the impression that ecological theology and ethics can simply be read from the pages of the Bible, once the text is rightly understood, and that the Bible can be defended against all the critical charges levelled against it and labelled a 'green' book with a clearly 'green' message. This kind of approach fails to do justice both to the ambivalence and difficulty of the biblical material and to the extent to which contemporary theological and ethical appropriation is necessarily a constructive endeavour, informed by the present context (including science, etc.) as well as by the traditions of Christian theology. By contrast, we have suggested that the critical ecojustice approach of the Earth Bible project, while generating much theologically pertinent material, does not sufficiently articulate how such creative and critical interpretation might contribute to the ecological reconfiguration of Christian theology – a theology in which the Bible will need to have some formative and authoritative place and which will need to be in some kind of demonstrable continuity with the Christian tradition.[12] The approach we have tried to develop, by contrast, may be broadly described as an attempt to construct an ecological theology which, while

---

12   Cf. the discussion of the Earth Bible project, its ecojustice principles and their relation to Christian doctrine in Conradie's essay in this volume and in Conradie 2004.

innovative, is nonetheless coherent (and in dialogue) with a scripturally shaped Christian orthodoxy – though that, of course, immediately raises questions about what will 'count' as orthodox, sufficiently faithful to the tradition to be authentically Christian yet sufficiently creative to reshape a tradition that has by and large been preoccupied with issues of human behaviour and salvation.

Any attempt to develop such a theological ecological hermeneutic will need to learn carefully from the history of Christian theological interpretation in order to consider the kinds of twists and turns that have been taken – for better or worse – as the biblical texts have been read through the centuries, and will need to foster engagement between biblical scholars and theologians in order to consider how the texts might fruitfully be interpreted now. It is these *desiderata* that inform the conception and structure of the present volume. We have not imposed upon, nor even suggested to, our contributors any particular hermeneutical method or theological stance; indeed some, for sure, will disagree with the particular way in which we have framed our approach to ecological hermeneutics. But the various contributions, for all their individual diversity, provide material which resources the kind of reflection we have sought to develop.

The Aims and Scope of the Volume

Two concerns are then crucial to the shaping of this collection of essays. The first is to bring biblical and theological perspectives into closer dialogue through ecologically orientated and hermeneutically informed reflection on the Bible. The second is to learn critically from the history of interpretation, recognising that earlier interpreters did not share our ecological concerns and awareness and may indeed have helped to reinforce the anthropocentrism of the theological tradition, but be ready also to find potentially fruitful interpretative perspectives in previous engagements with the biblical texts.

Part I of the book, introduced by Francesca Stavrakopoulou, contains a variety of readings of biblical texts, though these are unavoidably selective in terms of the range of texts that are included. In some cases their focus is on texts that have long been identified as pertinent to, or indeed problematic for, the themes of ecology (e.g. the essays by John Rogerson, Brendan Byrne, Vicky Balabanski and Edward Adams). In other cases they range more widely into bodies of literature whose ecological relevance has not been so fully considered (e.g. the essays by Katharine Dell, John Barton and Richard Bauckham). Jonathan Morgan's essay deals with the book of Leviticus, a text which, for a range of more and less obvious reasons, has been neglected in Christian theology generally as well as in ecological interpretation.[13] While our contributors take a range of perspectives and offer a diversity of possible interpretations, they are aware of the difficulties in finding ecologically relevant or

---

13 For this reason, this text was chosen as the focus for a doctoral thesis (being written by Morgan) within the project's overall concerns.

positive material in the Bible, and recognize that developing ecological interpretations of the texts requires some constructive and creative thought.

Part II of the book, introduced by Cherryl Hunt, deals with the history of interpretation, from Irenaeus (Francis Watson) and the early Church fathers (Morwenna Ludlow), through Thomas Aquinas (Mark Wynn), Martin Luther (Paul Santmire) to twentieth-century theologians such as Karl Barth (Geoff Thompson), Hans Urs von Balthasar (David Moss) and Jürgen Moltmann (Jeremy Law). The Orthodox tradition is considered in the essay by Andrew Louth. Here, then, it is even more inevitable that the diverse range of studies is highly selective and illustrative only in terms of what and who is covered. Despite a wide variety of approaches and concerns, our contributors are generally candid about the fact that these earlier writers did not share our ecological awareness and concerns, except in the case of the most recent and still contemporary writer to be considered, Moltmann. But this does not prevent these writers and traditions from offering significant material relevant to the task of developing an ecologically orientated theology.

The third and final part of the book, introduced by Christopher Southgate, is still more selective, as well as being briefer. What unites the essays in this section, by Harry Maier, Stephen Barton, Tim Gorringe and Ernst Conradie, is a concern to articulate in some way an approach or direction in contemporary biblical interpretation that represents some kind of ecological hermeneutic. In this respect, however, there is an overlap of concern with many of the essays in the previous section, where examinations of particular figures or traditions are undertaken not for purely historical interest but precisely because of the ways in which these might resource contemporary ecological hermeneutics. It is appropriate that the volume concludes with a programmatic and wide-ranging essay by Ernst Conradie because his methodological reflections are fundamental to the overall task and aims of the volume; his work has also been highly influential on the approach we have developed in our own project at Exeter. Conradie outlines the way in which he sees biblical interpretation functioning within the overall task of ecological hermeneutics, with 'doctrinal constructs' (such as 'stewardship') 'made' in the process of reading and interpreting, and serving 'to identify *both* the meaning of the contemporary context *and* of the biblical texts' (301).

The volume thus constitutes only an initial foray, or set of forays, into a field that will undoubtedly remain of high importance for the foreseeable future. Many more biblical texts could be engaged, and many more traditions and figures from the history of interpretation could fruitfully be examined. And, not least given the enormous amount of ecotheological literature produced in recent years,[14] there remain many possible directions for constructive theological and ethical engagement beyond those included here. Nonetheless, our hope is that this collection of essays makes a significant contribution to the field in a number of ways. First, in

---

14 For an extensive listing of bibliographical resources, see Conradie 2001.

generating hermeneutically aware and critical readings of biblical texts, readings that make constructive contributions to ecotheology without pretending that the Bible can straightforwardly or unproblematically be regarded as a 'green' text. Second, in indicating how valuable studies of the history of interpretation can be for ecotheology, even where that history is ambivalent in its impact and far removed from the specific issues of ecological concern. Third, in illustrating the potential for an ecological hermeneutics which crosses boundaries between biblical studies and theology to bring a diverse range of scholars together in making constructive attempts to address an issue of profound importance.

References

Adams, E. 2007 *The Stars Will fall From Heaven: Cosmic Catastrophe in the New Testament and Its World* (LNTS 347; London/New York: T&T Clark).

Anderson, B.W. 1984 'Creation and Ecology', in B.W. Anderson, *Creation in the Old Testament* (Philadelphia/London: Fortress/SPCK): 152–71.

Baranzke, H. and Lamberty-Zielinski, H. 1995 'Lynn White und das Dominium Terrae (Gen. 1.28b). Ein Beitrag zu einer doppelten Wirkungsgeschichte', *Biblische Notizen* 76: 32–61.

Barr, J. 1972 'Man and Nature – The Ecological Controversy and the Old Testament', *BJRL* 55: 9–32.

Beisner, E.C. 1997 *Where Garden Meets Wilderness: Evangelical Entry into the Environmental Debate* (Grand Rapids, MI: Acton Institute for the Study of Religion and Liberty/Eerdmans).

Berry, R.J. (ed.) 2006 *Environmental Stewardship: Critical Perspectives, Past and Present* (London/New York: T&T Clark).

Blenkinsopp, J. 2004 *Treasures Old and New: Essays in the Theology of the Pentateuch* (Grand Rapids, MI: Eerdmans).

Bouma-Prediger, S. 2001 *For the Beauty of the Earth: A Christian Vision for Creation Care* (Grand Rapids, MI: Baker Academic).

Conradie, E.M. 2001 *Ecological Theology: An Indexed Bibliography* (Study Guides in Religion and Theology 3; Bellville, South Africa: University of the Western Cape).

Conradie, E.M. 2004 'Towards an Ecological Biblical Hermeneutics: A Review Essay on the Earth Bible Project', *Scriptura* 85: 123–35.

De Vos, P., Wilkinson, L. and Calvin Center for Christian Scholarship 1980 *Earthkeeping: Christian Stewardship of Natural Resources* (Grand Rapids, MI: Eerdmans).

Dyer, K.D. 2002 'When is the End Not the End? The Fate of Earth in Biblical Eschatology (Mark 13)', in N.C. Habel and V. Balabanski (eds), *The Earth Story in the New Testament* (The Earth Bible, 5; London/Cleveland, OH: Sheffield Academic Press/Pilgrim Press): 44–56.

Earth Bible Team, The 2000a 'Guiding Ecojustice Principles', in N.C. Habel (ed.), *Readings from the Perspective of Earth* (The Earth Bible, 1; Sheffield/Cleveland, OH: Sheffield Academic Press/Pilgrim Press): 38–53.

Earth Bible Team, The 2000b 'Conversations with Gene Tucker and Other Writers', in N.C. Habel and S. Wurst (eds), *The Earth Story in Genesis* (The Earth Bible, 2; Sheffield/Cleveland, OH: Sheffield Academic Press/Pilgrim Press): 21–33.

Earth Bible Team, The 2002 'Ecojustice Hermeneutics: Reflections and Challenges', in N.C. Habel and V. Balabanski (eds), *The Earth Story in the New Testament* (The Earth Bible, 5; London/Cleveland, OH: Sheffield Academic Press/Pilgrim Press): 1–14.

Finger, T. 1998 *Evangelicals, Eschatology, and the Environment* (The Scholars Circle; Wynnewood, PA: Evangelical Environmental Network).

Granberg-Michaelson, W. (ed.) 1987 *Tending the Garden* (Grand Rapids, MI: Eerdmans).

The Green Bible. New York/London: HarperCollins, 2008.
Habel, N.C. 2000a 'Introducing the Earth Bible', in N.C. Habel (ed.), *Readings from the Perspective of Earth* (The Earth Bible, 1; Sheffield/Cleveland, OH: Sheffield Academic Press/Pilgrim Press): 25–37.
Habel, N.C. (ed.) 2000b *Readings from the Perspective of Earth* (The Earth Bible, 1; Sheffield/Cleveland, OH: Sheffield Academic Press/Pilgrim Press).
Habel, N.C. (ed.) 2001 *The Earth Story in Psalms and Prophets* (The Earth Bible, 4; Sheffield/Cleveland, OH: Sheffield Academic Press/Pilgrim Press).
Habel, N.C. 2008 'Introduction', in N.C. Habel and P. Trudinger (eds), *Exploring Ecological Hermeneutics* (SBLSS 46; Atlanta: SBL): 1–8.
Habel, N.C. and Balabanski, V. (eds) 2002 *The Earth Story in the New Testament* (The Earth Bible, 5; Sheffield/Cleveland, OH: Sheffield Academic Press/Pilgrim Press).
Habel, N.C. and Trudinger, P. (eds) 2008 *Exploring Ecological Hermeneutics* (SBLSS 46; Atlanta: Society of Biblical Literature).
Habel, N.C. and Wurst, S. (eds) 2000 *The Earth Story in Genesis* (The Earth Bible, 2; Sheffield/Cleveland, OH: Sheffield Academic Press/Pilgrim Press).
Habel, N.C. and Wurst, S. (eds) 2001 *The Earth Story in Wisdom Traditions* (The Earth Bible, 3; Sheffield/Cleveland, OH: Sheffield Academic Press/Pilgrim Press).
Hall, D.J. 1990 [1982] *The Steward: A Biblical Symbol Come of Age* (revised edn; Grand Rapids, MI/New York: Eerdmans/Friendship Press).
Horrell, D.G. 2010a 'The Green Bible: A Timely Idea Deeply Flawed', *Expository Times* 121: 180–86.
Horrell, D.G. 2010b *The Bible and the Environment: Towards a Critical Ecological Biblical Theology* (Biblical Challenges in the Contemporary World; London/Oakville, CT: Equinox).
Horrell, D.G., Hunt, C. and Southgate, C. 2008 'Appeals to the Bible in Ecotheology and Environmental Ethics: A Typology of Hermeneutical Stances', *SCE* 21: 219–38.
Horrell, D.G., Hunt, C. and Southgate, C. 2010 *Greening Paul: Rereading the Apostle in an Age of Ecological Crisis* (Waco, TX: Baylor University Press).
Lohfink, N. 1994 *Theology of the Pentateuch: Themes of the Priestly Narrative and Deuteronomy*, tr. L.M. Maloney (Edinburgh: T&T Clark).
Lucas, E. 1999 'The New Testament Teaching on the Environment', *Transformation* 16.3: 93–99.
McKibben, B. 1994 *The Comforting Whirlwind: God, Job, and the Scale of Creation* (Grand Rapids, MI: Eerdmans).
Moo, D.J. 2006 'Nature in the New Creation: New Testament Eschatology and the Environment', *JETS* 49: 449–88.
Orr, D.W. 2005 'Armageddon Versus Extinction', *Conservation Biology* 19: 290–92.
Palmer, C. 1992 'Stewardship: A Case Study in Environmental Ethics', in I. Ball, M. Goodall, C. Palmer and J. Reader (eds), *The Earth Beneath: A Critical Guide to Green Theology* (London: SPCK): 67–86.
Patrick, D. 2001 'Divine Creative Power and the Decentering of Creation: The Subtext of the Lord's Addresses to Job', in N.C. Habel and S. Wurst (eds), *The Earth Story in Wisdom Traditions* (The Earth Bible, 3; Sheffield/Cleveland, OH: Sheffield Academic Press/Pilgrim Press): 103–15.
Russell, D.M. 1996 *The "New Heavens and New Earth". Hope for the Creation in Jewish Apocalyptic and the New Testament* (Studies in Biblical Apocalyptic Literature; Philadelphia, PA: Visionary Press).
Southgate, C. 2006 'Stewardship and its Competitors: A Spectrum of Relationships between Humans and the Non-human Creation', in R.J. Berry (ed.), *Environmental Stewardship: Critical Perspectives, Past and Present* (London/New York: T&T Clark): 185–95.
White, L., Jr 1967 'The Historical Roots of Our Ecologic Crisis', *Science* 155: 1203–207.

Part I

Biblical Perspectives

Introduction to Part I

Francesca Stavrakopoulou

Ecological readings of biblical texts often deal with the twin matters of authority and accountability. For some, biblical portrayals of a humanity at the centre or apex of creation have been used to give divine authorization for the relegation of the rest of the world to a secondary, lesser status. Accordingly, the Bible has been held accountable by many eco-critics for the ethical devaluation of the environment that has served to legitimate its ongoing degradation and damage. But the Bible is often also regarded as an authoritative voice by Christians seeking to protect the environment from further damage, so that ethical appeals to its religio-cultural authority and influence are used to evoke in others a biblically and theologically accountable responsibility for the care of the non-human world. Collectively, the essays gathered in this section of the volume address questions about the authority and accountability of the Bible in these broad ways.

But among these contributions, several also engage a third matter alongside authority and accountability by exploring the extent to which it is *appropriate* to appeal to biblical literature in cultivating positive and negative attitudes to the environment. As will become apparent, many authors here emphasize that the essential otherness of the ancient worlds giving rise to the biblical texts must be taken seriously. While this can help disarm the more aggressive and environmentally damaging appeals to biblical images of a glorious anthropocentrism, it can also create notable difficulties in trying to use the Bible as an eco-friendly resource. Sophisticated eco-criticism demands a multivalent and creative approach to these ancient texts in order to render them more palatable – and useful – to modernist, Western concerns about the environment and humanity's role and place within it.

As is well known, the creation story in Genesis 1 has been given particular attention in the debate concerning the influence of the Bible on human attitudes to the environment. John Rogerson engages this debate head-on in recognizing that the language of subjugation used in Genesis 1 to describe the dominant relationship of humans over non-human creation is not easily softened within its biblical context: notions of supportive stewardship are not easily derived from this text. Rather, he argues, it is within the broader narrative context of Genesis 1–9 that a softer interpretation of humanity's relationship with non-human creation can and should be located. Read alongside the accompanying stories of humanity's bad behaviour, the subsequent flood and the world that emerges from the waters, Genesis 1 images a world in which humanity's coercion of non-human creation is to be performed with reciprocally beneficial generosity in a non-violent world – but this is not the world experienced by post-diluvian humanity. Instead, the world in which Noah and his meat-eating, conflict-ready descendants live is a 'compromise world', formed and marked by human violence and exploitation of the non-human creation which was never intended. Genesis 1 thus functions biblically as a prophetic critique of the actual state of human behaviour.

One of the most significant aspects of Rogerson's discussion is the scholarly honesty with which he engages the biblical text. For him, the language of domination and subjugation in Genesis 1 is plainly present; it can only be smoothed into a more palatable form for contemporary concerns by its interpretation within the broader frame of inter-textual and extra-textual, multivalent critique, which employs not only theological, ethical and eco-critical strategies, but philosophical and cultural perspectives too, in acknowledgment that the worlds of human existence envisaged in Genesis 1 and other biblical texts are not the worlds of contemporary human experience.

This crucial point is similarly emphasized by Jonathan Morgan, who reminds us that in engaging biblical texts, Western readers are crossing a cultural divide to enter ancient worlds in which the norms of our own culture are at a significant distance from those represented in the biblical literature. In considering the relationship between human and non-human species and the environments they share, he asks whether the biblical norm of animal sacrifice is inevitably and irreconcilably at odds with contemporary attempts to construct a biblically-based environmental ethic. In the eyes of most Western readers, it may be perceived to be so. But this is to misunderstand the religio-cultural interrelatedness of human and non-human animals within the cultures giving rise to the biblical material. By focusing on the worldview of Leviticus, and bringing it into dialogue with Genesis 1–11, Morgan argues that animal sacrifice functions as an act of humility, deriving from and responding to an awareness of both the anthropocentric ordering of creation and the human inclination towards, and perpetuation of, violence. The animal offering is not a passive, substitutionary victim of human–divine ritual exchange, but an empowered and empowering high-status member of the Israelite community, which performs a crucially liminal role humans would be incapable of performing for themselves.

The essential interrelatedness of human and non-human creation is also a focus of the writings attributed to the Hebrew Bible's prophets – but perhaps not as explicitly or self-consciously so as today's environmentally interested readers might hope. As John Barton points out, the biblical prophets conventionally located in the eighth–sixth centuries BCE are not so much concerned with environmental ethics as with inter-personal ethics. Large-scale land acquisition and agricultural exploitation are condemned, but for the sake of human flourishing, rather than environmental welfare. And yet the 'authentic' writings credited to these prophetic figures are given a more cosmic scope in their biblical reworking, expansion and reception in the exilic and post-exilic periods. Indeed, it is the biblical modelling of what has been called the 'cosmic covenant' that images a direct link between human conduct and universal – and not merely local or national – welfare, with God acting as guarantor and guardian of this relationship. The cosmos flourishes when in their appropriate environmental settings humans act harmoniously with one another; it becomes a disastrous 'world turned upside down' when bad behaviour brings about the divine destabilizing of cosmic order. But while prophetic portrayals of the cosmic covenant might offer contemporary readers with a care for the environment a more helpful portrayal of the symbiotic relationship between humanity and the world in which they live, they nevertheless prioritize divine–human and human–human relationships, with little direct emphasis on the 'goodness' of the non-human creation. The prophetic writings remain therefore limited in the extent to which they may be applied to modern eco-ethical strategies.

Thus, like Rogerson and Morgan, it is in Barton's view hermeneutically essential to recognize and accept the essential 'otherness' of the worldviews exhibited in the biblical texts – despite and because of the problems these texts might pose for contemporary readers seeking to reconcile or rehabilitate modernist concerns for the environment with the biblical heritage of the West. But not all biblical texts are as difficult in this regard. The wisdom literature of the Hebrew Bible is now increasingly perceived as a collection of fruitful texts from which to garner positive biblical perspectives on the environment. Katharine Dell explores the role of the biblical wisdom tradition within the ecological debate, focusing in particular on the books of Proverbs, Job, and Ecclesiastes. While these books tend to exhibit an anthropocentric interest, many texts within them are also sharply critical of anthropocentrism. Significantly, some portray a relationship between the natural world and God that does not involve humans at all – and might indeed suggest that humans can learn something from non-human creation about the dynamics of the relationship between the divine and created worlds. Though the relative absence of 'national' and 'salvific' themes more common elsewhere in the Hebrew Bible (such as temple, covenant, exodus and exile) might go some way to explain wisdom's concentrated focus on cosmological theology, there is also a strong sense in these texts of the inherent value of the natural world in and of itself, regardless of human interaction with it. Most important, perhaps, is the repeated and rich portrayal of what Dell describes as 'a complex web of life', in which God is both creator and sustainer of the created world, but in which humans and non-humans also play vital roles in enabling, maintaining and sustaining the world. At the very least, this worldview has the potential to engender a humility in contemporary readers which might go some way to temper the more environmentally destructive aspects of contemporary anthropocentrisms.

It might be argued that the New Testament's Christologies model another – and culturally more influential – paradigm of a tempered anthropocentrism to be welcomed by environmentalism. The figure (and refiguring) of Jesus in these texts engages complex ideas about the relationship between the divine and created realms, ideas which crucially locate a sense of the potential, limits and impacts of humanity within a broader, non-human frame, both 'earthly' and 'cosmic'. But again, some texts are more conducive to an environmentalist reading than others. As Richard Bauckham observes, the Synoptic Gospels' somewhat limited portrayal of Jesus' relationship with non-human creation might be thought to be of little interest or help in this regard. But for Bauckham, ecological dimensions of the Jesus story can be identified in the gospels of Matthew, Mark and Luke, and might indeed go some way to contributing to a biblically-based theological understanding of humanity's part in the rest of creation. The god of Jesus is the creator god familiar from the Hebrew Bible, who cares for birds and flowers as he also cares for the human creation – they are all a part of the same created community. Accordingly, Jesus' portrayed teaching about the Kingdom of God points not only to the place of non-human creation in the hoped-for Kingdom, but also indicates that, for the synoptic writers, the coming of the Kingdom signalled the redemption of the human relationship with the non-human creation: the coming of the Kingdom of God will not destroy and replace creation, but will instead renew it in accordance with the divine will. This is anticipated in some of the miraculous acts credited to Jesus in these texts (including the feeding miracles in the wilderness), and is also underlined in the depiction of the Kingdom of God as a peaceable kingdom, in which the conflict between human and non-human creation in the current world will be absent. Thus in the Synoptic Gospels, it is in the eschatological dynamics of Jesus' teaching that an ethical environmentalism might be most helpfully located and explored.

For Brendan Byrne, the eschatological imaging of cosmic re-ordering forms an important backdrop to Rom. 8.19-22 – another key biblical text in debates addressing the roles of the Bible in environmental ethics. In his essay, Byrne argues that the 'groaning' of non-human creation in this text is best understood as a difficult longing and eager anticipation of a better situation to come, an experience shared by humans caught in the eschatological overlap between the two ages. Thus for Paul, non-human creation is intimately bound up with the fate of humans, whether good or bad, so that human failure impacts negatively on creation, while human restoration will render the non-human creation positively transformed. This emphasis likely derives from the tradition articulated in Genesis 1–3, but finds distinctive expression in Romans in the (notably personified) imaging of non-human creation as an innocent but hopeful victim of divine punishment for human sin, a punishing process which renders non-human creation thwarted, on account of its role as the instrument of God's retribution. Once again, the interrelatedness of human and non-human creation comes to the fore, because according to Byrne, the solidarity between the two is evident in their sharing a 'common fate': their purposeful suffering and hopeful redemption. Importantly, this interrelatedness is not manifested directly, but rather mediated through the agency of God in both human and non-human creation.

In focusing on the letter to the Colossians, Vicky Balabanski offers nuanced reflections on the portrayal of what she terms the 'interconnectedness' of humanity and the rest of creation, and its implications for ecological hermeneutics. The crucial frame for her discussion is the distinctive Hellenistic cosmology the letter assumes in imaging the 'world' in which humanity exists. As she argues, this is a cosmology notably akin to the ideas about the cosmos and its angelic and astral components that are evident in the writings of Philo, whose own religio-cultural heritage contained concepts derived in part from Platonic, Stoic and Babylonian cosmologies. Within the letter's rich cosmological frame, it is in Christ that the cause, logic and goal of the invisible and visible cosmos, and the heavenly and earthly domains, are located and reconciled. This is both a 'cosmic Christology' and a 'Christological cosmology' which can offer contemporary readers an instructive understanding of the significance of the non-human cosmos and humanity's interaction with it: the cosmic Christ is the interconnection of *all* things – heavenly and earthly, material and spiritual. As such, Balabanski argues, 'the fabric of the material world cannot be viewed as spiritually irrelevant'; rather, it must be taken seriously in its divine significance, rendering redundant the tendency within Western Christianity to prioritize only the divine and the human at the cost of the rest of the cosmos. While the notion of a cosmic Christ may be more at home within Eastern Orthodox theologies, it can thus play a transformative, ecologically beneficial role in the theologies of Western Christianity.

Many of our contributors emphasize the solidarity of the divine and non-divine, and the human and the non-human, in searching out texts offering a plausible or persuasive biblical basis on which to construct an environmental ethic. But in some cases, this solidarity is set within the context of cosmic dissolution, and thus might be held to engender and even endorse a destructive attitude to the environment, particularly among some Christians awaiting the eschaton. Edward Adams deals with one such example in his discussion of 2 Pet. 3.5-13, a passage in which it is claimed that the heavens and the earth will be dissolved in fire, to be replaced by new heavens and a new earth. Adams explores whether this text can bear the interpretative load placed upon it by recent commentators who seek to characterize this vision as an image of transformation (renewal), rather than destruction – and argues it cannot. 'Special pleading' cannot rehabilitate this difficult text for a pro-environmentalist agenda; nor indeed should it be marginalized or ignored, as some might prefer. Rather, its portrayal of cosmic destruction and its new and subsequent creation should be recognized and addressed directly. In doing so, Adams argues that 2 Pet. 3.5-13 is not empty of eco-ethical potential: the intrinsic value of the earthly realm is not cheapened by this eschatological text, for the earth is not held to be inherently evil; the cosmic dissolution is not an end in itself, but a means to a new earthly future, as well as new heavens; and in 2 Peter (perhaps most importantly) the approaching end does not encourage or allow for the abandonment of humanity's ethical obligations.

In exhibiting a diverse range of approaches and emphases in their eco-critical engagement with biblical literature, these essays share a view that a biblically-based, contemporary environmental ethic cannot rely on a simplistic or selective reading of texts. As ancient and complex literature, the biblical texts are essentially distanced and therefore limited in their direct cultural relevance to contemporary socio-political and ecological concerns. It is only through constructive and critical use – that is, through the agency of human readers – that the biblical texts can contribute something to contemporary ecotheology.

This focus on human agency and responsibility dovetails with the Bible's own anthropocentrism. Several essays here engage explicitly with the benefits and limitations of this anthropocentrism, while others emphasize the biblical portrayal of humanity as a part of an interrelated cosmos, in which the human and non-human, the divine and non-divine, the material and non-material, are bound up together as a dynamic whole. But while this emphasis can go some way to reframe the human-centredness of the biblical literature, our contributors would likely agree that it is unable to liberate the non-human world from its reliance upon representation by humans – both within and beyond the Bible. After all, human concerns set the agenda for both biblical writing and interpretation, as much as they set the agenda for both environmental damage and protection. Any depictions of the 'environment', or of 'nature', and any construals of human responsibilities towards it, are of course human constructions, voiced by humans.

Chapter 1

The Creation Stories: Their Ecological Potential and Problems

John W. Rogerson

For most of the history of western civilization the Old Testament creation stories, especially those in Genesis 1, have been viewed with great respect because of the belief that they give an accurate account of how God created the universe. That belief was gradually abandoned by biblical scholars in the nineteenth century, but it enjoys currency today in the challenge to Darwin's theory of natural selection that is mounted by advocates of various types of 'creationism'. That debate is no part of the present chapter (see the illuminating account of the origins of 'creationism' in McCalla 2006). The concern here is rather with the debate that has raged around Genesis 1 in recent discussions about the ecological crisis faced by the world today.

Rightly or wrongly, an article published by Lynn White in 1967 has been taken as the starting point for a modern debate that has held Christianity in general and the biblical creation narratives in particular to be responsible for the current ecological crisis (White 1967). Writing as a professor of medieval history and a churchman, White stressed the need for greater knowledge of the history of technological change, and he sketched some key moments, as he saw them. He made a distinction between the Latin West, the site of the most significant developments, and the rest of the then-civilized world. Crucial to the march of technological progress, in White's view, was a belief in perpetual progress, derived from Judeo-Christian theology. This was further exacerbated by what White saw as an essentially anthropocentric view of the world that was contained in the biblical creation stories, and which taught that the universe was created solely for the benefit of humanity. If it was the case that modern science and technology were a realization of the Christian view of humanity's God-given mastery over the natural world, then Christianity, and by implication the biblical creation stories, bore a huge burden of guilt for the present ecological crisis.

White's charge – that a Christian anthropocentric view of the natural world was in some way responsible for the ecological crisis – was taken up by others (see the brief survey in Santmire 1985: 1–7) and linked specifically by Paul Santmire to the work of two prominent Old Testament scholars, G. E. Wright and Gerhard von Rad (Santmire 185: 187–92). Both were accused of downgrading the natural world by their emphasis on history, and the assertion that God had revealed himself to Israel through historical processes and traditions rather than through nature.

The discussion was not confined to North America. In 1972 the German writer on ecology Carl Amery published a book which held Judaism and Christianity to be responsible for the view that there could and should be unlimited and continuous economic and technological growth (Amery 1972). This produced a response from the Old Testament scholar Norbert Lohfink (1977: 156–71). Lohfink felt it necessary to deal with the interpretation of one particular verse in Genesis 1, a verse which seemed to 'justify' the criticism being made against Judaism and Christianity:

> Be fruitful and multiply, and fill the earth and subdue it: and have dominion over the fish of the sea and over the birds of the air and over every living thing that moves upon the earth. (Gen. 1.28)

Lohfink dealt first with the charge that the creation of humans in the divine image (Gen. 1.27) forged a gulf between humanity and the rest of the natural order. In fact, the passage had to be understood in the context of creation stories found among Israel's neighbours in the ancient world, in which human beings were created by the gods in order to do the hard and menial tasks that the gods did not wish to undertake themselves. The passage about the divine image in humanity was meant to bestow a dignity upon human beings, something lacking in the worldviews of Israel's neighbours. It had nothing to do with creating a gulf between humanity and the rest of nature.

Secondly, Lohfink distinguished between command and blessing in relation to the words about being fruitful and multiplying. He noted that they were preceded immediately by the phrase 'And God blessed them and said . . .'. There was therefore not a command to the whole of humanity for all time to continue to multiply. God's blessing was designed to enable the human species to become viable and was considered to have been fulfilled in Exod. 1.7, which describes the Israelites in Egypt as having been fruitful and having multiplied. Lohfink turned his attention next to the two Hebrew verbs *kabash* and *radah* in Gen. 1.28, verbs normally rendered as 'subdue' and 'have dominion'. The basic sense of *kabash*, he argued, was to put the foot on something, in the sense of claiming ownership. In Gen. 1.28, therefore, the translation 'subdue it [the earth]' gave a false impression. It had to do with taking possession of the earth, as in Josh. 18.1 where 'the land lay subdued before them' meant 'the land lay under their feet', i.e. they had taken possession of it. The verb *radah* had a semantic field that included accompanying, shepherding, leading, commanding. It belonged to the cluster of ideas common in the ancient world where the notions of ruler and shepherd were linked together. 'Have dominion', therefore, implied tender, sympathetic rule. Whether Lohfink made a convincing case for his understanding of *kabash* and *radah* is something that must be considered later.

One of Lohfink's most interesting arguments and one that, again, will be considered more fully later, was that those who took Gen. 1.28 to be a command to humanity to multiply for all future generations overlooked the fact that Gen. 1.29

presupposed the existence of a world in which humans would be vegetarians:

> Behold, I have given you every plant yielding seed which is upon the face of the earth and every tree with seed in its fruit; you shall have them for food.

Would those who made such play out of Gen. 1.28 also argue that in all future generations, humans everywhere should be vegetarians? Dismissing the idea as absurd, Lohfink went on to point out the important contrast between Gen. 1.30 with its vegetarianism, and Gen. 9.3, which gave permission to human beings to eat (kosher) meat, and which, in verse 2, described an enmity between humans and the other living creatures. This latter state of affairs corresponded to the world of human affairs, which meant that Gen. 1.28-30 was prophetic in envisaging a world in which humans and animals lived in mutual harmony. This fact was of fundamental importance for any understanding of Genesis 1.

What has been written so far can be taken as an introduction to the chapter. In what follows there will be four sections, dealing with the history of the modern idea of the subordination of nature to human interest, the interpretation of Genesis 1 in the context of the narrative structure of Genesis 1–9, a view of the current ecological crisis and a return to Genesis 1 in the light of this.

I

Any reconstruction of the history of ideas is bound to be subjective, and this will be true of what is said here. Also, the questions of influence, and how far alleged influences can be said to bear burdens of guilt for subsequent developments, are very slippery indeed. This section will confine itself to some observations drawn from Charles Taylor's *Sources of the Self*, published in 1989. Taylor's stated aim was to describe the phenomena of modernity, especially modern identity, stressing and exploring the significant differences between the moral world of 'moderns' and that of previous civilizations (Taylor 1989: x, 3, 11). A long section is devoted to Descartes and to how, in Taylor's view, Descartes transformed a tradition of introspection that went back through Augustine to Plato (139–58). Prior to Descartes, introspection ('inwardness' as Taylor calls it) had among other things viewed the natural world as an arena in which signs of God's presence and work could be discerned. The change brought about by Descartes was to use the faculty of reason that was disclosed by introspection as the main or even sole arbiter in determining what was true. This 'disengaged reason' as Taylor calls it (disengaged from the outside world) led to a radically different understanding of the world of nature. It was no longer something to be contemplated; it was objectified. It was to be understood mechanistically; it became 'disenchanted'. Here was that 'instrumental reason' which would underlie the advances in technology that would ultimately bring the world to an ecological crisis. As Taylor remarks in a later section

> We who think, and see, have a glimpse of how deep the roots are of our fragile consciousness, and how mysterious and strange its emergence is. This spiritual attitude is in exact contradiction to the Cartesian. There the dominant idea is of the purity of thinking being, of its utter heterogeneity from blind physical nature, and of its transcendently higher status. (347)

To what extent can Christianity and Genesis 1 be blamed for this transformation of the understanding of nature and all that flowed from it via Locke, the Deists and others? Taylor acknowledges that it was within Christian culture that these developments took place; that behind the Cartesian turn stood Augustinian inwardness. 'The disengaged subject stands in a place already hollowed out for God; he takes a stance to the world which befits an image of the Deity' (315). Yet what arises within Christian culture is transformed by what Taylor calls a mutation 'which will carry it outside Christian faith altogether' (315). But of course, this 'secularizing', rationalizing trajectory was not the only one to stem from Descartes, and Taylor devotes space to what he calls the 'Expressionist Turn', something exemplified in Herder, the German Romantics, and Wordsworth, to name but a few. Nature ceases to be merely a machine that can be observed, mastered and exploited for human ends. It becomes an enigma that can only begin to be understood if one participates in it. It is necessary for new forms to be created in poetry and art in order to bring to expression what arises from an engagement with nature in all its manifestations (see Taylor 1989: 379–81). What this brief reference to Taylor's wide-ranging and profound book indicates is that reconstructions of the history of ideas in relation to the alleged responsibility of Christianity for the ecological crisis cannot afford to be simplistic and one-dimensional if they are to be convincing, and to make a contribution to the ecological debate.

II

The fact that Gen. 1.29 appears to command human beings to use a vegetarian diet, while the permission to eat meat is given only after the flood, at 9.3, is no new discovery. The Babylonian Talmud records a discussion of the matter among Rabbis of the third century CE (*Sanh*. 59b). One of the points of discussion was whether the eating of fish was allowed before the flood, the point being that at Gen. 9.3 there is a specific warning that meat with blood in it is not to be eaten. If it was the case that fish had no blood, were humans allowed meat as food before the flood? Protestant commentators from the Reformation onwards were uncertain as to how to interpret the verse. Because it was stated that Abel brought the firstlings of his flock as an offering to God (Gen. 4.4) it was assumed that before the flood the earliest humans killed animals in order to sacrifice them, and that they may also have eaten part of what was sacrificed. The Puritan commentator Matthew Poole was representative of opinion with the words, 'It is neither affirmed nor denied that flesh was granted to the first men for food, and therefore we may safely be ignorant of it. It is sufficient for us that it was expressly allowed, Gen.ix.3' (Poole 1962 [1685]: 5). Scholars in the nineteenth century took a more robust view of the matter. Adam Clarke had no doubt that the first humans were vegetarians (Clarke 1825: *ad loc.*) and added the significant point 'it may be inferred from this passage, that no animal whatever was originally designed to prey on others'. A detailed discussion along similar lines was offered by Franz Delitzsch (1853: 113–15). The question of whether the animals were herbivores before the flood was rarely dealt with; the whole discussion was sometimes affected by the fact that there is no explicit reference to animals being allowed to eat meat in Genesis 9. Of course, this discussion was effected by the belief, that prevailed in the nineteenth and earlier centuries, that Genesis 1 was an authoritative account of how God had actually created the universe. Once this belief was abandoned it was possible to draw other conclusions, conclusions that arguably made it more likely that the original intentions of the biblical writer(s) were being understood.

Before this step is considered, however, a slight digression is necessary. The original charge of White was that the anthropocentric view of the creation narrative in Genesis 1 had led via Christianity to the modern view that humanity had the right to exploit the natural world for its own benefits. Lohfink sought to rebut that charge (in its German form) by arguing that Genesis 1 enjoined a pastoral, supportive role for the human created order, not a domineering, exploitative role. His defence raises two questions: did he succeed in rescuing Genesis 1 from the charges brought against it, and, second, if he did, did this decide the matter? It has to be allowed as a possibility that even if the writer(s) of Genesis 1 intended it to be read in the way that Lohfink suggested, the passage may still have been misunderstood by later interpreters, and this misunderstanding may have been responsible for the development of the alleged Christian anthropocentric view of things.

In answer to this first question, the view taken here is that Lohfink's discussion of the verbs *kabash* and *radah* is not convincing. Without going into a detailed examination of the fourteen occurrences of *kabash* and the twenty-four occurrences of *radah* in the Bible in Hebrew, there are no indisputable instances of the verbs being used in the way claimed by Lohfink.[1] If *kabash* indeed had a basic meaning of 'placing the foot upon', this is almost always in a hostile manner. Usage in the Bible leads inevitably to the 'basic meaning' of *kabash* being 'to subdue, to subjugate'. Similarly, the usage of *radah* points inevitably to the senses 'have dominion', 'rule', 'dominate' (see Brown *et al.* 1953: 921–22). If there is any way of 'softening' the implication of these verbs, it must be by way of interpreting them in the context of the narrative structure of Genesis 1–9, as will be argued shortly. With regard to the second question, it has already been argued in the previous section that the history of the roots of the ecological crisis is complex and many-faceted. Even if the crisis has its origins in Christian culture, there have been 'mutations' which have taken theory and practice into areas that cannot justifiably be called Christian.

---

1   For an exhaustive discussion of *radah* and *kabash* see Neumann-Gorsolke 2004: 204–29 and 274–300, respectively.

It is time to return to Gen. 1.29-30 and their implications in the light of the narrative structure of Genesis 1–9. If, as pointed out above, the vegetarian implications of Gen. 1.29 have long been noted and discussed, it is only comparatively recently that scholars have taken seriously the implication of Gen. 1.30 that the animals as well as the humans were not permitted to eat meat.[2] One of the most subtle and persuasive discussions of this subject is by Pierre Beauchamp (1987). For him, the verses concerning the animals (the non-human living creatures) are crucial because they help to define what it means to be human. In Gen. 9.2 it is stated that 'the fear of you and the dread of you shall be upon every beast of the earth . . .'. This is the prelude to humanity being granted permission to eat meat in the following verse. The issue is thus not merely one of what it is permitted to eat; it is about relationships between human and non-human living creatures. The fact that, after the flood, this relationship is one of fear and mutual enmity indicates that prior to the flood, the relationship was one of mutual harmony. The vegetarian regime in Gen. 1.29-30 is a way of describing a world that is in harmony with itself, a world without 'nature red in tooth and claw'. This is of importance for the understanding of the verbs *kabash* and *radah* because whatever they may mean in other contexts, in Genesis 1 they occur in the context of a non-violent world. Any coercive sense that they possess has to be understood in a non-violent way. Beauchamp writes of Genesis 1:

> It is able to believe that a mastery over the earth is possible without exercising a mastery over the other beings, who are intermediate beings between the master and the earth . . . The Bible does not think of peace between human beings without peace between humans and animals.[3] (1987: 170, 180; my translation)

In this connection it is noteworthy that in the visions of a renewed created order in Isa. 11.1-9 and 65.17-25 the vegetarian order returns, in the sense that animals that are normally carnivores or predators are depicted as lying down together, while the lion will eat straw like the ox. The child will not be attacked by the snake (Isa. 11.7-8; 65.25). These things exemplify the promise 'they shall not hurt or destroy in all my holy mountain' (Isa. 11.9; 65.25).

What is clear from these observations is that whatever else Genesis 1 may describe, it is not the world of our experience. That world, in which there is enmity between a meat-eating humanity and the animals, and among the animals themselves, comes into existence only after the flood. Gen. 9.1-7 is meant to be read over against Gen. 1.27-30. The latter is a prophetic text, describing an ideal that is not realized in the world of actual human experience. A reading of the opening chapter of Genesis in this way was impossible as long as it was believed that Genesis 1 was an account

---

2 For a contrary view and wide-ranging discussion see Neumann-Gorsolke, 2004: 233–70.
3 'elle a pu faire croire qu'un maîtrise de la terre était possible sans que fût exercée une maîtrise sur d'autres êtres, intermédiaires entre le maître et la terre . . . La Bible ne pense pas la paix entre les hommes sans la paix de l'homme avec l'animal.'

of how God brought the universe into being. This is no doubt one reason why commentators such as Poole preferred to be agnostic about whether Gen. 1.29 prescribed vegetarian fare for human beings. The abandonment of the belief that Genesis 1 is an accurate account of the creation of the universe has made possible a reading that is closer to the intention of the biblical writer(s). No doubt he or they also believed that Genesis 1 described how God created the universe; but the chapter was not intended to be natural science. It was myth in the sense of being a narrative set in beginning time whose purpose was to describe how and why things experienced by humanity came to be as they were. The narrative structure of Genesis 1–9 made it clear that the world of human experience was not as God intended it to be. That was the world of Genesis 1, a world that had been so corrupted by human wickedness that God had had to destroy it by means of a flood, after which a compromise world was set up, one which allowed for the fact that it contained, in the human species, an animal that was determined to exploit and dominate other living creatures. These other animals were now allowed to defend themselves on the basis of the fear that existed between them and human beings. Genesis 1 read in the context of Genesis 9 is not a mandate for the human exploitation of the world; it is a critique of the actual state of human behaviour. This does not mean, however, that it cannot be used in modern discussions about the ecological crisis, as will be shown in the concluding sections.

III

In his *Ökologie, Naturschutz, Umweltschutz*, the German environmental scientist Ragnor Kinzelbach outlines two main approaches to thinking about, and seeking to deal with, the current environmental crisis (Kinzelbach 1995). What is common to them is their analysis of the causes of the crisis, namely, over-population and over-production, and the consequent divergence of the human economic system from the ecosystems of the natural world so that the ecosystems are under threat from the economic systems. The first strategy for dealing with the problem he describes as *die ökologische Versöhnungsstrategie*, the strategy of reconciling the economic systems with the ecosystems. This involves the following goals, and means to their attainment. First, the protection of nature and its environments, including the protection of land, air and water and the animal and plant worlds, against the harmful effects of human use of these things (111). Secondly, a restriction on or reduction of population growth and a reversal of the cycles of economic over-production. Needless to say, this latter goal has consequences for the lifestyles especially of those who live in the affluent parts of the world (139–44). Third, a drastic recasting of financial systems so that it becomes clear who, and what practices, are responsible for environmental degradation, so that those responsible can be penalized financially.

On the matter of protecting the natural world Kinzelbach points out that this amounts to an intervention on the part of the human species. During the history of the world many species have become extinct either because of regional or global changes of temperature, etc., or because they have been unable to protect themselves against other species. The modern protection of species implies a recreation of the natural world in the image of those doing the protecting; and it can be added that if, say, aboriginal peoples were doing the recreating of nature in their image, it might work out differently from the results produced by modern Western environmentalists. Put another way, protection of nature is essentially protection of humanity (Kinzelbach 1995: 116), which does not invalidate it, but raises the question of the nature of the human species that is protecting itself via the protection of nature.

This assertion of the subjective element in nature preservation leads Kinzelbach to make observations about two assumptions which are often part of the 'reconciliation with nature' strategy. The first is that nature has intrinsic value; the second is that it maintains a kind of equilibrium that human economic activity has disturbed, and which human action must try to restore. Both assumptions are questionable, according to Kinzelbach. The first is based upon a sentimental view of nature which ignores its violent manifestations such as earthquakes, floods and outbreaks of deadly diseases. The second view, that concerning equilibrium, is too simplistic and needs to be replaced by a dynamic model in which the system is constantly changing by means of diversification and adaptation, something that has been going on for the entire history of the world. Kinzelbach makes a nice German distinction between *Da-Sein* and *So-Sein*, between what is actually in existence (*Da-Sein*) and what people would ideally like to exist or to remain in existence (*So-Sein*) (1995: 136–37). The strategy of 'reconciliation with nature' will be flawed if nature is seen as a benign system in harmony with itself. It must rather be seen as an ongoing and dynamic process, not a condition.

These observations lead to a second strategy outlined by Kinzelbach, and the one he prefers, *die ökologische Entwicklungsstrategie*, the ecological development strategy. What this boils down to is that humanity can only save itself and the world that it inhabits, first, by emancipating itself from nature, and secondly, by steering nature in a direction determined by human values. This, however, raises the question of the nature of humanity and its values, and calls, in the view of Kinzelbach, for a new conception of the nature of humanity and the structure of its society in the world of the future (1995: 166).

IV

Kinzelbach's alternative strategy, that the solution to the ecological crisis is for humanity to save itself from the world by emancipating itself from nature and by steering it in a direction determined by human nature, suggests a way of returning to Genesis 1 and the verbs *kabash* and *radah*. The element of coercion implied by the Hebrew verbs cannot be denied but, as argued above, that element of coercion appears in a different light when read in the context of the vegetarian, conflict-free world implied in Genesis 1. Kinzelbach's preferred option would be disastrous if the human values that steered the natural world were those of a humanity driven by greed and exploitation, a humanity that continued to fell rainforests, pollute the atmosphere and was indifferent to thousands of deaths each day in road accidents. This, of course, is not what is intended. As Kinzelbach says at the end of his book, 'the overcoming of the ecological crisis requires a new conception of the nature of humanity and of the structure of the world community of the future' (Kinzelbach 1995: 166, my translation).[4] This is arguably what Genesis 1, seen as a prophetic text, is about. Read against Gen. 9.1-4 it is a critique of the world that humanity's wickedness has brought about. It is a challenge to create a human society that will be capable of living in a world that is the kind of world that God intends.

One of the ways in which this is to be done in the Old Testament is by 'imposing' gracious behaviour on the natural world behaviour, drawn from the experience of the people of God as the recipients of divine graciousness. A *locus classicus* is Exod. 23.9-12 which reads as follows in my translation:

> A stranger you shall not treat harshly. You know what it is like to be a stranger, for you were strangers in the land of Egypt. Six years you may sow your land and harvest its produce, but in the seventh you shall let it lie fallow and leave it unattended. The poor of your people shall eat from it, and what remains may be eaten by the wild animals. You shall do the same to your vineyard and to your olive orchard. For six days you may do your work, but on the seventh day you shall desist, so that your ox and your ass may have rest and your slave and the stranger resting with you may refresh themselves.

The passage begins with a command that the Israelites must deal graciously with strangers, that is, Israelites or non-Israelites who are estranged from their families and taking refuge with those who are not their kin. The command is grounded in the fact that the Israelites were themselves estranged in Egypt. Also implied is the fact of their having been freed from Egyptian enslavement by the gracious act of God. Both their sympathy born of suffering and their gratitude for deliverance must be translated into generosity towards others. But not just towards others. This generosity must also be extended to the natural order.

The origins of the sabbatical year for agriculture have been sought in ancient tabu practices that set a boundary against the extent to which humans could use nature for their own purposes (Albertz 1998: 394). The addition of vineyards and oliveyards, and the injunction to allow the poor and wild beasts to eat the produce from the sabbatical year would therefore be later developments, as would the linking of these practices with the exodus story. But the end result is a theologizing which is impressive and calls for attention.

Because of the lack of fertilizers in ancient Israel, fields were fallowed every other year, which means that the sabbatical year was not an agricultural necessity made into

---

4 'zur Behebung der ökologischen Krise bedarf es eines neuen Entwurfes vom Bild des Menschen und von der Struktur der Weltgesellschaft der Zukunft.'

a theological virtue. No doubt it helped fields to recover their growing potential, but this was not the primary purpose. The primary purpose was to establish and preserve a triple relationship between God, the users of the land and the land itself, where the limits set upon the use of the land also contributed to human self-understanding by setting limits to human ambition. This is indicated by the later addition of vineyards and olive orchards to the text, things that do not need to be fallowed every seven years to assist their growing potential. These items are most likely to have been added to the text in the post-exilic period when land use in Judah seems to have switched from the growing of barley (its main cereal crop) to the production of oil and wine. The continuation of the passage to embrace the weekly sabbath moves in the same direction, that of imposing upon the use of domesticated animals – a practice derived from compassion and graciousness. The first stated beneficiaries of the sabbath rule in Exod. 23.12 are the ox and the ass.

There are, of course, other well-known passages in which compassion for aspects of the natural order are enjoined. Deut. 20.19-20 forbids the felling of fruit trees that belong to a city that is besieged in warfare. Trees which do not yield fruit may be used to build siege works, but trees are not otherwise to be felled. As the most recent research indicates, this injunction was not simply an expression of solidarity with the world of nature; it was also a way of expressing outrage at the military practices of the neo-Assyrian empire, which showed no mercy either to human foes or the world of nature. Eckhart Otto in his recent *Krieg und Frieden in der Hebräischen Bibel und in Alten Orient* not only quotes from Assyrian texts which boast about the wholesale destruction of fruit trees, and indeed of anything that produced food for human consumption; he also reproduces a scene from an Assyrian relief which shows Assyrian soldiers felling the fruit trees outside a besieged city (Otto 1999: 99–100). However, the Hebrew legislation is not simply an outraged human reaction against brutal practices; it is driven by the divine command for compassion rooted in God's act of compassion in freeing his people from slavery; and the same motive is behind the injunction in Deuteronomy 22 which commands compassionate treatment for straying and lost animals, animals that have fallen down in some way, mother birds with their young and asses that must not be made to plough with the much stronger oxen.

These passages are arguably the best commentary on the verbs *kabash* and *radah* in Genesis 1. The passages do not describe a humanity exploiting the natural world and its non-human creatures but rather a humanity exercising a gracious role in an otherwise cruel world, inspired by narratives and cultural memories about God's compassionate action in freeing a people from slavery. Taken together with Genesis 1 they offer a challenge to modern practice. Most of us do not possess slaves, or fields, or vineyards or domesticated animals that plough and carry heavy loads; but we are challenged to ask what narratives and values we need to bring to bear if we are to save the world by the way we treat and shape it. We cannot avoid the question 'what does it mean to be human?' if we agree with Kinzelbach that we need a new conception of the nature of humanity and the structure of the world community. The ecological crisis is as much a theological matter as a scientific one, which brings us back, although in a different way, to Lynn White's claim to see a connection between the Genesis view of humanity's place in the world and the present ecological crisis.

References

Albertz, R. 1998 'Sabbatjahr' in *Neues Bibel-Lexikon* (Vol. 3; Zürich and Düsseldorf: Benzinger): 394–95.
Amery, C. 1972 *Das Ende der Vorsehung. Die gnadenlosen Folgen des Christentums* (Reinbeck: Rowohlt).
Beauchamp, P. 1987 'Création et fondation de la loi en Gn 1,1-2,4' in F. Blanquart (ed.), *La Création dans l'orient ancien* (Paris: Cerf): 139–82.
Brown, F., S.R. Driver and C.A. Briggs 1953 [1907] *A Hebrew and English Lexicon of the Old Testament* (Oxford: Clarendon).
Clarke, A. 1825 *The Holy Bible* vol. 1 (London: Joseph Butterworth and Son).
Delitzsch, F. 1853 *Die Genesis ausgelegt* (Leipzig: Dörffling und Franke).
Kinzelbach, R. 1995 *Ökologie, Naturschutz, Umweltschutz* (Darmstadt: Wissenschaftliche Buchgesellschaft).
Lohfink, N. 1977 *Unsere großen Wörter. Das Alte Testament zu Themen dieser Jahre* (Freiburg: Herder).
McCalla, A. 2006 *The Creationist Debate: The Encounter Between the Bible and the Historical Mind* (London: T&T Clark).
Neumann-Gorsolke, U. 2004 *Herrschen in den Grenzen der Schöpfung. Ein Beitrag zur alttestamentlichen Anthropologie am Beispiel von Psalm 8, Genesis 1 und verwandten Texten* (WMANT 101; Neukirchen-Vluyn: Neukirchener).
Otto, E. 1999 *Krieg und Frieden in der Hebräischen Bibel und im Alten Orient. Aspekte für eine Friedensordnung in der Moderne* (Stuttgart: Kohlhammer).
Poole, M. 1962 [1685] *A Commentary on the Holy Bible* (Edinburgh: Banner of Truth Trust).
Santmire, H.P. 1985 *The Travail of Nature. The Ambiguous Ecological Promise of Christian Theology* (Philadelphia: Fortress).
Taylor, C. 1989 *Sources of the Self. The Making of the Modern Identity* (Cambridge: Cambridge University Press).
White, L., Jr 1967 'The Historical Roots of our Ecologic Crisis', *Science* 155: 1203–207.

Chapter 2

Sacrifice in Leviticus: Eco-Friendly Ritual or Unholy Waste?

Jonathan Morgan

In a fascinating scene early on in Nikita Mikhalkov's beautiful but little-known 1991 film *Urga: Close to Eden*, Sergei – a Russian, who in the opening moments falls asleep at the wheel and drives his truck into a lake in the middle of the Mongolian steppe – is offered hospitality by a local shepherd, Gombo, and his family. While Sergei rests, Gombo selects and catches a lamb and prepares to kill it. As Sergei looks on from a distance, Gombo turns the lamb over, sits with one leg across its body to hold it still and, after making a small incision in its belly, swiftly reaches inside the animal and manually disconnects the aorta from its heart. The camera cuts to Sergei and we see that he is severely unsettled by what he is witnessing.

As Gombo and his wife Pagma go about draining the blood, removing the organs and feet and skinning the lamb, Sergei becomes increasingly uncomfortable until, at the point where the couple instruct their young children to help with the work of preparing the animal, he turns away in dismay and disgust. Once the food is ready, Sergei refuses to join the family for the meal, choosing to remain outside and eat from a packed lunch salvaged from his truck. After it becomes clear that the family will not eat without him, and indeed that the lamb has been prepared in his honour, Sergei reluctantly enters the yurt and shares the food.

It is perhaps no surprise that *Urga* – a film about a clash of cultures, between technological and traditional ways of life – begins with two powerful scenes relating to death. In the other such scene, just prior to the meal, Sergei explains to Gombo, in a rather panicked way, that there is a human corpse in the grass near to his stranded vehicle. He is shocked and disconcerted to learn that not only is Gombo aware of this, but that his uncle is lying there by design – uncovered and face up in accordance with Mongolian tradition. Beliefs and practices relating to the beginning and end of life are often those held to be most significant within a culture and also those that carry the strongest weight of socialization. It strikes Sergei as almost inconceivable that anyone would deliberately leave a dead body outside, uncovered – to rot, be eaten by birds and seen by anyone who passes – or that anyone could kill an animal by tearing open its heart with their hands; yet Gombo is bemused by Sergei's scandalized responses to what are, for him, two thoroughly ordinary scenarios.

These two scenes, the meal scene in particular, are, I think, particularly instructive for an attempt to relate a contemporary agenda like ecological ethics to ancient texts regarding animal sacrifice. We must be aware that we, like Sergei, are crossing a cultural divide, that we approach the texts from a world that, while not totally discontinuous with that of the text, is significantly removed from it. Furthermore, we must recognize that the issues surrounding the sacrifice of an animal touch on a realm that we tend to interpret emotively, instinctively and in line with the norms of our own culture.

For example, when I recently explained to a friend over a drink that I was writing about ecological ethics and animal sacrifice, his immediate response was 'Surely they're diametrically opposed?' When I asked him to expand, he explained that in his mind being ecological was all about reducing waste, using resources responsibly and learning that we are not above and beyond nature, but inextricably part of the ecosystem. When I asked him why he thought animal sacrifice was at odds with this vision, he paused for a while and then said, 'Well, it shows that we think of animals as just another "resource" and as less morally significant than us. I mean, from what I've heard, it was done in a pretty gruesome way and happened an awful lot – neither of which seem particularly respectful.' He stopped, took a drink and then added, 'I wouldn't mind a sacrifice that was essentially a ceremonial preface to a meal, but aren't there some in the Bible where they just burn the whole lot up? That', he proclaimed with certainty, 'is just an unholy waste.'

In this essay I intend to question whether this kind of interpretation of animal sacrifice – one that I suspect is fairly typical of those held generally in modern, Western culture – constitutes an accurate reflection of the ritualistic practices mentioned in the book of Leviticus. Moreover, I argue that reflections on these practices, and their wider ideological and cosmological foundations in the priestly writings more generally, can offer an insight into the priestly understanding of the relationship between humans and non-human animals which is far more nuanced, intriguing and (potentially) ecologically valuable than that which is often derived from an unhelpfully narrow and superficial focus on their apparent assertion of human dominion over nature. It is my proposal that, rather than being a cruel, wasteful practice emanating from the logic of human domination, animal sacrifice can be seen to function in priestly thought as an act of humility, deriving from a keen sense of human perpetuation of, and culpability for, violence and corruption. In the light of this, I also question traditional assumptions regarding the substitutionary function, passivity and victimhood of the sacrificial animal.

The most fundamental challenge that I wish to pose to the kind of analysis with which my friend confronted me, is the notion that ancient Israelite sacrifice functions as an expression not of domination and disrespect, but of humility. In order to explore this proposition, we must firstly contextualize the human/non-human animal dynamic at work in Leviticus' sacrificial regulations within the more general priestly conception of the relationship between all animals. In order to do this we must examine various aspects of the myths of pre-history in Genesis 1–11.[1]

I

One of the most striking aspects of the priestly creation myth in Gen. 1.1–2.4a is its description of the vegetarianism of the first humans. Although (infamously) Gen. 1.28 instructs the humans to rule over both the earth and all non-human animals, the following verse makes it clear that they are not entitled to eat meat.

> God blessed them, and God said to them, 'Be fruitful and multiply, and fill the earth and subdue it; and have dominion over the fish of the sea and over the birds of the air and over every living thing that moves upon the earth'. God said, 'See, I have given you every plant yielding seed that is upon the face of all the earth, and every tree with seed in its fruit; you shall have them for food. And to every beast of the earth, and to every bird of the air, and to everything that creeps on the earth, everything that has the breath of life, I have given every green plant for food.' And it was so. (Gen. 1.28-30)[2]

The key emphasis seems to be that since death and killing are not aspects of this idealized vision of 'original' society, no animals, including humans, are carnivorous. Although it is obvious, it is perhaps also worth emphasizing that this deathless, vegetarian scenario signifies that animal sacrifice is also not an aspect of the priestly myth of origins.[3]

While the killing and eating of other animals is explicitly not part of the dominion that they are to exercise, humans are distinguished by virtue of being the only animals that eat fruits and grains, rather than simply green plants. In the light of verse 29, therefore, it seems likely that a major part of what is signified by the instruction in verse 28 to 'subdue the earth' is the tilling of the soil to make possible the raising of fruits and crops (MacDonald 2008: 18). At the heart of what is being communicated in these verses is the concept that humans are animals whose nature is to be cultured.[4]

Much to the disappointment of any reader looking for an excuse to stop eating broccoli, the message is not that humans shouldn't eat green vegetables because they

---

1 Working with an interpretative logic that is informed both by a theological emphasis on canon and by the likelihood of a priestly redaction and arrangement of the Pentateuch, I consider these chapters – both material which is usually classified as priestly and that traditionally attributed to other sources – as an invaluable resource for attempting to interpret and understand the priestly worldview.
2 Biblical quotations are from the NRSV, unless otherwise stated.
3 It is also interesting that while many scholars have noted the apparent presence of temple imagery in the Edenic narrative (e.g. see Wenham 1986; Stordalen 2000), there does not appear to be any representation of an altar. In this context, the apparent proposition of a mythic temple without an altar, and hence without cultic activity, is an intriguing one indeed.
4 A similar argument can be made with regard to God's clothing of Adam and Eve in Gen. 3.21 – an act (presumably) only made possible by the first animal slaughter.

are dull or tasteless – although there is certainly an argument for saying that the ancient Israelites were scornful of them[5] – but rather they are not listed as human food in this situation because they symbolize non-cultivated foodstuffs, not requiring of agricultural organization. This having been said, there is also crucial metaphorical significance in the allocation of seed-yielding plants to humans in the light of the call for them to 'be fruitful and multiply'. This dual identification of the consumption of 'seeds' with both cultural activity and sexual fecundity functions as an aspect of a complex subtext in the priestly material concerning the nature of human life and vocation.

Part of the reason why Gen. 1.28-30 has been disdained in recent times, especially within ecotheological discourse, is that it is seen as presenting a negatively anthropocentric understanding of creation that places humanity at the top of a hierarchy, perched above the creation as its local rulers. It is in my opinion a futile and disingenuous exercise to attempt to reinterpret the priestly creation myth in order to insulate it from all the potency of this type of critique. A hierarchical structuring of creation with human beings at the apex is irrefutably part of the priestly vision. However, there is more to this material than simply the endorsement of humanity as the ontological rulers of creation. As such, the interpretation I offer here is not intended so much as a 'restoration reading' as simply a broadened one.

Given the inescapability of the priestly vision of humanity's ruling status, the interesting question, the question that we must pursue, is precisely what kind of rule are humans expected to exercise within the priestly understanding, and just what kind of relationship between humans and the rest of creation does this dynamic propose?

II

Moving ahead to Genesis 9, we find a rather different situation to the one laid out in Genesis 1:

> God blessed Noah and his sons, and said to them, 'Be fruitful and multiply, and fill the earth. The fear and dread of you shall rest on every animal of the earth, and on every bird of the air, on everything that creeps on the ground, and on all the fish of the sea; into your hand they are delivered. Every moving thing that lives shall be food for you; and just as I gave you the green plants, I give you everything. Only, you shall not eat flesh with its life, that is, its blood. For your own lifeblood I will surely require a reckoning: from every animal I will require it and from human beings, each one for the blood of another, I will require a reckoning for human life. Whoever sheds the blood of a human, by a human shall that person's blood be shed; for in his own image God made humankind. And you, be fruitful and multiply, abound on the earth and multiply in it.' (Gen. 9.1-7)

---

5 See MacDonald 2008: 18, 28 n.6.

Here, in a passage that is very clearly intended to function as a postdiluvian parallel to Gen. 1.28-30, we find that the prohibition on eating meat has almost completely evaporated. It appears that only one solitary restriction, a prohibition on the ingestion of blood, stands to limit Noah and his sons' (and presumably their wives') consumption of flesh.

Between these two instances of the instruction for human beings to 'be fruitful and multiply, and fill the earth', of course, stands the Edenic myth, and thereafter, the vignettes that describe the proliferation of sin that causes God to grieve over his creation and to decide to cleanse the earth with water. In describing the condition of the antediluvian world, Gen. 6.11-13 states that

> The earth was corrupt in God's sight, and the earth was filled with violence. And God saw that the earth was corrupt; for all flesh had corrupted its ways upon the earth. And God said to Noah, 'I have determined to make an end of all flesh, for the earth is filled with violence because of them; now I am going to destroy them along with the earth'.

Following the disobedience of Adam and Eve, and first exemplified in the brutality of Cain's attack on Abel, violence begins to proliferate and pervades the pre-historical culture to the point where verse 11 describes the earth as 'filled with violence (ḥāmās)'. Having begun in human society, as a result of the human disobedience of divine regulation, violence has here become a part of the reality of the lives of 'all flesh' (Gen. 6.12). Although the floodwaters enact the (ritual) purification of the earth, the violence which brought about its corruption remains a reality of the postdiluvian world by virtue of its effect on all the animals – human *and* non-human – that survived the flood.

As many commentators have argued, this shifting of the boundaries with regard to human diet reflects a recognition of the need to control the violence that has redefined the existence of all animals.[6] In the same way that dietary distinctions defined the relationship of humans to non-human animals in Genesis 1, the postdiluvian recourse to meat eating represents the redefinition of that same relationship.

Whereas in the priestly creation myth humans were distinguished from other animals on the basis of an emphasis on their unique propensity for enculturation, now they are to some extent re-equated with them both through the implicit recognition of a shared tendency towards violence and the explicit reference to the consumption of green plants in Gen. 9.3. What distinguishes humans now is the fact that they are permitted to kill and eat animals whereas no one is permitted to kill (or eat) humans.

Where predation and self-defence were not an aspect of the vision of Gen. 1.1–2.4a, they are an unavoidable reality of the world of Noah and his family. The legitimation of the slaughter and consumption of other animals is apparently now a necessary aspect of the rule of humanity over the rest of creation. Part catharsis,

---

6 See Houston 1979: 165–66; 1993: 254–58; Rogerson 1991: 17–25, Anderson 1984: 161–69.

part self-defence, the practice of meat eating is envisaged as a regulatory measure. Whereas previously both humans and non-human animals were defined by their location within the perfection of the divine creation – 'and indeed, it was very good' – now, no natural harmony exists between the species. Where once a natural justice existed with regard to inter-special relations, there is now a need for boundaries to regulate violence. While the human activity of meat eating serves to regulate the activity of non-human animals, the prohibition of the consumption of blood stands to regulate human activity.

As Steven Mason has recently and convincingly argued, this paradigm shift in the relationship between humans and non-human animals is intimately bound up with the covenant God makes with Noah. In opposition to the traditional tendency to interpret God's commitment never again to flood the earth (Gen. 9:8-17) as a unilateral promise, Mason posits a bilateral aspect to the covenant as expressed in verses 1-7 (Mason 2007: 184–95). According to this interpretation, God promises to never flood the earth again on the condition that human beings take over the role of controlling the effects of violence by regulating the shedding of blood. Mason's proposal has much to commend it, not least the way in which it highlights the density and scope of the classic priestly commandment to 'be fruitful and multiply and fill the earth', frames the apparent connection between the threat from wild animals and human enemies (e.g. Lev. 26.6, 21-25) and provides an useful context within which the complex issue of the role of blood in the Hebrew Bible can be explored.

The context of Genesis 9 and the covenant with Noah are therefore vital in terms of setting animal sacrifice in a wider ideological and cosmological context. Central to this contextualization is the emphasis on the profundity of the impact of human sin on the wider created order, and on the relationship between humans and non-human animals in particular. Furthermore, it sets out and formalizes in covenant form the deep-rooted connections between the human calling to 'be fruitful and multiply', the need to regulate violence and the killing of animals. However, whereas in the case of killing animals for food the emphasis is on the maintenance of peace between humans and non-human animals for the explicit benefit and flourishing of humans, it is my proposal that the sacrificial killing of animals carries a more complex and ecologically interesting aspect.

III

Whereas Gen. 9.4 places only one limitation, that of not consuming animal blood, the system of rules regarding purity and sacrifice set out in Leviticus creates a far more regulated framework within which this dynamic must operate, reinterpreting and clarifying the situation further through a re-emphasis on the boundaries that make creation ordered and good. Just as in the dynamic envisaged by Genesis 9, the functioning of the tabernacle/temple[7] in Leviticus relies upon a fundamental recognition of the corrupting influence of human sin. Central to the texts that describe the sacrificial tradition stands the insistence that temple practice is a matter of profound seriousness, indeed of absolute necessity. The fundamental logic that the priestly instructions regarding sacrifice attest to, reinforce and indeed proceed from, is that regular, officially sanctioned sacrifice is a fundamental requirement for the proper functioning of Israelite society and that this is because of the ever-present reality of human corruption.

The centrality of this notion within the priestly worldview explains how Leviticus can begin its instructions concerning sacrifice with the words, 'When any of you bring an offering of livestock to the LORD . . .' (Lev. 1.2). Not only is it assumed that the priesthood, the sanctuary, the whole sacrificial system is necessary, but it is also assumed that the text's intended audience recognizes this, or at least accepts it to be the case without the need for demonstration.

The emphasis on the potency of impurity proceeds from the priestly understanding of the importance of the presence of YHWH at the heart of the community. While the whole earth is YHWH's to roam, and the land of Canaan his home in particular (Lev. 25.23), within the priestly tradition the tabernacle/temple is the primary location of the divine presence (Lev. 26.11-12). The holy of holies is envisaged as the space in which the human and divine realms meet, and whence the divine holiness radiates throughout the whole land, purifying and sustaining it (see e.g. Gorman 1997: 10, 13–14, 20).

Impurity, which is in this model the opposite of holiness, inhibits the permeation of holiness, and can, if things get bad enough, force YHWH to abandon the sanctuary and cause the people to be ejected from the land.[8] This possibility of abandonment and ejection, which essentially functions as the framework for the priestly interpretation of the exile, is a threat not just to the people, but to the wider flourishing of the land and all its inhabitants (see esp. Lev. 18.24-28; 26.19-33).[9] The sacrificial 'system' that we encounter as readers of Leviticus is a complex set of distinct yet related ritualistic practices which are only sketchily described and which tend to wriggle free from attempts at complete schematization. Perhaps the most accurate generalization we can make is that it is a way of dealing with the consequences of impurity, and thus avoiding the extreme scenario described in Leviticus 26.

Although it functions as a significant foundation for the notion, simply highlighting the fact that a recognition of the potency and perpetuity of human sin lies at the heart of Leviticus' conception of sacrifice does not go far enough to justify my claim that a sacrifice can be perceived as an act of humility. In order, therefore, to further

---

7   This composite phrase is used to express the dual emphases derived from both the narratological and historical locations of Leviticus.
8   The central motif in the book of Ezekiel – cf. Ezek. 8.6, 12; 9.9; 10.18-20; 11.9-12; 12.1-6, 17-20; 15.7; 20.38; 22.15; 39.23.
9   For an account of the potential ecological value of the conception of the land in Leviticus, see Morgan 2009.

expand the grounds of this claim, let us consider one particular type of sacrifice set out in Leviticus – the *ḥaṭṭa't*, usually translated 'sin offering'.

According to Leviticus chapters 4, 12, 15 and 16, the sin offering was necessary to rectify the situation where someone had either unintentionally committed an act prohibited by the law, was in need of purification as a result of childbirth or genital discharge or had, as in the case of Aaron's sons, committed a flagrant and deliberate violation. Jacob Milgrom has long argued that the translation 'sin offering' has fed the (incorrect) assumption that the ritual focuses on the individual offender and that the offering functions to rid them of their sin. Departing from this interpretation, he points out that the blood used in the offering is not applied to the offender, but in fact to various parts of the sanctuary (depending on the nature of offence). He argues that while the offender is purified variously by washing, by the passing of time or by the recognition of their fault, blood is required to purge the sanctuary which has become corrupted (Milgrom 1991: 254–61).

According to this interpretation, as well as being the earthly dwelling of YHWH and the location from which the divine holiness emanates, the tabernacle/temple is also the target of the polluting effect of impurity, which functions as a kind of miasma, attaching itself to the sanctuary and sancta, polluting them from a distance. Although Milgrom's clearly overstated insistence that the *ḥaṭṭa't never* serves to rid the impure party of their sin but rather *always* functions to cleanse the sancta of its effects has come in for criticism,[10] there seems little doubt that his basic proposition – that the priestly writers conceived of the sanctuary as the primary locus of the polluting effects of sin – is indeed a key concept at work in Leviticus (see Lev. 8.14-15; 15.31; 16.15-19).[11]

For Milgrom, the recognition of this miasmic quality within the priestly conception of sin serves as a sharp contrast between Israel and her neighbours. While he argues that the concept of pollution at a distance is common to many ancient Near Eastern traditions, he notes that the corruption in question is usually the result of the actions of demons. By contrast, in the Israelite priestly tradition, concern regarding autonomous, malevolent deities or spirits is eclipsed by the recognition of humanity as chief among the corrupting influences in the world (see Milgrom 1991: 261; 2004: 8–16).

I remain unconvinced by Milgrom's claim that the notion of autonomous elemental or spiritual forces in opposition to YHWH is total anathema to the priestly tradition, and am certainly uneasy about his repeated emphasis on the definite distinction between Israelite and 'pagan' religion. However, despite these concerns, it seems to me that Milgrom is right to emphasize both the anthropogenic nature of impurity and its communal affect.

Therefore, it is not simply the case that the people were to be reminded of the voracity and persistence of sin by the continual functioning of the tabernacle/

---

10   See Gilders 2004: 28–32, 109–141; Kiuchi 1987: 14–19; Grabbe 1997: 38–43; Jenson 1992:156–60; Willis 2009: 38–40.
11   See Rogerson 1998: 10–11, 255 n.8; 1980: 54.

temple, but also that the workings of the system bore testimony to the effects of all sin beyond the realm of the individual – indeed beyond the realm of human society. As with the wider priestly conception expressed in Genesis 9, the relentless and corrosive reality of human sin forms the framework within which the relationship of humans and non-human animals must be brokered. The foremost responsibility for managing the relationship falls to humans, not simply because of a recognition of their higher status, but, more significantly, because of their culpability with regard to the controlling dynamic.

This notion that the sacrificial system served, at least in part, to preserve the purity of the sanctuary for the benefit not just of the people, but all the inhabitants of the land – and indeed the land itself – brings us to the core of the claim regarding humility. Conceiving of the system in this way makes it clear that the priestly conception of animal sacrifice did not simply displace human responsibility and needlessly victimize disinterested animals. The animals concerned were not envisaged as external to the problem; they too were members of the community that would be affected by YHWH's abandonment of the sanctuary or the people being evicted by the land.

Some might baulk at this idea of the conception of animals as members of the community, interpreting it as a modern, fluffy fiction, but once again we must remind ourselves that, just like Sergei, we carry with us our unspoken cultural assumptions about the 'proper' relationship of humans to animals. The majority of animals used for sacrifice are what we would call 'farm animals': cattle, sheep and goats. While for the majority of modern, particularly urban, Westerners these animals inhabit a very different kind of space from people, the realities of ancient Near Eastern life would have meant (as is indeed the case in many non-urban, non-Western contemporary settings) that such animals lived in a fashion much more in line with our notion of 'domestic' animals. While they would have been far from modern Western pets, they would certainly not have existed (either physically or ideologically) in an environment completely separated from the family home.[12] It is worth reminding ourselves that the kind of alienation from the agricultural means of production that occupants of modern, Western cities have come to regard as normal would have been far from so for the majority of people since the birth of civilization.

Even if we accept, however, the notion that the practical relationship between an Ancient Israelite household and its animals, and the ritualistic conception of animals as part of the community affected by human sin, speaks to a more nuanced, more interesting relationship between humans and animals at work in the sacrificial system, we are still left with the question as to why an animal has to die.

The simple answer to the question as to why, for Leviticus, an animal has to die for a sacrifice to be performed, is that it does not. We must not forget that in Ancient Israel, 'sacrifice' and 'animal sacrifice' were not synonymous terms. Setting aside the broad gamut of activities to which the term sacrifice might be legitimately applied in

---

12   See Douglas 1966: 54–55; 1999: 149; Rogerson 1998: 13–14.

what we might think of as a more metaphorical sense, there are, of course, a large number of ritualistic sanctuary offerings and practices which do not require the shedding of animal blood.

Significantly, wheat, barley, oil, incense, wine, bread and salt[13] are all among the vegetarian sacrificial equipment sanctioned for use in various circumstances and for various purposes in Leviticus.[14] Furthermore, there are the certain sacrificial rituals which involve animals, but do not demand their death (e.g. the rites of cleansing in Lev. 14.1-7 and 48-53, or the mysterious *Azazel* ritual described in Lev. 16.1-22). Setting this important point regarding non-animal and non-lethal animal sacrifice to one side, in the light of what we have already observed I propose that there is a thread of reasoning by which we might examine those sacrificial activities wherein an animal was required to die in a way which has the potential to throw them into an unusual and interesting perspective.

Partly because of certain overarching theological conceptions that many Christians bring to the Hebrew Bible, and partly due to well-established ideas regarding sacrifice and ritual in various other periods and cultures, readers of Leviticus often tend towards interpreting the sacrificial animal as a substitute for the sacrificer. Even if they are not inclined to think of the animal as literally standing in for a human victim, often a vaguer conception of symbolic stead directs interpretation. Much is made in this context of the 'laying on of hands' (see Lev. 1.4; 3.2, 8, 13; 4.4, 15, 24, 29, 33; 8.14, 18, 22). Although many commentators have drawn attention to the fact that the texts that mention this procedure do not allow the reader to draw any firm conclusions regarding its ritualistic function (e.g. Kiuchi 1987: 112–19), it is interesting to note that many still affirm the assumption that it signifies a substitution.[15]

The notion of substitution can connote a variety of meanings, some of which will be more helpful than others in terms of interpreting animal sacrifice in Leviticus. My reticence to embrace the term derives from both the intense theological meaning with which it is loaded – meaning which easily has the potential to hijack an interpretation – and the fact that often the implicit logic of its application is that the sacrificial animal is essentially an expendable stand-in onto which impurity and/or guilt can be displaced in order to enable the cleansing (and survival) of the human sinner.

It is my conviction that this kind of interpretation fails to take both the status and the function of the sacrificial animal within the priestly tradition with the necessary seriousness. For a start, there is good reason to think of the animals that were suitable for sacrifice as possessing extremely high status. These were highly prized animals, not only practically but also ritualistically. The instructions are clear that,

---

13 Note how these are all classic symbols of cultural activity.
14 On the importance of vegetal and liquid offerings see McClymond 2008.
15 A fitting and interesting example is found in Wenham 1995 where the author provides a fairly nuanced survey of several possible meanings without demonstrating any one to be compelling, but then appears to revert to the assumption of a broadly conservative and one-dimensional interpretation. It is also interesting to note the appeal to the story of Abraham and Isaac (80) – a common yet, I believe, deeply flawed rhetorical move.

in order to be acceptable, animals used for sacrifice were to be 'perfect' (Lev. 22.21), 'without blemish' (Lev. 1.3, 10; 3.1, 6; 4.3, 23, 28, 32; 5.15, 18; 6.6; 9.2, 3; 14.10; 22.19; 23.12, 18.). This insistence is no doubt partly to ensure that weak or lame animals were not offloaded as offerings (Lev. 22.21-25) – a point which testifies to the fact that the inherent economic loss to the offerer was not an insignificant factor.[16] However, more fundamentally, the insistence on physical perfection seems to have been to ensure that the animal was seen as worthy of, and able to live up to, the cultic role required of it. In order to perform its ritualistic role, the sacrificed animal needed to be holy. This, in itself, given the seriousness with which the priests use holiness language and the lengths to which they themselves needed to go in order to be fit for their work, suggests interesting implications about the perceived status of such animals.

The role that a sacrificed animal must play is a liminal one; it is required symbolically to span two realms. In priestly thought, such liminality is a deadly serious matter. Clear boundaries separate life and death, order and chaos, the holy and the profane; even to approach, let alone transgress, the clearly defined boundaries between these realms is potentially to jeopardize the very fabric of created reality. In being able to transgress these boundaries and pass from one realm to the other, the animal somehow makes possible cleansing from contamination, the restoration of distinctions between things and thus the right reordering of society (see Davies 1977: 396–97).

It is only by virtue of being a member of the (covenant) community that desires the presence of God and would suffer from its withdrawal, but *not* a member of the community of (immediate) culpability for sin that the animal can play this vital role. Therefore, far from being a poor substitute, the sacrificed animal is a holy thing that performs a role on behalf of humans which they could not and could never perform for themselves. In this sense, if the concept of substitution is at all a helpful one in this context, we must be clear that rather than being about the importation of a more disposable alternative to bear the brunt of punishment, it is an exchange that involves the replacement of a less ritually capable and significant animal (the human) with a more ritually capable and significant one (the 'holy' sheep/bull/goat/bird).

By the same logic, while it is obviously not plausible to think of the selection process as being on a voluntary basis, it does not seem fitting to me to conceive of the animal as a 'sacrificial victim'. It could be argued that if there is a single 'sacrificial victim' it is the human, who is powerless to deal with the effects of their own sin. In making this recognition, we come to see that the flaw in the language of victimhood is its failure to account for the chronology of sacrifice. The sacrificial animal *begins* as a victim, suffering the actual and potential consequences of a particular sin (along with all the inhabitants of the land), but, through enabling the cleansing of the sanctuary and the offender, ends by dissolving the very context of the victimhood of

---

16 See Rogerson 1998: 14–15.

all concerned. The animal does not remain a victim in exactly the same way that the community as a whole is restored from a position of victimization.

IV

I began by sketching a series of assumptions that a modern, ecologically aware reader might bring to the sacrificial material in Leviticus regarding the antithetical nature of ecology and animal sacrifice. First, that animal sacrifice implies and necessitates assent to the conception of a destructive, anthropocentric, hierarchical, domination paradigm. Secondly, that animal sacrifice is unavoidably cruel and disrespectful to animal life. And third, that it is inherently wasteful. It is my hope that over the course of this brief chapter I have been able to meaningfully address and disrupt these assumptions.

I have argued that by means of close attention to the broader context of the priestly conception of the relationship between humans and non-human animals, and the nudging of things beyond the (often assumed) context of sacrifices as making satisfaction for individual sin, that the act of animal sacrifice can be described as an act of humility rather than hubris.[17] I have also sought to demonstrate that other assumptions regarding the low status, passivity and victimhood of the sacrificial animal are somewhat unjustified in the context of Leviticus' conception.

With regard to the question of waste, it was, in a sense, my intention to undermine this objection before it had ever been raised by presenting the scenes from *Urga* as a hermeneutical context. It seems clear to me that such a conception of wastefulness intrinsically assumes the definition of its opposite; that is, to say that something is wasteful is to assume that we know what the opposite of waste looks like. In claiming that sacrifices are a waste if they do not provide food, for example, my friend demonstrated a cultural predisposition regarding the unnecessity and inefficacy of sacrifice. The charge of wastefulness is severely weakened once the priestly conception of sacrifice is explored in depth and on its own terms.

At the broadest level, it has been my intention to convey the notion that careful attention to the precise role and function of the sacrificed animal serves to lead us still further from the conceptual paradigm wherein humans *use* other animals to rectify *their* problems. Not only is the world of Ancient Israelite priestly thought not ruled by issues of utility, but it relies on and expounds a conception of reality in which humans, non-human animals and the earth itself are inextricably bound up in a set of relationships with YHWH that require humans to commit to regulating

---

17   The scope of the concept of humility that I have utilized is illustrated in the appeal to a concern for the whole land (N.B. *humus*) and all its inhabitants. In this sense the distinction between 'humility' and 'hubris' can be seen to map onto the tensions in Genesis 1–11 between 'multiply' (*rabah*) and 'increase' (*tarob*), which Shemaryahu Talmon has argued carries an implicit concern regarding human self-aggrandizement and pride (1987: 114–15).

the proliferation of violence, which is the result of human sin, and require certain non-human animals to function as mediators and agents of purification on behalf of the whole community.

The hermeneutical complexities involved in drawing an obscure, Ancient, ritualistic text into conversation with contemporary ecological ethics cannot be overstated. However, for communities of faith, the challenge of continually rereading and reinterpreting sacred texts and instantiating their wisdom in the here-and-now is one which simply cannot be avoided and must not be abandoned. As I see it, the most fruitful way ahead involves the construction and utilization of bridges of imaginative analogy between our own location and that of the text, in full recognition of the fact that neither is ever fully known or truly independent of the other, but that both collide in their provisionality within the community of interpretation.

In the context of this kind of hermeneutical project, it is my conviction that, more than simply enabling a construction of a defence of the Levitical sacrificial system against accusations of negative ecological value, it is possible to discern, in the details of its conceptualizations of sin, human culture, non-human animal life and ecological interdependence and accountability, practices and principles that can serve as fruitful stimuli for contemporary ecotheological reflection.

Perhaps, in this context, Milgrom is not so far off the mark when he comments that in the Priestly writings 'we can detect the earliest groupings [sic] toward an ecological position' (Milgrom 2004: 13), or indeed when he offers the following reflection a few pages later:

> How would Israel's priests see our world today? Without hesitation they would spot the growing physical pollution of the earth: oil spills, acid rain, strip mining, ozone depletion, nuclear waste. [Likewise] they would be aghast at the unending moral pollution of the earth. How long [they] would cry out, before God abandons God's earthly sanctuary? (33)

References

Anderson, B. 1984 'Creation and Ecology', in B. Anderson, *Creation in the Old Testament* (Issues in Religion and Theology 6; London/Philadelphia, PA: SPCK/Fortress): 152–71.
Davies, D. 1977 'An Interpretation of Sacrifice in Leviticus', *ZAW* 89: 388–98.
Douglas, M. 1966 *Purity and Danger: An Analysis of Concepts of Pollution and Taboo* (London: Routledge and Kegan Paul).
Douglas, M. 1999 *Leviticus as Literature* (Oxford: Oxford University Press).
Gilders, W.K. 2004 *Blood Ritual in the Hebrew Bible: Meaning and Power* (Baltimore, MD: Johns Hopkins University Press).
Gorman F.H., Jr 1997 *Divine Presence and Community: A Commentary on the Book of Leviticus* (ITC; Grand Rapids, MI: Eerdmans).
Grabbe, L. 1997 *Leviticus* (OTG; Sheffield: Sheffield Academic Press).
Houston, W. 1979 '"And Let Them Have Dominion . . .": Biblical Views of Man in Relation to

the Environmental Crisis', in E.A. Livingstone (ed.), *Studia Biblica 1978. I. Papers on Old Testament and Related Themes* (JSOTSup 11; Sheffield: JSOT Press): 161–84.

Houston, W. 1993 *Purity and Monotheism: Clean and Unclean Animals in Biblical Law* (JSOTSup 140; Sheffield: JSOT Press).

Jenson, P.P. 1992 *Graded Holiness: A Key to the Priestly Conception of the World* (JSOTSup 106; Sheffield: Sheffield Academic Press).

Kiuchi, N. 1987 *The Purification Offering in the Priestly Literature: Its Meaning and Function* (JSOTSup 56; Sheffield: JSOT Press).

McClymond, K. 2008 *Beyond Sacred Violence: A Comparative Study of Sacrifice* (Baltimore, MD: Johns Hopkins University Press).

MacDonald, N. 2008 'Food and Diet in the Priestly Material of the Pentateuch', in R. Muers and D. Grumett (eds), *Eating and Believing: Interdisciplinary Perspectives on Vegetarianism and Theology* (London: T&T Clark).

Mason, S. 2007 'Another Flood? Genesis 9 and Isaiah's Broken Eternal Covenant', *JSOT* 32: 177–98.

Milgrom, J. 1991 *Leviticus 1–16: A New Translation with Introduction and Commentary* (AB 3; New York, NY: Doubleday).

Milgrom, J. 2004 *Leviticus: A Book of Rituals and Ethics* (A Continental Commentary; Minneapolis, MN: Fortress).

Morgan, J. 2009 'Transgressing, Puking, Covenanting: The Character of Land in Leviticus', *Theology* 112: 172–80.

Rogerson, J. 1980 'Sacrifice in the Old Testament: Problems of Method and Approach', in M.F.C. Bourdillon and M. Fortes (eds), *Sacrifice* (London/New York: Academic Press): 45–59.

Rogerson, J. 1991 *Genesis 1–11* (OTG; Sheffield: JSOT Press).

Rogerson, J. 1998 'What Was the Meaning of Animal Sacrifice?', in A. Linzey and D. Yamamoto (eds), *Animals on the Agenda: Questions about Animals for Theology and Ethics* (London: SCM): 8–17.

Stordalen, T. 2000 *Echoes of Eden: Genesis 2–3 and Symbolism of the Eden Garden in Biblical Hebrew Literature* (Leuven: Peeters).

Talmon, S. 1987 'The Biblical Understanding of Creation and the Human Commitment', *Ex Auditu* 3: 98–119.

Wenham, G. J. 1986 'Sanctuary Symbolism in the Garden of Eden Story', in *Proceedings of the Ninth World Congress of Jewish Studies*, Division A, Jerusalem, 19–25.

Wenham, G. J. 1995 'The Theology of Old Testament Sacrifice', in R. Beckwith and M. Selman (eds), *Sacrifice in the Bible* (Carlisle/Grand Rapids, MI: Paternoster/Baker).

Willis, T.M. 2009 *Leviticus* (AOTC; Nashville, TN: Abingdon).

Chapter 3

Reading the Prophets from an Environmental Perspective

John Barton

Once at the beginning of Lent I preached a sermon about repentance, as might be expected. In it I stressed that repentance should not begin with a sense of one's own inferiority, but rather of one's human dignity. We are sorry for our shortcomings, I said, because we recognize what we are capable of and so of having fallen short of it, not because we think of ourselves as worms in the first place. After all, I said, not much can be expected of worms in any case.

After the service I was approached by a woman in the congregation who seemed rather angry. 'You're obviously not a gardener,' she said – which is true – 'or you wouldn't have been so rude about worms. Worms do exactly what they're meant to, and they're absolutely vital. We expect a lot of them, and they never disappoint us. Humans are really inferior to worms.'

This showed how one can take something for granted without reflecting how it will play out in someone else's mind. I had taken it as read that we look down on worms, but of course we shouldn't: they are essential to our life, and they do indeed carry out their tasks to perfection. I reflected ruefully that others have not made the same mistake. Haydn's *Creation*, for example, has a great section on the creation of the worms, for bass solo. But the Bible does tend to be fairly dismissive of them, as when Second Isaiah disparagingly addresses Israel as a worm (Isa. 41.14). The unexpected attack on what I had said, however, reminded me of other things the prophets say about animals, in which, like the defender of worms, they contrast the way animals fulfil their divine vocation with the way humans do not. One thinks immediately of Isa. 1.3: 'The ox knows its owner, and the donkey its master's crib; but Israel does not know, my people do not understand.' Or Jer. 8.7: 'Even the stork in the heavens knows its times; and the turtle-dove, swallow, and crane observe the time of their coming; but my people do not know the ordinance of the Lord.' There is here an awareness of the good order of nature which contrasts with the bad behaviour of human beings. This might contribute in some small way to discussion about the environment, by suggesting that the prophets were aware of the orderliness of creation when uninterfered with by human beings, as a backdrop to what was their more obvious concern, the sins and failings of humankind and especially of their own nation, Israel.

At the same time it is difficult to find very much else that bears on environmental issues in those words of the prophets that most scholars consider 'authentic', that is, to have actually been spoken by the prophets under whose name they now appear. I think that the great prophets of the eighth to the sixth centuries BCE concerned themselves much more obviously with interpersonal ethics than with environmental ethics, and this is certainly how they have mainly been received, both in Judaism and in Christianity. It would be anachronistic to look to them for a concern to protect the environment in the terms in which this is understood nowadays: they simply did not have that at the forefront of their interests, and of course they thought of environmental disasters, such as drought and famine, as natural or, rather, God-given disasters, not as the result of bad agricultural techniques or anything of that kind.

However, even the interpersonal ethic that was the prophets' major concern did have components that for us at least can have environmental implications. It is clear that for them there was a kind of ideal for human society, represented in the idea of every man sitting under his vine and under his fig tree (e.g. Zech. 3.10). The ideal was that of the independent peasant farmer, secure on his own ancestral land, and not seeking to upset the balance in society by trying to increase that land by pushing others off theirs. This is crystal-clear in Isaiah 5, where the prophet attacks those who are grabbing land: 'Ah, you who join house to house, who add field to field, until there is room for no one but you, and you are left to live alone in the midst of the land!' (Isa. 5.8). The consequence of this practice, something like what we think of as enclosure, is not only personal but also environmental damage: 'The LORD of hosts has sworn in my hearing: Surely many houses shall be desolate, large and beautiful houses, without inhabitant. For ten acres of vineyard shall yield but one bath, and a homer of seed shall yield a mere ephah' (Isa. 5.8-10). Micah says similar things: 'Alas for those who devise wickedness and evil desires on their beds! When the morning dawns, they perform it, because it is in their power. They covet fields, and seize them; houses, and take them away; they oppress householder and house, people and their inheritance' (Mic. 2.1-2). Again, the punishment for this takes a tit-for-tat form, in which those who have in this way transgressed the ancient laws against removing their neighbour's landmark (cf. Deut. 27.17) will see their own ancestral land shared out among the invading troops when God intervenes by sending in the Assyrians, saying, 'We are utterly ruined; the LORD alters the inheritance of my people; how he removes it from me! Among our captors he parcels out our fields' (Mic. 2.4). This will leave 'no one to cast the line by lot in the assembly of the LORD' (2.5) – in other words, no one who by virtue of being a landowner has rights to participate in the city's assembly.

Underlying all this is the kind of attitude we find in the story of Naboth's vineyard in 1 Kings 21. The prophet Elijah condemns King Ahab for getting Naboth killed in order to take over his vineyard, presumably implying that the property of convicted criminals became the king's. But Ahab sins in the first place by wanting the vineyard and trying to get it even by what might strike us as legitimate means, offering Naboth its full value or an equivalent piece of land somewhere else. What is wrong with this is that it would result in ancestral land being alienated from the family it belongs to. This is not seen as a matter of commercial justice – for then Ahab's offer would in principle be perfectly reasonable – but as an attack on the family and tribal structures of the people. God, in effect, has given Naboth's family this piece of land, and Naboth is not at liberty to sell it. Thus the ideal behind the story, as behind the prophecies of Isaiah and Micah, is the inalienability of the family possession, truly the ideal of a nation of peasant farmers. Whether it is legitimate to deploy these examples nowadays to attack the accumulation of massive estates I am not sure, but they certainly have force where actual land-*grabbing* is in question and people are forcibly put off the land on which they have always lived. There is some sense here of the ideal human scale for agricultural life, a defence of the small-holding against massive farms that are inhuman in their scale. I think the prophets in general share this ideal, even though it is mostly in Isaiah and Micah that it surfaces visibly. There is implicit in all the prophets of the eighth century a dislike of growing urbanism, with its rootless people, and a defence of traditional agricultural values.[1]

I said that there is not much in the words of the prophets generally agreed to be authentically theirs that bears on environmental issues, and I think we have now probably exhausted what there is. It has little to say to us on most of the environmental issues we face today, which were far from the awareness of the prophets: they did not think about sustainability or pollution, of course, but mainly about the justice or injustice for human beings of the system of land distribution. That is not to say, however, that there is no relevant material in the prophets, for there is a good deal in the material that is widely judged 'inauthentic'. It is often in oracles and paragraphs in the prophetic books that most scholars think later than the prophets whose names they bear that we do find a concern for nature in its own right, and about human responsibility for maintaining and nurturing it.

The pioneering work on this material was done in 1992 by Robert Murray in his important book *The Cosmic Covenant*, the subtitle of which draws on a World Council of Churches initiative of the time: *Biblical Themes of Justice, Peace and the Integrity of Creation*. Murray's basic argument in this book is as follows. Within the Old Testament, and especially in the prophetic corpus, we find speculations about a covenant older and more all-embracing than any of the covenants Old Testament scholars have traditionally studied – the covenants with Abraham or David, or the covenant made through the mediation of Moses on Mount Sinai. Those covenants are to do with people or peoples. The covenant with Abraham is a divine promise that Abraham's descendants, taken to be the people of Israel, will grow and prosper. The covenant with David speaks of the choice of the royal dynasty of Judah, and would in time come to be seen as having its longer-term fulfilment in the coming of the Messiah. The covenant of Sinai establishes the Mosaic legislation as the basis for the ongoing life of Israel as a people. But alongside these covenants, Murray

---

1   On Naboth and Micah see the comments in Wittenberg 2001.

argued, there is another covenant, in which God develops a particular relationship with the created world and its fruitfulness. This covenant tends to be mentioned in rather 'late' texts, that is, in passages in the prophetic books that have been added to the authentic words of the prophets, and in later narrative sources such as the Priestly Document (P) in the Pentateuch. But its origins are probably in fact older than those of the other covenants, being part of the set of ideas Israel shared with many other ancient Near Eastern nations. In the ancient world generally there was a belief in divinely ordained order in the universe, and the Israelite texts in question are a reflection of that.

According to Murray we can see the idea of what he calls a 'cosmic' covenant underlying a late passage such as Isaiah 24, usually referred to as 'proto-apocalyptic' and coming perhaps from as late as the third century BCE.

> Now the LORD is about to lay waste the earth and make it desolate, and he will twist its surface and scatter its inhabitants . . . The earth shall be utterly laid waste and utterly despoiled, for the LORD has spoken this word. The earth dries up and withers, the world languishes and withers, the heavens languish together with the earth. The earth lies polluted under its inhabitants; for they have transgressed laws, violated the statutes, broken the everlasting covenant. Therefore a curse devours the earth, and its inhabitants suffer for their guilt; therefore the inhabitants of the earth dwindled, and few people are left. The wine dries up, the vine languishes, all the merry-hearted sigh. The mirth of the timbrels is stilled, the noise of the jubilant has ceased, the mirth of the lyre is stilled. No longer do they drink wine with singing; strong drink is bitter to those who drink it. The city of chaos is broken down, every house is shut up so that no one can enter. There is an outcry in the streets for lack of wine; all joy has reached its eventide; the gladness of the earth is banished. Desolation is left in the city, the gates are battered into ruins. For thus it shall be on the earth and among the nations, as when an olive tree is beaten, as at the gleaning when the grape harvest is ended.[2] (Isa. 24.1-13)

The 'everlasting covenant' that has been broken here is surely not the Sinai covenant, which was incumbent only on Israel, but some covenant that embraces the whole human race, and its breach has universal consequences in terms of desolation for the whole earth, not simply for Israel. Breaking the covenant results in turning the whole physical world upside down, producing a resurgence of primeval chaos, not simply the kind of military conquest of Israel that the prophets themselves mostly foresaw but a cosmic upheaval.

Here we find what we lack in the authentic words of the prophets, a link forged between human conduct and cosmic, rather than merely national, disaster. Although, as I said, much of the relevant material is in texts later than the prophets themselves, Murray thinks that it often rests on much more ancient sources, which were to some extent elbowed out of the way by the prophets and the 'deuteronomists', the zealous

---

2 On this passage see also Charles 2001.

monotheistic party responsible for orientating so much in the Old Testament as we now have it towards the covenant made through Moses. The theme of 'the world turned upside down' surfaces in many prophetic passages, as here in Jeremiah:

> I looked on the earth, and lo, it was waste and void [*tohu wabohu*, the phrase used in Genesis 1 for the primeval chaos], and to the heavens, and they had no light. I looked on the mountains, and lo, they were quaking, and all the hills moved to and fro. I looked, and lo, there was no one at all, and all the birds of the air had fled. I looked, and lo, the fruitful land was a desert, and all its cities were laid in ruins, before the LORD, before his fierce anger. (Jer. 4.23-6)

Thus human misconduct – the content of which is unfortunately unspecified – has the result that not just human society but the physical world itself is affected.

Now if people in ancient Israel in general believed that there was a covenant between God and the world, not only between God and human beings or even only between God and Israel, a number of things in the prophetic books become more comprehensible; and that applies even to the prophets themselves, who probably had these ideas as part of their mental make-up even though they do not surface explicitly in their authentic words but only in rather later texts. For example, it is quite common to find that human sin is supposed to affect the fertility of the land. This is perhaps clearest of all in the early post-exilic prophet Haggai, speaking around 520 or so about the crop failures that were blighting the life of the community trying to resettle in Judah after the Babylonian Exile:

> You have looked for much, and lo, it came to little, and when you brought it home I blew it away. Why? Says the LORD of hosts. Because my house lies in ruins, while all of you hurry off to your own houses. Therefore the heavens above you have withheld the dew, and the earth has withheld its produce. And I have called for a drought on the land and the hills, on the grain, the new wine, and the oil, on what the soil produces, on human beings and animals, and on all their labours. (Hag. 1.9-11)

The human sin that has produced this dire effect is the neglect of the prophetic call to rebuild the ruined Temple: more on that later. But the nexus between sin and physical environmental disaster is very clear. Haggai continues the theme in chapter 2:

> Before a stone was placed upon a stone in the LORD's temple, how did you fare? When one came to a heap of twenty measures, there were but ten; when one came to the wine vat to draw fifty measures, there were but twenty. I struck you and all the products of your toil with blight and mildew and hail; yet you did not return to me, says the LORD Consider from this day on . . . Since the day that the foundation of the LORD's house was laid, consider: Is there any seed left in the barn? Do the vine, the fig tree, the pomegranate, and the olive tree still yield nothing? From this day on I will bless you. (Hag. 2.15-19)

The restoration God promises in many late prophetic texts is also presented, Murray argues, in terms of a renewed covenant with the physical world. This is strikingly seen in an oracle in the book of Hosea, in chapter 2, which again most commentators think does not go back to Hosea himself but is a later reflection on the restoration of Israel after the Exile. But again it draws on very old themes of the reintegration of the whole creation. The passage is quite obscure but Murray translates it as follows: 'On that day I will cause response, declares YHWH – I will cause heaven to respond, and it will respond to earth, and earth will make response of corn, of wine and of oil, and they shall make response to Jezreel' (Hos. 2.21-22; Murray 1992: 30). There is here a kind of 'marriage of heaven and earth', parallel to Hosea's own marriage, which in turn is a symbol for God's marriage to Israel. Underlying this is a very ancient idea of the god's marriage to his creation, such as we find in the mythology of both Egypt and Mesopotamia, and which is one way of conceptualizing the 'cosmic covenant'. It implies a restoration of a primal harmony between human beings and the animal and physical worlds. A passage just before this spells this out similarly: 'I will make for you a covenant on that day with the wild animals, the birds of the air, and the creeping things of the ground' (Hos. 2.18). Thus in these images the world as it were turns back the right way up again, with a harmonious relationship between the human and animal creations.

There is a similar vision of cosmic harmony in the famous passage in Isaiah 11 about the 'peaceable kingdom', with the wolf living with the lamb, and so on. Here again the whole world, not just Israel, is to be as full of the knowledge of God as the sea is full of water. Right order is restored, the order as it was at creation, when animals and humans alike were vegetarian, according to Genesis 1. The fact that lions can't survive on a vegetarian diet was not realized, or else it was assumed this would somehow be redressed; though another great paean of praise to creation, Psalm 104, says that the lions roaring for their prey are seeking their food from God (Ps. 104.21), a rather more realistic picture.

Murray sees his rediscovery of the 'cosmic covenant' as having definite implications for the modern ecological debate:

> When the Bible's teaching on God's creation and our place in it is duly digested, I believe that it cries out to us 'you are brothers and sisters of every other human being, and fellow-creatures of everything else in the cosmos; you have no *right* to exploit or destroy, but you have *duties* to all, under God to whom you are responsible.' (Murray 1992: 174)

He believes that a reading of the Old Testament prophetic books that attends to the later passages succeeds, paradoxically, in rediscovering themes that were present in very ancient times, before the biblical prophets themselves began their work, and that these themes are much more relevant to our modern debates than much in the overt teaching of the classical prophets themselves which is less focused on the obligations peculiar to Israel and more concerned with how the human race should relate to the physical and animal world.

I think Murray's work is fascinating, and deserves to be much more widely known than it is: I hope its reissue in 2007 will have this result. Let me however raise some issues that we might encounter in trying to apply it to the modern situation.

First, the prophets of Israel were not announcing a programme of reform, but primarily spoke of what God had done and would do of his own initiative. They criticized what the people had, in their view, done wrong, but on the whole they were not proposing ways in which they could act better, or at least were not saying that it would now make any difference if they did. This is true, at any rate, of the great prophets of the eighth and seventh centuries: Amos, Hosea, Isaiah, Micah and Jeremiah. As we saw earlier, with Haggai (as also with his contemporary Zechariah) there is a clear desire to propose courses of action that would result in God changing tack and blessing rather than destroying the nation. But in the earlier prophets the focus is very much on coming judgement, and the moral teaching is given to explain the disaster that can no longer be avoided, rather than to provide a programme for future conduct – in other words, theodicy is more of a concern than reform.

Nevertheless, there is no reason why we should not do as later generations in Israel certainly did, and take up the prophetic critique as providing some guidelines for our own concerns today. As we have seen, it is in later prophecies, where there generally is more interest in the future conduct of the prophets' audience, that we find the theme of the cosmic covenant emerging most clearly. If we ask why there should be any connection at all between how human beings act towards their environment and what outcomes God brings about, we can see a clear conviction that there is an ideal state of harmony between humankind and the universe, expressed in a fraternal relationship with the physical and animal world as well as in good relations between people and peoples, that will dispose God to give blessing rather than curse in the physical environment. Thus the rediscovery of the 'cosmic covenant' does have some quite positive benefits. Of course there is the much wider question whether God ever in fact intervenes to do things of any sort in the world, and hence whether the theological basis of the cosmic covenant makes any difference. One could perfectly well imagine a secularized version of it, and it could be argued that this is, in effect, what most people with an interest in environmental issues believe: that there is a natural principle that connects human action with the environment through normal causal nexuses, without any need to bring God into the picture. Nevertheless, for a theist with any kind of commitment to the Bible, the religious version of this idea, in which God is somehow the guarantor and guardian of this natural principle, is likely to be attractive. Old Testament studies in recent years has become much more able to accommodate such ideas than it used to be, with a much greater awareness of the concerns for natural justice and universal moral principles that united Israel with its wider ancient Near Eastern context, and much less stress on the features that made it distinctive. Biblical study is gradually recovering from a kind of Barthianism that denied all continuities with the environing culture, and is instead coming to see the Old Testament as a very sophisticated version of much that was common in the ancient world. In this newer context the idea of a cosmic covenant that antedates the covenant on Sinai, and was part of the mental furniture even of the prophets, becomes more attractive, even as it also suggests that the Old Testament has much more to contribute to questions such as environmental ones than an earlier generation of scholars was ready to believe. Certainly it undermines the accusation, which once seemed considerably more plausible, that the Old Testament disenchanted the world to such an extent that it allowed space for human exploitation of the planet – the accusation in the famous essay of Lynn White Jr that has occupied so many theologians over the years.[3] In significant ways the Old Testament was fully aware of the need for human care for the physical environment, which it saw as grounded in God's own creative intentions.

But secondly, how is the cosmic covenant maintained and fostered? Here there is a real divergence between the Old Testament picture and modern concerns. We saw in Haggai that the natural order will become responsive to human need, not when humankind stops exploiting it or when some kind of ethical standards are implemented, but rather once the Temple is rebuilt. This reminds us of something that is much stressed by Murray, namely that in the ancient world – and Israel was no exception to this – cosmic order was maintained through ritual. What went on in temples helped to sustain the cosmos in right order. Murray fascinatingly shows how traces of this idea can still be found in the Old Testament even though on the surface it is often more exercised about what we should call 'moral' issues. After outlining the prophetic role in cursing the enemies of Israel, he continues:

> The establishment of *shalom* is the positive side of the 'rituals of control': the side of blessing as against cursing, of attracting good power as against exorcizing evil power. The rituals of *shalom* will have affirmed the supremacy of *sedeq*, right order in the cosmos and on earth, and symbolized the 'marriage of heaven and earth' so as to ensure the right functioning of nature and right relationships between all the inhabitants of earth. The existence of rituals with these objects is far less hypothetical than that of the 'control rituals' just described, for the latter have not survived in Judaism in anything like their original form, whereas the *shalom* rituals, which clearly centred in the autumn festival (and, indeed, formed its main theme and *raison d'être*) lived on in the feasts of New Year and Tabernacles as described in the Mishnah, and their themes remain recognizable in the High Holydays to this day. (Murray 1992: 82–83)

Ritual in Israel as in many other cultures had the function of *world-maintenance*: it ensured that the natural order would continue in a benign way.

Here, it seems to me, we encounter an aspect of the Old Testament's cosmic covenant that is likely to strike the average modern person, whether religious or not, as hard to engage with. The way to maintain the world in good order for us is a matter of how we actually treat it, and has nothing to do with *ritual* actions. It is here that we encounter the great divide between the Old Testament world and our

---

3   White 1967. See the discussion in Barr 1972.

own. The way to ensure good crops, according to Haggai, is to build the Temple and get the sacrificial system up and running again. In Joel we may even have a liturgy for restoring fruitfulness to the land after the depredations of a plague of locusts, involving prayer, fasting and weeping. Such ideas continued well into early modern times: an interesting set of liturgies was devised in Elizabethan England for fasting ceremonies in time of national pestilence. But this is all quite out of keeping with modern ecological concerns. We do well in turning to the Old Testament to realize that it does come from a non-modern culture, and cannot be simply applied to our world without adjustment. There are indeed themes about 'Peace, Justice, and the Integrity of Creation', but they work with a very different mindset from ours.

Thirdly, attention to the cosmic covenant should not obscure the extent to which the prophets are concerned with human ethics, and are pioneers in this, actually trying to wrest their audience's attention away from ritual and towards the well-ordering of human society. Peace and harmony on earth, for the great classical prophets, are achieved through justice and righteousness, and though these terms (*mishpat* and *sedaqah*) have definite cosmic overtones, they are still to be encountered primarily in the way humans behave towards each other. A clear case of this can be found in Isaiah 33, another probably late oracle, but one that does not work so much with a cosmic covenant as with a covenantal structure embracing the human realm. We begin, admittedly, with images of cosmic collapse reminiscent of Isaiah 24 or Jeremiah 4, discussed earlier: 'The land mourns and languishes; Lebanon is confounded and withers away; Sharon is like a desert; and Bashan and Carmel shake off their leaves' (Isa. 33.9). This causes panic: 'The sinners in Zion are afraid; trembling has seized the godless: "Who among us can live with the devouring fire? Who among us can live with everlasting flames?"' (Isa. 33.14). But the answer is: 'Those who walk righteously and speak uprightly, who despise the gain of oppression, who wave away a bribe instead of accepting it, who stop their ears from hearing of bloodshed, and shut their eyes from looking on evil, they will live on the heights; their refuge will be the fortresses of rocks; their food will be supplied, their water assured' (Isa. 33.14-16). It is when people behave like this that all goes well for them and the earth yields its goodness. Here, therefore, it is ethical conduct rather than ritual that ensures the goodness of the created order. Very much the same picture emerges outside the prophets, in a psalm such as Psalm 72, where ethical conduct on the part of the king secures the blessings of fertility for his land. When he 'delivers the needy when they call, the poor and those who have no helper. He has pity on the weak and the needy, and saves the lives of the needy. From oppression and violence he redeems their life; and precious is their blood in his sight' (Ps. 72.12-14), then there will be 'an abundance of grain in the land, may it wave on the tops of the mountains' (v. 16). The king in this psalm does not maintain order in the universe through right rituals, but through justice and righteousness in the social sphere. And this is very much the main message of the prophets, despite the presence of the ideas about the cosmic covenant that Murray so well digs out and analyzes. In the end it is interpersonal ethics that is the main burden of the prophetic message, with ideas about the integrity of the created order an important but secondary theme.

So although I hope in this essay to have suggested some perhaps unexpected ways in which the books of the prophets do offer some constructive ideas for an environmental concern, I think in the end that it is probably elsewhere in the Old Testament that one would need to look for a more sustained presentation of this theme. It is probably above all the Priestly document in the Pentateuch, and perhaps also the wisdom literature – Proverbs and Job – where one finds more sustained interest in the maintenance of the created order, in respect for everything that God made and declared to be very good. The prophets, for all that they do draw on the traditions of the cosmic covenant, are on the whole more concerned with social than with environmental ethics, and have their eyes fixed on the human rather than the natural world. It is paradoxical that only a generation or so ago this made them seem much closer to our own ethical concerns, further away from ancient Near Eastern speculations about the order of the universe, whereas now it distances them somewhat from the things that really interest us, certainly if we are exercised (as who is not nowadays?) by environmental issues. Concern for 'peace, justice, and the integrity of creation' is quite central to modern ethical discussion, and it may be that parts of the Bible other than the prophets have the most to contribute to this theme. On the other hand, the foregrounding of these questions does force us to ask whether we have analyzed the prophets correctly, as I have tried to show; and it has the effect of rehabilitating large swathes of prophetic oracles which, because they are probably not 'authentic' to the prophets under whose names they appear, have traditionally been neglected by Old Testament scholars.

References

Barr, J. 1972 'Man and Nature – The Ecological Controversy and the Old Testament', *BJRL* 55: 9–32.
Charles, N.J, 2001 'A Prophetic (Fore)Word: "A Curse Is Devouring Earth" (Isaiah 24.6)', in N.C. Habel (ed.), *The Earth Story in the Psalms and the Prophets* (The Earth Bible, 4; Sheffield/Cleveland, OH: Sheffield Academic Press/Pilgrim Press): 123–28.
Murray, R, 1992 *The Cosmic Covenant: Biblical Themes of Justice, Peace and the Integrity of Creation* (reprinted 2007; London: Sheed & Ward).
White, L., Jr 1967 'The Historical Roots of our Ecologic Crisis', *Science* 155: 1203–207.
Wittenberg, G.H, 2001 'The Vision of Land in Jeremiah 32', in N.C. Habel (ed.), *The Earth Story in the Psalms and the Prophets* (The Earth Bible, 4; Sheffield/Cleveland, OH: Sheffield Academic Press/Pilgrim Press): 129–42.

Chapter 4

THE SIGNIFICANCE OF THE WISDOM TRADITION IN THE ECOLOGICAL DEBATE

Katharine J. Dell

> But ask the animals, and they will teach you;
> the birds of the air, and they will tell you;
> ask the plants of the earth, and they will teach you
> and the fish of the sea will declare to you.
> Who among all these does not know
> That the hand of the Lord has done this?
> In his hand is the life of every living thing
> And the breath of every human being.
>
> *(Job 12.7-10)*

In their book *Deep Ecology*, Bill Devall and George Sessions suggest that 'A celebratory deep ecology, drawing from Scripture, might begin with a passage such as this:' (1985: 91) and they quote Job 12.7-8. In this passage from Job, one of the three wisdom books of the Old Testament,[1] the suggestion is that human beings might well have something to learn not only from animals, but birds, plants and fish as well. These non-humans are aware of the omniscient hand of God in all things, in the created order and in the life of every sentient being. In a sense this passage is anthropocentric in that a dialogue takes place involving human beings, i.e. between Job and his so-called friends. Yet it is almost an attack on anthropocentrism in that a key message of this passage is that human beings do not always have all the answers. Another key point is that there is a relationship between the natural world and God which does not involve human beings, and in fact may have a lot to teach them. A passage such as this immediately introduces us to the value that a study of the wisdom literature is going to have in the quest for an ecological hermeneutic.

---

1   I shall confine my comments in this article to the three main wisdom books of the Old Testament, Proverbs, Job and Ecclesiastes. The debate might well be illuminated further by reference to Sirach, the Wisdom of Solomon, wisdom psalms and other literature on the periphery of the genre. See Dell 2000 for a discussion of the definition of wisdom and its parameters.

If there is a corresponding negative to be drawn out here, it is that the wisdom literature has only slowly been brought into the environmental debate. Due to the focus on Genesis and to some of the less positive sentiments about dominion that can be traced back, in modern times, to the seminal article of Lynn White Jr (1967),[2] it has been assumed that this kind of view is a consistent one throughout the Old Testament when it comes to creation ideas. However, the wisdom tradition stands apart as having its own worldview regarding God as creator, a rich tradition of observation of the natural world and of the interaction of human beings with both. Reasons for this relative neglect may include a devaluation of the wisdom literature in general when it was regarded as containing a more 'foreign' theology than mainstream Old Testament views on covenant and salvation history.[3] However, such prejudices are well behind us and increasingly wisdom is coming into the environmental debate. James Barr, for example notes the place of creation in the wisdom tradition and the delight taken in it, although he also says of the wisdom literature, in slight denigration, 'the sorts of scientific and technological interests that it reveals are not explicitly derived from the specific revelation of God to Israel' (1972: 68). A more positive and significant contribution is found in the work of Robert K. Johnston (1987) who still regards the wisdom literature as in some sense commentary on Genesis, but who provides useful insights into the relation between wisdom and ecology. Interest has deepened in the last couple of decades in the work of Norman Habel (Habel and Wurst 2001; Habel 2003), Celia Deane-Drummond,[4] William P. Brown (1999) and Bill McKibben,[5] among others.

It is a well-established point in modern hermeneutical theory that it is partly in the way the text is 'read' that leads to a particular emphasis. Thus wisdom has been regarded as very much 'life from the human side' in contrast to divine revelation.[6] It has a pragmatism and realism that is firmly grounded in concern for human beings and their relationships. However, this has also led to it being read in a one-sided and

---

2 White blames the emphasis on 'dominion' in the Genesis creation story and our perception that we are made in God's image as the root of our arrogant attitude to our environment in the past and lack of care for the world in which we live. The belief that the natural order was created for the sake of human beings is at the root of the problem in his view. Of course he has been attacked from many quarters, not least for misrepresenting Genesis (see Barr 1972). This article sounds dated today when the environment is at the centre of global concern and it shows how much can change in 50 years.

3 See for example Bright 1967, 136: 'Some parts of the Old Testament are far less clearly expressive of Israel's distinctive understanding of reality than others, some parts (and one thinks of such a book as Proverbs) seem be be only peripherally related to it, while others (for example Ecclesiastes) even question its essential features.'

4 Deane-Drummond (2000, 2004, 2006, 2008), is coming from a more doctrinal angle, but has some very helpful reflections on the relationship of creation and wisdom, the latter in the two senses of practical, ethical wisdom and divine, personified Wisdom.

5 McKibben (2005) draws together his views on the current ecological crisis and explores them in relation to Job 38–39. This lively book forms an important bridge between scholarly insights and the wider world. He urges the need for new ways of looking at the world, as was the result for Job after his challenge.

6 Von Rad referred to it as 'Israel's wisdom deriving from experience' (1965: 418).

anthropocentric way in many quarters and in this paper I wish to affirm the three-way interaction of human beings, God and nature that I believe is central to the ethos of the wisdom debate and to the wider Old Testament when considered with regard to ecological issues.[7] In terms of the questions that ecologists ask of texts, this too will lead to some fresh readings and insights. Of course it needs to be borne in mind that biblical authors did not have our environmental awareness in scientific terms,[8] and yet they had strong connections to the land and to the non-human world around them which many of us today have lost. Their outlooks and presuppositions can therefore be illuminating for our own concerns and guide us in attitudes we might adopt towards our environment.

Unusually in the Old Testament, in the wisdom literature God is perceived solely as creator rather than in any of his more salvific roles.[9] He is also guarantor of the order that underlies creation and that the sages believe can be perceived and experienced in the world.[10] It was Walter Zimmerli who coined the phrase, 'Wisdom thinks resolutely within the framework of a theology of creation' (1964: 148). The work of Leo Perdue (1991, 1994) has in recent times attempted to spell this out in more detailed terms. He speaks, following Gerhard von Rad (1965), of a dialectic between an anthropology that sees human beings at the centre of creation and a cosmology that puts the divine at the centre. A dialectic between these two poles conveys the dynamic nature of the relationship between God and the created order and insists that divine and non-divine aspects are given equal place. The use of the word 'anthropology' suggests that this model is anthropologically conceived and we might wish to bring the non-human creation into the picture here. 'Creation' is essentially about the making of order out of chaos and the wisdom literature seeks to explicate that order as it is identifiable in the world. It is almost a pre-scientific attempt to list, order, categorize and control the world.[11]

I have drawn attention elsewhere (Dell 1994) to three essential ecological principles that are applicable in an evaluation of biblical texts. The first is concerned with

---

7   The essential three-fold nature of this interaction is spelt out in the work of my own research student, Hilary Marlow (2009). I am grateful to her for reading a draft of this article and making helpful suggestions for improvement.
8   The ancient Israelites saw the world as much more of a unity than we do today. As Hermisson comments, 'ancient wisdom starts from the conviction that the regularities within the human and the historical-social realm are not in principle different from the ones within the realm of nonhuman phenomena' (1978: 44).
9   It is often pointed out that there is no mention of Moses, the Exodus or David in the wisdom literature – Solomon, however, is wisdom's 'patron' (Prov. 1.1; 10.1; Eccl. 1.1; 1.12).
10 Von Rad (1972) stressed the importance of the 'act-consequence' relationship in wisdom in which every act has a consequence within an order that can be known. While he has been criticized as being over-prescriptive in this judgement, there is some truth in the 'black and white' worldview of the proverbial material and the strong sense of order found there. Cf. Schmid 1968.
11 In ancient Egypt onomastica or lists were used to range items and there may be hints of that in this material, in Proverbs 30 in particular. Listing phenomena was a way of pinpointing, arranging and controlling them.

nature's complex interrelated processes and the interaction of human beings with those processes and with each other. To this we might add interaction with the divine as the essential third strand of any theologically orientated evaluation. The second is about the well-being and flourishing of all human and non-human life in its richness and diversity. Ideas of the essential goodness of creation (cf. Genesis 1), and awe at the sheer wonder of the created world (cf. Psalm 104) come under this heading. The third is that of the sustaining of life – it is often forgotten that the picture of God as creator in the Old Testament is also essentially that of sustainer. Although God overcomes the creature of chaos at creation and creates the world *ex nihilo*,[12] he also sustains it upon its course, constantly providing for it from the beginning until the end. Essentially, God is the creator of the natural world, not part of nature itself. As Bernhard W. Anderson stresses, God transcends the whole of creation. He writes: 'While heaven and earth reveal the glory of deity, Israel refused to suggest that the creation is a direct self-revelation of Yahweh, as though it were an emanation of his being or as though he were a power immanent within it' (1975: 32). This is a very important distinction in relation to the 'nature religions' of the surrounding world of the time in which gods often represented an aspect of nature, e.g. Baal in the Canaanite pantheon was the god of thunder. While we find portrayals of Yahweh as having a powerful voice that 'thunders' (e.g. in Psalm 29, which may well have been an old Canaanite hymn adapted for Israelite use), he is never embodied in an aspect of nature. Rather, elements of storm god and fertility deity enrich his portrayal without threatening his transcendence over such elements. This is where essential interaction with human beings comes in since humans have a key role, although not an exclusive one,[13] in the continuation and sustenance of the created world. The non-human world too has a vital role to play in maintaining this sustenance. The triangle of responsibility comes out strongly here.

These three ecological principles help to give us a nuanced framework through which to look at key texts from the wisdom tradition that might inform an ecological hermeneutic in a positive way. The first of 'interaction', both within nature and with humans and between both and the divine, comes across in the wisdom literature in the sheer use of nature imagery and interest in the natural world that is revealed there. In Proverbs, human life is over and over illuminated by a pithy proverb, likening

12 May (1994) makes the distinction between a developed doctrine of creation *ex nihilo*, which he ascribes not to Hellenistic-Jewish achievement in the post-exilic period as commonly assumed by scholars, but to a controversy between Greek philosophy and early Christianity. He admits however that older, unsophisticated, implicit statements of this concept exist in the Old Testament itself so that a line runs from biblical ideas of creation to this more developed doctrine.
13 Job 38.25-30 reminds us that God provides rain for the wilderness where no human habitation is found, hence confirming that nature is of value in itself without human involvement (see pp. 64–66) and indeed human beings have tended to take over non-human ecosystems and hence change them, assuming a responsibility dictated by an anthropocentric outlook. McKibbin (2005) makes the point that by exercising our power over oceans, atmospheres and animals, we are gradually destroying our planet.

some aspect of human character to the natural world: 'The north wind produces rain, and a backbiting tongue, angry looks' (Prov. 25.23), for example. God's interaction is shown by the fact that he is behind the scenes, directing the action, presupposed even if not specifically mentioned.[14] The proverbs contain basic observations, similes, metaphors and antithetical comparisons all of which use animal, plant or other references to illuminate some aspect of human behaviour. Let us look briefly at one example of each of these. An example of a short proverb springing from basic observation of animal behaviour is Prov. 6.6: 'Go to the ant, you lazybones; consider its ways, and be wise.' The lazy person is instructed to look at an insect who is a paradigm of discipline and hard work, which is of course the ideal of the diligent wise person who is the opposite to the aforementioned 'lazybones'. An example of a simile using plant imagery is Prov. 11.28: 'Those who trust in their riches will wither, but the righteous will flourish like green leaves.' The healthy leaf is a symbol of vitality and well-being, such as describes the righteous, who by inference trust in God rather than in ephemeral matters such as 'riches'. An example of a metaphor is in Prov. 15.19: 'The way of the lazy is overgrown with thorns, but the path of the upright is a level highway.' The metaphor of thorns is a frequent one, denoting a bumpy path rather than a smooth one. Once again the lazybones is under attack. Antithetical comparison is a keynote of the wisdom literature. This is characterized by the use of the phrase 'Better . . . than . . .', e.g. Prov. 15.17: 'Better is a dinner of vegetables where love is than a fatted ox and hatred with it.'

So on one level the approach here in Proverbs is anthropocentric, in that the sages are attempting to shed light on human character and yet at the same time they are telling us something profound about their detailed observation of the non-human world around them, a world with which they interact every day. In many ways they interact more profoundly with the natural world and are not so divorced from that world as we are in our modern cities today. As von Rad wrote, 'While present-day man lives his life very much isolated from the world, and is determined by the feeling of otherness and foreignness to it, Hebrew man felt it to be much more personally related to himself' (1965: 428).

The sages particularly liked joining together in a proverb two things that had apparently nothing to do with each other – the bringing together itself made for an interesting and sometimes profound observation. For example, 'Like clouds and wind without rain is one who boasts of a gift never given' (Prov. 25.14). This likens two completely unlike situations by the link of disappointment when what is promised does not appear in reality. This is about both perceiving and imposing an order on the world so that human behaviour can be understood as part of a wider order that links the natural world and the divine realm. Similar techniques of proverbial types are found in Job and Ecclesiastes. In Job they are often phrased as a question, e.g. 'Does the wild ass bray over its grass, or the ox low over its fodder?' (Job 6.5). This suggests the answer,

---

14   The issue of how theological or secular the proverbs are is a well-worn debate. See the discussion in Dell 2006, where the stress is on the more theological side of the argument.

no, since if these animals have their desire – i.e. food – there is no need for complaint. Job makes considerable use of similes, e.g. Job 9.25-6: 'My days are swifter than a runner; they flee away, they see no good. They go by like skiffs of reed, like an eagle swooping on the prey.' Here the days are personified, another common technique in Job. In Eccl. 7.6 there is a clear simile using plant imagery: 'For like the crackling of thorns under a pot, so is the laughter of fools.' A metaphor example from Job is the use of a ploughing metaphor used of the wicked: 'Those who plough iniquity and sow trouble reap the same' (Job 4.8). Another technique, found particularly in Job, is the use of personification of non-human elements in order to shed light on human life or experience. An example is the personification of day and night as witnesses to Job's conception and birth (Job 3.1-10). In Ecclesiastes too there are simple comparisons with the natural world, as in 10.1 where folly in the context of wisdom is likened to dead flies in the context of fine ointment: 'Dead flies make the perfumer's ointment give off a foul odour; so a little folly outweighs wisdom and honour.'

There are two key texts I wish to look at in connection with this first principle of interaction, that is Prov. 30.15-33 and Eccl. 1.4-9. In Prov. 30.15-33 we find considerable use of animal and plant imagery used in creative listings, often using techniques of numerical heightening as a means of comparison. This idea of putting together images that apparently have no link at all is at the heart of this clever technique perfected by the wise. Ranged together the separate images form a wider whole and the human and animal world are interchangeable. The passage divides into subsections, the first being verses 15-16, which is about things that are not satisfied. The image of a leech is used. Leeches suck people dry of blood and are a good image for the endless need for more. The leech is portrayed as having two daughters who also are never satisfied. This is where a numerical heightening technique comes in: the four 'never satisfied' items that are put together are Sheol, the place of the dead that never ceases to gobble up victims; the barren womb that always wants a child; the earth that is always needing water; and the raging fire that goes on increasing and intensifying unless it is checked. By putting these four things together there is illumination between them and we can see how the human and non-human worlds are not distinguished one from another – they are completely interchangeable. Verses 18-19 form another unity and bring together four unlike things under the catchword 'way'. Two images are from the natural world – the eagle and the snake whose habits are beyond the understanding of the writer. Then the passage turns to a human invention – the ship – but its passage through the sea, which apparently behaves according to its own rules, and then on to human relationships.

Verses 21-23 form another group of four, this time of unnatural occurrences that threaten 'order'. Here all the images are human ones and show an interest in human hierarchies. However in verse 24 the concern switches to animals again. Here four items are ranged together that are small but 'exceedingly wise'. The industrious ant is held up as an example again, badgers are praised for their ingenuity in making their homes in the rocks, locusts march in rank despite having no leader and lizards are small but aspire to more when they are found in the palaces of kings. This ranking has a slightly tongue-in-cheek, humorous feel to it. The imagery is rich and allows the imagination free rein. Deane-Drummond comments on this passage that 'by paying attention to the quiet witness of such creatures . . . human beings learn of the possibility of a different form of society' (2008: 94). She sees these creatures as representing the 'voice of the earth' speaking to humans. However, her emphasis on the human parallel, in my view, draws attention away from the sheer delight in the insect world that is expressed. Verses 29-31 provide the final set of numerically heightened images. The four here are three animals, which are then likened to the king. It is often, of course, in the fourth image that the climax is found. Here one imagines a mighty lion, which is likened to a strutting rooster and a he-goat. The king's similar striding perhaps has an air of arrogance to it, as with these animals. This shows once again the complete interlinking of worlds, albeit always in a human context.

The book of Ecclesiastes gives us an insight into nature's own complex interrelated processes in its description of the 'cycles' of sun, moon and wind in Eccl. 1.4-9. A human comparison is brought in in verse 4 with the mention of human generations in contrast to the earth's permanence, although the emphasis is on a simple watching of the world on its course (see Dell 2009). It is basically the observation that everything goes around – the sun rises and goes down. In the ancient world the sun had a resting place overnight as there was no concept of the roundness of the world. The wind too blows in all directions on its own circuits. Water flows to the sea and then returns to its source.[15] The message is that everything on the earth comes around, except the earth itself, which is permanent. Human life is a part of that equation. The wider context of verses 2, 3 and 8 suggest a world-weariness and feeling of pointlessness about life, although I would argue that verses 4-9 themselves are more neutral and are simply observation rather than evaluation in a negative vein. Human intervention in such natural cycles arguably puts them under threat and human beings need to make sure that protection of natural processes is a prime concern.[16]

The second principle of the flourishing of all life, gives us a sense of the awe that human beings have when they consider the created world and the God who first created and now sustains it. This involves ideas of the essential goodness of God's intention for the world and all its creatures (cf. Genesis 1). An important presupposition of the proverbs is that life is essentially good, for example, Prov. 16.20:

---

15   An alternative translation for 1.7 is, 'To the source from which the rivers come, there they flow to run again', following Min (1991). Min recognizes the problem that it is common knowledge that waters do not flow backward from the sea to the water source, but posits that the author of Ecclesiastes may have understood evaporation of water into the air which then falls as rain at the source of the water (as propounded by Ibn Ezra in relation to this passage).

16   McKibben writes, 'What we are doing is very simple – we are taking over control of the physical world around us. The most basic laws remain beyond our grasp – gravity still causes objects to fall, atoms still repel at close distances, the sun still revolves around the earth. But nature on the scale immediately and constantly visible to us – the world of animals, of rainfall, of trees, of waves – may soon answer to us, as our crude alterations of atmospheric chemistry begin to guide the most fundamental processes of terrestrial life' (2005: 57).

'Those who are attentive to a matter will prosper, and happy are those who trust in the LORD.' Reaching towards an intention of goodness is something with which the environmental thinker should be dealing.

A sense of awe at the created world is found in Job 28, ostensibly a hymn to Wisdom, but arguably, rather, a hymn in praise of the created world (see Dell 2001). There is a description of all the precious metals to be found in the bowels of the earth and praise of human ingenuity in finding them. The irony that the earth provides 'bread' (v. 5) but underneath contains gold and fine sapphires (v. 6) is brought out. The point of comparison is with Wisdom, which cannot be found however hard it is sought.[17] However, this should not detract from the sheer awe at the created world that is found here. Strong animals are described such as falcons and lion – even they have not found Wisdom. Human beings probe all things – 'hidden things they bring to light' (v. 11) – this is the closest the Bible comes to a description of scientific endeavour. Yet no one knows the way to Wisdom – it is not in the 'land of the living' (v. 14) and the place of the dead has only heard a 'rumour' of it (v. 22). It is not in the sea, it is unable to be valued versus gold or glass – and yet in the process all those wonders are themselves described. Its price is beyond coral, crystals or pearls, chrysolite or gold (vv. 16-19) – and yet those wonders come from the earth too. This list of fine stones and metals comprises the richness of the earth's gifts. The comparison with the inaccessibility of Wisdom then, while seeming to downgrade all these wonders in the process of the comparison itself, also reveals the wonders of the world at the same time. It is the earth that is full of these bounties and that is to be praised. Human beings also have a role in that they have used their ingenuity to find out such hidden things. The climax comes in verse 23 that God does know the way to wisdom for he 'sees everything under the heavens' (v. 24).[18] His work as creator is described and clearly his lordship over all is an important theme here.

---

17 Fretheim, in his important book on creation theology which stresses its relational aspect and brings in the non-human, likens Wisdom to a person with ever deeper dimensions, 'a being that is always in the process of becoming . . . Those in search of wisdom will always be finding ever new dimensions of reality to be studied and will always be at least one step behind. As with persons, wisdom is forever inexhaustible' (2005: 210).

18 Habel (2003) makes an important point about biodiversity and the changing nature of species, according to a Darwinian model, which requires us to see creation as a more continuous process. He suggests that God discovers wisdom in the natural ordering of the Earth and hence looks to the Earth for this wisdom. He likens God to a sage seeking out wisdom in the Earth. This however could suggest limitation of the divine mind of the world that Job 28.24 arguably qualifies. Deane-Drummond struggles with this distinction when, having supported Habel's view, she writes, 'Certainly from the perspective of the book of Job, it seems to make more sense to speak primarily of creaturely wisdom as being that which God discovers in creation, rather than that which is imposed by God. Yet, God's ability to create in the first place according to a "design" and purpose, and then assess that wisdom and confirm it, implies wisdom in God that is *beyond* that which God discovers as existing in the world that God creates' (2008: 95). Perhaps the idea of wisdom existing in the divine mind (Perdue 1994) and a wisdom that is continually changing and being discovered by God (Habel) are not completely in tension and can be seen as facets of the mystery that is Wisdom herself.

However, he is also responsible for creating and sustaining the wonders of the earth, in the presence of which human beings stand open-mouthed in awe.

This same awe at the processes of both life and death is also found in somewhat more cynical vein in Eccl. 3.18-21. The thematic link with Job 28 is the limits of human knowledge. The comparison here is between the fates of humans and animals respectively. The context is that both die and thus one has no advantage over the other. The question comes in verse 21: 'Who knows whether the human spirit goes upward and the spirit of animals goes downward to the earth?' The author does not know the answer here and perhaps there is a slight hint that in fact, in line with the former verses, humans and animals are the same in their fate and so perhaps this distinction cannot be made after all. People have a tendency to denigrate animals below humans but, rather like in Job 12.7-8, they may have something to teach us. And who knows where the human and animal spirit goes? The author's advice is to stop worrying about afterwards and get on with the enjoyment of hard work! One key way in which human beings can flourish is to develop a sense of purpose in their work, a facet of human life that Ecclesiastes emphasizes.

The third principle of the sustaining of life – a process initiated by God but continued by his creatures – brings us right up to the present and our human duty of care. In the whole creation and sustaining process there is a dark side, as God has the freedom to act as he likes and he can bring weal as well as woe (e.g. Job 1.10). One way in which he appears to exercise this freedom is in the use of natural disaster, such as earthquake and fire, to exercise judgement (cf. Amos 1.7, 10, 12, 14; 2.5; 8.8). However the wisdom tradition in general is confident that God tends to act according to the rules he has established – or at least the earlier wisdom tradition had this confidence (as demonstrated in Proverbs) which was somewhat undermined by the time Job and Ecclesiastes were written. I wish in this section to look at two key texts: Job 38–39 and Proverbs 8.

Job 38–39 gives us a fascinating insight into some of the wild animals created by God and sustained by him for no better purpose than for the sheer sake of it, demonstrating to Job that God's world is far richer and more free than he ever imagined. This conveys the idea that the natural world has inherent value in and of itself and as God's creation, whether or not there are any humans to interact with it (see Attfield and Dell 1996). Job 38 consists of a series of rhetorical questions to Job, designed to make him feel small. He was clearly not present at creation and doesn't know the technicalities of it. God, by contrast, was and does! However, as well as being a 'put-down' of Job, it is also an immensely rich account of God's action in creation and that as a continuous, not once-only, process. The language of foundation, measurements, stretching a line, sinking bases and placing a cornerstone is that of building a house. The sense of sheer joy is found in verse 7: 'when the morning stars sang together and all the heavenly beings shouted for joy.' Creation involves ordering chaos, reining in that which is likely to get out of hand, hence the image of shutting in the sea (v. 8) and prescribing bounds for it (v. 10). This is an act of continual restraint on God's part that happened both once for all at creation, but also goes

The Significance of the Wisdom Tradition in the Ecological Debate 65

on being done to sustain the planet and all its creatures.[19] We find similar imagery to that in Eccl. 1.5-7 in the cycle of the day in verse 12, although it is interesting that such a process is likened, in verse 13, to the overcoming of the wicked. God's all-encompassing power over every corner of the earth is described in verses 16-18, 19-21 and 22-24, recalling God's knowledge of Wisdom's hiding place in Job 28.

God is also the provider of all sustenance – in verses 25-27, 28-30 of rain that waters the land – and is the bringer of life to desolate places. These places contain no human habitation – the wilderness is wholly independent of humanity and yet God causes it to rain. In fact even the observation of this gratuitous rain is of no use to humans – such rain is simply part of God's scheme.[20] The description is rich in the way it turns to the stars in verses 31-33. God has the power to do all things – he can command floods and lightning and he can provide wisdom to humanity (vv. 34-38). From Job 38.39 begins the long description of different animals – mainly wild ones and certainly strong ones – which God created and which he sustains. This section rejoices in the habits of animals that behave according to set orders set in motion by God and whose lives follow cycles such as birth and death. We find rich descriptions of lions, ravens, mountain goats, wild asses, wild oxen, the ostrich, the horse, hawks and eagles. The wildness of these animals suggests something untamed and free, which is how God is being described here too.[21] These animals exist and function without any reference to the human world – they are simply answerable to their divine creator.[22] There is a sense of awe at the sheer variety and diversity of this world – and some of the animals behave in ways that humans beings would find chaotic, e.g. the ostrich leaving her eggs to hatch alone (Job 39.14-15) – and yet such animal habits are rejoiced in as part of the wider tapestry of God's magnificent creation. In this thought-world, the very existence of the created world and all that is in it is a process utterly dependent upon God as creator and sustainer. It does not exist apart from him as a separate working entity, but rather is dependent upon him in a continuous sense.

The description of the animals in Job 38–39 is a unique opportunity in the biblical

---

19 Peacocke (2001) makes the important point that, in the light of our knowledge of biological evolution, any modern statement of God as creator must assert that God is continuously creating in a dynamic sense. He writes, 'The traditional notion of God *sustaining* the world in its general order and structure now has to be replaced by one with a dynamic and creative dimension – a model of God giving continuous existence to a process that has an inbuilt creativity, built into it by God and manifest in a "time" itself given existence by God' (23).
20 Palmer comments on this verse in the context of human assumption of their stewardship of nature and the occasional inappropriateness (as here) of that presupposition, that 'God is directly involved with the land and has no gardener. Humanity is irrelevant. Its position is neither to have dominion over the land, nor to tend and dress it. The "desolate wasteland sprouts with grass" without human aid' (1992: 70).
21 Fretheim expresses the paradox that there is order in creation and yet some disorder is allowed for by God. He writes, 'Amid the order there is room for chance. The world has ostriches and eagles, raging seas and predictable sunrises, wild weather or stars that stay their courses. God creates space for creaturely freedom at various levels of complexity' (2005: 244).
22 Dyrness makes the point that in these speeches it is clear that non-human creation doesn't need to have a relation to human lives – 'we are relieved of the pressure to make creation at every point useful for human society' (1987: 52–53).

tradition to see God and nature in partnership quite apart from the involvement of human beings. It is not a particularly palatable picture – it is nature in the raw involving blood and death and, while the description inspires awe, it also repels and alienates the human perspective. There is no transformation of the natural world in Job as in Isaiah 40.4. This is a celebration of the wild and the untamed, of noble creatures nurtured by God but remaining wild. This description certainly expands Job's horizons, but whether it expands his *moral* horizons (Brown 1999) is debatable. It is also not stated that this creation is 'innocent' (Santmire 2006). In my view these descriptions serve to overwhelm Job with the wonders of creation, to make him see other possibilities that lie outside a human-centred worldview, hence to displace him from his usual 'world', and to teach him more about God's created world, particularly a world that is on the margins of his own experience. However, these speeches are, more crucially, about the beauty and non-conformity of the created world and there is an essential element of playfulness, whim and caprice in God's delighting in what he has made. They are also about God's power in nature, none more so than in the descriptions of Behemoth and Leviathan in chapters 40–41, great creatures that represent both the chaos overcome by God at creation and the constant care of God on nature's behalf in the face of chaotic forces. These creatures, even if they are based on hippopotamus and crocodiles, are representative of animals that remain untamed and apart from human experience and control.

One of the keynotes of the wisdom tradition is contradiction. Individual proverbs contradict one another from time to time (e.g. consecutive and conflicting proverbs on silence in Prov. 17.27-28). That sense of contradiction is particularly brought out in Ecclesiastes where the speaker comments on proverbial sayings and puts them in the wider context of 'vanity'. Job also draws out the contradiction between traditional guarantees and fresh experience, which leads to contradiction and a deep sense of questioning. The sense of dialectic runs through the material and, as commented above, that dialectic need not simply be regarded as two-way – divine/human – but three-way – divine/human/non-human. Contradiction suggests openness to revision and elaboration and openness to change. The very presence of Job and Ecclesiastes within the wisdom tradition itself shows how the tradition managed to break out of its own certainties and fixed system. In Proverbs 8 the sense of dialectic spoken of by Perdue (1994) – between cosmology and anthropology – is apparent. A figure that stands at the heart of this dialectic in Proverbs is Woman Wisdom, as described in Proverbs 8, who mediates between the divine and the human. And yet she also rejoices in the inhabited world and is described as having been present and delighting in the world at the very beginning.[23] This is therefore a helpful paradigm with which

---

23 Fretheim stresses the importance of 'delight' in the relationship between God and Wisdom – it shows God involved in a dynamic and interactive relationship, it shows Wisdom delighting in humanity and hence realizing God's purposes for creation. He writes, 'Delight is not amusement in the sense of an activity different from work but a dimension of the relationship itself and including work and all participants – God, wisdom and creation' (2005: 217).

to end and from which to reflect on our own dialectic with God and nature.

In Proverbs 8, Wisdom first seems to relate to human beings – their well-being depends upon hearing her call and she represents knowledge and justice. This is the same Wisdom described in Job 28 as being beyond human knowledge. Here, however, Wisdom, in female guise, is on offer to human beings if they will take hold of her and embrace her. From verse 22 the link with God's creative acts is apparent, although she is never doing the creating. Rather she stands beside God admiring his work. This need not be taken literally[24] but can be regarded as an extended poetic metaphor for describing God's creative act. However, the use of this poetic technique conveys the mediation between God's creation and the humans and non-humans within that world. Wisdom forms a bridge between the work of God and the delight that is taken in 'his inhabited world . . . and the human race' (v. 31). This is therefore a profound image of the dialectic between creator and created that is at the heart of the wisdom worldview.

So what of a practical nature can human beings take away from these rich images found in the wisdom literature? The sense of interaction with God and nature comes across here. We human beings are a part of a complex web of life, the key to which is the need to sustain the world that we inhabit. God is both creator and sustainer of the world, but we have a major role in sustaining it[25] and enabling all its processes to continue, processes which are open to constant change. However, the study of the wisdom material has given us a timely reminder that we are not the only inhabitants of this universe and has prioritized the wilderness image of places of habitation well beyond the human domain. Contradiction and reinvention characterize the creative process, the natural world and human life. Embracing the contradiction and the dialectic leaves us open to the possibilities of change. It is clear from the speeches of God in the book of Job that not all of creation should be seen as subordinated to human interests, a lesson we will still do well to learn as we continue to live unsustainably in the world. McKibben (2005) gives us a timely reminder that the voice from the whirlwind calls us to humility on the one hand and joy on the other – the need to restrain our desires for control of the planet and for ever increasing levels of consumerism and find our rightful place in the world of nature by restraining our greed and appreciating our environment afresh. Just as the way to wisdom is a mystery (Job 28) so full awareness of the created world is not known to us, only to God. We rightfully seek to discover this world, but our desire to control it and change it and so often spoil it needs to be kept in check. The study of the wisdom

---

24   Some scholars have seen evidence of vestiges of a goddess figure here, e.g. Lang 1975. Fretheim (2005) also sees her as both divine and a creature, which in my view is an overstatement – she is 'created' but in a special role and relationship with God.

25   There is a slight tendency from those writing from an environmental angle to downgrade the role of human beings and present humans as the 'baddies' who have destroyed much of the planet. However, it has to be acknowledged that, as McKibben puts it, 'our peculiar brains set us apart from the rest of creation. We have powers unique to ourselves; to refuse them would be like a bird refusing flight. Luckily . . . there are whole huge categories of activity for which reason is utterly suited and which do not also spell destruction for the rest of the ecosystem' (2005: 67).

world-view engenders a certain humility that we are indeed a part of a complex set of processes, of God's world, of which we are a crucial part, but which has the right to exist completely independently of ourselves.

References

Anderson, B.W. 1975 'Human Dominion Over Nature', in M. Ward (ed.), *Biblical Studies in Contemporary Thought* (Somerville, MA: Hadden): 27–45.
Attfield, R. and K. J. Dell (eds) 1996 *Values, Conflict and the Environment* (Aldershot: Avebury).
Barr, J. 1972 'Man and Nature: The Ecological Controversy and the Old Testament', *BJRL* 55: 9–32.
Bright, J. 1967 *The Authority of the Old Testament* (London: SCM).
Brown, W. P. 1999 *Cosmos and Ethos: The Genesis of Moral Imagination in the Bible* (Grand Rapids, MI/Cambridge: Eerdmans).
Deane-Drummond, C. 2000 *Creation Through Wisdom* (Edinburgh: T&T Clark).
Deane-Drummond, C. 2004 *The Ethics of Nature* (Oxford: Blackwell).
Deane-Drummond, C. 2006 *Wonder and Wisdom* (London: Darton, Longman & Todd).
Deane-Drummond, C. 2008 *Eco-theology* (Toronto: Novalis).
Dell, K. J. 1994 'Green Ideas in the Wisdom Tradition', *SJT* 47: 423–51.
Dell, K. J. 2000 *Get Wisdom, Get Insight: An Introduction to Israel's Wisdom Literature* (London: Darton, Longman & Todd).
Dell, K. J. 2001 'Plumbing the Depths of Earth: Job 28 and Deep Ecology', in N. C. Habel and S. Wurst (eds), *The Earth Story in Wisdom Traditions* (The Earth Bible, 3; Sheffield/Cleveland, OH: Sheffield Academic Press/Pilgrim Press): 116–25.
Dell, K. J. 2006 *The Book of Proverbs in Social and Theological Context* (Cambridge: Cambridge University Press).
Dell, K. J. 2009 'The Cycle of Life in Ecclesiastes', *Vetus Testamentum* 59: 181–89.
Devall B. and J. Sessions 1985 *Deep Ecology* (Salt Lake City, UT: G M Smith).
Dyrness, W. 1987 'Stewardship of the Earth in the Old Testament', in W. Granberg-Michaelson (ed.), *Tending the Garden: Essays on the Gospel and the Earth* (Grand Rapids, MI: Eerdmans): 50–65.
Fretheim, T. E. 2005 *God and the World in the Old Testament: A Relational Theology of Creation* (Nashville, TN: Abingdon).
Habel, N. 2003 'The Implications of God Discovering Wisdom in Earth', in E. van Wolde (ed.), *Job 28: Cognition in Context* (Leiden: Brill): 281–97.
Habel, N. and S. Wurst 2001 *The Earth Story in Wisdom Traditions* (The Earth Bible, 3; Sheffield/Cleveland, OH: Sheffield Academic Press/Pilgrim Press).
Hermisson, H-J. 1978 'Observations on the Creation Theology in Wisdom', in J. G. Gammie, W. A. Brueggemann, W. L. Humphreys and J. M. Ward (eds), *Israelite Wisdom: Theological and Literary Essays in Honour of Samuel Terrien* (Missoula, MA: Scholars Press): 43–57.
Johnston, R. K. 1987 'Wisdom Literature and Its Contribution to a Biblical Environmental Ethic', in W. Granberg-Michaelson (ed.), *Tending the Garden: Essays on the Gospel and the Earth* (Grand Rapids, MI: Eerdmans): 66–82.
Lang, B. 1975 *Frau Weisheit: Deutung einer biblischen Gestalt* (Dusseldorf: Patmos).
McKibben, B. 2005 *The Comforting Whirlwind: God, Job, and the Scale of Creation* (Cambridge, MA: Cowley).
Marlow, H. F. 2009 *Biblical Prophets and Contemporary Environmental Ethics: Re-reading Amos, Hosea and First Isaiah* (Oxford: Oxford University Press).
May, G. 1994 *Creatio ex Nihilo: The Doctine of 'Creation out of Nothing' in Early Christian Thought* (Edinburgh: T&T Clark).
Min, Y-J. 1991 'How Do the Rivers Flow? (Ecclesiastes 1:7)', *The Bible Translator* 42: 226–31.
Palmer, C. 1992 'Stewardship: A Case-study in Environmental Ethics', in I. Ball, M. Goodall,

C. Palmer and J. Reader, *The Earth Beneath: A Critical Guide to Green Theology* (London: SPCK): 67–86.

Peacocke, A. 2001 'The Cost of New Life', in J. Polkinghorne (ed.), *The Work of Love: Creation as Kenosis* (London: SPCK; Grand Rapids, MI/Cambridge: Eerdmans): 21–42.

Perdue, L. 1991 *Wisdom in Revolt* (Sheffield: Almond).

Perdue, L. 1994 *Wisdom and Creation* (Nashville, TN: Abingdon).

Santmire, H. P. 2006 'Partnership with Nature according to the Scriptures: Beyond the Theology of Stewardship', in R.J. Berry (ed.), *Environmental Stewardship* (London/New York: T&T Clark): 253–72.

Schmid, H. H. 1968 *Gerechtigkeit als Weltordnung* (BHT 40; Tübingen: Mohr Siebeck).

von Rad, G. 1965 *Old Testament Theology* (vol. 1; Edinburgh and New York: Oliver and Boyd).

von Rad, G. 1972 *Wisdom in Israel* (London: SCM).

White, L., Jr 1967 'The Historical Roots of our Ecologic Crisis', *Science* 155: 1203–207.

Zimmerli, W. 1964 'The Place and Limit of Wisdom in the Framework of Old Testament Theology', *SJT* 17: 146–58.

Chapter 5

READING THE SYNOPTIC GOSPELS ECOLOGICALLY

Richard Bauckham

Few of those who have written about the ecological dimension of the Bible have found much to say about the Synoptic Gospels.[1] It may be that, as Robert Murray (1997: 126) comments, Jesus' relationship to the non-human creation is not 'a salient theme in the gospels', but, alternatively, it may be that, especially when the Gospels are read with their relation to the Old Testament in mind, there are significant references to the non-human creation that have not been given the attention they deserve. It may be that, in the case of the Gospels, the eyes of modern urban readers still need to be opened to that dimension of human life, our relationship to the non-human environment and its creatures, that to the biblical writers was self-evidently of huge importance.

In this essay I shall explore two approaches to identifying the ecological dimensions of the story of Jesus in the Synoptic Gospels. (I shall not be concerned to distinguish 'the historical Jesus' from the Jesus of the Gospels, but with the way in which the Gospels depict Jesus and his story.) The first approach attempts to make explicit the Palestinian ecological context that the Gospels largely take for granted, in the hope of discovering something of Jesus' relationship with it. The second approach works with the theme of the Kingdom of God, unquestionably the central theme of Jesus' teaching and ministry in the Synoptic Gospels, in order to show that the Kingdom includes the whole of creation and that some of the acts in which Jesus anticipated the coming Kingdom point to the redemption of the human relationship with the rest of creation.

Jesus in his Ecological Context

In a chapter called 'Jesus and the Ecology of Galilee', Sean Freyne (2004: 24–59) has recently characterized the 'micro-ecologies' that distinguished the three regions

---

[1] Notable exceptions include Faricy 1982: 40–48; Northcott 1996: 224–225; Leske 2002; Loader 2002; Jones 2003. My own previous contributions are: Bauckham 1994; 1998; 2009a; 2009b.

of Galilee – Lower (including Nazareth), the Valley (including Capernaum and the lakeside) and Upper (including Caesarea Philippi) – along with the 'different modes of human interaction with, and different opinions about the natural world' that the three different environments produced (Freyne 2004: 40). Freyne sees Jesus' ministry as taking place successively in these three regions, and suggests ways in which the ecological character of each may have influenced Jesus' thought and teaching. It has to be said that many of these suggestions are very speculative, while some are illuminating and others at least plausible.

It is probable, for example, that the term 'the sea', used by Mark and Matthew to refer to the lake of Galilee, reflects the usage of those who lived beside it and were unconcerned with the Mediterranean, while the story of the stilling of the storm reflects the threat of the mythological abyss on the part of people whose lives were dominated by water, its possibilities and dangers. It is also plausible that Jesus' faith in the creator God of the Hebrew Scriptures, who cares for his creation and overcomes the ever-threatening chaos, engaged at this point with the consciousness, at once realistic and mythic, of the local fishermen who were his disciples (Freyne 2004: 53). (The stilling of the storm will be discussed further in the last main section of this essay.)

On the other hand, I am not tempted by this suggestion:

> One is tempted to ask whether Jesus' healing ministry, attested in all the gospels, might have given him a special appreciation of the climatic conditions of the Lake area, and the quality of its water, prompting a visit to its source [Mount Hermon]. (Freyne 2004: 56)

Nothing in the stories of Jesus' healings offers the slightest hint of a regard for the health-giving quality of the water of the lake. There is nothing like Elisha's command to Naaman to wash in the Jordan (2 Kgs 5.10) or the Johannine Jesus' command to the blind man to wash in the pool of Siloam (Jn 9.7). Freyne does not answer the question he says 'one is tempted to ask', but one may also question whether such an excessively speculative question is even worth asking. It seems to be a strained attempt to forge a link between Jesus and some aspects of the lake of Galilee and Mount Hermon that we know interested some ancient writers. This example is among the least plausible of Freyne's suggestions.

Freyne is surely right in general to argue that Jesus' thought and teaching were influenced by his natural environment, its diversity and the various ways Galileans made a living from it. He was not a bookish intellectual but a man consciously embedded in his rural environment. But Freyne is also right to insist that we need not play off Jesus' direct experience of his environment against the rootedness of his beliefs in the Hebrew Scriptures and Jewish religious tradition (especially, in this case, faith in God as Creator of all things). The parables, he says,

> are the product of a religious imagination that is deeply grounded in the world of nature and the human struggle with it, and at the same time deeply rooted in the traditions of Israel which

speak of God as creator of heaven and earth and all that is in them (Freyne 2004: 59, cf. also 48).[2]

It is also important to note that Freyne does not, like some nineteenth-century writers,[3] depict Jesus' relationship to nature as a romantic idyll. Many of Jesus' references to the non-human world are to the hard work of making a living from the soil or the lake, and the parables also show awareness of the increasingly precarious state of small landowners, hard-pressed or deprived of their land as large estates became more numerous (Freyne 2004: 45–46).[4]

Freyne's method is a historical one, drawing on archaeology and literary sources to reconstruct the ecology of Galilee in Jesus' time. As in much historiography, historical imagination is required to make the links with Jesus. But Edward Echlin's approach is more creatively imaginative. He speaks of 'imaginative contemplation' in which we can make the 'implicit' in the Gospels (as in the rest of the Bible) 'explicit' (Echlin 1999: 26–27, 30, 32, 54–55).

> When we contemplate the testimonies to Jesus looking for insights we will catch glimpses in the depths, in the small print, in what is hidden, between the lines, tacit and silent. (Echlin 1999: 29; cf. 54)

The following passage, imagining Jesus' early years in Nazareth, shows how Echlin takes up hints in the Gospels to paint the sort of picture they make no attempt to provide, but which Echlin, a former Jesuit, aptly places in the tradition of the imaginative meditations in Ignatius Loyola's *Spiritual Exercises*:

> With imagination we may place ourselves in hilly Nazareth with its few hundred families and their sheep and goats, oxen, cattle and donkeys. In those green and brown and stony hills we may imaginatively observe the growing Jesus (Lk. 2.40, 52) learning, especially from his mother, about the useful elder trees, the scattered Tabor oaks and Aleppo pine, the nettle, bramble, mallow, and startling yellow chrysanthemums of April, the galaxy of weeds and herbs and wild flowers which he later compared to Solomon's attire. Grapes grow and grew in Nazareth's old town, their branches nourished by the everlasting vine. Jesus wondered at their rapid growth, their ripening in the burning sun, and their harsh winter pruning, he learned about apples, almonds and pomegranates, he saw figs swarming from rocks offering two, even three crops of dripping sweetness. When they began to put out leaves, as did the other trees, he knew that summer was here (Lk. 21.20).[5] (Echlin 1999: 55)

---

2 Similarly Echlin 1999, 76: Jesus' 'sensitivity to nature, so vivid in his parables, derived from living close to the natural world and from familiarity with the Jewish Scriptures and their metaphors of cosmic order'.
3 See especially Renan 1905 [1863]: 42–44.
4 On this point with regard to the parables, see also Shillington 1997: 9–11.
5 It is interesting to compare this account of Jesus' environment in his early years in Nazareth with Renan's (1905: 17–18). Renan's is more romantically aesthetic, Echlin's more ecological.

This may seem novelistic, but something like this must indeed have been the case for Jesus, as for any boy growing up in the villages of Lower Galilee. In principle, this kind of filling in of the environmental context of Jesus that the Gospels take for granted or ignore is no different from the way that historical Jesus scholars routinely fill in the social, economic, political and religious contexts of first-century Jewish Palestine to which events of the Gospel narratives relate. Imaginative as it is, an exercise like this could, paradoxically perhaps, also be an exercise in historical realism.

The wealth of references to flora, wild and cultivated, and fauna, wild and domesticated, as well as to common farming practices, in the Synoptic teaching of Jesus has, of course, often been taken to indicate Jesus' closeness to the natural and rural world of Galilee, but I know of no systematic study of the matter. In an admittedly rapid survey, I find the following animals mentioned, each at least once: bird, camel, chicken (cock and hen), dog, donkey, dove, fish, fox, gnat, goat, moth, ox, pig, raven, scorpion, sheep, snake, sparrow, viper, vulture, wolf (21 in total). Of these, eight are domestic animals. None is especially surprising in a rural Palestinian environment. The following are the plants to which the Synoptic teaching of Jesus refers: bramble, fig tree, herbs (mint, dill, cummin, rue and others), mulberry, mustard plant, reed, thorn, vine, weed, wheat, wild flower. Methods of making a living from this environment, mentioned in Jesus' teaching, include arboriculture, viticulture, shepherding, trapping animals, netting birds and the various stages of growing and processing wheat and other grains. Of course, this basic information could be expanded to include the frequency of mention of the various items, and evidence of familiarity with natural and farming processes, animal behaviour and so forth. References to the weather and its bearing on the farming activities of Jesus' Galilean contemporaries are another such topic for which the information could be assembled and discussed.

Most of these references, of course, function in the teaching of Jesus not as literal references but as figurative comparisons, and even the factual references are made for the sake of a religious point. Broadly similar phenomena are common in the prophets, the psalms and wisdom literature. So the question arises whether such material in the teaching of Jesus derives from direct observation of nature and farming or from the scriptural and oral traditional sources of Jesus' reflection and teaching. Vincent Mora (1991: 184–92), writing specifically about the animals in Matthew's Gospel, argues that almost all of these are used as symbols with deep roots in the Hebrew Scriptures. This is, course, true for some of the material, such as the image of shepherd and sheep, but certainly not for all. To take just two examples of Matthean animals, that foxes have holes (Mt. 8.20) and that pigs can be savage (Mt. 7.6) are not observations to be found in the Hebrew Bible or in Jewish traditions known to us. As we have already noted that Freyne observes, there is no need to think of direct observation and traditional usage as exclusive alternatives.

With the range and frequency of allusions to nature in the Synoptic teaching of Jesus it is perhaps instructive to compare the comparative rarity of such allusions in the Pauline letters. In the whole Pauline corpus (including the Pastorals) these animals occur: dog, lion, ox, snake, sheep (and Passover lamb), viper, wild animals, along with a general reference to birds, animals and reptiles. Only the following plants occur: olive tree, vine, wheat and other grains. Although ancient cities were much more closely connected with the natural and cultivated environment outside them than modern cities are, it does seem likely that the contrast between Jesus and Paul in this respect reflects the urban context of both Paul and his readers and hearers, by contrast with the mostly rural context of Jesus' life and ministry.[6] The contrast shows that the range and frequency of allusions to nature in the Synoptic teaching of Jesus are not merely what one might expect from any Jewish teacher acquainted with the Scriptures and Jewish religious traditions.

This whole issue merits much closer and more careful study. But, even if we suppose that Jesus' teaching drew extensively on his own close familiarity with the nature and farming practices of rural Galilee, we may still ask what the significance of this might be. With few exceptions, all these references have a figurative function: they do not seem to function to teach Jesus' hearers anything about the natural world itself or human relationships with it, but serve to make points about God and human life. However, there are some suggestions in the literature that could indicate otherwise. C. H. Dodd, having observed that the parables are realistic stories, true to nature and to life,[7] rather than artificial allegories, writes:

> There is a reason for this realism of the parables of Jesus. It arises from a conviction that there is no mere analogy, but an inward affinity, between the natural order and the spiritual order; or as we might put it in the language of the parables themselves, the Kingdom of God is intrinsically *like* the process of nature and of the daily life of men. Jesus therefore did not feel the need of making up artificial illustrations for the truths He wished to teach. He found them ready-made by the Maker of man and nature. (Dodd 1961: 20)

Claus Westermann understands the way parables work differently from Dodd, but he also argues that, like the 'comparisons' in the Old Testament with which he compares them, the parables of Jesus, by drawing their comparisons from the world of creation, 'assign great significance to God's creation in the context of what the Bible says about God' (Westermann 1990: 202). These are claims that need much fuller investigation before they can be confidently accepted or rejected.

Freyne makes a related but somewhat different point:

> Part of the genius of Jesus' parable-making is his ability to take everyday experiences, such as sowing and reaping and weave these into narratives that are at one and the same time highly

---

6   Of course, Galilee included the Herodian cities of Sepphoris and Tiberias, but the absence of any reference to these in the Gospels' accounts of Jesus' ministry very probably indicates that he deliberately avoided visiting them.
7   On the realism of the parables, see especially Hedrick 1994: 39–56.

> realistic in terms of his hearers' world and their experiences *and* deeply resonant of Yahweh's activity on behalf of Israel as this had been described in the psalms and the prophets. For peasant hearers their everyday work and experiences were being elevated to a symbolic level with reference to God's caring presence to Israel, as was the case also with the proverbial wisdom in the Hebrew Scriptures. The element of surprise and dislocation that many of these stories contain was intended to challenge the hearers to reconsider their understanding of God and his dealings with Israel, and to experience his presence in the world of the everyday, the world of home, village, field, sky and mountain. (Freyne 2004: 59)

This feature of the parables of Jesus could be highlighted by a comparison with the rabbinic parables. Though these share motifs with the parables of Jesus, they are much less connected with the everyday world (natural and occupational) of ordinary people. This down-to-earth and small-scale character of the stories Jesus told could also be associated with Jesus' miracles (healings, exorcisms and nature miracles) and significant acts (such as eating with sinners): both in his teaching and his activity Jesus proclaimed and embodied the kingdom of God in small-scale instances within the lives of ordinary people. These people's relationship to the natural world was a constant and determining feature of their lives, and this is reflected both in Jesus' parables and in his nature miracles.

Closeness and sensitivity to the natural environment would not, of course, make Jesus a modern ecologist. Echlin is clear about this: 'What emerges from the gospels is a villager within the Jewish tradition of holistic compassion and sustainable organic husbandry with people and animals on the land, working with and not against the ways of nature' (Echlin 1999: 78).

In other words, Echlin sees Jesus as embodying the best of the Jewish tradition, informed by the Hebrew Bible, with regard to attitudes to other living creatures and the environment. But this requires that we look for signs of the creation theology of the Hebrew Scriptures within the Synoptic teaching of Jesus. This is the starting point for the next section of this essay, in which we shall ask how creation theology might relate to the central theme of Jesus' teaching and ministry: the Kingdom of God.

The Kingdom of God as the Renewal of Creation

Jesus evidently endorsed the creation theology of the Hebrew Bible, centred on the belief that God created all things (cf. Mt. 19.9; Mk 10.6) and, as 'Lord of heaven and earth' (Lk. 10.21; Mt. 11.25), cared for the whole of his creation. As we shall see, this was the presupposition of his teaching about the Kingdom of God. But creation theology also appears explicitly at a number of key points in Jesus' theology:

1. To support his command to love enemies, Jesus uses the notion of imitation of God: 'so that you may be children of your Father in heaven; for he makes his sun rise on

the evil and on the good, and sends rain on the righteous and on the unrighteous' (Mt. 5.45).[8] The God who generously and mercifully pours his blessings on all people without distinction is the Creator who, according to Psalm 145, 'is good to all, and his compassion is over all that he has made' (Ps. 145.9). He is the source of all the blessings of the natural world, including sun (Ps. 19.4-6) and rain (Pss 65.9-11; 104.13; 147.8; Lev. 26.4).

2. 'Are not two sparrows sold for a penny? Yet not one of them will fall to the ground apart from your Father. And even the hairs of your head are all counted. So do not be afraid; you are of more value than many sparrows' (Mt. 10.29-31; cf. Lk. 12.6-7). While the point of this saying is to reassure the disciples of God's providential care for them, this rests on the assertion that God's providence embraces even the sparrows, whom humans value so cheaply that a pair costs a penny in the market. It is God who preserves each sparrow's life, and so not one sparrow can be caught in a hunter's net without his knowledge and consent. Jesus' words here reflect the view of the Hebrew Scriptures that God's caring responsibility embraces each living creature he has made (Job 12.10; Pss 36.6; 104.29-30).[9]

3. 'Look at the birds of the air; they neither sow nor reap nor gather into barns, and yet your heavenly Father feeds them. Are you not of more value than they? . . . Consider the lilies of the field, how they grow; they neither toil nor spin, yet I tell you, even Solomon in all his glory was not clothed like one of these. But if God so clothes the grass of the field, which is alive today and tomorrow is thrown into the oven, will he not much more clothe you . . .' (Mt. 6.26, 28-30; cf. Lk. 12.24, 27-28). Again, this is an argument from the lesser (wild flowers and birds) to the greater (human), but again the lesson for Jesus' hearers cannot be had without the premise that God cares for birds and wild flowers. That God feeds the birds (as he does all living creatures) is explicit in the Hebrew Bible (Ps. 147.9; Job 38.41; cf. Pss 104.27-28; 145.15-16). Humans can trust in God's provision because they too are members, even if eminent members, of the community of God's creatures for whom he generously provides.

4. Probably Jesus' hearers would also have understood his parables of growth (Mk 4.3-8, 26-32; and parallels) in terms of Jewish creation theology. They would not have supposed the growth of grain or mustard plants to be some kind of autonomous natural process, but as due to the blessing of God (cf. 1 Cor. 3.6). Only through the blessing of God is his creation fruitful (Deut. 7.12; 26.15; 28.4-5; Pss 65.9-11; 67.6; 107.38; cf. Gen. 1.22, 28). So in these parables the comparison is between God-given growth in creation and the God-given growth of the Kingdom of God, or, we might say, between the divine work of creation and the divine work of salvation and renewal. Also worth noticing at this point is the fact that the Psalms feature so prominently among the biblical sources of Jesus' creation theology. They would, of course, have been among the Scriptures best known to both Jesus and his hearers.

---

8   Biblical quotations are from the NRSV unless otherwise stated.
9   On this passage, and the Lukan parallel, see Bauckham 1998: 42–44.

From these indications of the importance of creation theology to Jesus the question arises as to its relationship to his proclamation of the coming Kingdom of God, which the Synoptic Gospels consider the overriding theme of his mission and teaching. Misunderstanding at this point has been fostered both by the tendency of scholars (enshrined in the so called 'criterion of dissimilarity') to stress only what appears to be novel in the teaching of Jesus vis-à-vis Judaism, and also by the perception of some kind of opposition between creation and eschatology, as though the eschatological Kingdom comes to abolish and replace creation. Instead, we should recognize the continuity between Jesus' teaching and the Scriptures and traditions of Judaism, without which what was novel in his teaching cannot be understood, and, crucially, that the Kingdom of God in the teaching of Jesus represents not the abolition but the renewal of creation.

Just as Jesus' creation theology seems rooted especially in the Psalms, so also is his understanding of the Kingdom of God, though Isaiah and Daniel are also important in this case. Most treatments of the background to the Kingdom of God in the Gospels give no great prominence to the Psalms, but Bruce Chilton's work especially remedies this failure (Chilton 1996: 23–44). The kingship and rule of God are more prominent in the Psalms than in most other parts of the Hebrew Bible, and they are closely related to creation. It is as Creator that God rules his whole creation (Ps. 103.19-22). His rule is over all that he has made, human and otherwise (Pss 95.4-5; 96.11-13), and it is expressed in the kind of caring responsibility for creation that we have already seen reflected also in the teaching of Jesus (Psalm 145). All non-human creatures acclaim his rule now (Pss 103.19-22; 148) and all nations must come to do so in the future (Ps. 97.1), for God is coming to judge the world, that is, both to condemn and to save (Pss 96.13; 98.9). His own people Israel's role is to declare his kingship to the nations (Pss 96.3, 10; 145.10-12). When God does come to judge and to rule, all creation will rejoice at his advent (Pss 96.11-12; 98.7-8). (These last three sentences show how close these Psalms are to the message of Isaiah 40–66, where the rule of God is also central.)

The kingship and rule of God in the Psalms have both a spatial and a temporal dimension. They are cosmic in scope, encompassing all creation, by no means confined to human society. They are also eternal, established at creation and set to last forever (Pss 93; 145.13; 146.10). Yet God's rule is widely flouted and rejected by the nations, and so it is still to come in the fullness of power and in manifest glory. The God who rules from his heavenly throne (Pss 11.4; 103.19) is coming to establish his rule on earth. It is this coming that Jesus proclaims. His distinctive phrase, 'the kingdom of God comes', stands for the expectation of the Psalms and the prophets that God himself is coming to reign (Meier 1994: 298-99).

The cosmic scope of the Kingdom can be seen in the opening three petitions of the Lord's Prayer in Matthew's version:

> Our Father in heaven,
> hallowed be your name,

>   your kingdom come,
>   your will be done,
>   on earth as it is in heaven. (Mt. 6.9-10)

The phrase 'on earth as it is in heaven' should probably be understood to qualify all three of the petitions. Presently, God's name is perfectly hallowed, his rule perfectly obeyed, and his will absolutely done in heaven, but all are neglected or contested on earth. Probably the emphasis is on humans coming to hallow God's name, to acknowledge God's rule and to do his will, but we should recall that in the Hebrew Bible non-human creatures also do these things, often when humans fail to do so (e.g. praising God's name: Ps. 145.5, 13; acclaiming his rule: Pss 103.19-22; 145.10-11; doing his will: Jer. 8.7). Moreover, the coupling of 'heaven' and 'earth' cannot fail to evoke the whole creation, everything God created at the beginning (Gen. 1.1; 2.1, 4). God, it was standardly said, is the Creator of heaven and earth, and this is the basis on which his Kingdom must come on earth as it is in heaven. The Kingdom does not come to extract people from the rest of creation, but to renew the whole creation in accordance with God's perfect will for it.

As well as proclaiming and explaining the Kingdom of God, Jesus instantiated it in the many activities of his ministry. These included the miracles of healing, exorcisms and the so-called 'nature' miracles. They also included significant acts such as his demonstration in the temple, sharing meals with sinners, blessing children, washing the disciples' feet and riding a donkey into Jerusalem. All these activities are to be understood as proleptic instances of the coming of the Kingdom, helping to define how Jesus understood the rule of God, but more than just symbols of its coming. In such activities the Kingdom was actually coming, but in anticipatory fashion, in small-scale instances. Their small-scale nature comports with the way most of the parables represent the Kingdom by events set in the ordinary world of Jesus' hearers. Just as a mustard plant, in the parable, grows to the dimensions of the mythical world tree, so, when Jesus stills the storm, a squall on the lake evokes the vast destructive power of the mythical abyss. Just as the extraordinary generosity of God in his coming Kingdom is figured, in the parable, when a master serves dinner to his slaves, so it takes place when Jesus pronounces the forgiveness of a notorious sinner who washed his feet.

The activities of Jesus were small-scale anticipations of the Kingdom that heralded its universal coming in the future. What is notable about them, for our purposes, is the way that their holistic character points to the coming of the Kingdom in all creation. Jesus brought wholeness to the lives of the people he healed and delivered: reconciling them to God, driving the power of evil from their lives, healing diseased bodies, making good crippling disabilities, restoring social relationships to those isolated by their misfortune, while of those who had everything he required much. At least some of the nature miracles anticipate the transformation of human relationships with the non-human world in the renewed creation. In the feeding miracles God's generous provision for his people through the gifts of creation takes place even in the barren wilderness, as had happened in the first exodus (Ps. 78.15-16,

23-25) and was expected for the new exodus (Isa. 35.1, 6-7;[10] 41.18-19; 51.3; cf. Ezek. 34.26-39). When Jesus walks on the water and stills the storm, God's unique sovereignty over the waters of chaos is evoked, with the expectation that in the renewed creation the destructive powers of nature will be finally quelled. While most of Jesus' activities focused on humans and human society in relation to God, there are sufficient indications that Jesus and the evangelists also embraced the fully inclusive understanding of God's rule over all creation that is so prominent in the Psalms.

Jesus and the Peaceable Kingdom

In the Hebrew Bible the desirable relationship between humans and other creatures is sometimes portrayed as peace. As Murray points out, this may be either peace *from* or peace *with* (Murray 1997: 34, 105). Both speak to the threat that dangerous animals posed both to human life and to human livelihood (in the form of domestic animals). Peace *from* is the more pragmatic possibility, secured in the covenant with Noah by the fear of humans that came to characterize other creatures (Gen. 9.2). Peace *from* could also be secured simply by the absence of dangerous animals, like the absence of invading armies that is sometimes linked with it (Lev. 26.6; Ezek. 34.25, 28; cf. Hos. 2.18). The more positive state of peace *with* wild animals is a return to paradisal conditions. This is the relationship with dangerous animals that is portrayed in the well-known description of the messianic kingdom in Isa. 11.6-9. This passage has often been misunderstood by modern readers as a picture simply of peace between animals. In fact, it depicts peace between the human world, with its domesticated animals (lamb, kid, calf, bullock, cow), and those wild animals (wolf, leopard, lion, bear, poisonous snakes) that were normally perceived as threats both to human livelihood and to human life. Humans appear in their most vulnerable form, as children, just as most of the domestic animals do (lamb, kid, etc.). This is a picture of reconciliation of the human world with the wild world, healed of the fear and violence that had been accepted, as a pragmatic compromise, in the Noahic covenant.

It is likely that the ecotopia envisaged in Isaiah 11 is the key to understanding the reference to wild animals in Mark's brief account of Jesus in the wilderness:

> He was in the wilderness forty days, tempted by Satan;
> and he was with the wild animals;
> and the angels ministered to him. (Mk 1.13: my translation)

Here Jesus goes into the wilderness, the realm outside of human habitation, in order to establish his messianic relationship with the non-human creatures. The order in which the three categories of them appear is significant. Satan is simply an enemy of

---

10   It is noteworthy that in Isaiah 35, the transformation of nature accompanies the healing of the blind, the deaf, the lame and the dumb (a passage to which Mt. 11.6 and Lk. 7.22 allude).

Jesus and the angels simply his friends, but the wild animals, placed by Mark between the two, are enemies of whom Jesus makes friends. Jesus in the wilderness enacts, in an anticipatory way, the peace between the human world and wild nature that is the Bible's hope for the messianic future. Mark's simple but effective phrase ('he was with the wild animals') has no suggestion of hostility or resistance about it. It indicates Jesus' peaceable presence with the animals. The expression 'to be with someone' frequently has, in Mark's usage (3.14; 5.18; 14.67; cf. 4.36) and elsewhere, the sense of close, friendly association. (It may also be relevant that Genesis describes the animals in the ark as those who were 'with' Noah: Gen. 7.23; 8.1, 17; 9.12.) Mark could have thought of the ideal relationship between wild animals and humans, here represented by their messianic king, as the restoration of dominion over them or as recruiting them to the ranks of the domestic animals who are useful to humans. But the simple 'with them' can have no such implication. Jesus befriends them. He is peaceably with them.[11]

A passage that evokes a very different aspect of messianic peace with the non-human world is the story of the stilling of the storm. According to Mark's version (4.35-41), Jesus 'rebuked the wind, and said to the sea, "Peace! Be still!" Then the wind ceased, and there was a dead calm' (4.39). The story evokes a mythical image that is widely reflected in the Hebrew Bible: the primeval waters, the destructive powers of nature imaged as a vast tempestuous ocean, which God in creation reduced to calm and confined within limits so that the world could be a stable environment for living creatures. These waters of chaos were not abolished by creation, only confined, always ready to break out and endanger creation, needing to be constantly restrained by the Creator. For ancient Israelites the waters of the mythical abyss were not simply a metaphysical idea. In an event such as a storm at sea, the real waters of the sea became the waters of chaos, threatening life and controllable only by God. In the case of this story, a squall on the lake of Galilee is enough to raise the spectre of elemental chaos.

When Mark says that Jesus 'rebuked the wind and said to the sea, "Peace! Be still!"', he recalls the most characteristic ways in which the Hebrew Bible speaks of God's subduing the waters of chaos. The 'rebuke' is God's powerful word of command, as in Ps. 104.7: 'at your rebuke the waters flee'. The word that silences the storm occurs, among other places, in Job 26.12: 'By his power he stills the sea'. What Jesus enacts, therefore, is the Creator's pacification of chaos. In this small-scale instance he anticipates the final elimination of all forces of destruction that will distinguish the renewed creation from the present (cf. Isa. 27.1; Rev. 21.1).

A third instance in which Jesus anticipated the peaceable kingdom is his entry into Jerusalem riding a donkey (Mk 11.1-10 and parallels). As Matthew (21.5) makes explicit, Jesus here enacts the prophecy of Zech. 9.9-10.[12] According to the prophecy, following the Messiah's victory ride on the donkey, he will 'command peace to the

---

11   I have argued at length for this interpretation of Mk 1.13 in Bauckham 1994. Among recent studies, this view is also taken by Marcus 1999: 167–68.
12   There may also be allusion to Gen. 49.10-11, interpreted as a reference to the Davidic Messiah. Here the Messiah's donkey occurs within a context of paradisal plenty.

nations'. The peace is among humans, but a peaceable animal, the donkey, helps to bring it about.[13] In ancient Near Eastern cultures, horses were associated with war, but a king in peacetime might be expected to ride a mule, not a donkey (cf. 1 Kgs 1.33).[14] Jesus rides the animal that was every peasant farmer's beast of burden.

Michael Northcott (1996: 224) writes that, in the Gospels, 'Jesus is portrayed as one who lives in supreme harmony with the natural order'. This is not entirely true. The harmony is marred by the destruction of the Gerasene pigs (Mk 5.10-13 and parallels) and by the cursing of the unfruitful fig tree (Mk 11.12-14, 20-21; Mt. 21.18-21). It is, of course, the demons who destroy the pigs, but Jesus lets them do so, presumably because the destruction of the pigs was of lesser concern than the deliverance of a man from demon-possession.[15] The fig tree suffers from symbolizing the failure of the temple authorities to do the good that God expected of them. In both cases we are reminded that Jesus anticipates the Kingdom within a still unredeemed and unrenewed world. The glimpses of paradisal harmony are no more than small-scale instances pointing to the eschatological future. They do, however, show that the Gospels take seriously the Messiah's task of healing the enmity between humans and the rest of God's creation.

Concluding Comment

This exploration of the ecological dimensions of the Synoptic Gospels has remained within their first-century Jewish thought world. I have not attempted the further hermeneutical task of relating this to the very different ecological context in which twenty-first century people find themselves. The suggestions made here do not have direct ethical implications, but may contribute to the formation of a Christian theological understanding, rooted in the whole canon of Scripture, of what it means for God's human creatures to be part of God's whole creation. The earthly Jesus, his teaching and story, can hardly be irrelevant to such an understanding. But the enterprise of reading the Gospels ecologically has barely begun.

References

Bauckham, R. 1994 'Jesus and the Wild Animals (Mark 1:13): A Christological Image for an Ecological Age', in J.B. Green and M. Turner (eds), *Jesus of Nazareth: Lord and Christ: Essays on the Historical Jesus and New Testament Christology* (Grand Rapids, MI: Eerdmans): 3–21.
Bauckham, R. 1998 'Jesus and Animals I: What did he Teach?' (chapter 4) and 'Jesus and Animals II:

---

13 Cf. Bishop 1955: 212: 'In this case both animal and Rider implied the same idea of peaceable progress.'
14 Davies and Allison 1997: 116–17, provide relevant references but seem curiously unable to distinguish a donkey from a mule.
15 On the story of the Gerasene demoniac, see Bauckham 1998: 47–48.

What did he Practise?' (chapter 5), in A. Linzey and D. Yamamoto (eds), *Animals on the Agenda: Questions about Animals for Theology and Ethics* (London: SCM): 33–60.

Bauckham, R. 2009a 'Reading the Sermon on the Mount in an Age of Ecological Catastrophe', *SCE* 22: 76–88.

Bauckham, R. 2009b 'Jesus, God and Nature in the Gospels', in R.S. White, *Creation in Crisis: Christian Perspectives on Sustainability* (London: SPCK): 209–24.

Bishop, E.F.F. 1955 *Jesus of Palestine* (London: Lutterworth).

Chilton, B. 1996 *Pure Kingdom: Jesus' Vision of God* (Grand Rapids, MI: Eerdmans/London: SPCK).

Davies, W.D. and D.C. Allison 1997 *A Critical and Exegetical Commentary on the Gospel According to Saint Matthew*, vol. 3 (ICC; Edinburgh: T&T Clark).

Dodd, C.H. 1961 *The Parables of the Kingdom* (revised edition; Glasgow: Fontana).

Echlin, E.P. 1999 *Earth Spirituality: Jesus at the Centre* (New Alresford: Arthur James).

Faricy, R. 1982 *Wind and Sea Obey Him* (London: SCM).

Freyne, S. 2004 *Jesus, a Jewish Galilean: A New Reading of the Jesus-story* (London: T&T Clark).

Hedrick, C.W. 1994 *Parables as Poetic Fictions: The Creative Voice of Jesus* (Peabody, MA: Hendrickson).

Jones, J. 2003 *Jesus and the Earth* (London: SPCK).

Leske, A.M. 2002 'Matthew 6.25-34: Human Anxiety and the Natural World', in N.C. Habel and V. Balabanski (eds), *The Earth Story in the New Testament* (The Earth Bible, 5; London and New York: Sheffield Academic Press/Cleveland, OH: Pilgrim Press): 15–27.

Loader, W. 2002 'Good News – For the Earth? Reflections on Mark 1.1-15', in N.C. Habel and V. Balabanski (eds), *The Earth Story in the New Testament* (The Earth Bible, 5; London and New York: Sheffield Academic Press/Cleveland, OH: Pilgrim Press): 28–43.

Marcus, J. 1999 *Mark 1–8* (AB 27; New York: Doubleday).

Meier, J.P. 1994 *A Marginal Jew: Rethinking the Historical Jesus*, vol. 2: *Mentor, Message, and Miracles* (New York: Doubleday).

Mora, V. 1991 *La Symbolique de la Création dans l'Évangile de Matthieu* (Lectio Divina 144; Paris: Cerf).

Murray, R. 1997 *The Cosmic Covenant* (Heythrop Monographs 7; London: Sheed & Ward).

Northcott, M.S. 1996 *The Environment and Christian Ethics* (Cambridge: Cambridge University Press).

Renan, E. 1905 [1863] *Renan's Life of Jesus* (tr. William G. Hutchinson; London: Walter Scott).

Shillington, V.G. 1997 'Engaging with the Parables', in V. George Shillington (ed.), *Jesus and His Parables: Interpreting the Parables of Jesus Today* (Edinburgh: T&T Clark): 1–20.

Westermann, C. 1990 *The Parables of Jesus in the Light of the Old Testament* (Edinburgh: T&T Clark).

Chapter 6

An Ecological Reading of Rom. 8.19-22: Possibilities and Hesitations

Brendan Byrne, SJ

Recent endeavour to rest ecological concern upon a biblical basis has asked a lot of a small passage in Romans 8 (vv. 19-22) where Paul makes reference to the groaning of creation. Whether Paul can be recruited for the ecological cause on so slender a base remains a question. Paul would doubtless be startled to discover all that has been wrung out of the tortured sentences and mysterious allusions in this text. His major concerns in the letter far more evidently bear upon such matters as the necessity of faith in the Gospel (rather than observance of the Mosaic law) for justification, and the fate of the bulk of Israel that has proved resistant to such faith. Interest in the fate of the non-human remainder of creation is at best tangential. When, then, we interpret this text in an ecological sense we are pushing it well beyond what would appear to be Paul's main concerns, though not, I would argue, counter to the intent of the text. From a hermeneutical point of view, we are reading the text as Scripture. We are therefore engaging with it from a wider horizon of discourse, informed by the concerns peculiar to our own time, notably the global situation.

What has been missing in more recent enquiry into Rom. 8.18-22 is a consideration of it within the wider running context of Paul's letter to Rome. Such a consideration can, I believe, enhance the hermeneutical possibilities of the text in the direction of ecological concern. In a recent book chapter and now in his published commentary on Romans (Jewett 2004; 2007: 508–10), Robert Jewett has offered a reading of Rom. 8.18-22 – and the corruption and redemption of creation which it mentions – within the context of the Roman imperial ideology, the most familiar element of which would be the celebrated *Fourth Eclogue* of Virgil. Harry Hahne has studied the passage from the perspective of the corruption and redemption of the natural world as a motif in Jewish apocalyptic literature (Hahne 2006). Both authors, from complementary directions, fill out the background to Paul's rather sudden introduction of the non-human created world, and its longing and groaning, at this point in Romans 8. What I offer here is a consideration of the text within the broader argument of the letter itself and in respect to several themes that run throughout its length: the complex ('overlap') eschatology of believers' present existence; the interplay of grace and sin, and the symbolic role of Adam as instrument of sin; the consequences for 'creation' of human existence as embodied. It is from a wider view building upon consideration of these motifs that I propose to approach the references to 'creation' in Romans 8.

It is generally agreed that Paul states the theme of his letter to Rome in a lengthy statement describing the power of the Gospel in 1.16-17:

> For I am not ashamed of the Gospel: it is the power of God leading to salvation for every one who has faith, to the Jew first and also to the Greek. For in it the righteousness of God is revealed, from faith to faith, as it is written: 'The person who is righteous by faith will live' [Hab. 2.4].

This programmatic statement makes clear that the letter is primarily about 'salvation'. It is a defence of the power of the Gospel – and the Gospel alone – to bring to salvation all who respond to it in faith, because through faith believers receive as gift the righteous status upon which salvation depends (Rom. 5.9-10; 10.9-13). In the light of our current concern the question that immediately presents itself is whether 'salvation' as here asserted includes the non-human remainder of creation or envisages human beings alone. Until recently, and especially as a consequence of the Reformation controversy, interpretation has hardly stopped to examine this question, so confident has been the assumption that Romans is all about how human individuals find salvation through the grace of God. Too rarely, perhaps, have interpreters paused to consider that human existence for Paul is embodied existence – something that, as Paul insists in 1 Corinthians 15, extends beyond the barrier of death. The difficulty of conceiving of a human bodily existence that did not in some sense relate to the non-human material remainder of creation as its necessary physical context suggests from the start that the 'salvation' thematically asserted as the objective of the Gospel must in some way include that non-human remainder within its scope. Nonetheless, Paul's notion of salvation operates within a complex reconfiguring of post-biblical Jewish eschatology, to which we must now devote some attention.

The Overlap of the Ages

Behind the argument that Paul develops in Romans is the sense shared with Jewish apocalyptic eschatology of two ages or 'aeons': the 'present age' and the 'age to come' (Byrne 1996: 20–21). In the present age the created world and human beings within it have become corrupted and dominated by sin, with a destiny to death and decay. How the world got into this state Paul does not explain, though he seems to presuppose in his readers awareness of a tradition, stemming ultimately from Genesis 3, in which the first human being, Adam, plays a significant role (Scroggs 1966; Levison 1988). This 'present age' stands under God's wrath (Rom. 1.18; 5.9; cf. 1 Thess. 1.10), a wrath that is very soon to break out destructively and which is already to some extent 'revealed' in the perverted state of human bodily existence (Rom. 1.18-32).[1]

According to the Gospel, in the person and work of Jesus Christ, God has begun to establish upon earth a new age in which human beings can be rescued ('saved') from the present time and reclaimed for the original intent of the Creator. For Paul this divine rescue operation has not burst upon the world unannounced. It is the working out of a liberation proclaimed long ago in the Scriptures (Rom. 1.2). In fact, it fulfils a promise made to Abraham, to whom the originally universalist design of the Creator was announced and in whose person and responses to God its realization is prefigured (Rom. 4.1-23).[2]

What complicates things for Paul is the fact that, contrary to conventional Jewish apocalyptic expectation, these two 'ages' have not followed each other in orderly sequence; they in fact overlap and co-exist at the present time (Dunn 1998: 464). God has intervened in Christ to mount an eleventh hour rescue of the human situation before the full operation of divine wrath comes into play. The eschatological justification leading to entrance into the new age is available here and now for all who accept in faith the divine offer of righteousness made in the proclamation of the Gospel (Rom. 3.21-26). This means that, as far as relations with God are concerned and as attested by the gift of the Spirit, believers already live the life of the new age. As far as their bodily existence is concerned, however, they are still anchored in the present age. It is this situation of having to live currently in both ages that creates the spiritual and ethical dilemmas confronting the present life of believers that Paul addresses in Romans 5–8 (Byrne 1981).

Paul's Sense of Life in the Body in Romans

In this part of the letter (Romans 5–8) Paul addresses three factors arising out of the continuing tug of the old age upon believers in their bodily life: first, suffering; then, mortality; and, third, the necessity and possibility of living righteously in the present 'overlap' time where people no longer live 'under the law'. Paul addresses the issue of suffering in the first half of chapter 5 (vv. 1-11) and revisits it in the latter half of chapter 8 (vv. 18, 31-39). Suffering is not to be interpreted as an indication of God's wrath. On the contrary, in the context of God's action in giving up the Son for our justification (Rom. 4.25; 5.6-10; 8.32) and the union with Christ thereby established (Rom.8.17), it is a sure index of hope: that God will bring to completion that saving work already begun at such cost (Gieniusz 1999). Likewise (Rom. 5.12-21), though

---

1   On the hermeneutical and ethical issues raised for contemporary interpretation by Paul's adherence to a conventional Hellenistic Jewish view linking idolatry and sexual perversion in pagan society, see Byrne 1996: 70.
2   I leave aside here the huge issue for Paul arising out of how to account for Israel, the Sinai covenant, and the Law and the righteousness it purported to offer.

death has become a universally prevalent factor of human existence as a legacy of Adam's sin and the universal sinfulness thereby unleashed (Rom. 5.12), sin and death will not have the last word. In Christ, as counterpart to Adam ('Last Adam' [1 Cor. 15.45]), God has introduced into the world a 'much more' powerful legacy of righteousness leading to life (Rom. 5.15-17). Finally, whereas in the old era human existence had fallen under the grip of 'Sin' (*hamartia*) personified as an overbearing slavemaster imposing a fatal necessity to sin, through faith and their baptizmal union with Christ, believers have been set free from such slavery and brought into a new obedience of righteousness leading to life (Rom. 6.1-23).

Believers have to live out this new situation, however, as 'flesh', and flesh is where they remain vulnerable to the still present threat of the slavemaster Sin. When Paul's argument takes an anthropological turn in Romans 7, it is not easy to get a grasp upon why he at times speaks about human existence as 'flesh' (Rom. 7.5, 14, 18, 25; 8.3-9 [passim], 12, 13) and at times as 'body' (Rom. 7.24; 8.10, 11, 13, 23). Flesh is clearly the more pejorative quantity. While it can refer simply to the physical aspect of human life (2 Cor. 12.7; Gal. 4.14), it more usually has overtones of vulnerability, leading to hostility to God and resistance to the Spirit (Rom. 8.6-8); as 'flesh' human beings have bad relationships: with God, with each other and with each one's own best interest. Human bodily existence is material but essentially relational: it is as *sōma* that believers relate to surrounding physical world and also to each other (Byrne 1983). Whereas as 'flesh' relating is always bad, as *sōma* it can go either way: in the direction of alienation from God and death, or, under the influence of the Spirit, in the direction of freedom and eternal life. So Paul can speak of our 'former self' (literally, 'our old man') being concrucified with Christ in order to take away the 'body of sin', that is, presumably, to destroy our bodily subjection to Sin (Rom. 6.6); he can also urge his audience, not 'to allow Sin to reign in your mortal bodies' but to offer 'your members as instruments of righteousness to God' (Rom. 6.12).

In regard to this latter, positive aspiration, in Paul's view the Law is no help at all (Rom. 7.5); it simply anchors people in the conditions and slavery of the old age – a situation dramatically illustrated in the dilemma of the 'I' described in the latter part of chapter 7 (vv. 14-25). This comes to a climax with the plaintive cry: 'Who will deliver me from the body of this death?' (v. 24b), that is, from a bodily existence trapped in a servitude to Sin that will inevitably lead to (eternal) death.

In the first part of chapter 8, as a kind of answering second panel of a diptych, Paul describes the new possibility brought about by God's redemptive act in the sending of the Son (Byrne 1996: 213, 234–41). This has liberated human beings from the power of Sin dominating the flesh and created the possibility of living bodily life under the influence not of the flesh but of the Spirit (Rom. 8.1-4). In Rom. 8.12-13, Paul concludes on a kind of exhortatory note:

> So then, my brothers (and sisters), we are people under an obligation – not to the flesh, to live according to the flesh. For if you live according to the flesh, you will die. But, if in the Spirit you put to death the deeds of the body, you will live.

Why did Paul write (or dictate) in that penultimate phrase 'deeds of the body' – as though the body were the cause of all the trouble? Why did he not write, 'deeds of the flesh'? Was it a lapse that Tertius (Rom. 16.22) did not advert to? Or did Paul mean 'body' under the negative aspect? Presuming that he did mean 'body', perhaps we have to understand here deeds that believers do in the body under its aspect of still being anchored in the conditions of the present age and still liable to be determined by it, that is, by its enslavement under Sin. We remember that in verse 3, Paul speaks of God in the Christ act having 'condemned' Sin in the flesh. This reference to Sin's 'outing' and condemnation as the real villain is not necessarily the same thing as its complete removal or elimination.

Later in Romans 8, in the verse (v. 23) coming immediately after the passage that is our fine point of focus, Paul will speak of believers awaiting 'the redemption of the body'. As is widely recognized, this phrase is not to be interpreted in a proto-Gnostic sense as redemption 'from' the body, as though bodily existence were the whole problem. Rather it refers to the redemption – that is, the costly liberation – of believers' bodily existence from the continuing conditions of the present age: suffering, death and the threat of sin. The 'cost' may be physical death itself (cf. Rom. 8.10b). For Paul, however, death is not the end of life in the body but the gateway to bodily life fully under the influence of the Spirit (cf. 1 Corinthians 15): human existence as God intended from the start that it should be, patterned upon the risen humanity of Jesus (cf. Rom. 8.29).

In the meantime, as he begins the parenesis that brings to a conclusion the main body of his letter to Rome (12.1–15.13), Paul exhorts his audience to offer their bodies 'as a living sacrifice, holy and pleasing to God, the worship you owe as rational beings' (Rom. 12.1). Present bodily life, though vulnerable and mortal (Rom. 8.10), is capable of being lived out in a way totally pleasing and acceptable to God – a pattern of life regulated not by going back to the Law but through discernment of God's will, and what is 'good and acceptable and perfect' (Rom. 12.2d). This discernment is made possible through believers' not being conformed to this present age but transformed through the renewal of their mind (Rom. 12.2c). The exhortation recognizes that believers have to live their bodily life in the context of two ages but insists that they do not have to live determined by the conditions of the present one: with renewed 'mind' they can live in the present the values of the new.

What I have been trying to uncover in this review of Paul's wider argument in Romans is a context that makes Paul's sudden appeal to 'creation' in the middle of chapter 8 somewhat less surprising. In the context of his continuing consciousness of human existence as bodily existence and hence of related existence, including relation to the non-human created world, that reference, when it occurs, becomes less anomalous. All through this part of Romans Paul has been dealing with the issues and dilemmas created by the overlap of the ages and the necessity for believers of living a bodily life within the opposing 'tugs' of those two ages.

The Groaning of Creation: Rom. 8.19-22

The passage that is the specific object of our enquiry occurs at a point where Paul, pursuing his overall case for hope in the present 'overlap' situation (Romans 5–8), explicitly confronts once more (cf. Rom. 5.1-4) the phenomenon of suffering. After an opening thematic assertion (v. 18) to the effect that the sufferings of the present time pale into insignificance (literally, 'do not bear comparison') with 'the glory that is to be revealed in us', the small passage on 'creation' appears as the first of three subsections each of which features a subject that 'groans': ('creation' [vv. 19-22]; 'ourselves' [vv. 23-25]; 'the Spirit' [vv. 26-27]). In each case the 'groaning' is not simply a negative reaction to pain. It provides grounds for hope in the sense of expressing a 'divine restlessness' with the present state of affairs, offering a well-founded anticipation of a much better situation ('glory') soon to come (Byrne 1996: 255). Paul rounds off the 'groaning' sequence by evoking the sense of believers' being caught up in the inexorable unfolding of God's salvific plan (vv. 28-30).

The logical flow in the sequence making up the first 'groaning' passage (vv. 19-22) is not all that obvious at first glance. Paul works to his conclusion, the groaning of creation (v. 22), by first (v. 19) pointing to an eager longing on the part of creation, and then, in a little parenthesis (vv. 20-21), explains why creation has this eager longing, which expresses itself in a groaning (v. 22) that he sees to be the outward manifestation of hope. Along with most interpreters, I take 'creation' (*ktisis*) here to refer to the non-human remainder of creation (Byrne 1996: 255–56; Hahne 2006: 176–81). Paul's argument then rests upon a biblical and post-biblical tradition, stemming ultimately from Gen. 1.26-28, that sees creation in this sense as intimately bound up with the fate of human beings for good and for ill. When human beings fail, that failure redounds negatively upon creation (cf. Gen. 3.17-19; *4 Ezra* 7.11-12; 9.19-20). Conversely, human restoration will be reflected in a transformation of the non-human created world (cf. Isa. 11.6-9; 43.19-21; 55.12-13; Ezek. 34.25-31; Hos. 2.18; Zech. 8.12; *1 Enoch* 45.4-5; 51.4-5; *4 Ezra* 8.51-54; *2 Apoc. Bar.* 29.1-8; Byrne 1996: 256; Hahne 2006: 35–168). It is on the basis of this 'common fate' that Paul, personifying 'creation', can speak of its 'eager longing' (*apokaradokia*) for the revelation of the sons (and daughters) of God' (v. 19), that is, for the outward manifestation in risen glory of the filial status in regard to God of those who already, as beneficiaries of Christ's redemptive act, experience the reality of that status in a hidden way (Rom. 8.15-16, 23; Gal. 3.26-28; Byrne 1996: 257).

The background to this eager expectation on the part of creation is explained in the little parenthesis making up Rom. 8.20-21. Most interpreters find in the reference to creation's 'subjection to futility' an allusion to the element of the second creation story Gen 2.4b–3.24 where the earth is cursed as a consequence (and punishment) for Adam's sin (Gen. 3.17-19). 'Futility' (*mataiotēs*) has the general sense of 'worthlessness', 'purposelessness' (BDAG: 621). It is difficult to pinpoint precisely what Paul means by 'futility' in the context under discussion, though it is probably safest to see the term retaining its basic sense of 'inability to attain its true purpose' (Cranfield 1975: 413–14). The motif occurs elsewhere in Paul (in the form of the cognate verb in the passive) only in Rom. 1.21 (with an echo in Eph. 4.17) in regard to the human lapse into idolatry (worshipping the creature rather than the Creator [v 24]). In Rom. 1.21, however, it is the human side of the interaction (the mind) that becomes 'futile' rather than the objective created world, as in Rom. 8.20. What is common to both occurrences is the sense that because of human failure something – the human mind in the first case, the non-human created world in the second – has been frustrated from attaining its true purpose. In Gen. 3.17-19 the consequence of YHWH's cursing of the earth is that what had previously been a garden providing all manner of delightful food for the human couple without any labour on their part has been rendered a difficult and harsh terrain from which they have to wrest their food with wearying toil and effort. In other words, the kind of harmonious relationship between human beings and the natural world proper to life in a garden has been replaced by one more redolent of situations where the two are virtually in conflict. In this sense it is perhaps not drawing too long a bow to relate the subjection to 'futility' in Rom. 8.20 to the contemporary sense of environmental degradation – at least in the context of the wider Adamic 'sin story' that, as I shall argue, runs through the central chapters of the letter.

But who is 'the subduer' (*ton hypotaxanta*) 'on account of' (*dia*) whom creation, against its own will (*ouch hekousa*) underwent subjection to futility (v. 20b)? While most interpreters recognize an 'Adamic' aura behind the elusive references in this text, a minority find here a precise reference to Adam, or to humankind as represented by him (Byrne 1996: 258, 260–61). However, the unmistakable divine passive in the reference to subjection *hypetagē* earlier in the verse and the fact that God is certainly the agent of the cursing of the earth according to Gen. 3.17-19 have led most to see here a reference to God – even though such a reference does put a strain upon the *dia ton* . . . phrase, which has then to be understood in a rarely occurring instrumental sense rather than in the causal sense that it far more normally has (Fitzmyer 1993: 508). Within the overall allusion to the so-called 'Fall' story and hence the sin of Adam, what seems to be uppermost in Paul's mind is responsibility for the bringing about of the negative situation (the subjection of creation to 'futility'). He wants to deflect this responsibility from creation, which neither wanted it (*ouch hekousa*) nor deserved it. The subjection came about as a consequence of human sin and as punishment for that sin. Perhaps in trying to wrest meaning from Paul's highly cryptic phrases here we can offer some distinctions in regard to 'causality' for the 'subjection': God was the agent of the subjection (the *hypotaxanta* corresponding to the divine passive in *hypetagē*); Adam was its cause in the sense of meriting this punishment; creation, as the instrument of the divine retribution, was compelled to be the innocent victim in the entire transaction.

In 'compensation', so to speak, for its being required to play this retributory role, God gave creation the 'hope' spelled out in v. 21 (reading *hoti* at the start of the statement in a declaratory sense: Byrne 1996: 261). That is, creation would be set free from its bondage to decay ('futility') to share in the 'freedom' (from such bondage) associated with the glory of the children of God. On the solidarity or 'common fate' principle linking it with human beings, the non-human creation cherished the hope that when the fall of human beings would be reversed and they (or at least some) would attain the likeness to God ('glory') that was the original intent of the Creator in their regard, and it also would share this freedom and glory from corruption and decay.

It is in view of this hope given it by God that creation awaits with 'eager longing' the revelation of God's sons (and daughters) (v. 19), a revelation that will occur when the status of divine filiation now attested only through the Spirit (Rom. 8.14-16) will be made externally manifest through the liberation of human bodily existence (the awaited 'redemption of the body' [v. 23]) in resurrection. The reversal of human beings' bondage to mortality ('decay') and attainment of the 'glory' that was the Creator's original intent in their regard will signal to creation that its own time for liberation has arrived.

Having explained why creation has this eager longing, Paul can now (v. 22) round off this first stage of his argument for hope by pointing to its 'groaning' manifestation as an object of common knowledge (*oidamen gar*). Ever since the 'Fall' (cf. Gen. 3.17-19) right up to the present (*achri tou nun*), the entire non-human creation has been groaning, not simply because it has had to bear the consequences of Adam's sin, but also in view of the hope that the Creator bestowed upon it when 'subjecting it to futility' as a way of punishing human sin. It is suffering but not suffering to no purpose. As in the case of the suffering of the justified as expressed in Rom. 5.3-5, it is suffering a suffering redolent of hope.

It is natural to interpret the 'groaning together' (*systenazei*) of 'all creation' in the sense of a response to the pain inflicted upon the earth by (sinful) human misuse. While there is no need from an exegetical point of view to exclude the sense of a groaning in response to injury and pain, the wider flow of the argument in Rom. 8.18-30 as a whole favours understanding this 'groaning' (along with the later references to the groaning of 'ourselves' [v. 23] and the 'inexpressible groans' of the Spirit [v. 26]) primarily as an index of hope (Byrne 1996: 255; Hahne 2006: 202–203). Hence, when ecologically attuned present-day readers find in the 'groaning' of creation a response to the pain inflicted upon the earth by (sinful) human misuse, there is need for some nuance and clarification. Neither in the 'Fall' story of Gen. 3.17-19 nor in the apparent allusion to it behind Rom. 8.20-21 is there any suggestion of direct human action in respect of creation in a destructive sense. Adam's sin, while it may involve reaching out to a forbidden creature (Gen. 2.16-17; 3.6), was essentially an act of disobedience towards God. In the Genesis myth and the tradition stemming from it the 'subjection' inflicted upon creation came about as an action of God designed to punish human beings for their sin. There is no 'straight line' between human action and the effect upon the non-human created world. The punitive causality, if one may speak in such terms, runs through God.

The 'Sin Story' in Relation to Creation

Such being the case, a reading of Rom. 8.19-22 that wishes to derive from the text a reflection upon destructive human behaviour in regard to the non-human creation will have to do so on the basis of a somewhat broader view of human sinfulness and its consequences according to Paul. Besides the focus upon grace and faith, Paul's letter to Rome offers a sustained and sophisticated analysis of human sin, which in its central chapters it portrays under the image of a slavery from which humans are powerless to escape. The Adamic aura hovering about Rom. 8.19-22 draws this text into association with the Adamic allusions that first become explicit in connection with the onset of sin and death in Rom. 5.12-21, but which run far more widely beneath the surface of the argument. Adam was significant for Paul not simply as the individual who fathered the race but also as representative symbol of unredeemed human existence, enslaved to selfishness as the radical core of sin and, in consequence, relating poorly both to God and to the wider created world. 'In Adam' Paul sees told the 'sin story' of the human race, over against which God's action in the Christ-event has counterpoised a (much more powerful) 'grace story' (Byrne 2003). Throughout a substantial block of the argument in Romans (5.12–8.4) Paul portrays sin (*hamartia*) as a tyrant slavemaster into whose grip Adam has delivered the human race, the consequence being an ineluctable compulsion to sin that can only be broken by God's act in Christ (Rom. 8.3-4).

It is in this wider sense, I believe, that the Adamic allusions in Rom. 8.19-22 can most properly be related to ecological concern. In the 'overlap of the ages' situation where human bodily life continues to be anchored in the conditions of the 'old age', vulnerable to weakness ('flesh'), suffering and death, the Adamic 'sin story' continues to exert its tug upon human beings. While, as the imagery suggests, Paul is more interested in the radical core of sinfulness rather than its outward manifestation in specific acts, there is no reason why ecological misbehaviour and abuse of the environment, whether on an individual or communal scale, should not be seen as outward manifestations of what he would recognize as a radical slavery to 'Sin'.

The 'Grace Story' in Relation to Creation

So much for the negative. But what of the positive? As is widely recognized, Paul's negative allusions to the Adam story and to the onset of sin and death that it encapsulates, serve as a foil over against which to assert the superior force (the 'much more' [*pollō mallon*]: Rom. 5.9, 10, 15, 17; cf. 20b) of the grace story told in Christ, which is the basis of hope. Is it possible to relate this story, focused upon Christ as 'Last Adam' (cf. 1 Cor. 15.45), to a positive future for the world resting again on human bodily solidarity with the non-human creation?

In several respects things are even more tricky here than in the negative case, where, as I pointed out, neither Paul in Rom. 8.19-21 nor the Genesis text lying behind it envisaged *direct* human agency for ill upon the non-human world. The 'grace story' is precisely grace: the gift of God made concrete in the life and especially the sacrificial self-gift in death of Jesus Christ (Rom. 5.15, 17). In respect of that gift, which is in effect the 'new creation' (2 Cor. 5.18; Gal. 6.15), human beings can 'do' nothing: all they can do is to open themselves up to receive through faith the justification that it offers and the promise of salvation that it holds out (Rom. 1.16-17; 3.21-26; 4.21-25; 5.1; 10.5-13).

Pure receptivity is not the whole story, however. Faith may be the sole channel of justification (Rom. 3.28) but Paul also insists that in the 'overlap of the ages' era, while living in the 'space' between justification and the salvation still to come, believers must live a life of 'obedience' (Rom. 6.1–7.6). This is not an obedience to the Law, but an obedience which is really the self-sacrificing obedience of Christ (Rom. 5.19; Phil. 2.8) welling up within them as a consequence of their baptizmal union with him (Rom. 6.4, 11; cf. Rom. 15.1-3). In this way there is 'fulfilled' (*plērōthē*) within them 'the righteous requirement of the Law' as they 'walk' not according to the flesh but according to the Spirit (Rom. 8.4). As I have argued elsewhere (Byrne 1981: 569, 576), the passive 'fulfilled' here carefully preserves the divine initiative, the sense that all Christian obedience is the product of the Spirit's working within the believer the continuing obedience of Christ. At the same time, the righteousness created in this way as a response to grace does lead to 'salvation' (Rom. 1.16-17), as believers, in accordance with Paul's exhortation, 'offer their members (*melē*)' as 'instruments (*hopla*) of righteousness' to God (Rom. 6.13). 'Members' takes up the reference to 'mortal body' in the preceding verse ('Let not then Sin reign in your mortal body . . .' [v. 12]), making it clear that Paul has in mind the bodily life of believers in the 'overlap' era. Such human bodily life, though not fully 'redeemed' (Rom. 8.23), can nonetheless be part of the 'new creation' (2 Cor. 5.17) that is being brought into being through the action of the Spirit.

In this sense, I believe, it is possible to speak of an Adamic existence relating – as a response to grace – to the non-human created world in a positive, unselfish, non-exploitative way on the model of the 'Last Adam' (1 Cor. 15.45), who did not 'please himself' (Rom. 15.3; Phil. 2.6-8). Once again, as in the negative case, it is necessary to read the specific text (Rom. 8.19-22) within a general awareness of Paul's sense of life in the body and in the context of the wider flow of his letter to Rome. In this way a positive reading can emerge to balance the negative side of the story.

'Balance', however, is not quite accurate, since throughout the letter Paul has insisted upon the 'superiority' of the grace side at the expense of sin (Rom. 5.6-11; 5.15-21; cf. 8.31-32). It is because of the 'much more' stemming from God's act in Christ that there is hope for salvation, the central affirmation of Romans 5–8, and indeed of the letter as a whole. Can the 'salvation' in question, for which there is hope, include the non-human created world? Since for Paul it does involve the bodily life of human beings it must surely do so. Also, unlike other Pauline passages where the motif of resurrection is more explicit, '(t)he passage implies the redemption and transformation of the present material world, rather than the destruction of the world and the creation of a new one' (Hahne 2006: 208; cf. Byrne 2000: 201–202). It would, then, be exegetically naïve, as well as hermeneutically irresponsible, to conclude that even if human beings destroy the world, God will ultimately recreate or rescue it.

On the basis, however, that human action impinges upon the world for good (as a response to grace) and for ill (as a manifestation of captivity to sin), we can acknowledge that, in Pauline terms, the future of the world (salvation) does to some extent lie in human hands. It is not *simply* God's gift and it remains ours to lose. Hope for the future in this sense takes human action into account. It remains hope in God but it is also hope in the prevailing power of God's grace *working through*, not around or above human cooperation. If righteousness for Paul is ultimately about fidelity – divine and human – then Paul's exhortation to believers that they offer 'their members as instruments of righteousness to God' (Rom. 6.13) can be taken as, in part at least, an encouragement to behave not only responsibly towards the environment but with an unselfish, non-exploitative fidelity that mirrors and indeed is an extension of the divine fidelity (righteousness) behind the entire Christ-event (cf. 2 Cor. 5.21). In this way, I believe, we may include the future of the world in the broad sweep of the Gospel as proclaimed by Paul in Romans.

References

Byrne B. 1981 'Living Out the Righteousness of God: The Contribution of Rom. 6.1–8.13 to an Understanding of Paul's Ethical Presuppositions', *CBQ* 43: 557–81.
Byrne B. 1983 'Sinning Against One's Own Body: Paul's Understanding of the Sexual Relationship in 1 Corinthians 6.18', *CBQ* 45: 608–16.
Byrne B. 1996 *Romans* (SP 6; Collegeville, MN: Liturgical Press).
Byrne B. 2000 'Creation Groaning: An Earth Bible Reading of Romans 8.18–22', in N. C. Habel (ed.), *Readings From the Perspective of the Earth* (The Earth Bible, 1; Sheffield/Cleveland, OH: Sheffield Academic Press/Pilgrim Press): 193–203.
Byrne B. 2003 'Paul's Adam Myth Revisited', in D. Reid and M. Worthing (eds), *Sin and Salvation* (Task of Theology Today III; Hindmarsh, South Australia: Australian Theological Forum): 41–54.
Cranfield, C.E.B. 1975 *A Critical and Exegetical Commentary on the Epistle to the Romans*: Vol. 1 *Introduction and Commentary on Romans I–VIII* (ICC; Edinburgh: T&T Clark).
Dunn, J.D.G. 1998 *The Theology of Paul the Apostle* (Grand Rapids, MI; Cambridge, UK: Eerdmans).
Fitzmyer, J.A. 1993 *Romans: A New Translation with Introduction and Commentary* (AB 33; New York: Doubleday).
Gieniusz, C.R. 1999 *Romans 8:18-30: Suffering Does Not Thwart the Future Glory* (Atlanta, GA: Scholars Press).
Hahne, H. 2006 *The Corruption and Redemption of Creation: Nature in Romans 8.19-22 and Jewish Apocalyptic Literature* (LNTS 336; London: T&T Clark).
Jewett, R. 2004 'The Corruption and Redemption of Creation: Reading Rom. 8:18-22 Within the Imperial Context', in R. A. Horsley (ed.), *Paul and the Roman Imperial Order* (Harrisburg, PA; London and New York: Trinity Press International): 25–46.
Jewett, R. 2007 *Romans: A Commentary* (Hermeneia; Minneapolis, MN: Fortress).
Levison, J.R. 1988 *Portraits of Adam in Early Judaism: From Sirach to 2 Baruch* (Sheffield: JSOT Press).
Scroggs, R. 1966 *The Last Adam: A Study in Pauline Anthropology* (Philadelphia: Fortress; Oxford: Blackwell).

Chapter 7

Hellenistic Cosmology and the Letter to the Colossians: Towards an Ecological Hermeneutic

Vicky S. Balabanski

One of the most formidable gulfs between the ancient world and ourselves is how vastly different the cosmological framework implicit in a biblical text may be from our own. In order to develop a contemporary ecological hermeneutic, it is imperative to have some explicit interaction between the ancient cosmology or cosmologies implied in a biblical text and our contemporary cosmological framework. To draw ecological meaning from ancient scripture, cosmology is one of the areas needing to receive some careful and nuanced attention.

One context in which this issue has been raised is the 'Earth Bible' project. This is a South Australian-based project, though with national and international contributors from several continents, and a variety of social locations, including Africa and South America. It began in 1998, under the guidance and facilitation of Norman Habel, a biblical scholar best known for his commentary on Job (1985), but whose often prophetic work has led him to fall foul of conservative church authorities at various times. The strategy of the project was a collaborative one, which called together a team of scholars in the fields of Old and New Testament, as well as systematic theology, and sought to identify not only those biblical texts apparently friendly to the earth, but also those which are problematic. The aim was to read the Bible *in solidarity with* the Earth; and here, 'Earth' is used as an inclusive term encompassing the whole web of life, or ecosystem, of which humanity is a part. This differed in approach from other ecological biblical hermeneutic strategies, in that it did not focus on

> what a given text may say about creation, about nature, or about Earth. In this context, Earth is not a topos or theme for analysis. We are not focusing on ecology and creation, or ecology and theology. An ecological hermeneutic demands a radical change of posture in relation to Earth as a subject in the text.[1] (Habel 2008: 3)

1   The Earth Bible team, of which I am a member, drafted and reviewed essays which set out to engage with small sections of the biblical witness from the perspective of the Earth. Habel, in dialogue with both theologians and ecologists over several years, had developed a series of 'eco-justice' principles which became the central strategy by which these essays found a coherent focus. These principles were not framed in theological terms, but rather in terms that allowed cross disciplinary dialogue.

In order to achieve this 'radical change of posture', it is necessary to give attention to what presuppositions we hold about the nature of the universe, the *kosmos*, and how humanity relates to the *kosmos*. In an early essay in the Earth Bible series, 'An Earth Bible Reading of the Lord's Prayer', I raised the issue of implied cosmologies, and stated that ancient cosmologies may be more diverse than had been presumed (Balabanski 2000: 153–54). This present essay takes up the issue of ancient cosmologies. The Earth Bible eco-justice principle of interconnectedness is fundamental to this reading, and is further explicated by it ('Earth is a community of interconnected living things that are mutually dependent on each other for life and survival' [Habel and Balabanski 2002: xx].

Assumptions of this Study

There are several assumptions which this study makes. The first is that the cosmology of Plato's *Timaeus* is relevant to first century Asia Minor and to the Letter to the Colossians, despite the fact that it was written circa 348–338 BCE, some four hundred years before this letter.[2] It is clear that *Timaeus* had been interpreted and adapted by the period of the first century CE, so that this era of Plato's heritage has come to be distinguished from the earlier period. These Platonic interpreters, known to us as Middle Platonists, incorporated concepts and insights from other philosophical schools, particularly Stoicism. French classics scholar Rémi Brague demonstrates just how influential Plato's cosmology was, even for those who took different views (Brague 2003: 36). He recognizes that the Timaean model of the cosmos became dominant only after a long history, but nevertheless argues that Stoic philosophy, at least in relation to cosmology, takes its impetus from the model of Plato's *Timaeus* (25). This was a syncretistic period, and *Timaeus*' influence has been identified in many philosophical streams, whether positively, as in Philo's work (Runia 1986) or negatively, as in the writings of Epicurus. Brague (2003: 39) points out that Epicurus may have intended to parody aspects of *Timaeus*.

The second assumption relates to the Letter to the Colossians. This study accepts that Colossians is not primarily the work of Paul, largely on the basis that the cosmology of Colossians differs from the cosmology of the undisputed letters. There are various considerations giving weight to this indication of authorship: the Letter itself states that the Colossians have not met Paul in person (2.1), that the authorship is joint (1.1) and that the Letter was not penned by Paul himself (4.18), so these factors may have influenced the articulated cosmology of the Letter. Moreover, the Letter is very interested in affirming the leadership of Epaphras (1.7-8; 4.12-13), in a way that suggests a dating still close to that of Paul's own lifetime, given that Epaphras was the one who brought the Gospel to them originally. George van Kooten has

---

2   For text of *Timaeus* (*Tim.*) see Bury 1929/1999.

persuasively argued in his monograph on Pauline and deutero-Pauline cosmology (2003) that Colossians reflects a different cosmology to that of the genuine Pauline epistles, and I will discuss the basis of this claim presently. At this point it is necessary only to note that this paper assumes that the cosmic Christology of this letter is not Pauline.

The third assumption is that the cosmology of the Colossian hymn, whatever its source, is shared by the rest of the Letter. This has also been argued convincingly by van Kooten, who states that there is no reason that the hymn could not have been composed by the author of the Letter (2003: 115). Without entering into the source question, it is important to decide whether one holds that the cosmological views of the hymn differ from those of the central part of the Letter, and I accept that there is a consistent cosmological perspective across the Letter.

Ancient Cosmology as an Interpretative Framework

Since the late 1990s, there has been increased interest in exploring cosmological questions as they arise in Pauline writings. Two monographs in particular can be mentioned: Edward Adams, *Constructing the World: A Study in Paul's Cosmological Language* (2000), and George H. van Kooten, *Cosmic Christology in Paul and the Pauline School: Colossians and Ephesians in the Context of Graeco-Roman Cosmology, with a New Synopsis of the Greek Texts* (2003). A third monograph is also pertinent to the field, namely *The Wisdom of the World: The Human Experience of the Universe in Western Thought*, by Rémi Brague (2003). A fourth monograph also makes an important contribution to the area, as it explores both biblical and Greco-Roman cosmology in relation to ecology. It is by the Dutch environmental scientist and philosopher Jan J. Boersema, entitled *The Torah and the Stoics on Humankind and Nature: A Contribution to the Debate on Sustainability and Quality* (2001). Boersema sets out compelling reasons why engaging in the cultural-historical background of environmental problems and their perception is important, and he pursues this particularly in relation to the creation, Sabbath and purity traditions of the Hebrew Scriptures, and in the Greek cosmologies which shaped Christian thinking.

In 2004 I presented a paper to the ecological hermeneutics consultation at the annual SBL meeting in which I argued that the cosmological language of Colossians evokes Stoic cosmology to a greater extent than has been recognized; this gives the cosmological framework for the Christological cosmology in which Christ permeates creation (Balabanski 2008: 151–59). This current essay seeks to explore further aspects of the cosmological background to Colossians in order to pursue its implications for ecological hermeneutics.

How did Hellenistic Cosmology Shape the Hearing of the Christian Proclamation?

Hellenistic cosmology can be understood as an aspect of ancient philosophy. The philosophy of the ancient Greeks embraced the study of logic, mathematics, physics, astronomy and linguistics, and in these ways engaged in seeking to understand the inner logic of the cosmos. Though ancient 'science' began with observation, experiment and analysis, as contemporary scientific method does today, it did not view its task as limited to that which is apprehensible via the senses. Rather, it sought to draw connections between disparate phenomena and, via inductive logic, to move towards synthesis, where the underlying meaning which brought the world into harmony could be glimpsed. This was viewed as a significant part of the quest for wisdom.

A prominent aspect of philosophy was the discourse about how events were connected with one another. Ancient Greek philosophers gave a great deal of attention to 'causes' – what was the primary or 'first cause' (*Tim.* 29E, 68E), and what were auxiliary or secondary causes (*Tim.* 46–47). The underlying principle was that there was a unified cosmos which was created rationally, so examining the observed effects could lead someone trained in logic to discern the causes. Much thought was therefore given to discerning what an observed phenomenon – an effect – might indicate about the cause or causes which brought it about. Aristotle categorized causes into four rubrics, all of which could be logically demonstrated to lead to an effect.[3] Many subsequent philosophers shared this concern to link an effect to its cause or causes, for it could bring the thinker closer to reaching a measure of understanding, if not control, of the causes and thus situate the thinker more securely in the world. The chaotic and irrational were constant possibilities in the world, but the wise person sought to discern the unifying logic of the cosmos and to attune himself to it.

These reflections are pertinent to the task of seeking to comprehend the cosmology behind the Letter to the Colossians. Where was Christ positioned in relation to the cosmos? And what new position did the Colossians see themselves as gaining through their connection with Christ?

It is not just that the cosmology itself is different from a contemporary cosmology. It also played a different and much more prominent role for the recipients of this letter. They expected their new religious path to address all aspects of life – cosmology, and the related area of calendars, as well as feast and fast days. In a world perceived as essentially integrated in every facet, the adoption of a new religious allegiance had to be connected intellectually and experientially with the received wisdom. They expected to be taught religious practices, because every effect has a

---

3   These were the material cause, the formal cause, the efficient cause and the final cause. The most famous illustration is that of a bronze statue, whereby the bronze is the material cause, the figure is the formal cause, the artist the efficient cause and the purpose of the creation the final cause. Aristotle *Physics* 2.3-9 (194b-200b); also *Metaphysics* 1.3.1. (933a-b); 5.2.1-3 (1013a-b).

cause or causes, and how one lives is directly connected with how one experiences the phenomenal world. One could not ignore one's ritual responsibilities and hope that the outcome would be good. If all things are connected, and there is a unifying wisdom which binds the visible world and the invisible world together, each action is potentially significant.

We see from the Letter to the Colossians that the community is carefully cultivating the ethical and community practices that they have been taught – the 'love for all the saints' (1.4), the 'spiritual wisdom and understanding' (1.9) that leads to virtue. They are also following certain practices that were not explicitly taught, but which seemed to them to be an outworking of the same wisdom, namely the ancient Jewish purity regulations, as practised in the Diaspora. This included avoidance of substances that defile (2.21), and dietary restriction (2.16, 21, 23). It also included a different calendar of religious practices from those which they had once observed, with the introduction of the 'sabbath' cycle in addition to the lunar observance (2.16). The seven-day week was not widely established in the wider society until the beginning of the fourth century CE (Evans 1999: 269), and the adoption of it must have shaped the routines of the new believers quite significantly, as well as shaping the perception which their non-Christian neighbours now had of them. It must have seemed patently obvious to the new believers, grafted as they were onto the ancient Jewish faith with its messianic revelation, that they could not continue to practise their ritual observations according to the old ways and the Greco-Roman calendar. But neither could they cease to practise such things altogether, for the connection between inward and outward, between cosmic and individual was affirmed by their new understanding of wisdom. Omitting such practices, which affirmed their piety, humility and their subjection of the demands of the flesh (2.23), had apparently not appeared to them to be an option.

There is a further issue for the believers at Colossae that seems to have been related to cosmology, namely 'self-abasement' and 'worship of angels' (2.18). Angels were firmly part of the cosmological systems in Hellenized Asia Minor of the first century; scholars have demonstrated their centrality to religious practices in this region (Stuckenbruck 1995: 181–204). However, they were also firmly established via cosmology. Plato's *Timaeus* describes God creating the Cosmos as a Living Creature endowed with soul and reason (30B). In a series of steps, God creates four classes of creatures: the first is deemed heavenly (39E), namely the stars, which are wrought out of fire and able to move about the heavens (40A). To these God delegated the task of fashioning human beings as mortal living creatures, weaving together the immortal with the mortal (41C, D). In this cosmogony, the stars are the ones who, like angels affecting God's will, fashion humans, sustain them with food (41D) and receive them again when the mortals waste away (41D). This gives these 'gods', the stars, particular claim over the ones whom they have fashioned, as the divine speech in *Tim.* 41C indicates:

> But if by my doing these creatures came into existence and partook of life, they would be

made equal unto gods; in order, therefore, that they may be mortal and that this World-all may be truly All, do ye turn yourselves, as Nature directs, to the work of fashioning these living creatures, imitating the power showed by me in my generating of you.

The stars therefore had precedence over the mortal creatures that they had fashioned. Just as a patriarch commanded honour and obedience from his progeny, so too did the stars, for those who shared this cosmology. If the Colossians continued certain practices that acknowledged the role of angels/gods/stars in their heritage, they would be acting according to the cultural script of Greco-Roman patriarchal society.

Cosmological concepts transcend the boundaries of religious affiliation. In transferring their allegiance to the God of Israel, the Father of the Lord Jesus Christ, the Colossians were not divested of the categories in which they thought of the material world. Rather, they were in the process of revising their understanding of the powers and forces within whose jurisdiction they lived. The Letter can therefore be seen as a stage in a longer process of reconfiguring their concept of themselves in relation to the cosmos.

Approaching the Colossians' problems implicit in the Letter via Hellenistic cosmology makes it unnecessary to postulate an influx of false teachers into this situation, or a community that is unusually concerned with astrology and angels.[4] I am suggesting that the Colossian believers had received the Pauline Gospel (though not from Paul himself [2.1] and since then had been seeking to interpret it as a full system of religious practices. For areas of uncertainty, they could turn to the cosmological wisdom which had its roots in the Timaean model and which had already been integrated with Jewish thought by Philo. This is not to suggest that Philo's writings were known to this community directly, but rather that many of the ideas were current. David Runia has demonstrated that the cosmology of Colossians has striking similarities to the cosmology of Philo (Runia 1993: 84–86), and this could only be the case if the ideas which Philo set out in an elegant and scholarly way already had currency in Hellenized Jewish circles.

It would be straightforward to conclude that the cosmology evoked by Colossians is fully elucidated against this background of Platonic cosmology. However, the cosmological shifts that occurred in the intervening years make such a claim only partially true. Runia discusses these shifts in more detail than there is scope for in this paper, looking at Plato's successors, the influence of Aristotle, the creative interpretation of *Timaeus* by the Stoics, and then its diminished influence under the Peripatetics, Epicureans and Cynics (Runia 1986: 41–49).[5] It seems to have been later Stoic philosophers, particularly Panaetius of Rhodes (c.185–109 BCE) and Posidonius

---

4   Morna Hooker, who does not reconstruct false teachers at Colossae, sees this as a minority position, though it is also supported by N.T. Wright and R. Yates (Hooker 2003: 117).

5   One shift occurred relatively quickly; *Timaeus* was interpreted non-literally but rather didactically by subsequent leaders of the Academy. Aristotle interpreted Plato's cosmogony literally, however, and both criticized and reinterpreted it in a way that later interpreters found very difficult to disentangle (Runia 1986: 45).

of Apamea (c.135–50 BCE), who played an important role in the reaffirmation of Platonic thinking, though stamped with distinctive Stoic concepts in the areas of physics and theology. To give a full account of the rise of Middle Platonism, with its more religiously tinted, orientalizing approach to philosophy, is beyond the scope of this paper. However, one factor that has not been sufficiently noted by those dealing with the history of these ideas is the impact of the Babylonian planetary theory on Greek astronomy. Greek astronomers contemporary with Plato had not found an approach for calculating planetary positions from theory. During this period of the rise of Middle Platonism, Babylonian planetary theories with quantitative, predictive capacity, based not on geometrical models, but on arithmetic rules, came to the attention of Greek astronomers (Evans 1999: 259). Such a development must have encouraged and enabled the heightened interest in astrology in this period, and fostered respect for oriental wisdom.

This heightened respect for oriental wisdom may in itself have played a role in fostering the spread of the Gospel. Whether or not this is so, we can see that the Letter to the Colossians was written into a context which was open to a synergy of ideas.

The writer of the Letter to the Colossians did not seek to dissuade the recipients from integrating their cosmology with their Christology. The opening section affirms their desire to be 'filled with the knowledge (*epignōsis*) in all wisdom (*sophia*) and spiritual understanding (*sunesis pneumatikē*)' (1.9). The word *epignōsis* and its cognate verb *epiginōskō* occur three times in the first ten verses, and again in chapters 2 and 3 (2.2; 3.10). There is no sense in which the writer is seeking to minimize the Colossians' desire for an integrating wisdom. Rather than seeking to dissuade them, he is confirming them in this direction. This is even more striking in chapter 2, where the author desires for the readers 'all the riches of the full certainty of knowledge (*sunesis*), for understanding (*epignōsis*) the mystery of God, namely Christ' (2.2). Christ is shown to be the key to comprehending the cosmos itself. The Colossian hymn had claimed in Stoic language that in Christ all things were created, all things hold together and all things are reconciled. There could hardly be a grander image of Christ as the cause, the logic and the goal of the visible and invisible cosmos. The undisputed Pauline letters had already made some of these claims for Christ (Gal. 4.3-10; 1 Cor. 15.23-28; Rom. 11.36), but Paul maintained in his undisputed letters that the present order of the cosmos is in the process of being subjugated, and saw the present world as passing away (van Kooten 2003: 107–109). Colossians' cosmology not only affirms the present coherence of the cosmos in Christ, but identifies Christ *ontologically* with the cosmos. In the undisputed letters of Paul, Christ is seen messianically, shaped by the Danielic vision of the subjugation of the powers and kingdoms. In Colossians, the framework has shifted to a Timaean one.

In *Timaeus*, prior to the creation of humanity and prior to the creation of heavenly bodies, the cosmos comes into existence as a 'Living Creature endowed with soul and reason owing to the providence of God' (30B). It goes on to state that this

Living Creature embraces and contains within itself all the intelligible Living Creatures, just as this Universe contains us and all the other visible living creatures that have been fashioned. For since God desired to make it resemble most closely that intelligible Creature which is fairest of all and in all ways most perfect, He constructed it as a Living Creature (*zōon*), one and visible, containing within itself all the living creatures which are by nature akin to itself. (30D)

Plato portrays this as being a process of bringing order out of disorder.

Zeno of Cittium, the founder of Stoicism, gave this image of the cosmos as a Living Creature a revised and more central position in his cosmological framework. He opposed the dualism between matter and spirit in Platonism and Aristotelianism, and developed a philosophy in which matter and spirit are identical in a cosmic body. Michael Lapidge describes the cosmology vividly:

> Stoic cosmology was one of the most imaginative and compelling intellectual constructs devised in antiquity to explain the structure and appearance of the universe: its conception of the divine and fiery mind penetrating all parts of the universe, of the resulting cosmic sympathy between all these parts, of the chain of fate in which every event is linked to every other, and of the fiery conflagration into which the universe dissolves at certain times – these striking theories attracted many adherents to Stoicism . . . .. (Lapidge 1989: 1379–380)

He goes on to state that the fundamental orientation of Stoic cosmology can be described as biological, in that for the Stoics, the universe was a living being or organism (*zōon*; Lapidge 1989: 1381).[6] For those who shared a Stoic cosmological framework, the immanence of this Living Creature, in which all creation exists, became a touchstone of their thinking. This living being was permeated by an all-pervasive fiery *pneuma*, according to Chrysippus' writings; as in the body, so in the universe, the pervasive motion of spirit creates a tensional force, which holds the universe together (Lapidge 1989: 1383). This concept did not remain unique to Stoic thought, but is evident in many authors of the Middle Platonic period, including

---

6   There are, to my knowledge, at least three areas of contemporary scientific enquiry that have analogies with ancient Stoic cosmology. The first and most obvious relates to the biological and geophysical sciences, namely the concept of the earth as a body. This has re-emerged in recent years in public discourse via James Lovelock's Gaia hypothesis. Although this concept has been hailed as 'new', we can see that it has its antecedents in ancient philosophy. The hypothesis, which highlights the feedback processes that connect ecosystems, provides a heuristic tool for the earth sciences and has prompted fruitful discussion and research. The second and third are related to the fields of astronomy and astrophysics. The second is the analogy between the Stoic concept of 'Cosmic sympathy' and contemporary research into dark matter. The third concerns the primordial cosmic structures such as those observed in the cosmic microwave background radiation that are believed to have precipitated the formation of galaxies, and the tiny seed magnetic fields postulated to have existed in the early universe and to have stretched during the rapid phase of cosmic expansion known as inflation. In the Stoic framework there are such seeds, known as *logoi spermatikoi*, which account for exceptional causation.

Cicero and Vergil, to name just two who were not self-professed Stoics (Lapidge 1989: 1386–92).[7]

The shift from Pauline eschatology, in which the present order of the cosmos is in the process of being subjugated and the present world is passing away, to a Timaean framework, against which the present coherence of the cosmos in Christ is affirmed, represents a shift in the relative weight given to eschatology and cosmology. In Pauline thought, the emphasis lies with eschatology, whereas for the writer of the Letter to the Colossians, the emphasis lies with cosmology.[8]

Such a distinction is not perfect, however, as Timaean cosmology has its own cyclical eschatology, which looked for the end of the present order in cosmic conflagration and potential *palingenesia*, renewed birth and repetition of all things (*Tim.* 22 C, D). John J. Collins discusses *ekpurōsis* (conflagration) (Collins 2004: 59–70), and points out that destruction/purification of the world by fire is envisaged in Zoroastrian myth, Greek tradition and even in the Apocalypse of Asclepius, associated with the Hermetic corpus but also an example of cosmic eschatology in the Egyptian tradition: 'It reflects the syncretism of late antiquity, where ideas circulated widely and the coherence of cosmos and history was widely assumed' (Collins 2004: 70). An illustration of this on a philosophical level is found in the writings of Sextus Empiricus, a physician in the late second century CE, who writes of the universe as a living being, and connects this view with both Plato and Zeno:

---

7   Given the blended nature of Greco-Roman cosmology in the first century, it is difficult to state with accuracy what elements can be deemed to be Stoic, and what elements are Middle Platonic. If I were to venture a list of distinguishing Stoic characteristics, it would include:

   i. The emphasis on the corporeality of reality, including god; matter and spirit are identical. Only four groups are deemed to be incorporeal: *lekta* – meanings, or intellectual intentions behind human thoughts; the void beyond the universe, space; and time.
   ii. The conviction that mind is not external to matter; it is the active principle, the creative force permeating the universe and holding it together.
   iii. The immanence of god/logos/spirit in creation.
   iv. The interconnection of all cosmic parts by means of 'sympathy'; a movement in one part of the universe would have a reciprocal and corresponding movement elsewhere.
   v. The downplaying of chance in the world of nature in favour of a chain of causes.
   vi. The affirmation that reason and the senses make certain knowledge possible.
   vii. The concept that there are cosmic cycles of the universe, ending with conflagration.

8   This is not to deny that there are some future (unrealized) eschatological references in Colossians, particularly the future revelation of Christ and of the believers in glory (3.3-4), though the nature of that revelation is debated. See Still 2004: 129. Other unrealized references, according to Still and others, include 1.5, 26-27; and 3.6, 24-25. Nevertheless, the 'vertical axis' of this eschatology, depicted as current reality which crosses spatial and temporal boundaries, is more vivid and pronounced that the 'horizontal axis' of chronology. Hence the author of Colossians can refer to the raising of the believers with Christ through baptism as a past event (2.12; 3.1; aorist passive constructions).

> Plato sets forth virtually the same argument as Zeno. For Zeno says that the universe is the most beautiful product executed according to nature, and in all probability a living being, endowed with soul, both intelligent and rational. (von Armin 1968–1978: I, 110)

The writer of Colossians, by identifying the one through whom, in whom and for whom the creation came into being as Christ, is giving Christ the same pre-eminent position vis-à-vis the invisible and visible world as this Living Creature has in the Timaean model, and expressing this conviction in Stoic terms. Such a move already had currency in Hellenistic Judaism in relation to the Logos of God, as we see in Philo's *De opificio mundi (Opif)*:

> If you would wish to use a formulation that has been stripped down to essentials, you might say that the intelligible cosmos is nothing else than the Logos of God as he is actually engaged in making the cosmos. (*Opif.* §24; Runia 2001: 51)

So in making this interpretative move, the author of Colossians seems to be laying claim to the cosmological framework of Plato's *Timaeus*, but claiming that the Living One is to be known and identified in the person of Jesus Christ.[9] In Colossians we have therefore a cosmic Christology, and seen from another angle, a Christological cosmology. I see this as a bold deutero-Pauline move, enabled by the Timaean cosmological framework, shaped by Stoic thought and motivated by the drive towards synthesis which characterized philosophical thought in the ancient world.

Ecological Hermeneutical Potential

At this point I want to turn to the question of ecological hermeneutics, and ask whether the cosmic Christology of Colossians offers contemporary readers the potential for a renewed understanding of the significance of the non-human cosmos.

It is almost a truism that the duality of matter and spirit lies at the heart of Western thought, and that the Christian faith is shaped and determined by such fundamental binary opposition. In Colossians, however, we have a Christology which allows us to see something different. 'All things in heaven and on earth' (1.16) are shown to be connected via Christ, not only in their origin and their purpose, but also in the soteriology of reconciliation (God was pleased to reconcile *all things* to himself, via

---

9   In this scheme, the Living One is created. Christian patristic reflection, though strongly influenced by Middle Platonic thought, came to insist on the uncreatedness of Christ, most particularly in the Arian controversy, in which Colossians played an important role. See Stead (1964: 16–31), who sets out the complexity of this debate, discusses aspects of the reception of *Timaeus* (though not the Living One) and illustrates the close link between differing cosmologies and Trinitarian theologies.

Christ [1.20].[10] All things therefore have divine significance, matter and spirit alike. Greek philosophy is more diverse than is often recognized with regard to binary thinking, and so too is Christology. The more holistic attitude to the world that is often associated with Eastern religion and philosophy has its counterpart in Stoic thinking, and in the Letter to the Colossians.

However, Christian doctrine does not arise directly from scripture, bypassing the intervening centuries, but comes mediated via Church history and tradition. The tradition of the Church fathers is shaped by Middle Platonism, which integrated aspects of Stoic thought, but not primarily its cosmology. We find ourselves therefore at a conceptual distance from Stoic cosmology, and indeed in Western Christian thinking at a conceptual distance from cosmic Christology.

Yet it is the cosmic Christ who has direct ecological implications. The Jesus of the Gospel traditions can model a lifestyle of simplicity and respect for all creatures, but he does not directly give a framework for reconfiguring our relationship with the Earth based on mutuality rather than hierarchy.[11] However, if one holds a cosmic Christology, the fabric of the material world cannot be viewed as spiritually irrelevant. It cannot be merely the arena for God's dealings with humanity. In embracing a cosmic Christology, Christian practice also cannot remain an individual piety, which takes neither responsibility for others nor for just dealings with other species, as 'all things' were created in him and for him.

However, it is this very cosmic Christology which is largely foreign to Western Christianity and to Protestant theology most particularly. Jesus is proclaimed as 'Lord', 'Saviour', 'Friend', but not as the one through whom and for whom the world was created, nor as the reconciler of a broken and exploited cosmos. And it is precisely Western Protestant theology which recent scholarship has implicated in some of the damaging practices of the transnational corporations, justified by an eschatology that looks for a new heaven and new earth (Maier 2002: 171–74).

Cosmic Christology remains problematic for many, perhaps most, Western evangelical Christians. It seems as though proclaiming a Christ who is 'bigger than Jesus' (Robinson 1973: 10) is seen to be relativizing the particularity of the revelation in the crucified and risen man Jesus. The author of Colossians would vigorously disagree, given that the 'blood of his cross' (1.20) is cited as the instrument of cosmic reconciliation. Some contemporary evangelical thinkers also disagree (Bauckham 2003: 134–35). Yet the fact remains that contemporary Western Christians have

10 The author of the Letter assumes the need for the reconciliation of all things due to cosmic disorder. *Tim.* 29A had affirmed the goodness of the cosmos, but subsequent thinkers accounted for the problem of evil by adopting what was a logical possibility in Platonic thought, namely a bad or ignorant Demiurge (Creator); this is reflected in the rise of Gnosticism (van Kooten 2003: 5). For the author of the Letter to the Colossians, the cosmos was in need of reconciliation with God; the principles, powers and elements of the present cosmos have been restored from disharmony to peace with God under Christ their head (Col. 2.10; van Kooten 2003: 129–35).

11 John's affirmation that the Word became *flesh* (Jn 1.14) does open up ways of connecting Christ with the web of life. See Habel 2009: 93–94.

significant difficulty in connecting the individual and historically particular with the universal and transcendent. The role of the Cosmic Christ has therefore largely been occupied by the third person of the Trinity in Western theology.

Stoic cosmology is not directly comparable to standard Christian theology as it has developed particularly in the West, because is it both monist and materialist.[12] Yet it is fruitful to recognize that the earliest Christians in Asia Minor, and possibly elsewhere, may have been much closer to holding a Stoic cosmology than we are today. For those of us who profess Christian faith and are concerned with ecological hermeneutics, it can be positive to recognize that Stoic cosmological concepts, at least as they come to us via the Letter to the Colossians, are not pantheistic, but function christologically.

I do not know whether it is possible to reinvigorate cosmic Christological thinking in Western Christian thought. It is certainly prominent in Eastern Orthodox theology, with Christ Pantocrator represented in the cupola of each church, and the tradition of iconography requiring a different set of assumptions about the connection between matter and spirit. Western tendencies in theology and in worldview more generally are oriented towards thinking primarily in historical rather than symbolic categories, with the individual and the particular taking the most prominent place. Because of this, the Cosmic Christ may be a concept that remains too foreign for the majority of Western Christians to embrace. Yet the ecological implications of ignoring this theology are profound. In a world-view in which only God and humans have significance, utilitarianism can come to govern everything else, and the natural world can be viewed as being there simply for maintaining and entertaining humans. One Western scholar who has developed a significant ecotheology of the Cosmic Christ is Sally McFague, who shows that the dimensions of place and space, which are neglected in traditional Christian theology, must become increasingly significant as 'an ecological sensibility demands that we broaden the circle of salvation to include the natural world' (1993: 180). In order to effect this shift in perspective, McFague writes that we need to see ourselves in relation to our 'home', Earth, by learning ecology, 'words about home' (*oikos*, home, *logos*, word) (McFague 2008: 48–49).

Some practical implications arise specifically from the cosmic Christology of Colossians. Most Christians understand the Body of Christ ecclesiologically (Rom. 12.5; 1 Cor. 12.27) or sacramentally (1 Cor. 10.16). In Colossians, Christ is *also*[13] the head of the body, the church (Col. 1.18), but his body is understood ecologically as the *kosmos*; in him 'all things hold together' (1.17). If we can hear this perspective, we can expect to experience the divine in all creation, not just in the Church or in the Eucharist. The various understandings of Christ's body need to be connected with one another; the Church must be committed to Christ's body, our ecological home, and

---

12   Monistic and materialistic worldviews are not by definition opposed to Christian thought. John W. Cooper states that 'nowadays most biblical scholars strive to outdo one another in emphasizing that Hebrew anthropology, like the Hebrew mind and Hebrew worldview in general, is decidedly antidualistic and enthusiastically holistic or monist'. He goes on to point out that this can be closely linked with materialism (2000: 34).
13   MacDonald 2000: 61.

our participation in the sacraments must help us perceive the world sacramentally. Christ's body, wounded on the cross (1.20), makes peace and reconciles, and this same suffering Christ is now perceived in the woundedness of creation. We are called to cultivate practices that connect us with the wounded world, and with each other.[14]

Conclusions

At the opening of this essay I claimed that in order to draw ecological meaning from ancient scripture, cosmology is one of the areas needing to receive some careful and nuanced attention. I then proposed that cosmological concepts transcend the boundaries of religious affiliation, and I examined aspects of Plato's cosmology in *Timaeus* and the Stoic framework of Zeno and subsequent Stoic thinkers. This formed the background to examining aspects of the Letter to the Colossians, as the believers at Colossae, in transferring their allegiance to the God of Israel, the Father of the Lord Jesus Christ, did not divest themselves of the categories in which they thought about the material world. Rather, they were in the process of revising their understanding of the powers and forces within whose jurisdiction they lived. The Letter to the Colossians can therefore be seen as a stage in a process of reconfiguring their concept of themselves in relation to the cosmos. The writer of Colossians, by identifying the one through whom, in whom and for whom the creation came into being as Christ, is giving Christ the same pre-eminent position vis-à-vis the invisible and visible world as the Living Creature has in the Timaean model, and expressing this conviction in Stoic terms. I went on to argue that cosmic Christology has significant ecological potential, although it is more difficult for Christians shaped in the Western tradition of the Church than in the Eastern tradition to access this potential.

The cosmic Christology of Colossians deserves to be given much more significant weight in constructing a contemporary theology that is aware of the interconnectedness of the Earth. The earliest Christians in Colossae, and possibly elsewhere in Asia Minor, expressed their faith against the conceptual framework of Stoic cosmology, which they understood Christologically. For those of us who profess Christian faith and are concerned with ecological hermeneutics, this ancient interconnected cosmology can be in dialogue with a contemporary scientifically informed cosmology, and in this way, help us to find new ways of recognising our connection with *all things*.

References

Adams, E. 2000 *Constructing the World: A Study in Paul's Cosmological Language* (SNTW; Edinburgh: T&T Clark).
Balabanski, V.S. 2000 'An Earth Bible Reading of the Lord's Prayer', in N.C. Habel (ed.), *Readings*

---

14   For example, see Habito 2006.

From the Perspective of the Earth (The Earth Bible, 1; Sheffield/Cleveland, OH: Sheffield Academic Press/Pilgrim Press): 151–61.

Balabanski, V.S. 2008 'Critiquing Anthropocentric Cosmology: Retrieving a Stoic "Permeation Cosmology" in Colossians 1.15-20', in N.C. Habel and P. Trudinger (eds), *Exploring Ecological Hermeneutics* (SBLSS 46; Atlanta, GA: SBL): 151–59.

Bauckham, R. 2003 'Where is Wisdom to be Found? Colossians 1.15-20 (2)', in D. Ford and G. Stanton (eds), *Reading Texts, Seeking Wisdom* (London: SCM): 129–38.

Boersema, J.J. 2001 *The Torah and the Stoics on Humankind and Nature: A Contribution to the Debate on Sustainability and Quality* (Leiden/Boston: Brill).

Brague, R. 2003 *The Wisdom of the World: The Human Experience of the Universe in Western Thought* (tr. T.L. Fagan; Chicago and London: University of Chicago Press).

Bury, R.G. (tr.) 1929/1999 *Plato's Timaeus* (Plato IX, Loeb Classical Library 234; Cambridge, MA: Harvard University Press).

Collins, J.J. 2004 'Cosmology: Time and History', in S.I. Johnston (ed.), *Religions in the Ancient World: A Guide* (Cambridge, MA and London: Harvard University Press): 59–70.

Cooper, J.W. 2000 *Body, Soul and Life Everlasting: Biblical Anthropology and the Monism-Dualism Debate* (Grand Rapids, MI: Eerdmans).

Evans, J. 1999 'The Material Culture of Greek Astronomy', in *Journal for the History of Astronomy* 30: 237–308.

Habel N.C. 1985 *The Book of Job* (London: SCM).

Habel N.C. 2008 'Introducing Ecological Hermeneutics', in N.C. Habel and P. Trudinger (eds), *Exploring Ecological Hermeneutics*, (SBLSS 46; Atlanta, GA: SBL): 1–8.

Habel, N. 2009 *An Inconvenient Text: Is a Green Reading of the Bible Possible?* (Adelaide: Australasian Theological Forum).

Habel, N.C. and Balabanski, V. (eds) 2002 *The Earth Story in the New Testament* (The Earth Bible, 5; London and New York/Cleveland, OH: Sheffield Academic Press/Pilgrim Press).

Habito, R.L.F. 2006 *Healing Breath: Zen for Christians and Buddhists in a Wounded World* (Boston, MA: Wisdom Publications).

Hooker, M. 2003 'Where is Wisdom to be Found? Colossians 1.15-20 (1)', in D. Ford and G. Stanton (eds), *Reading Texts, Seeking Wisdom* (London: SCM): 116–28.

Lapidge, M. 1989 'Stoic Cosmology and Roman Literature, First to Third Centuries AD.', *ANRW* II.36.3: 1379–429.

MacDonald, M.Y. 2000 *Colossians and Ephesians* (SP 17; Collegeville, MN: Liturgical Press).

McFague, S. 1993 *The Body of God: An Ecological Theology* (Minneapolis, MN: Fortress).

McFague, S. 2008 *A New Climate for Theology, the World and Global Warming* (Minneapolis, MN: Fortress).

Maier, H.O. 2002 'There's a New World Coming! Reading the Apocalypse in the Shadow of the Canadian Rockies', in N.C. Habel and V. Balabanski (eds), *The Earth Story in the New Testament* (The Earth Bible, 5; London and New York/Cleveland, OH: Sheffield Academic Press/ Pilgrim Press): 166–79.

Robinson, J.A.T. 1973 *The Human Face of God* (London: SCM).

Runia, D.T. 1986 *Philo of Alexandria and the* Timaeus *of Plato* (Philosophia Antiqua; Leiden: Brill).

Runia, D.T. 1993 *Philo in Early Christian Literature: A Survey* (CRINT; Assen: Van Gorcum).

Runia, D.T. 2001 *On the Creation of the Cosmos According to Moses: Introduction, Translation and Commentary* (Leiden: Brill).

Stead, G.C. 1964 'The Platonism of Arius', *JTS* 15: 16–31.

Still, T.D. 2004 'Eschatology in Colossians: How Realized is it?', *NTS* 50: 129.

Stuckenbruck, L.T. 1995 *Angel Veneration and Christology: A Study in Early Judaism and in the Christology of the Apocalypse of John* (WUNT 2.70; Tübingen: Mohr Siebeck).

van Kooten, G.H. 2003 *Cosmic Christology in Paul and the Pauline School: Colossians and Ephesians in the Context of Graeco-Roman Cosmology, with a New Synopsis of the Greek Texts* (WUNT 2.171; Tübingen: Mohr/Siebeck).

von Arnim, H. (ed.) 1968–1978 *Stoicorum veterum fragmenta* (Vols.1–4; Stuttgart: Teubner).

Chapter 8

Retrieving the Earth from the Conflagration: 2 Peter 3.5-13 and the Environment

Edward Adams

2 Peter 3.5-13 is, at first sight, one of the least eco-friendly texts in the New Testament. A fiery destiny is predicted for 'the present heavens and earth' (v. 7). We are told that 'the heavens will be set ablaze and dissolved, and the elements will melt with fire' on the coming day of the Lord (v. 12); after the fire, there will be 'new heavens and a new earth' (v. 13). The eschatological scenario projected in these verses appears to offer little incentive for environmental care. Indeed, the writer's exhortation to wait for and 'hasten' the coming of the fiery day of God (v. 12) might seem to encourage practices that lead to environmental decline and ruination. Keith Dyer (2002: 56) thinks that this passage 'presents irretrievable problems for an ethical response to ecological problems'. Yet, various efforts have been made to read the text in a way that supports a biblically based environmentalism.[1] Such attempts largely consist of exegetical and interpretative arguments aimed at showing that what is in view is not the earth's destruction but its transformation. In this essay, I will consider these arguments, concluding that the dissolution of the earth, along with the heavens, is indeed envisioned. However, I will suggest that, even on a destructionist interpretation of it, the environmental implications of this text are perhaps somewhat less egregious than may appear.

2 Pet. 3.4-13

In our passage, the writer is countering the eschatological cynicism of his opponents.[2] The 'false teachers', as he labels them (2.1), are active within the congregations addressed, undermining traditional apostolic teaching, especially with regard to the Lord's coming. In his polemic, the author portrays the adversaries as 'scoffers' of the last days whose coming (of which the author speaks in the future tense) is a sign

---

1   Bouma-Prediger 2001: 76–77; Finger 1998: 3–6; Heide 1997: 46–55; Lucas 1999: 97; Moo 2006: 466–69.
2   The writer presents himself as Peter, but most commentators doubt that the apostle was the actual author of the epistle.

that the last phase of history has arrived (3.3).

The content of their eschatological mockery is cited in verse 4: 'Where is the promise of his coming? For ever since the fathers fell asleep, all things continue as they were from the beginning of creation!' The promise under attack is usually taken to be Jesus' own promise (or the promise attributed to him) to return within a generation (Mk 13.30 + par.), but it is more likely to be Old Testament prophetic expectation of God's eschatological coming (e.g. Isa. 64.1-3; 66.15-18; Zech. 14.1-5; Mal. 3.1-4), which the early Christians applied to Jesus' return.[3] This fits with the mention of 'the fathers', a term regularly used of the Old Testament fathers,[4] and also with 1.20-21, which implies that the opponents denounce Old Testament prophecy. The scoffers reject the hope of the Lord's coming because of the great length of time that has elapsed since it was originally expressed (v. 4a). The excessive time of waiting, beyond all reasonable expectation, indicates that the promise is unlikely ever to come true (Adams 2005: 113–14). The temporal objection is buttressed by the assertion that all things continue just as they were from the creation of the cosmos. On the standard interpretation of verse 4b, this clause expresses a dismissal of the possibility of divine intervention in the world.[5] The opponents' outlook is thought to resemble Epicurean scepticism (see esp. Neyrey 1980): Epicureans rejected divine involvement in the cosmos or human history. However, if the false teachers were radical sceptics in the Epicurean mould, it is difficult to imagine how they could have belonged to the believing community.[6] The assertion of verse 4b is much better understood as an affirmation of cosmic stability and immutability, reflecting philosophical belief in the imperishableness of the cosmos.[7] Like Plato (*Timaeus* 32–3) and Philo (*De aeternitate mundi*), the adversaries held that the world is created and indestructible. The idea of the parousia is thus to be rejected because it involves the impossible prospect of cosmic destabilization and collapse.[8]

The author answers the objections of his opponents in verses 5-9, dealing first, in verses 5-7, with their cosmological argument. In response to the claim that the created cosmos continues unceasingly without major change, he argues that the adversaries have deliberately ignored the fact that there was an occasion, the occasion of the flood in the time of Noah, when the created world was destroyed. The flood shows that the world is not imperishable. As God destroyed the world once before, so he will do so once more. In these verses, the writer correlates creation, flood and the final day of judgement: by word and water God created the world; by word and water

---

3   As argued in Adams 2005. This view is also now taken by Peter Davids in his new commentary on 2 Peter (2006: 266). For the influence of the Old Testament and early Jewish hope of God's coming on the New Testament expectation of Jesus' return, see Adams 2006.
4   E.g. Mt. 23.30, 32; Lk. 1.55, 72; Jn 4.20; 6.31; Acts 3.13, 25; Rom. 9.5.
5   E.g. Bauckham 1983: 294; Horrell 1998: 139, Kraftchick 2002: 152–53
6   For further difficulties, see Adams 2005: 115–16.
7   So Bigg 1910: 119. For a fuller defence of this view, see Adams 2005: 116–21.
8   In Old Testament prophecies of God's coming, the divine advent is often accompanied by massive upheavals in nature: e.g. Mic. 1.2-4; Nah. 1.3-5; Hab. 3.3-15; Zech. 14.4-5.

he destroyed it; by word and fire, he will destroy it again. In verses 8-9, he responds to their temporal argument by showing that God's sense of time is very different to ours: 'with the Lord one day is like a thousand years, and a thousand years are like one day' (cf. Ps. 90.4). He further argues that the seeming delay of the parousia is due to God's forbearance: by appearing to postpone the day of judgement, God is allowing people time to repent.

The writer assures his readers in verse 10 that, despite the apparent delay, the day of the Lord will come. When it arrives, it will do so suddenly: 'like a thief' (cf. Mt. 24.43; Lk. 12.39; 1 Thess. 5.2, 4; Rev. 3.3; 16.15). On that day, the heavens will pass away with a loud noise, the elements will be dissolved with fire, and 'the earth and all its works will be found'. In verses 11-13, the author moves from apologetic to moral application.

> Since all these things are to be dissolved in this way, what sort of persons ought you to be in leading lives of holiness and godliness, waiting for and hastening the coming of the day of God because of which the heavens will be set ablaze and dissolved, and the elements will melt with fire? But, in accordance with his promise, we wait for new heavens and a new earth, where righteousness is at home.

In the course of the appeal, he repeats his description of the fiery dissolution from verse 10, but now mentions 'new heavens and a new earth'. The 'promise' of which he speaks is almost certainly that contained in Isa. 65.17 and 66.2, verses which specifically foretell the creation of 'new heavens and a new earth' (Kelly 1969: 368). The coming destruction is thus not an end in itself; it prepares the way for a new situation. Unlike John the Seer in Revelation 21–22, the author makes no attempt to describe the new created order; he simply notes that the new creation will be an environment in which righteousness flourishes (in contrast to the corruption that marks the world at present [1.4].

Destruction or Transformation?

It is generally accepted that 2 Pet. 3.4-13 has to do with the future of the cosmos. It has become fashionable to interpret the language of cosmic catastrophe in Mk 13.24-27 (talk of sun and moon being darkened, cosmic structures convulsing and stars falling at the coming of the Son of Man) as metaphorical for localized socio-political change and as referring to events on the immediate historical horizon, usually the events surrounding the fall of Jerusalem in 70 CE.[9] Reading the catastrophic and cosmic language in this way is an effective way of nullifying its apparent anti-environmental force. But, I have not as yet come across any scholarly attempt to rescue 2 Pet. 3.4-13

---

9   E.g. France 2002: 530–37; Hatina 1996; Wright 1996: 339–67; Bird 2008: 56–58.

for biblical environmentalism that employs this interpretative strategy.[10] In my view, it is a mark of good exegetical sense that such an approach has not (so far!) been adopted. That the writer is presenting a scenario that is universal and cosmic in scope is very hard to deny. Even if it is insisted that the language (especially the language of fire) is to some extent 'figurative', that the text is about cosmic events is crystal clear. It is noteworthy that even N.T. Wright, the main contemporary advocate of the socio-political interpretation of biblical cosmic catastrophe language, acknowledges that this passage presents an 'end-time scenario' and a 'cosmic drama' (2003: 462).

Writers who have sought to retrieve 2 Pet. 3.4-13 for a biblically based environmentalism have done so mainly by trying to argue that the passage does not describe the destruction of the existing earth but rather its transformation. Whether this text envisages destruction (and re-creation) or transformation is a longstanding interpretative debate,[11] but it is deemed to have particular relevance to the environmental question. As Thomas Finger puts its, the conviction that God will transform the present earth, rather than destroy it, means that 'this earth must be precious to God, and that proper stewardship of nonhuman nature is a task with eternal consequences' (1998: 27). By advocating a non-destructionist reading of 2 Pet. 3.5-13, scholars such as Finger also endeavour to bring it more into line with Paul's hope for the liberation of creation expressed in Rom. 8.18-25, which, as Douglas Moo states, 'clearly implies that the destiny of the natural world is not destruction but transformation' (2006: 463).

At least five distinct exegetical and interpretative arguments are used in support of a non-destructionist interpretation of 2 Pet. 3.4-13.

First, it is argued that the analogy with the flood indicates something less than destruction. The author states that at the time of the flood, the world that then existed 'perished' (*apōleto*, 3.6), but as Gale Heide notes, the flood, as described in Genesis 6–9, 'did not destroy the earth completely' (1997: 53). Fish presumably continued to exist and geological features, such as mountains, remained. Every animal species was spared, along with some human beings, by virtue of being in the ark. In other words, 'much of what existed previously in creation survived' (Heide 1997: 54). The comparison drawn between the flood and the fiery judgement suggests that

---

10 The claim that 2 Peter 3 is about the destruction of Jerusalem was, however, made over a century ago by J.S. Russell as part of his general thesis that the parousia happened in the events in 70 CE. See Russell 1887: 319–26.

11 The issue tends to be presented in dichotomous terms: either total annihilation (destruction into nothing) followed by new creation *ex nihilo*, or transformation. For the annihilationist reading, see, for example, Overstreet (1980: 365): 'Heaven and earth shall be annihilated. In nuclear fission some waste products are always left over. But when God causes this catastrophic event, the destruction will be complete and total.' The scholars with whom I am engaging in this essay (Bouma-Prediger, Finger, Heide, Lucas and Moo) operate with the annihilation/transformation dichotomy. I will argue that the author of 2 Peter envisages destruction, but not absolute annihilation, a concept that would have been inconceivable to him.

the latter, like the former, is about the cleansing of creation from unrighteousness not its complete destruction (Heide 1997: 55).

Secondly, it is maintained that fire is not primarily a destructive agent in 2 Pet. 3.5-13. Moo points out that fire in the Old Testament 'is often a metaphorical way of speaking of judgment', and even if sometimes the reference is to physical fire, the fire need not be totally destructive (2006: 468). Ernest Lucas notes that 'fire is used as a metaphor of judgement which does not simply destroy, but *purifies*, e.g. Isaiah 21-26; Malachi 1-4' (1999: 97). The purpose of the eschatological fire in 2 Peter 3, according to Lucas, is to 'purge the created order of all evil'(1999: 97). Similarly, Heide suggests that fire in this text is 'the cleansing agent for the stain of sin upon the earth . . . rather than a means for indiscriminate disintegration' (1997: 54).

Thirdly, it is argued that the preservation of the earth is implied in the final clause of verse 10. It is noted that the reading adopted by the KJV and some other versions, 'the earth and everything in it shall be burned up', finds little acceptance nowadays. Most commentators agree that the original reading is: 'the earth and all its works will be found'. On this construal, according to Bouma-Prediger, the earth is 'discovered, not destroyed' (2001: 77). Finger, in line with a number of recent commentators, argues that being 'found' refers mainly to God's assessment of human beings: he maintains that the earth is 'found, or discovered; not to be destroyed, but so that the human works done upon it may be judged' (1998: 5).

Fourthly, it is noted that the word for 'dissolve' in verses 10, 11 and 12 is *luō*, which 'does not necessarily have to refer to annihilation'; according to Heide, the thought is more that of 'breaking down into component parts' or 'release from bondage' (1997: 53). Some form of physical alteration is meant, but not 'a total eradication of all physical substance.' Similarly Moo thinks that the word points not to annihilation 'but a dissolution or radical change in nature' (2006: 468).

Finally, the point is made that the word for 'new' in the phrase 'new heavens and a new earth' is not *neos*, which means 'previously non-existent', but *kainos*, which means 'new in quality' (Lucas 1999: 97). According to Finger, it is not necessary to think of the new state as 'created entirely from scratch' (1998: 6); the wording is consistent with the idea of a transformation of the existing heavens and earth.

A cumulative case is thus built for seeing 2 Pet. 3.4-10 as about 'renewal through transformation, not a total destruction of the old and its replacement by something quite different' (Lucas 1999: 97). The case looks impressive, but on closer scrutiny none of these arguments for a non-destructionist interpretation of the passage holds up.

First, it is true that in the Genesis account of the flood, creation is not totally destroyed, but, as J.N.D. Kelly points out, 'Jewish apocalyptic and speculation dependent on it read this frightening development into the story' (1969: 359). In 1 *Enoch* 10.2, 'the whole earth' is said to have perished at the flood. 1 *Enoch* 83.3-5 depicts the heavens as collapsing onto the earth, and the earth itself as being swallowed by the abyss.¹² Most commentators agree that the author of 2 Peter goes beyond Genesis and imagines the flood as bringing about the destruction of the whole universe: this is implied by the contrast between the 'heavens . . . and earth' of 'long ago' in verse 5 and 'the present heavens and earth' in verse 7 (Horrell 1998: 177). As well as post-biblical flood tradition that sees the flood as destroying the earth or the whole cosmos, the writer also seems to be influenced by the notion of parallel cosmic destructions by water and fire, an idea found in Stoicism of the period (Seneca, *Naturales Quaestiones* 3.28.7). One may readily agree that the analogous relation of flood and final act of judgement suggests that the latter, in line with the former, is about the cleansing of creation from sin and evil, but the cleansings take place, for our author, *by means of destruction* not instead of it.

Secondly, it is also true that fire is sometimes a metaphor for judgement in the Old Testament. For example, Zeph. 1.18 speaks of the whole earth being consumed 'in the fire of his passion'; here fire clearly functions as a metaphor for God's wrath (cf. Isa. 30.27; Jer. 40.4; Zeph. 3.8). But since the writer obviously understands water as a literal agent of destruction in the flood, we can be sure that he thinks of fire as a 'real' destructive force in the coming judgement. Moreover, it is doubtful that the background to the author's expectation of a fiery cosmic destruction is to be found in the Old Testament. As Richard Bauckham notes, in Old Testament texts where fire is an instrument of judgement, its function is mainly to consume the wicked (1983: 300); nowhere in the Old Testament is the total destruction of heaven and earth by fire predicted or visualized (Adams 2007: 97 n. 201; van der Horst 1994: 234–36). In Second Temple Jewish literature, the idea of the complete destruction of the cosmos by fire comes to expression in the Sibylline Oracles (2.196-213; 3.75-92; 4.171-92; 5.206-13, 512-31; Adams 2007: 88–95), but it does so under the influence of Stoic cosmology (Van der Horst 1994: 239). At the time of 2 Peter, the expectation of a cosmic conflagration was commonly viewed as a typically Stoic idea. The doctrine of world conflagration, or *ekpurōsis*, as it was known, was taught by Zeno, the founder of Stoicism, and his immediate successors, Cleanthes and Chrysippus.¹³ It was abandoned by several leading figures of middle Stoicism but was affirmed by first-century CE Roman Stoics including Seneca and Epictetus. Philo (*Aet.* 8) attributes the theorem to the great mass of Stoic philosophers in his day. Given the Stoic provenance of the notion, it seems reasonable to suppose, as many have concluded, that it was from this source that the author of 2 Peter derived it. This is not to say that the writer bought into the cyclic dimensions of the Stoic theory, according to which the cosmos is destroyed and regenerated endlessly: the author presses the Stoic conception into a linear scheme and imagines the conflagration as a one-off and final act of judgement. If a Stoic background to 2 Pet. 3.10-12 is accepted, there need be no distinction between destruction and purification, since in Stoic thought the fire

---

12 On 'the abyss' as a reference to the primeval waters, see Dennis 2008: 174–75, rightly correcting Adams 2007: 214.
13 On the Stoic conflagration see Adams 2007: 114–24; Long 1985.

that devours the cosmos is both destructive and purifying (it was evidently called a *katharsis* or purification [Lapidge 1978: 180]), consuming all material things and purging the world of evil.

Thirdly, it is correct that the last line of verse 10, on the best textual evidence, does not speak of the destruction of the earth. The meaning of the reading, 'the earth and all its works will be found', which should be regarded as original,[14] is not easy to determine, but as Finger argues, it most likely relates to God's judgement of humans. The point being expressed, as Horrell states, is that '[a]ll the deeds and works of human beings will be laid bare before God'.[15] But this clause should not be interpreted to mean that the earth is preserved through or protected from the fire. The destruction of the earth along with the heavens is expressed in the opening phrase of verse 11: 'since all these things are to be dissolved in this way . . .' The words 'all these things' (*toutōn pantōn*) pick up the references to the heavens, the elements and the earth in verse 10. As Bauckham (1983: 324) points out, the dissolution of the earth is also implied in verse 7 ('the present heavens and earth have been reserved for fire') and in verse 13 ('a new earth').

In my view, the earth's dissolution is further implied in verse 10 with the mention of the elements being dissolved with fire (cf. v. 12, 'the elements will melt with fire'). The meaning of the word *stoicheia*, translated 'elements', is debated. Most commentators take the word as referring to the heavenly bodies: sun, moon and stars. Some (e.g. Horrell 1998: 180; Finger 1998: 6) see a double reference to the cosmic bodies and the spiritual powers thought to be controlling them. However, the application of the term *stoicheia* to the heavenly bodies is not securely attested until after the New Testament period (*EDNT*: 3.278). The most natural meaning of *stoicheia* in 2 Pet. 3.10-12, when the epistle was written, would have been the physical elements of which, it was believed, all earthly things are composed: earth, air, water and fire. Commentators tend to reject a reference to the four material elements because that would seem to entail the absurdity that fire is dissolved by fire. However, no illogicality is involved if the background of thought is Stoic cosmology, since Stoics distinguished between the element fire and the cosmic fire into which all things are resolved at the conflagration (Adams 2007: 115). The author's division of cosmic reality into the heavens and the elements (especially in v. 12, where there is no additional mention of the earth) fits with the standard Stoic division of the cosmos (with the four elements comprising all things in the earthly realm, and ether constituting the substance of things in the supra-terrestrial realm).

Fourthly, it is indeed the case that the word *luō* means more to break down into component parts than to annihilate or obliterate from existence, but the former still has to do with destruction (specifically disintegration) and the latter would not have been considered a conceivable meaning at the time of writing. In Greco-Roman

---

14 So Bauckham 1983: 316–21; Neyrey 1993: 243–44; Horrell 1998: 180–81; Kraftchick 2002: 163.
15 Horrell 1998: 181. See further Adams 2007: 228.

discussion of whether the cosmos will perish or endure forever, 'destruction' was understood as resolution into some originating principle or breaking down into constituent parts, and not as reduction to nothing. Philo (*Aet.* 6) is quite clear on this point:

> Nothing in fact is so foolish as to raise the question whether the world is destroyed into non-existence. The point is whether it undergoes a transmutation from its ordered arrangement through the various forms of the elements and their combinations being either resolved into one and the self-same conformation or reduced in complete confusion as things are when shattered.

The idea of the total resolution of the cosmos and all matter into nothingness is given serious expression in the mid-second century CE and beyond, largely in heterodox circles on the fringes of the mainstream Church. It was apparently part of Valentinian cosmological teaching (Irenaeus, *Against Heresies* 1.7.1), and it is found in certain Nag Hammadi treatises (*Orig. World* 126-7; *Great Pow.* 46). Among the church fathers, it was accepted by Tertullian (*Against Hermogenes* 34), who, unlike Valentinians and 'Gnostics', looked for a new creation *ex nihilo*. But it would be anachronistic to use this notion of destruction as the benchmark for determining whether 2 Pet. 3.5-13 is about the dissolution of the cosmos.

The author of 2 Peter uses the word *luō* in a standard destructionist sense, and so it is correctly translated 'dissolve' or 'destroy' (BDAG: 667). The cluster of verbs used in verses 10 and 13 (*parerchomai*, 'pass away'; *puroō*, 'set ablaze'; *kausoō*, 'burn up'; *tekō*, 'melt') is clearly meant to portray violent destruction. The writer appears to envisage destruction by reduction into the primal element fire, as in the Stoic theory of *ekpurōsis*. To interpret his language as rhetorical hyperbole for non-destructive transformation is to ride roughshod over the writer's careful and 'scientifically' appropriate use of terms and to rob his argument of its force as a response to the assertion that the cosmos is indestructible.

Finally, the observation that the word for 'new' is *kainos* not *neos* is not all that significant since the words were plainly being used interchangeably at this time (BDAG: 496–97, 669). The contrast with 'the present heavens and earth' in verse 7 clearly indicates that the author is thinking in terms of a new created order not just a transformation of the present cosmic order.

In sum, therefore, the case for a non-destructionist reading of 2 Pet. 3.5-13 is not very strong and is marked to a certain extent by special pleading. What the author envisions here is the violent dissolution of the heavens and earth and their creation anew. His vision differs markedly from Paul's view of the cosmic future in Rom. 8.18-25 and it should not be made to conform to the Pauline text.

Beyond Retrieval?

Is 2 Pet. 3.5-13, then, beyond retrieval for a biblically informed environmentalism? And does it really matter if the text is deemed irrecoverable? It would be easy to dismiss this passage as expressing a marginal and extreme viewpoint out of harmony with other biblical voices. But the fact is that 2 Pet. 3.5–13 is not alone in the biblical canon in affirming the dissolution of creation (see Ps. 102: 25-27; Isa. 51.6; Mk 13.31 + par.; Heb. 1.10-12 [citing Ps. 102.25-27]; Rev. 21.1), so it is not out on a limb in this regard, though no other biblical passage depicts the destruction of heaven and earth so graphically and violently. Those seeking to derive from the Bible a positive environmental ethic need to acknowledge that the Bible has more than one way of conceiving the cosmic future and that the various statements cannot be pressed into a singular vision of non-destructive transformation.

Although 2 Pet. 3.5-13 cannot be considered a pro-environmental text, there are certain considerations which, even in a destructionist interpretation of the passage, mollify its apparent anti-environmental thrust.[16]

First, we can be confident that the expectation of cosmic destruction here articulated does not entail a negative assessment of the present creation as innately evil. According to N.T. Wright (1992: 285), the very idea of the world coming to an end betokens a world-negating, dualistic cosmology. But this was not the case for the Stoics, whose cosmology was firmly monistic. The main Stoic proponents of *ekpurōsis* regarded the conflagration as a wholly positive event (Adams 2007: 120–21). Chrysippus maintained that at *ekpurōsis*, the cosmos turns into light or brightness (Philo, *Aet.* 90). He insisted that the universe does not die (Plutarch, *Moralia* [*On Stoic Self-Contradictions*] 1052c); rather it grows to its acme and is regenerated. As Pieter van der Horst states, for Stoics, the conflagration 'is an act of god in his benevolent providence. It is a blessing, not an evil' (1994: 234). It was perhaps this positive assessment of the conflagration within Stoic cosmology that made it theologically acceptable to the writer of 2 Peter. He clearly views the destruction and re-creation of the cosmos as a positive action of God, bringing judgement, establishing righteousness and fulfilling divine promise. Old Testament and Second Temple Jewish writers can also affirm the destructibility or end of the world without assuming that the earth is inherently bad (Adams 2007: 28–32). The book of Genesis, in its finished form, holds together belief in the intrinsic goodness of creation (Gen. 1.4, 10, 12, etc.) and belief in the mortality of the earth (Gen. 8.22). The writer of 2 Peter alludes to Genesis 1 in 2 Pet. 3.5-6, and we can be sure that he agrees with the verdict of Genesis 1 that creation is intrinsically good.[17]

Secondly, the dissolution of the earth is not envisaged as an end in itself; it prepares

---

16   What follows expands and develops Adams 2007: 258–59.
17   True, the writer believes that there is corruption in the world, but like Paul in Rom. 8.20-21, he sees corruption entering the world by means of a 'fall' event ('because of desire', 2 Pet. 1.4).

the way for a new earthly future. The writer's vision stands in sharp contrast to later 'Gnostic' conceptions of the end in which there is no material re-creation after the annihilation of the material order (MacRae 1983: 323). For the writer of 2 Peter, the dissolution of heaven and earth is part of a process of renewal, which brings about a new heavens and new earth in continuity with what has gone before. In Stoicism, the new cosmos was conceived as an exact (or near-exact) replica of the preceding world (Long 1985: 25–26). It is doubtful that the author expected the new cosmic creation to be an exact replication of the present world, but it is very likely that he thought of it as in some sense a restoration and perfection of the original creation.

For the author of 2 Peter, the new heavens and earth are not a *creatio ex nihilo* but a *creatio ex vetere*, a creation out of the old. Material continuity between the present cosmos and the new eschatological creation is assumed, on the basis of the physical continuity that obtained between the antediluvian and postdiluvian worlds, and on the basis of the preservation of matter through conflagration and regeneration as pictured in Stoic cosmology. For the writer of 2 Peter, matter is not to be dumped into eternal nothingness but *recycled*.

Thirdly, living in the light of the end and re-creation, for this author, does not mean the abandonment of ethical obligations; he issues a moral appeal precisely on the basis of the coming end and renewal (vv. 11-12). In verse 14, pressing further his moral petition, he indicates that as believers await the new heavens and new earth, they should 'strive to be found by him at peace'. The verb 'strive' points to strenuous effort (and thus rules out *passive* waiting). Commentators tend to take 'peace' as meaning the condition of being reconciled to God[18] or the state of holiness or purity that flows from salvation.[19] In the Old Testament, 'peace' (Hebrew, *shalōm*) covers wholeness and well-being in the widest sense; it has a social and public significance 'far beyond the purely personal'.[20] Peace is a traditional quality of the eschatological order (Isa. 9.6-7; 32.15-20; 52.7; 60.17-22; etc.) and it embraces harmony with human beings and harmony with the wider creation (especially Isa. 32.15-20; 61.17-22). One wonders whether the broader notion of peace is being evoked in 2 Pet. 3.14, especially when one considers the immediate eschatological context. If so, the injunction to 'strive to be found at peace' might be interpreted as a call to work for wholeness in the present world wherever possible in anticipation of the peace that God himself will establish in the new creation. Since *shalōm* in its eschatological manifestation has an environmental dimension, might not striving for peace be taken to entail the exercise of environmental as well as social responsibility? This would of course be going beyond what the author himself had in mind (it would be absurd to attribute to him an ecological awareness), but it might be seen as an appropriate contemporary extension of his appeal.

But what of the exhortation to 'hasten' the coming of the day of God? Does this

---

18 E.g. Bauckham 1983: 327.
19 E.g. Neyrey 1993: 250.
20 See Beck and Brown 1976: 776–83.

not encourage the exploitation of the earth and its resources so as to accelerate the inevitable demise of the present creation? From the author's viewpoint, how one may hasten the day of the Lord is by living godly, holy and peace-seeking lives. The abusive treatment of God's creation is hardly consistent with such a lifestyle. It would be a twisted and pernicious misapplication of the writer's injunction to use it to legitimate the shameless neglect and misuse of the environment.

What about the sense of imminence that attaches to the expectation of the earth's fiery future? Does this not act as a disincentive to meaningful reparative and preservative environmental action? The time signals in this passage are decidedly mixed. On the one hand, there are strong indications of imminence (vv. 3, 12-13), but on other, there is the acknowledgement that the end may be a long way off (v. 8). Readers are thus encouraged to live in expectancy of the end while recognizing that the present world may continue to exist for thousands of years to come. This tension between urgency and long-termism, it seems to me, leaves space for Christian involvement in the wider socio-political world and its problems and for the development of an ethic of environmental care.

Conclusion

2 Pet. 3.5-13 remains a problematic text from an environmental perspective. Attempts to retrieve the passage for the environment based on the claim that what is envisioned is transformation and not destruction fail to persuade. The eschatological scenario depicted involves the destruction of the earth along with the material heavens; the scenario (in and of itself) is hardly one that inspires pro-environmental action. Yet, as I hope to have indicated, relating this passage in a positive way to the environment is not a completely lost cause. The text almost certainly presupposes the created goodness of the earth, which I regard as the primary biblical motivation for environmental concern (along with the stewardship of the earth implied in the 'creation mandate' of Gen. 1.26-28). The thought of the creator 'recycling' the old to produce the new, conserving and reprocessing matter, has positive environmental resonances. And the 'peace' for which readers are called to strive in verse 14 can be legitimately extended to include harmony with the environment. None of this is to suggest that 2 Pet. 3.5-13 can safely be re-labelled an eco-friendly text, but it perhaps shows that the text is not completely devoid of features which are retrievable for a biblical theology and ethic of the environment.

References

Adams, E. 2005 '"Where is the Promise of His Coming?" The Complaint of the Scoffers in 2 Peter 3.4', *NTS* 51: 106–22.
Adams, E. 2006 'The Coming of God Tradition and Its Influence on New Testament Parousia Texts',

in C. Hempel and J.M. Lieu (eds), *Biblical Traditions in Transmission: Essays in Honour of Michael A. Knibb* (JSJSup 111; Leiden: Brill): 1–19.

Adams, E. 2007 *The Stars Will Fall From Heaven: Cosmic Catastrophe in the New Testament and Its World* (LNTS 347; London: T&T Clark).

Bauckham, R.J. 1983 *Jude, 2 Peter* (WBC 50; Waco: Word).

Beck, H. and Brown, C. 1976 'Peace', in C. Brown (ed.), *New International Dictionary of New Testament Theology, Volume 2* (Exeter: Paternoster): 776–83.

Bigg, C. 1910 *A Critical and Exegetical Commentary on the Epistles of St. Peter and St. Jude* (ICC; Edinburgh: T&T Clark).

Bird, M. 2008 'Tearing the Heavens and Shaking the Heavenlies: Mark's Cosmology in Its Apocalyptic Context', in J.T. Pennington and S.M. McDonough (eds), *Cosmology and New Testament Theology* (LNTS 355; London: T&T Clark): 45–59.

Bouma-Prediger, S. 2001 *For the Beauty of the Earth: A Christian Vision for Creation Care* (Grand Rapids, MI: Baker Academic).

Davids, P.H. 2006 *The Letters of 2 Peter and Jude* (Grand Rapids, MI: Eerdmans).

Dennis, J. 2008 'Cosmology in the Petrine Literature and Jude', in J.T. Pennington and S.M. McDonough (eds), *Cosmology and New Testament Theology* (LNTS 355; London: T&T Clark): 157–77

Dyer, K. 2002 'When is the End not the End? The Fate of Earth in Biblical Eschatology (Mark 13)', in N.C. Habel and V. Balabanski (eds), *The Earth Story in the New Testament* (The Earth Bible, 5; London and New York/Cleveland, OH: Sheffield Academic Press/Pilgrim Press): 44–56.

Finger, T. 1998 *Evangelicals, Eschatology and the Environment* (The Scholars Circle 2; Wynnewood, PA: Evangelical Environmental Network).

France, R.T. 2002 *The Gospel of Mark: A Commentary on the Greek Text* (NIGTC; Grand Rapids, MI/Carlisle: Eerdmans Paternoster).

Hatina, T.R. 1996 'The Focus of Mark 13.24-27: The Parousia, or the Destruction of the Temple', *BBR* 6: 43–66.

Heide, G.Z. 1997 'What is New About the New Heaven and the New Earth: A Theology of Creation From Revelation 21 and 2 Peter 3', *JETS* 40: 37–56.

Horrell, D.G. 1998 *The Epistles of Peter and Jude* (Epworth Commentaries; Peterborough: Epworth).

Kelly, J.N.D. 1969 *A Commentary on the Epistles of Peter and Jude* (BNTC; London: A. & C. Black).

Kraftchick, S.J. 2002 *Jude, 2 Peter* (ANTC; Nashville: Abingdon).

Lapidge, M. 1978 'Stoic Cosmology', in J.M. Rist (ed.), *The Stoics* (Berkley/Los Angeles/London: University of California Press): 160–85.

Long, A.A. 1985 'The Stoics on World-Conflagration', *The Southern Journal of Philosophy* 23: 13–37.

Lucas, E. 1999 'The New Testament Teaching on the Environment', *Transformation* 16.3: 93–99.

MacRae, G. 1983 'Apocalyptic Eschatology in Gnosticism', in D. Hellholm (ed.), *Apocalypticism in the Mediterranean World and the Near East: Proceedings of the International Colloquium on Apocalypticisim, Uppsala, Aug 12–17 1979* (Tübingen: Mohr Siebeck): 317–25.

Moo, D. 2006 'Nature in the New Creation: New Testament Eschatology and the Environment', *JETS* 49: 449–88.

Neyrey, J.H. 1980 'The Form and Background of the Polemic in 2 Peter', *JBL* 99: 407–31.

Neyrey, J.H. 1993 *2 Peter, Jude: A New Translation with Introduction and Commentary* (AB 37C; New York: Doubleday).

Overstreet, R.L. 1980 'A Study of 2 Peter 3:10-13', *Bibliotheca Sacra* 137: 354–71.

Russell, J.S. 1887 *The Parousia: A Critical Inquiry into the New Testament Doctrine of Our Lord's Second Coming* (London: T. Fisher Unwin, new edition).

van der Horst, P.W. 1994 '"The Elements will be Dissolved with Fire": The Idea of Cosmic Conflagration in Hellenism, Ancient Judaism, and Early Christianity', in P.W. van der Horst, *Hellenism, Judaism, Christianity: Essays on Their Interaction* (Kampen: Kok Pharos): 227–51.

Wright, N.T. 1992 *The New Testament and the People of God. Christian Origins and the Question of God Volume One* (London: SPCK).

Wright, N.T. 1996 *Jesus and the Victory of God. Christian Origins and the Question of God Volume Two* (London: SPCK).

Wright, N.T. 2003 *The Resurrection of the Son of God. Christian Origins and the Question of God Volume Three* (London: SPCK).

Part II

Insights from the History of Interpretation

Introduction to Part II

Cherryl Hunt

The essays in Part I explored the possible contributions, and potential problems, arising from biblical texts considered from an ecotheological perspective. Our area of enquiry now moves to consider Christian theological thought from the second century to the twentieth. With the entire history of Christian interpretation to choose from, this section necessarily provides only a sample of the resources within the tradition for exploring a fruitful ecological hermeneutic. Our various contributors each examine how individual thinkers, or particular approaches, in the history of interpretation have read and used the Bible in relation to what are now perceived to be ecologically relevant themes; in most cases this reading centres on the relationship between God and creation as a whole, and the particular status and role of human beings in relation to the rest of creation. In this respect the focus is often, following Lynn White Jr's article, on theological construals of the creation narratives in Genesis.

As Francis Watson points out, Christian theology has always been characterized by an ongoing reshaping in response to the challenges thrown up by each successive age. Noting that the ecological crisis has highlighted the weaknesses of the anthropomonistic tendencies of the Christian tradition's 'fall–redemption' model, Watson stresses the need to remember that 'the gospel story is grounded in creation as well as fall'. His focus is on Irenaeus's rebuttal of Valentinian Christianity, in particular their belief that Valentinians, as truly spiritual beings, had no enduring connection with a physical world which was the product of an inferior demiurge. Irenaeus uses John's Gospel and the Genesis creation stories in an intertextual reading to form a theological hermeneutic which both rebuts the Valentinian argument and stresses the integral place of humanity within the community of creation. The Irenaean reminder of the foundational nature of creatureliness is a possible resource for an ecological hermeneutic and a timely challenge to the tendency to view creation as 'merely the stage on which the real drama of fall and redemption is played out'.

In contrast to Irenaeus's positive approach towards creation in its totality, some strands of the Christian tradition have left a more ambiguous legacy; in some cases, indeed, they are now viewed as irremediably anthropocentric, offering no support for contemporary ecotheological reflection. However, just as in Part I some authors found resources for such reflection within some initially unpromising texts, so here our contributors find useful approaches in what might initially appear hostile territory. Morwenna Ludlow's essay, focusing on a selection of the early Church Fathers, looks at how they read Gen. 1.1-2 and 1.26 and how *they* classified their readings – as literal, allegorical or spiritual, descriptions which often differ from modern definitions. This exploration illustrates how influenced the Fathers were by contemporary philosophical and cultural assumptions regarding the superiority of reason over emotion – and reason's concomitant right to assume a superior position in the hierarchy thought to be necessary to harmony within the creative order. These assumptions led the Fathers to perceive as natural a position of human dominion over other life forms, a concept they saw as supported by the biblical account of human creation in the image of God. However, Ludlow finds some positive resources for ecotheological reflection within the more distinctively Christian features of patristic discourse on these passages, arising both from Genesis itself and from understandings of the Incarnation: namely the *goodness* of creation, the co-materiality of human and non-human emphasizing the interconnectedness of all life, and the concomitant effects of human sin upon the whole.

Moving on into the Middle Ages, we have Mark Wynn's examination of Thomas Aquinas. Despite what many have seen as Aquinas's anthropocentric position on the dominion of higher, rational human beings over other animals, Wynn finds, in the Thomistic concept of God as subsistent existence, grounds for arguing for the goodness of all creation and the directedness of all creatures towards God. Moreover, it is by no means evident from Aquinas's text that the goals of other creatures are always to be subordinated to the goals of human beings. Significantly, Aquinas's writings indicate that the entire community of creatures together resembles God more closely, in some respects, than does any individual creature, even rational human beings. The human goal may be taken to be that of imaging God by means of our participation within a community of diverse creaturely types, where each type flourishes according to the possibilities which are inherent in its own nature.

As Paul Santmire shows, despite the possibility of considering nature as 'the biophysical dimension of creation' within Luther's theology of creation, Luther's writings provide a similarly ambiguous legacy to that of Aquinas. His anthropocentric portrayal of creation as a 'building' for the use of humanity and its being cursed due to Adam's sin, the central position he gave to human salvation, his prioritization of 'hearing' the Word over 'seeing' it, and his consequent rejection of the theology of glory in favour of the theology of the cross, are apparently eco-negative features. These are, however, balanced by Luther's sense of the divine immanence, the Word of God in nature, and his seeing creation as a means of gracious provision for humanity to share (rather than a possession to be exploited). Furthermore, an enhanced sense of nature's glory is accessible to the believer. Santmire, while acknowledging the problematic aspects of Luther's thought, proposes an appropriation of Luther's theology which balances the the-anthropocentrical strand of his thought with a the-cosmocentrical dimension based on his affirmations of the goodness of creation and of God's presence in it.

Another theologian whose work is often cited as being irremediably hostile towards ecotheological reflection is Karl Barth. Geoff Thompson acknowledges Barth's emphasis upon the Christocentricity of the biblical witness and the concomitant focus on the fulfilment of the covenant between God and *humanity*, not to mention his aversion to natural theology. Nevertheless, he sees Barth's determination to turn away from anthropocentrism as a key point of contact between his work and that of twenty-first century ecotheologians. Barth's description of non-human creation as a 'stage' and the 'external basis' of the covenant needs to be understood in the light of his portrayal of a far- from-passive, creation-praising God, and his insistence that humanity's dominion was limited in scope; rather than having a God-like right to dispose of the entirety of creation, humans are merely given dominion over the animals. This is tightly linked to their commission to be loyal *servants* of the earth and its vegetation. They may be integral to the goal of the creative and redemptive project, but they are far from being its sum.

In a similar fashion, David Moss begins by acknowledging that Hans Urs von Balthasar 'said little, if anything' about the environmental crisis. Rather, Moss argues that if Balthasar's thinking is to be appropriated to the cause of ecological reflection then it will be through an understanding of the theophanic character to nature, which always remains to be Christologically decoded. Thus, a Balthasarian contribution to an ecological hermeneutic should emerge not from a search for responses to the present crisis but rather, more fundamentally, from an attitude of wonder towards nature's beauty, and an ability to perceive 'the whole in the fragment', to see beyond the particular instance within nature to the One who is its origin and maintains it. We need to 'begin with beauty', to recover the sense that 'those transitory experiences of the truth, goodness and beauty of the cosmos are intelligible only by way of reference to a transcendent order of Being that is absolutely true, good and beautiful'. This 'hermeneutic of beauty' is needed to see the good, to read the stamp of God upon creation; the observers are 'trained by it in giving themselves away in love'.

Less ambiguous resources for reflection on ecotheology are to be found in the theology of Eastern Orthodoxy and, within the Protestant tradition, the writings of Jürgen Moltmann. Andrew Louth, drawing on both ancient and more recent Orthodox thinkers including St Maximos and Sergii Bulgakov, reminds us that Orthodox theologians have consistently seen the human drama of fall and redemption as being set within a larger story stretching from creation to transfiguration and deification. Viewing the world as having been created out of nothing, by the mediation of God's creative Word, leads to an attitude of praise and an ability to see the presence of God within creation. Furthermore, Orthodox interpretations of the creation of humanity itself see the human and the larger cosmos as interconnected: the cosmos is affected by human sin and the same sin hinders human perception of God within creation. The human is intended to be the priest of creation, 'interpreter of the cosmos', not its exploiter; the Incarnation enables the realization of this human role and a recognition of the holiness of both human and non-human creation, which can motivate a change in our attitudes towards our environment. Together, both human and the rest of creation approach a transfiguration, not into something new but into a state where they realize their true identity in union with God.

As Jeremy Law reminds us, Jürgen Moltmann has for some time been concerned with the environmental crisis, which he sees as a consequence of a crisis of values and therefore a subject on which theology can and should comment. Moltmann finds Cartesian anthropological theology a contributor, rather than an antidote, to this crisis, but he finds in the promissory nature of scripture a reason to seek answers therein. Further, he finds there a mandate to take the trajectory of biblical teachings beyond their original meanings to apply them to contemporary contexts, albeit a trajectory constrained by exegetical considerations. Following an examination of five key biblical motifs that Moltmann employs in his ecotheological reflection, Law goes on to outline central themes within his reflections, including a perichoretic Trinitarian panentheism and a concept of creation in God, together with a cosmic Christology that includes a vision of Christ as redeemer of the evolutionary process itself and of the whole cosmos; Law summarizes the impulse towards Christian action within Moltmann's works, as anticipation of the new creation leading to 'resistance and protest against that which contradicts this future'.

It might be said that some of our contributors are providing an apologetic for their subjects, attempting to salvage from committedly anthropocentric writings and attitudes some positive, more holistically creation-centred features to contribute to Christian reflection on the environment. In some cases the same can be said as is said of the biblical writers – it is understandable and to some degree inevitable that these theologians did not speak directly to an ecologically threatening situation which they did not have to face. Moreover it is notable that, in every case, the resources that our contributors find our subjects to provide lie in their meditations on the relationships between Creator and creation, Creator and humanity, and between humanity and non-human creation. The dyadic God–human focus of much Western theology is actually just one side of a triangle of relationships and the ecologically important baseline – the relationship between humans and non-human creation – is from a theological perspective totally dependent for its character upon the other two sides. This points the way for our formation of ecological hermeneutics: rather than proof-texting to seek a basis for how we should act along the human–non-human side of the triangle, those committed to working with the biblical texts should take a comprehensive approach towards scripture as a whole and build a model that takes account of the whole network of relationships. In contrast to an often anthropocentric theological tradition, an ecological hermeneutic should not focus entirely or even mostly on the God–human relationship but neither should it conflate God-human with God–non-human relationships; the human is in some respects distinct from the non-human in the biblical witness and an adequate ecological hermeneutic will recognize this and work with it. The essays here, taken together, illustrate more clearly all three sides of the creational triangle and offer diverse ways of developing an ecological hermeneutic in which creation is restored to its crucial place in the matrix of relationships between God, humanity and the non-human world.

Chapter 9

IN THE BEGINNING: IRENAEUS, CREATION AND THE ENVIRONMENT

Francis Watson

Preamble: Environmental Hermeneutics

There is an 'environmental crisis', and a 'crisis' is an emergency requiring immediate action if disaster is to be averted. Some of this action can be undertaken only by experts. It takes special training to launch a lifeboat, or operate a fire engine or design an energy-efficient light bulb. But immediate action may also be required from the crisis's potential victims. They must become aware that they *are* potential victims, and take whatever forms of evasive or remedial action that are open to them. They must grasp that the ship is sinking or that the building is on fire or that the planet is at risk, and act instantly in such a way as to minimize the threat to life – their own and others'. Similar considerations apply to perpetrators of the crisis, those whose misguided actions pose a threat to public safety and well-being. (Indeed, perpetrators and victims may be the same people.) Those who are at risk or who put others at risk must undergo a conversion from the mistaken belief that all is well to the recognition that disaster is imminent. All other considerations must be set aside.

Rather than speaking of a singular 'crisis', however, we might prefer to speak of a plurality of 'environmental problems'. The use of the plural would acknowledge that the issues that make up the singular 'crisis' are actually distinct. These issues may well be interrelated, and they may possibly be traceable back to a single underlying cause. Yet they are different. The terms 'recycling', 'conservation' and 'renewable energy' all represent current environmental imperatives, but each has its own distinct context and rationale. They are related, but they are not the same thing; they are responses to different problems. Only one of them directly responds to the problem of 'global warming' or 'climate change', and even there this is not the exclusive motivation: the problem with *non*-renewable energy is not only that it appears to promote global warming but also that it is finite. To speak of 'problems' rather than a 'crisis' is not to downgrade the seriousness of the issues. 'Problems' may be said to be 'serious' or 'urgent', and in their different ways our environmental problems may all be serious and urgent ones. Yet, unlike a crisis or an emergency, a *problem* allows time for critical reflection and informed debate.

The crisis model engenders eco-theologies, eco-justice, eco-warriors and eco-congregations, and there are good pragmatic reasons for all of them. Yet there is also room for an alternative approach, although it may lack the *eco-* prefix. In such an approach, it is acknowledged that environmental problems demand to be taken into account in our ongoing reshaping of the ethical, religious and intellectual traditions we inhabit. This reshaping is happening anyway. Traditions are always reshaped as they are handed on, for their transmission is constantly interrupted by new challenges that require adjustment and adaptation. There is nothing uniquely problematic or threatening about present encounters between an old tradition and 'contemporary issues', for the tradition is *constituted* in part by its previous encounters with once-contemporary issues of previous generations. Adapting to contemporary issues is what traditions do best, although the outcome may not please everyone. In such encounters between old and new, what is required is not just to reinterpret the tradition in the light of the contemporary issue but also to reinterpret the issue in the light of the tradition. An 'issue' is always an interpretative construct, and a construct may require *re-construction* if it is to be accommodated within a new context. Environmental problems may be construed quite differently within, say, Christian, Marxist or feminist perspectives, and these particular encounters will also be affected by other current encounters in which the tradition in question is being reshaped.

From the perspective of Christian faith, the 'environment' will be understood as 'creation', that is, as originating in the creative act of the triune God who is the subject and object of the fundamental biblical and credal narrative. Equally, however, a Christian understanding of 'creation' will now be affected by the current concept of 'environment', with its connotations of fragility, finitude, interdependence and inherent worth. Neither concept will remain unaffected by the other. In particular, the concept of 'environment' provokes some searching questions about the way in which Christian tradition has tended to understand 'creation'. These are *theological* questions, internal to Christian faith, and yet they are occasioned and incited by developments from outside its own immediate sphere.

What are these questions for and within Christian faith, provoked by contemporary environmental concern? In general, they have to do with the relationship of the human to the nonhuman world. What is meant by human 'dominion' over the animals, and is it subject to ethical constraints? Does the nonhuman world have any inherent value, or is its value measured exclusively by its usefulness for humans? Is biblical 'anthropocentrism' ethically problematic? Is there biblical warrant for an ethic of 'reverence for life' and for the practices that might follow from it? How do such issues fit into the wider field of Christian faith and practice? If there are difficulties in accommodating them, why is this the case, and can or should anything be done about it? To repeat, these are questions *internal* to Christian faith yet provoked from the outside, by the wider public debate about the environment. Of course, Christian faith *may* be directly questioned from the outside about its attitude to the environment. Yet there are no neutral criteria of ecological rectitude by means of which the Bible or 'Christianity' could be weighed in the balance and found wanting. Nor are there objective criteria to hand that would enable us to identify environmentally friendly fragments within the biblical witness, to be presented as 'positive resources' for anyone who cares to use them. Where texts are uprooted from the fragile biblical ecology and transplanted into some alien value system, they are subjected to exploitation and abuse. In the long run, internally shaped questions and answers will be of greater *public* significance than superficial interrogations of the Bible on the basis of external criteria that tolerate no counter-questioning or dissent.

And so we approach at last the specific topic of this essay. Public debate about the environment has indirectly served to expose a seriously deficient construal of Christian faith and the biblical witness. We may identify this construal as the *fall/redemption model*. In this model creation is affirmed, but not as an integral part of the main story. Creation is merely the stage on which the real drama of fall and redemption is played out. Humans are indeed created, but far more important is the fact that they are fallen, and more important still is the fact that though fallen they are also redeemed. Within this model, Christian self-understanding moves to and fro between the poles of sin and salvation, guilt and grace, law and gospel. Sin, guilt and the law represent a standing before God that is superseded by gospel, grace and salvation, and yet in such a way that the supervenient present preserves the recollection of the past. Within this model, I am to understand myself as a redeemed sinner – *redeemed*, indeed, but a *sinner* nevertheless. The entire biblical narrative depicts the transition from the one state to the other, and the machinery that makes it possible. This is not just 'anthropocentrism'. Anthropocentrism is inescapable for humans: since we are neither angels nor earthworms, our primary perspective on the world is a human one, it is bounded and shaped by the determinants of specifically human existence. Anthropocentrism is compatible with broad horizons. The fall/redemption model is not so much anthropocentric as *anthropomonistic*. The drama of sin and salvation is all-consuming. The created order provides the drama's theatre, staging and scenery, but it is the problematics of the divine–human relationship that provide the exclusive focus of attention. It is as though the Bible started at Genesis 3. In consequence of its theological marginalization, creation is secularized. It is assumed that those preoccupied with it absent themselves from the scene of the real, eternally significant action. Their gaze is directed outward, when it should be directed upward and inward.

This fall/redemption model is, of course, an ideal type that has never actually existed in pure, unqualified form. Yet it does serve to identify an anthropomonistic *tendency* within Christian life and spirituality (and not just in its protestant forms). The anthropomonistic tendency is flawed and problematic quite apart from current environmental concerns. Yet the current concerns expose its limitations with particular clarity. They relate to a realm – that of the 'natural order' – in which the Christian community appears to have no stake. Where Christians seek to challenge this perception, it proves surprisingly difficult to show that human responsibility to the environment is integral to their own core concerns. For anthropomonism, the only environment that counts is that of the divine–human relationship, understood in terms of sin and salvation. Humans share a creaturely status with the rest of creation, but far more important is what makes them unique. With the minor exception of some fallen angels, humans *alone* are capable of sinning, and indeed have always already realized that capacity. And humans *alone* are the objects of redemption. For anthropomonism, humans are unique and uniquely solitary, cut off from the community of creation.

In response to this flawed rendering of the biblical story, it is not enough merely to point to the fact that Genesis 3 is preceded by Genesis 1–2, and that the three chapters are closely connected. What is at issue is the coherence and logic of the core Christian narrative, which finds its goal and centre in the composite gospel account of the life, death and resurrection of Jesus. Where the gospel story is set against the background of 'the fall', the result is not lacking in coherence. What must be shown is that the gospel story is grounded in creation as well as fall, that the Genesis creation narrative is a plausible and necessary beginning for a story that reaches its culmination in Jesus. Creation is not just the stage on which the real drama is enacted, but is itself the opening act of the drama. What Jesus does is oriented towards humans not just in their unique fallenness but also in the creatureliness they share with the rest of the natural or created order.

Such a telling of the Christian and biblical story is not an innovation. On the contrary, it is as old as the Christian Bible itself, and is integral to the construction of a scriptural collection that includes four gospels and the Book of Genesis. Irenaeus of Lyons is one of the chief architects of the Christian canon, and his account of the place of creation within the story it tells remains highly instructive.

Gospels and Creation: A Johannine Key

As its traditional title indicates, Irenaeus's main work is directed *Against All Heresies* (*AH*). The heretics in question include Marcionites, Ebionites, Encratites and Gnostics (a term that Irenaeus can associate with a quite specific group, although his usage is not consistent).[1] But the 'heresy' that he knows best, and to which he keeps returning, is the one he ascribes to followers of Valentinus. Book 1 of his work opens with a detailed account of a Valentinian system, and much of the second and third books too are devoted to responding to its characteristic claims. Irenaeus's strategy is not a purely negative one. He refutes not only by exposing internal implausibilities and inconsistencies, but above all by constructing an alternative account of the matter in question. It is the encounter with Valentinian theology that generates his own constructive theological thinking.[2]

At the heart of Irenaeus's project is the need to demonstrate that the God revealed in Jesus is the God who created heaven and earth. This identification was denied

---

1   *AH* 1.29.1; 2.31.1; 4.6.4; 4.33.3; 4.35.1. On this see Logan 2006: 8–56.
2   On the relationship of this system to its predecessors, see Logan 1996, which focuses especially on the *Apocryphon of John* and *AH* 1.29-30. The recently published *Gospel of Judas* may also belong to the oldest accessible stratum of these 'Christian demiurgical traditions'.

by Valentinian theology, which announced the advent in Jesus of a previously unknown God above the creator deity of Genesis and Jewish scripture. This creator or demiurge previously believed himself to be the one true God, and repeatedly and mistakenly declared himself to be such in scripture (*AH* 1.5.3). But now, through Jesus, he knows better – and so do we. In himself, Jesus is already no ordinary human being but the special workmanship of the creator, miraculously born and deriving nothing from his mother. At his baptism, however, there descended upon him a being from the 'Pleroma', the truly divine sphere above the creator: Christ, or the Saviour, who embodies that many-sided divine sphere in its entirety, and who discloses it to us through his temporary union with Jesus. Thus, in Jesus, his life and his teaching, we encounter the God above the god of this world – not on account of Jesus himself but on account of the Christ or Saviour who spoke and acted through him. At the crucifixion, the heavenly Saviour left Jesus in order to return to the world above – an event which is to be distinguished from Jesus' own subsequent exaltation to the demiurge's right hand (*AH* 1.6.1; 1.7.2; 3.16.1). What the Saviour reveals is not just the superior God or the heavenly world *per se*, but also and above all our own stake in it. To our amazement, we discover from him that we ourselves have a transcendent origin and destiny. We (the enlightened elite, as opposed to the common Christian majority) are not of this world or its creator deity. He is responsible for our souls and our bodies, but not for the true spiritual self that originated in a complex train of events in the world above. Essentially, and to cut a long story short, our spiritual selves derive from the pre-mundane encounter between the Saviour and one 'Achamoth' (or 'Sophia'), our mother, the divine victim of a fall within the world of divinity itself.[3] (She is also incidentally the mother of the inferior creator-deity of Genesis, although his ontological status is inferior to ours [*AH* 1.5.1].) Unbeknownst to the creator, his mother secreted a spiritual seed within the animate, fleshly human creatures that he made in his own image and likeness. We are that seed, temporarily fallen into the world of the demiurge but destined to return to the Pleroma: that is the good news that the Saviour reveals through Jesus.[4]

Irenaeus's refutation of this theology was historically so successful that it is hard for most later Christians to recognize it as a possible though misguided construal of

---

3 Achamoth-Sophia (*AH* 1.4.1-5) derives from the Sophia who belongs to the Pleroma but who temporarily fell from it (1.2.1-4).

4 *AH* 1.5.6; 1.7.1. Here and elsewhere in this paper, my account of Valentinian theology restricts itself to evidence drawn from Irenaeus himself. As Dennis Minns notes, 'It should not be too readily supposed that [Irenaeus] resorts to cheap misrepresentations of his opponents' views in order to score rhetorical victories' (1994: 26–27). One reason for trusting Irenaeus's account is that he considered 'the accurate reporting of the views of his opponents . . . to be one of his most effective weapons against them' (26). Minns also notes, however, that Irenaeus is 'incapable of achieving any kind of imaginative, sympathetic insight into a world-view in which the phenomenal world is negatively assessed. He takes it as a given that the created world, in all its rich diversity, is a place of wonder and delight . . .' (25). Is that a limitation, or a theological virtue?

Christian faith. It hardly looks Christian at all. Yet Christian is what it intends to be. Beneath the surface of the extravagant mythology lies an early version of what we are calling the fall/redemption model of Christian faith. Admittedly, this version of the model is in many respects quite different from the more familiar later ones. Yet analogies may be traced even in the differences. Through the lapse of a heavenly being or of our earthly parents, we are fallen beings: in spite of the difference, Valentinian and orthodox Christianities agree on that. In both cases, our fallenness is a more fundamental truth about ourselves than our createdness. In both cases, we therefore have little stake in the created order, for our gaze must be directed not outward but upward and inward in view of our redemption through Jesus. In both cases, redemption is seen as the supreme work of deity, and is only tenuously linked to our creatureliness. In both cases, our origin and destiny lie beyond the bounds of this world in the outworking of the divine predestination; this world is merely the stage on which the drama of our redemption is enacted. To draw attention to these parallels is in no way to minimize the stark differences between early and later versions of the fall/redemption model. In their tendency to detach redemption from creation, however, they are on common ground. For that reason, Irenaeus's response to the Valentinian version of the model is of more than merely historical interest.

At the beginning of book 3 of his work, Irenaeus tells how the single gospel proclaimed by the apostles has taken fourfold written form. Initially, he provides a brief introductory note about the circumstances in which he believes each gospel to have been written. Matthew wrote for Jews, Mark recorded Peter's preaching in Rome after his death, Luke recorded Paul's preaching and finally John wrote his gospel in Ephesus (*AH* 3.1.1). Later, Irenaeus will seek to justify the church's selection of precisely four gospels (no more and no fewer), by way of an analogy with the four living creatures that surround the throne of God – one with the face of a lion, the second with the face of a calf, the third with the face of a man, the fourth with the face of an eagle (Rev. 4.7).[5] Just as in heaven there are four and only four creatures around the throne of God, offering God their differentiated yet harmonious worship, so on earth there are four and only four gospels in the church, differentiated yet at one in their teaching. Additional gospels are ruled out on principle – Irenaeus knows of a Valentinian Gospel of Truth and of a Gospel of Judas (*AH* 3.11.9; 1.31.1). Also ruled out at the other extreme is Marcion's use of just one gospel, Luke, or rather, that part of it that he did not excise (*AH* 3.11.7). Yet Irenaeus's problems are not solved merely by selecting the right texts. Everything depends on how they are interpreted. According to Irenaeus, Matthew, Mark, Luke and John 'have all declared to us that there is one God, Creator of heaven and earth, announced by the law and the prophets, and one Christ, the Son of God' (*AH* 3.1.2). These gospels speak of the Creator and his Christ, of the one God and the Son of God. But it is one thing

---

5   *AH* 3.11.8. For theological analysis of this symbolism, see Watson 2006: 102–109.

for Irenaeus to assert this, another to demonstrate it. Valentinians started from the same texts yet reached opposite conclusions: for them, the Christ is the being who descended from the Pleroma on the occasion of Jesus' baptism, revealing through him the unknown Father, and thereby exposing the creator of heaven and earth as an ignorant and subdivine being, the product of a cosmic accident.

Within the Valentinian hermeneutic, the Father is *not* the Creator. The gospels have little or nothing to say of creation. Even in Jn 1.3 ('All things came into being through him . . .'), the reference is not to Jesus as creator of the world but to the Logos as the originator of the lower levels of the Pleroma (*AH* 3.1.2). If Jesus had wished to affirm the Creator, the God of the Jews, he would not have spoken of his Father as unknown: 'No-one knows the Father except the Son and anyone to whom the Son chooses to reveal him' (Mt. 11.27; *AH* 3.1.2). Where on the other hand Jesus speaks of heaven as the throne of God, of earth as his footstool, and of Jerusalem as the city of the Great King (Mt. 5.35), he is clearly speaking of a well-known deity thoroughly at home in the cosmos and worshipped in Jerusalem: and this is not the Father but the Demiurge (*AH* 4.2.5-4.1). Similarly, we are told that 'no-one has ever seen God', but that 'the only Son [or God], who is in the bosom of the Father, has made him known' (Jn 1.18; *AH* 4.20.6, 11). In Jewish scripture, however, a number of people *do* see 'God': Abraham, Jacob, Moses, Isaiah, Ezekiel and others. This visible deity is no doubt the creator, but he cannot be the invisible Father made known in Jesus (*AH* 4.20.5). It is true that the gospels as they stand imply connections between Jesus and the creator-God of the Jews, for example in their citations of prophetic texts. But that is to be expected, for Jesus himself was the creature of the Demiurge. In addition, the evangelists were Jews and may either have shared Jewish prejudices themselves or at least accommodated their message to the prejudices of their audience (*AH* 3.1.1; 3.2.2; 3.5.1-2; 3.12.6). In modern parlance, Jewish features of the texts are 'culturally conditioned' or 'apologetically motivated'. The truly spiritual reader of the gospels is not deceived by their superficial Jewish features, but penetrates behind them to their secret disclosures of the heavenly Christ.

Given this hermeneutic, it will not be possible to *demonstrate* that the four gospels all attest one God, Creator of heaven and earth, perhaps by amassing unambiguous proof-texts. The Valentinian hermeneutic cannot be refuted merely by appealing to a 'literal sense' in opposition to the arbitrariness of 'allegorical interpretation', for it has already taken that literal sense into account. It can only be refuted by way of an alternative hermeneutic that offers a more persuasive reading of the texts as a whole. The Irenaean reading will be no less of an interpretative construct than the Valentinian one; the two readings will be incommensurable, and not subject to assessment by neutral exegetical criteria.

Irenaeus finds the key he needs in the Johannine motif of the Word. Rather than starting at the beginning of the Johannine prologue, with an anonymous Logos whose identification with Jesus is initially far from obvious, Irenaeus works backwards from the declaration that 'the Word became flesh and dwelt among us . . .' (Jn 1.14), claiming that none of the heretics quite knows what to do with this text.

The Logos-become-flesh can only be Jesus. Jesus is the Logos, and the Logos is Jesus: this simple equation replaces the complex differentiations between Jesus, the heavenly Christ or Saviour, and the Logos (*AH* 1.9.2-3; 3.11.3). The identification is still clearer in view of the preceding verses as Irenaeus reads them. There we read of the coming into the world of 'the true Light', who enabled those who received him 'to become children of God' (1.12), and 'who was born not of blood nor of the will of the flesh nor of the will of man but of God' (1.13). The variant reading that Irenaeus here follows – 'who *was* born' rather than 'who *were* born' – is crucially important, referring as it does to the miraculous conception of Jesus himself.[6] Where verse 13 is read as a singular reference to the Light rather than a plural reference to the children of God, it creates the strongest possible connection between Johannine incarnational christology and the Lukan and Matthean virginal conception tradition. The Word is the fleshly Jesus who derived his enfleshed existence from Mary his mother, and so the opening of the fourth gospel harmonizes perfectly with the openings of the first and the third. Only the second gospel opens with Jesus' baptism, and a christology that focuses on this event may now find itself at a disadvantage.[7] A Johannine incarnation fused with a Lukan annunciation provides a more substantial basis for christology than the later descent of the Spirit – although admittedly that event is important enough to be attested in all four gospels.

We continue to follow Irenaeus's backward reading of Jn 1.1-14, which for him constitutes the 'Johannine prologue'. (Verses 15-18 represent 'the testimony of John', and thus a transition to the passage that follows [Jn 1.19-34].[8]) Reading back from verses 12-13 to verse 11, we learn that 'he came to his own home' and that 'his own people received him not' – referring to Jesus' rejection by his own people, culminating in his crucifixion. And we learn that he, the true Light, 'was in the world, and the world was made by him . . .' (v. 10). Having achieved his crucial lateral connection between the fourth gospel and the first and third, Irenaeus can now link the fourfold gospel and its protagonist back to Genesis (*AH* 3.11.2). The link to Genesis is confirmed by the assertion that in the Word 'all things were made, and without him was nothing made' (v. 3) and by the reference to the Word's divine being 'in the beginning' (v. 1; *AH* 3.8.3; 3.11.1, 8). In Irenaeus's reflection on this Johannine material, a scriptural canon is taking shape – not just a list of included writings, but a theological structure. We recall that his purpose is to show that, for all four evangelists, 'there is one God, Creator of heaven and earth, announced by the law and the prophets, and one Christ, the Son of God' (*AH* 3.1.2). The gospels are connected in many and various ways to the law and the prophets, and Irenaeus will

---

6   *AH* 3.16.2; 3.19.2; 5.1.3. On this reading see Metzger 1975: 196–97. The fact that this reading may not have been 'original' does not affect the argument here.
7   The significance of Mark for a (heretical) christology oriented towards Jesus' baptism is noted in *AH* 3.11.7.
8   *AH* 3.10.2. Here and in *AH* 3.11.4, Irenaeus seeks to connect the Johannine 'testimony of John' with Luke 1.

explore these in his fourth book, directed especially against Marcion.[9] Yet explicit references to the God revealed in Jesus as the Creator of heaven and earth are scarce. Irenaeus cannot make his case by amassing unambiguous texts. Instead, he creates a theological hermeneutic out of the Johannine prologue. The hermeneutic still needs to be tested. If, for example, Genesis knows nothing of a creation of all things through the Logos, then the Valentinian claim that the Johannine text actually refers to the origins of the Pleroma will remain unrefuted. Yet Irenaeus has at least established a foothold in the biblical texts, a base for further theological and exegetical operations. He has begun to show that an impressive Platonizing myth of fall and redemption may not do justice to the apostolic and prophetic writings.

Re-enacting Genesis

Does Genesis support Irenaeus's claims? If we reread its opening chapters in the light of the Johannine prologue, is it plausible that the divine agency at work in the creation of heaven and earth is the same as the divine agency at work in the incarnation of the Word? Irenaeus's affirmative answer focuses primarily on the Genesis narrative insofar as it relates to humans. His rendering of the biblical narrative of creation and incarnation remains 'anthropocentric'. Yet the crucial question is how the being of *anthrōpos* is understood, and what kind of 'centre' this being constitutes. By emphasizing creatureliness as fundamental rather than accidental, Irenaeus excludes the claim that human existence is a life in exile from one's true home, and restores the human being to the community of heaven and earth. This restoration takes place only in the context of the creation/incarnation sequence, which Irenaeus develops by way of a series of parallels between the two.

At the very moment when the creation of humans is first announced, God appears to become plural: 'Let *us* create man after *our* image, after *our* likeness' (Gen. 1.26 LXX). Whom does God address here? Is God a community? Elsewhere in scripture, we read of God's *hands*: 'The sea is his, for he made it, for his hands formed the dry land' (Ps. 95.5). God does not possess physical hands, however. According to Irenaeus, God's 'hands' are the Son or Word and the Holy Spirit (the Wisdom present with God in creation, according to Prov. 8.22-31; *AH* 4, *pref*. 4; 4.20.1-3; 5.1.3). 'Let us create . . .' addresses the Son and the Spirit, the 'hands' through whom creation is accomplished. Furthermore, it is said that humans are to be created on the basis of a divine archetype, 'according to our image'. According to the apostle Paul, Jesus Christ is 'the image of the invisible God' (Col. 1.15; cf. 2 Cor. 4.4). If he is humanity's archetype, he is so by virtue of his incarnate life, already envisaged at the dawn of creation. Creation in the image of God is creation with a view to Jesus Christ (*AH* 5.1.3; 5.2.1). Elsewhere Paul tells us that humanity redeemed and

---

9 *AH* 4.6.2; 4.8.1; 4.13.1; 4.33.2; 4.34.1.

sanctified in Christ is 'being renewed in knowledge according to the image of its creator' (Col. 3.10; *AH* 5.12.4). Creation in the image of God refers us not only to the origin of human being but also to its goal, which is to be 'conformed to the image of [God's] Son' (Rom. 8.29).[10] In view of these intertextual links, it is inconceivable that the Creator is anyone other than the Father of Jesus. Irenaeus's christological interpretation of the Genesis image motif ensures that the humanity sanctified in Christ remains rooted in the created order.[11]

Genesis narrates the creation of humans not once but twice, and Irenaeus again has a Pauline template to hand as he turns from the first account to the second (Gen. 2.7). According to Paul, Adam was 'a type of the Coming One' (Rom. 5.14), that is, Christ (*AH* 3.22.3). As a result, Paul can construct a series of analogies between Adam and Christ – analogies which typically also involve contrasts. 'As in Adam all die, so also in Christ shall all be made alive' (1 Cor. 15.22). While life is the opposite of death, the *as/so* format ensures a focus not only on the contrast but also on the analogy, which consists in the fact that the individual figures of Adam and Christ both determine universal destiny. For Irenaeus's purposes, this Pauline template is the perfect vehicle for his argument about the single divine agency operative in both creation and incarnation. It enables him to develop his well-known account of 'recapitulation' – a term that can refer simply to a summing-up or gathering-together, but that is most characteristically used to assert the *re-enactment* in Christ of what initially occurred in Adam.[12]

The second Genesis account tells how 'the Lord God formed man of dust from the ground, and breathed into his nostrils the breath of life; and man became a living being' (Gen. 2.7). The first part of this statement speaks of the origin of human physicality, and Irenaeus argues that this was re-enacted in the incarnation. In the following citation, bold print highlights the *as/so* format, italics identify scriptural material from Romans or Genesis, and underlining indicates the points of analogy. While Irenaeus's initial venture into this analogy keeps close to Pauline language, the second is more independent:

> . . . And the original *form*ation was re-enacted in him [Christ]. For **as** <u>by one man's disobedience</u> sin gained entrance, and through sin death held sway, **so** also <u>by the obedience of one man</u>, righteousness being established, life comes to fruition in those persons who in times past were dead. And **as** the first-formed man Adam had his existence <u>from</u> <u>uncultivated and still virgin</u> soil *(for God had not yet sent rain, and there was no man working the ground)*, and was formed by the hand of God (. . . *And the Lord took dust from the earth and formed*

---

10 *AH* 5.6.1. In Irenaeus's anthropology, 'Man himself is still in the making. It is not his unmasking that is wanted, but his finishing; not the liberation of the spirit from the body sought by the gnostics and by pagans generally, but the life of communion vouchsafed to us in Christ' (Farrow 1999: 51).

11 For the christological interpretation of the 'image of God' motif, see Watson 1997: 277–304.

12 On 'recapitulation' and its hermeneutical significance, see Holsinger-Friesen 2009.

man), **so**, re-enacting Adam in himself and deriving <u>from</u> Mary who was <u>still virgin</u>, the Word himself fittingly submitted to an origin that re-enacted Adam's.[13]

Genesis 2 is linked to Luke 1, itself interpreted in the light of Johannine incarnational christology. The Word took flesh within the womb of Mary the Virgin, and the theme of virginity is unexpectedly anticipated in the 'still virgin soil' of Genesis. If the attribution of virginity to soil seems far-fetched, we should recall that the fruitful soil is an obvious metaphor for the womb and that the Genesis text explicitly draws our attention to the absence of the male ('there was no *man* . . .') and to the lack of a fertilizing element ('rain'). The incarnation of the second Adam re-enacts the creation of the first, for the same divine agency is at work in both cases.[14]

Gen. 2.7 speaks not only of human materiality but also of the original bestowal of life. Having formed a human figure out of dust, the Lord God 'breathed into his face the breath of life, and the man became a living being'. This too is re-enacted in the incarnation:

> **As** at the <u>beginning</u> of our <u>formation</u> in Adam, *the breath of life* which came from God, <u>united</u> to what had been <u>formed</u>, <u>brought the man to life</u> and manifested him as a rational being; **so** at the <u>end</u>, the Word of the Father and <u>the Spirit of God</u>, <u>united</u> with the original substance of Adam's <u>formation</u>, <u>made man living</u> and perfect, receptive of the perfect Father; in order that **as** *in the natural man we all were dead*, **so** *in the spiritual man we may all be made alive*.[15]

The incarnation corresponds to the first creation, as the end to the beginning. The original breath of God anticipates the soteriological role of the Spirit of God in the incarnation of the Word (cf. Lk. 1.35; Mt. 1.18, 20). The Word becomes flesh, but it is through the presence of the Spirit who was to be poured out on *all* flesh that this event has its fundamental soteriological significance. In the incarnation of the Word the original bestowal of life is *re-enacted*, and the same agency must therefore underlie both events.

To underline the point, Irenaeus immediately reverts from Genesis 2 to Genesis 1:

> For at no time did Adam escape the hands of God, to whom the Father said, *Let us make man in our image and likeness*. Therefore at the end, *not by the will of the flesh, nor by the will of man*, but by the good pleasure of the Father, his hands perfected a living man, so that Adam might be created according to the image and likeness of God.[16]

---

13 *AH* 3.21.9-10. Scriptural allusions are to Rom. 5.19a, 12, 19b; 1 Cor. 15.45; Gen. 2.5, 7.
14 In this context, Irenaeus is refuting the Ebionite denial of the incarnation and virgin conception.
15 *AH* 5.1.3. Pauline allusions here are to 1 Cor. 15.22, 46.
16 *AH* 5.1.3. The Johannine allusion is to Jn 1.13, again in its singular form.

Here Gen. 1.26 becomes a prophecy of the incarnation, and conversely the incarnation is shown to be grounded in the original creation of Adam, which it re-enacts.[17]

Elsewhere further analogies are drawn between Genesis 1–3 and the gospel narrative. Where they derive from Genesis 3, the re-enactment will also contain an element of reversal, as in the case of Mary's obedience in relation to Eve's disobedience (*AH* 3.22.4; 5.19.1), or Jesus' victory over Satan in relation to Adam's defeat (*AH* 5.21.1-2). Just as in Paul, however, the emphasis is still on the formal analogy created by the *as/so* format. As the gospels point us back to Genesis (by way of the Johannine prologue), so Genesis points us forward to the gospels.[18] This intertextual pattern is absolutely fundamental to Christian canonical scripture, which in Irenaeus's work is still under construction. The effect is to establish creation and human creatureliness as the foundation of the scriptural and credal narrative.

Conclusion

To be human is to be a creature and a member of the community of creation. It is also to be made in the image of God, that is, to participate in the fulfilment of human creatureliness in Jesus, the incarnate Word. Or so we are taught by Irenaeus's theological hermeneutics. The interpretative moves that make up this hermeneutics are in many cases astonishingly creative and imaginative; they do not compel assent, however. While the Valentinian version of the fall/redemption model has had its day, 'orthodox' versions of this model still flourish – as do construals of Christian faith that appear to have learned little from Genesis. Yet it may be timely to consider again the Irenaean theology, with its insistence that creation represents the beginning, end and overarching context of the Christian and scriptural account of the world. No theology of the classical Christian past will directly help us to address the environmental problems of the present. Yet such a theology might help to shape an ethos within which one learnt to take the environment seriously, as creation – and to do so without ceasing to be Christian.

---

17 As Farrow notes, however, Irenaeus's concept of recapitulation 'does something more than reserve for Jesus a pride of place at the apex of salvation history . . . Its first task is to signify that no realm whatever lies beyond the pale of his domain, that there are no autonomous times or spheres over which he is not the Lord' (1999: 54). At this point Irenaeus coincides with Barth.

18 This to-and-fro movement is characteristic of Irenaeus's theological style. As von Balthasar notes, for Irenaeus 'a line of thought is equally true whether it is followed from below to above or from above to below, from front to back or from back to front' (1984: 43). 'The most characteristic feature of this particular theologian' is 'his ability . . . to see things in their relation to one another, in a compact concentrated whole' (50).

References

Balthasar, H. Urs von, 1984 *The Glory of the Lord: A Theological Aesthetics. Volume II, Studies in Theological Style: Clerical Styles* (Edinburgh: T&T Clark).
Farrow, D. 1999 *Ascension and Ecclesia: On the Significance of the Doctrine of the Ascension for Ecclesiology and Christian Cosmology* (Edinburgh: T&T Clark).
Holsinger-Friesen, T. 2009 'Irenaeus and Genesis: A Study of Competition in Early Christian Hermeneutics' (JTISup 1; Winona Lake: Eisenbrauns).
Logan, A.H.B. 1996 *Gnostic Truth and Christian Heresy: A Study in the History of Gnosticism* (Edinburgh: T&T Clark).
Logan, A.H.B. 2006 *The Gnostics: Identifying an Early Christian Cult* (London: T&T Clark).
Metzger, B.M. 1975 *A Textual Commentary on the Greek New Testament* (London & New York: United Bible Societies).
Minns, D. 1994 *Irenaeus* (London: Geoffrey Chapman).
Watson, F. 1997 *Text and Truth: Redefining Biblical Theology* (Edinburgh: T&T Clark).
Watson, F. 2006 'Are There Still Four Gospels?', in A.K.M. Adam, S.E. Fowl, K.J. Vanhoozer and F. Watson, *Reading Scripture With the Church: Toward a Hermeneutic for Theological Interpretation* (Grand Rapids, MI: Baker): 95–116.

Chapter 10

POWER AND DOMINION: PATRISTIC INTERPRETATIONS OF GENESIS 1

Morwenna Ludlow

In current environmental debates, Christian biblical interpretation has often been held partly responsible for modern Western attitudes to the natural world. In particular, attention has fallen on readings of Gen. 1.26 in which God is described as giving humans 'dominion' over other creatures. Setting the modern theological and ecological debate to one side, this paper will give an historical analysis of some church fathers' interpretations of the first chapter of Genesis. The first part – 'power' – will be a very brief survey of readings of Gen. 1.1-2 with the aim of reviewing what kind of interpretation the fathers are attempting (literal, figurative, allegorical?) and in what kind of contexts (homilies for a mixed audience, more specialized philosophical treatises?). The paper's second part – 'dominion' – will focus on Gen. 1.26, analysing the fathers' understanding of the relationship of humans to other animals, in the light both of the *imago dei* theme and of late antique concepts of human and animal nature. Throughout, I will focus my comments on the writings of Origen, Basil, Gregory of Nyssa and Augustine and I will conclude by offering some brief suggestions as to the significance of their exegesis of Genesis in the context of current environmental debates.

I. Power

In the beginning (*en archē*) when God created the heavens and the earth, the earth was a formless void and darkness covered the face of the deep, while a wind from God (*pneuma theou*) swept over the face of the water (Gen. 1.1-2).

What is the beginning of all things except our Lord and 'Saviour of all' (1 Tim. 4.10) Jesus Christ 'the first born of every creature' (Col. 1.15)? In this beginning, therefore, that is, in his Word, 'God made heaven and earth' as the evangelist John also says in the beginning of his Gospel: 'In the beginning was the Word . . .' Scripture is not speaking here of any temporal beginning, but it says that the heaven and earth and all things which were made, were made 'in the beginning', that is, in the Saviour (Origen *Homilies on Genesis* [Hom. Gen.] I).

This extract apparently gives a classic 'allegorical' interpretation of Gen. 1.1-2. However, two points should make one pause. First, although his *Homilies* do contain much explicitly allegorical interpretation, Origen does not announce the above reading as such. Secondly, it is not his only reading of the verses: his (earlier) *Commentary on John's Gospel* not only rejected the Christological sense of *archē* for Gen. 1.1, but offered *seven* different possible meanings of the word! In fact, Origen rules several of these out – his main concern in the *Commentary* is to combat misreadings of Genesis which would undermine the unique glory and beauty of God's creative act. Hence Origen denies the possibility of any substance co-existing with God, whether immaterial or material. The work is detailed, exploratory, very aware of philosophical and religious alternatives to the views it proposes. By contrast, Origen's *Homilies on Genesis* were first preached in a liturgical context and were probably intended for a more general audience. Their concern is the clear delivery of a theological message, rather than delving into philosophical technicalities; the emphasis is often on salvation and ethics. This, rather than a change of mind, probably explains the differences in approach to the word *archē*.

Origen's exegesis in these works (and his *Commentary on Genesis*, unfortunately now lost) set the agenda for later readings, but by the fourth century his use of allegory had already met with criticism. Thus Basil's writings on Genesis – his *Homilies on the Hexameron (Hex.)* (the six days of creation) and two sermons *On the Origin of Humanity I & II (De crig.)* – proclaim themselves to be uninterested in it (see below). In these works Basil also launches some scathing attacks on pagan philosophy: he claims to be opposing the divisive foolishness of pagan philosophers with the plain unified truth of Scripture (Courtonne 1934: 143–44, Basil *Hex*. I.2). However, the matter is not that simple. First, Basil makes extensive use of pagan sources: he is unlikely to have been reliant merely on text-book compilations (Courtonne 1934: 157–58; Henke 2000: 62–97). Secondly, although Basil has been criticized for a sketchy treatment of and weak arguments against non-Christian cosmological theories, he does at least engage directly with them (Courtonne 1934: 143–61). It is best to treat Basil's *Homilies* as a work intended for a mixed audience, some of whom will respond to the colourful examples, others to the arguments and to the echoes of famous texts. They do not present one coherent argument, but the sermon genre explains their structure (like a 'harlequin's tunic' [Courtonne 1934: 160]), the tendency to draw morals from the biblical text and the focus on key theological ideas, like the fundamentals of the theology of creation, to which we will now turn.

Basil examines several possible meanings for Gen. 1.1, but his main theological point is clear: the cosmos was caused by God's good intention; there is nothing co-existent with God, whether an eternal evil principle, or eternally existing unformed matter (I.7). He believes the message of Genesis 1 is, in essence, simple and he claims to be avoiding too much technical language for fear that it would not serve 'the edification of the church' (I.8). Although Basil eschews a Christological reading of 'in the beginning', he is willing to accept that Gen. 1.2 refers to the Holy Spirit (II.6; the LXX Greek *pneuma theou* could naturally be translated 'God's spirit'). However, in the light of his general attitude to allegory in the *Homilies* and in the way he supports his argument (with reference to a Syriac version of the text), he seems *not* to think that this is an 'allegorical' interpretation.

Gregory of Nyssa had a complex relationship with his brother Basil. He says that his work *On the Hexameron* (*In Hex.*) depends on what Basil taught – even to the extent of rejecting allegorical interpretation. However, Gregory's very method implies that his work completes what Basil left undone (64b-c; 68c-b; 121d).[1] Furthermore, it is even more debatable in Gregory's case than in Basil's whether allegory has been completely left behind. Much more than Basil's, Gregory's work is focused on a 'systematic vision of the world' (Alexandre 1976: 159): he assumes that the 'ordered linkage' (*akolouthia*) of Moses' texts reflects such a structure in the world, and he aims to reflects that structure in the order of his own text (68d). Although using some of Basil's ideas, Gregory analyses in more detail the exact nature of God's creative action. Despite these differences, however, Gregory too desires to combat the sort of ideas that would limit divine power and thus affirms that 'in the beginning' means that everything came to be in a 'global' and 'instantaneous' creative act (Alexandre 1976). Gregory avoids a Christological interpretation of verse 1 and is much more circumspect than Basil about the spirit in verse 2. (Gregory seems to equate God's Spirit with the divine nature [81b].)

How does Augustine's approach compare? It is well known that Augustine's attitude to exegesis developed in the course of his career. For a while he sympathized with the way in which the Manichees ridiculed the idea of an anthropomorphic God, which they claimed to find, for example, in Genesis 1 (*Confessions* [*Conf.*] III.vii.12). But the discovery of spiritual exegesis was a turning point: 'I was delighted to hear Ambrose . . . saying, as if he were most carefully enunciating a principle of exegesis: "The letter kills, but the spirit gives life" [2 Cor. 3.6]. Those texts which, when taken literally, seemed to contain perverse teaching, he would expound spiritually . . .' (*Conf.* VI.iv.6). In fact, Augustine grew increasingly anxious about the excessive use of spiritual interpretation; but he never returned to the extreme literalism of the Manichees and continued to condemn it vociferously.

In his *Commentary on Genesis Against the Manichees* (*Gen. Man.*) Augustine outlines what he calls a historical meaning, according to which, he asserts, 'in the beginning' means 'in Christ'. He complains that the Manichaean reading of Gen. 1.1 raises inappropriate questions about time and God, such as 'what did God do before he created?' (*Gen. Man.* 1.2.3; cf. *Conf.* XI.xii.14). Augustine adds, however, that 'in the beginning' also means that God created time (*Gen. Man.* I.2.3). He seems to assume that the 'spirit' in verse 2 is the spirit of God, being concerned to combat a Manichean reading which saw the spirit as a material substance dwelling in the sea (*Gen. Man.* I.5.8-9).

In his *Unfinished Literal Commentary on Genesis* (*Gen. imp.*), Augustine assesses

---

1   *In Hex.* numbers in my text refer to divisions in Migne's PG 44, also used by Lecaudey and Rousselet.

the possibility of plural *literal* meanings of the text. For example, does 'in the beginning' indicate the beginning of time, or of all matter, or the origin of creation 'in Christ'? He does not reject the last idea, but seems more keen on a non-Christological reading (*Gen. imp.* 3.8). Again, in the completed *Commentary on Genesis According to the Letter* Augustine raises a very similar series of questions about Gen. 1.1, but now he seems to prefer the *Christological* reading (*The Literal Meaning of Genesis* [*Gen. litt.*] I.1.1). More explicitly than in his earlier writings (or than the other writers we have examined) he asserts that the *pneuma* of Gen. 1.2 is the Holy Spirit. Indeed, in it 'we recognize the complete indication of the Trinity' – that is, it 'completes' the allusion made to the Son as 'beginning' in Gen. 1.1 (*Gen. Man.* I.6.12).

There are I think three important conclusions which arise from this very brief survey of these fathers' readings of Gen. 1.1-2. First, they are not in agreement as to the meaning of 'in the beginning' and several writers raise the possibility of the verse having more than one *literal* meaning. They are, however, unanimous in ruling out meanings which would undermine the singularity of the power of God's creative act (e.g. the existence of uncreated matter out of which God formed the world; the co-existence with God of time or a spiritual realm). Secondly, while some of the writers are ambivalent about taking Gen. 1.1-2 to refer to the Son or Spirit, none of them seems to regard such a reading as an allegorical reading. Indeed, it is Augustine in his *last* commentary on Genesis – a work which is a self-proclaimed literal interpretation – who is the most certain about identifying 'God', the 'beginning', and the 'spirit' with the persons of the Trinity. Thirdly, then, although such a theological reading of the verse would hardly be described as literal by most modern scholars, one should at least pay attention to what the fathers say about their own exegesis: whether we think such readings are literal or not, clearly the fathers regarded them as something different from what they (or others) did when they read Scripture allegorically.

II. Dominion

> Then God said, 'Let us make humankind [*anthrōpon*] in our image [*kat' eikona hēmeteran*], according to our likeness [*kath' homoiōsin*]; and let them have dominion [*archetōsan*] over the fish of the sea, and over the birds of the air, and over the cattle, and over all the wild animals of the earth, and over every creeping thing that creeps upon the earth.' So God created humankind in his image, in the image of God he created them; male and female he created them. God blessed them, and God said to them, 'Be fruitful and multiply, and fill the earth and subdue it [*plērōsate tēn gēn kai katakurieusate*]; and have dominion over [*archete*] the fish of the sea and over the birds of the air and over every living thing that moves upon the earth'. (Gen. 1.26-28, LXX)

In his *Homilies on Genesis*, Origen thinks that Gen 1.20-26 refers not only to the historical creation of creeping and flying things and beasts of the land, but also to the presence of certain impulses in the human mind (I.11). 'Creeping things' signify evil thoughts, flying things good ones. Land animals represent 'the impulses and thoughts of our mind which are brought forth from the depth of our heart', that is the impulses of 'humans' outer nature' (*exterioris hominis*). The outer nature is *not* the human body; rather, 'lower' emotions and thoughts were associated with bodily functions (such as appetites for food or sex) but were not thought by most late antique writers to be material in themselves. Origen is clearly referring to Paul's distinction between 'outer' and 'inner' human nature (*ho exō hēmōn anthrōpos, ho esōthen* [*anthrōpos*]: 2 Cor. 4.16), which is a theological distinction, not a contrast between material and immaterial.

In *Hom. Gen.* I.11 Origen is quite clear that he is working in parallel with a historical reading (animals) and a spiritual reading (different kinds of thought and impulse). When he comes to Gen. 1.27, however, Origen argues that 'the image of God' *must* be understood 'spiritually': he attacks those interpreters who assume it means that God looked like humans (I.12). Instead, Origen asserts, people are made in the image of God as to their immaterial nature, not their bodies. Furthermore, they image God as to the *interior* aspect of their human nature – that is, the good inner nature, not the lower impulses, thoughts and emotions of the 'exterior nature'. Finally, humans are, strictly speaking, created *in* or *according to* the image of God: Christ himself is the true image of God (I.13). Not only is this idea consistent with Origen's teaching elsewhere, but emphasizing that Christ is the true image of God allows Origen to draw an appropriately homiletic message. Humans were created not *as* God's image (a state which cannot be lost), but merely *according to* God's image. They lost their God-likeness in the Fall, but can regain it in Christ: Origen bids his congregation to keep their eyes on Christ the image of God, in order to be renewed in God's likeness (I.13).

Origen, then, associates conformity with the image of God not just with the immaterial aspect of human nature, nor just with human rationality, but also with the evaluative or theological concept of the 'inner man', which he associates especially with the qualities of incorruptibility and immortality (I.13). These were lost in the Fall, but Christ the true image possesses them fully and will communicate them to those who love him. One result of interpreting the 'image of God' in these spiritual terms is that Origen appears to interpret humans' dominion over animals in a similarly spiritual way – that is, humans' inner nature is granted dominion over the passions and thoughts of their outer nature (I.12).

This is an interpretation which Origen himself declares to be 'spiritual' and in the *Homilies* such a reading is usually associated with the use of allegory. However, he apparently also assumes that, by virtue of being created 'in the image' of God, humans are superior to literal fish, birds and beasts. Furthermore, he asserts that the rest of creation was created '*for* humanity' (I.12). He even seems to hint that one can take an allegorical interpretation not just of the text of Genesis, but also of the very structure (the 'text') of the natural world: that world is in itself an indication of the 'world-in-miniature which is human nature' (*minorem mundum id est hominem*). Origen uses this concept to express his belief that humanity 'sums up' – and is therefore superior to – the rest of creation. He seems little interested in animals for their own sakes: the constant allegorical identification of the animals with human impulses reinforces this impression.

It is precisely this allegory which Basil rejects in his *Homilies on the Hexameron*:

> I know the laws of allegory, though less by myself than from the works of others. There are those truly, who do not admit the common sense of the Scriptures, for whom water is not water, but some other nature, who see in a plant, in a fish, what their fancy wishes, who change the nature of reptiles and of wild beasts to suit their own meanings, like the interpreters of dreams who explain visions in sleep to make them serve their own ends. For me grass is grass; plant, fish, wild beast, domestic animal, I take all in the literal sense. (IX:1, tr. Jackson, altered slightly by present author)

However, Basil still shows little interest in animals in themselves: he relates many stories about animals (some of them scarcely credible!) in order to draw a moral from them. For instance, from the migrations of various types of fish, Basil concludes:

> if beings deprived of reason (*ta aloga*) are capable of thinking and of providing for their own preservation . . . what shall *we* say, who are honoured with reason (*logō*), instructed by law, encouraged by the promises, made wise by the Spirit, and are nevertheless less reasonable (*alogōteron*) about our own affairs than the fish?' (VII.5)

Other animals are used as an example of divine providence: Basil notes the sea urchin which can predict inclement weather: 'it is the Lord of the sea and of the winds who has impressed on this little animal a manifest proof of His great wisdom . . . [God] is present everywhere and gives to each being the means of preservation. If God has not left the sea urchin outside His providence, is He without care for you?' Finally, throughout the *Hexameron* Basil multiplies his examples of animal and plant life in order to impress on his audience the beauty, variety and fecundity of creation (see e.g. VII.1-2).

His *Homilies on the Hexameron* conclude with only brief comment on the creation of humans; the theme is picked up by two sermons *On the Origin of Humanity I & II* (sometimes mistakenly attributed to Gregory of Nyssa: on Basil's authorship see Harrison's comments in Basil of Caesarea 2005: 14–16). Although Basil denies that the animals can be read allegorically as the passions of the 'outer man', he does accept Origen's point that humans image God only as to their invisible nature (*De orig.* I.7). But he omits Origen's notion of Christ as the true image and understands humans' inner nature less in terms of qualities (a moral or theological similarity) and more in terms of their rational capacity (an ontological similarity, resting on the immaterial, invisible nature of both the human mind and God). The mind, Basil asserts, is one's true self (I.7).

Basil connects the rational mind very closely with 'dominion': humans patently are physically weaker than animals, therefore they have dominion in that aspect which distinguishes them from, and according to which they are stronger than animals – the rational mind (*De orig.* I.6, 9, 10). Humans should not 'fill the earth' by occupying every space, but 'by authority [*exousia*], which God has given us to dominate [*kata to kurieuma*] the earth' (I.14).

Basil argues, however, that humans' ability to exercise this rational authority properly is severely undermined if they are not themselves ruled by reason; faintly echoing Origen's allegory, Basil chides his audience: 'Do you truly rule real beasts if those within you are untamed?' (*De orig.* I.19; cf. I.9). A later writer, John Chrysostom, follows this line of thought through to its logical conclusion by suggesting that in the Fall humans lost their full authority over other animals. God has permitted the use of farm animals as a concession, but human fear of wild beasts is designed by God to prevent excessive human pride (Reuling 2006: 129–30, 142).

For Basil himself, speculation about the effects of the Fall on humans' relations with animals was restricted to the idea that it ended vegetarianism: as there was no death before the Fall, there could have been no carnivores. Meat-eating, however, was provided by God as a concession to human weakness (just as doctors prescribe delicacies for recovering invalids). This subtle tension is characteristic of Cappadocian theology: meat-eating falls short of an ideal state, but as a God-given concession it is not in itself a bad thing (Basil *De orig.* II.7; see Harrison's comments in Basil of Caesarea 2005: 27–28). Ascetics who give up meat are thus not condemning its consumption; rather, they are pointing prophetically towards the possibility of another way of life. Throughout this discussion of vegetarianism it is notable that Basil's concern is not for the well-being of animals, but rather for human spiritual health. In sum, Basil connects the *imago dei* very closely with humans' dominion over animals. According to his reading, the second half of verse 26 ('let them have dominion') explains the first ('Let us make humankind in our image, according to our likeness'): it is because of the fact that humans are created in the image of God that they are given dominion; it is *only* with respect to the aspect of human nature that images God (the rational mind) that they have it. This, however, raises a theological problem: if humans still have rational souls – that is, if they still possess the image of God – how is it that they are so sinful? This problem is only partially addressed by Chrysostom's argument that human dominion over animals is now limited. As we have seen, Origen's solution made Christ the true image of God; humans were created merely *according to* that image, implicitly explaining how they could have lost their image-likeness. It is possible that Basil rejects this solution because of the subordinationist/Arian implications of emphasizing Christ as God's image. His answer (at least in *On the Origin of Humanity*) is to distinguish the divine *image* from humans' *likeness* to God:

> By our creation [*ktisis*] we have the first and by our free choice [*prohairesis*] we accomplish the second ... For I have that which is according to the image in being a rational being, but I become according to the likeness in becoming Christian' (II.16). In these sermons, this allows Basil to stress the importance not only of good behaviour but of Christian baptism: 'As you have that which is according to the image through your being rational, you come to be

according to the likeness by undertaking kindness [*chrēstotes* – a pun on the word *Christos*]. Put on Christ [i.e. in baptism], draw near to him and thus to God . . . the creation story is an education in human life'. (II.17)

Although the theological reasoning is somewhat different, the theological message is strikingly similar to Origen's.

With their homiletic lessons, brief allusions to philosophical theories and entertaining references to animal behaviour, Basil's two sermons on human origins contain a similar blend of material to his *Homilies on the Hexameron*. Gregory of Nyssa's treatise *On the Making of Humanity*, like his treatise on the Hexameron, has a contrasting style to his brother's work: both of Gregory's works are more reflective than Basil's – more complex, more concerned with a detailed resolution of puzzling features of the text, more focused on drawing a coherent argument (rather than a useful moral) from Scripture. Just as Gregory's treatise on the Hexameron puzzles over the exact nature of the divine creative act, so *On the Making of Humanity* worries at the problem left by Basil's accounts of human origins: if humanity was created in/according to the image of God, why is humanity currently so sadly lacking in God-like qualities (*De hom.* XVI)?

Gregory believes (as did Basil, in fact) that rationality is inextricably connected with human free will and thus with sin: if humans habitually sin, it must indicate a defect in their reason as well as their passions. Gregory disassociates the divine image from rationality *per se* – that is, with a faculty which humans have by definition of being human and which they keep, come what may; rather, he identifies it with certain qualities which mirror God, but which are liable to be lost: e.g. wisdom, virtue, free will, purity, kingship, blessedness, beauty (Behr 1999: 225; Ludlow 2000: 54–55). These qualities are regarded not as immaterial aspects of the soul, but characteristics of the ways in which humans (should) act as embodied beings. One interesting consequence of this is that Gregory connects the image with human physicality, arguing not that humans physically resemble God, but that their upright posture and ability to speak are perfectly fitted to (or facilitate) their kingly role (VIII–IX). Seemingly, then, the image of God resides not in the human body or soul, but in humanity's *function or purpose* in the world. After the Fall humanity still retains this purpose even if it fails to achieve it.

For Gregory, humans, as 'rational animals', have the function both of summing up the whole of creation and mediating between non-human creation and its Creator (see especially Behr 1999). To this end Gregory develops an idea implicit in Basil: that humanity is both different from and in a continuum with the rest of creation. In both writers this sense of (dis)continuity is conveyed by reflection on the quality of plant, animal and human life – particularly on the nature of 'soul' (*psuchē*). These reflections are informed both by Greek philosophy and by the Septuagint text of Gen. 1.30: 'everything that has the breath of life [*psuchēn zōēs* – literally 'soul of life']' (cf. Gen. 1.20, 24). Because fish (*ichthues*) are not mentioned (in the LXX) until 1.26-28, the *herpeta* (literally 'creeping things', cf. Gen. 1.30 above) created in 1.20-21 are understood by

Basil as reptiles etc. Basil notes that *herpeta*, not fish, are described as having a 'living soul', thus he concludes: fish are guided by bodily motions, while in creeping things 'the soul (*psuchē*) enjoys supreme authority [*hēgemonian*]' (*Hex.* VIII.1). He supports this with evidence that most quadrupeds have memory and keener sense perception. Furthermore, they 'express by cries their joy and sadness, recognition of what is familiar to them, the need of food, regret at being separated from their companions, and numberless emotions. Aquatic animals, on the contrary, are not only dumb; it is impossible to tame them, to teach them, to train them for man's society' (*Hex.* VIII.1 – an interestingly anthropocentric definition of animal capabilities!). Crucially, these abilities do not amount to the possession of reason, according to Basil (*Hex.* VIII.2); on the other hand, even fish demonstrate a remarkable ability to take precautions for their own preservation (as we saw above). Thus Basil describes a continuum of creatures' increasing awareness and interaction with their environment.

This idea is made even more explicit in Gregory who uses the common Greek distinction between the nutritive, the appetitive (or sensitive) and the rational (or intellectual) soul. The appetitive soul includes the nutritive; the rational includes the other two, thus: 'this rational animal, man, is blended of every form of soul; he is nourished by the vegetative kind of soul, and to the faculty of growth was added that of sense . . . Then takes place a certain alliance and commixture of the intellectual essence with the subtle and enlightened element of the sensitive nature: so that man consists of these three' (*De hom. opif.* VIII.5, citing 1 Thess. 5.23, Mk. 12.30; see Behr 1999: 227–28).

Gregory's repeated emphasis on this point develops Basil's notion that humanity is a microcosm – a mini-creation – encapsulating both materiality and the whole range of created immaterial functions ('souls'). However, interpretations differ as to the extent to which Gregory sets humanity apart from creation. According to one reading, Gregory thinks that humanity unites two inherently *opposed* aspects of creation – the material and the immaterial. A true microcosm (according to classical Greek philosophy) would hold these together in a static harmony. However, the image of God means that humanity has been given the chance to choose freely between a life dominated by the material and a life dominated by the immaterial (Corsini 1972). This interpretation emphasizes a dynamic, transformative view of the world, but at the expense of rather a negative interpretation of material nature: it gives little weight to Gregory's belief that all animal life is, in various ways, ensouled. It assumes that the conception of humanity as *imago dei* is set against that of humanity as microcosm. By contrast, John Behr has suggested that Gregory balances the two (1999: 233, citing *De hom. opif.* XVI.2). Behr stresses the intimate communion (*koinōnia*) between humans' intellectual and bodily aspects in Gregory's theology: even knowledge of the world and other people is mediated through the senses; rational thought is expressed through physical speech (1999: 229–30). This is how humans were always intended to be: materiality was *not* added as a result of the Fall. On the other hand, humans' nature as image-bearing is *also* their natural (albeit God-given) state. Thus, humanity's natural and proper role in creation is as a mid-way point (*methorios*) or mediator communicating divine beauty from God to creation and, as Harrison asserts, raising up creation's praise to God in priestly fashion (Behr 1999: 231; Harrison 1990: 468 n. 92).

It would be foolish to deny that Gregory thinks that humans have a God-given dominion over creation: the image of God lies in humanity's kingship and Gregory asserts, for example, that creation is a royal palace for humankind, its king (*De hom. opif.* II). Gregory, for all his general appreciation of the natural world does not take a theological interest in animals in their own right. His most lyrical celebrations of natural beauty assume it is best when humans are there to share it (*De hom. opif.* I.5; *Letter 20 to Adelphius*). However, his vision of humanity as *methorios* or half-way point does offer a new perspective on the concept of dominion.

Augustine's interpretations follow the development of his career as we might expect: his first, most 'allegorical', commentary on Genesis contains a vociferous attack on Manicheans who assumed that 'image' refers to the 'shape of our bodies' and thus denied humanity was made in the image of God (*Gen. Man.* I.17.27-28). Instead, Augustine argued, one must take a 'spiritual' understanding: '[image] is said with reference to the interior man, where reason is to be found and intelligence; and it is from this that he gets "authority over the fishes . . .".' His explanation here seems to echo Basil's: the image is precisely 'the power by which [human nature] surpasses all cattle, all animals', for humans evidently do not surpass such beasts in physical power.

In response to the question of why humans are now attacked by wild animals, Augustine replies (like Chrysostom) that human dominion is an ideal state, which was lost in the Fall. Even now, humans have control over domestic animals; eventually, when they are 'set free' humans will regain dominion over all other creatures (*Gen. Man.* I.18:29). Thus, Augustine firmly believes that human dominion over animals is part of the natural order – not the social order to which human kingship over other humans belongs (Clark 1998: 73). In a surprising echo of Origen, Augustine adds to this literal understanding a 'spiritual' interpretation of dominion as reason's control of emotions (*Gen. Man.* I.20.31; cf. *Gen. Man.* II.11.16). Both readings are connected by an implicit assumption that perfect harmony (the perfection of paradise, the perfected soul) is not only compatible with, but *requires* a hierarchy.

In his *Unfinished Literal Commentary on Genesis* the 'spiritual' reading of dominion as control over passion is absent. There is theological interpretation, but in it Augustine is more concerned with Christology: he wants to show that 'let us make' indicates the Father's making of humanity through the Son and that humanity is made *according to* the image and likeness of God, which is the Son. Later, in *The Literal Meaning of Genesis* Augustine corrects both of these readings to avoid misinterpretations which might sideline the Spirit: God the Trinity created humanity in the image of God as Trinity (*Gen. imp.* 16.57-60; *Gen. litt.* III.19.29). The emphasis on Trinitarian theology in this work follows the pattern we saw earlier. What is clear from the book titles, however, is that Augustine regards these theological speculations as *literal* interpretations of the text.

With regard to animals, in the unfinished commentary Augustine (somewhat off-handedly) admits a 'certain connection' between humanity and the other creatures made on the sixth day: 'they are all of them together land animals, after all' (*Gen. imp.* 16.55). However, he puts far more emphasis on the fact that humans and other animals are different 'because of the pre-eminence of reason, with respect to which man is made to the image of God and his likeness' (*Gen. imp.* 16.55; *Gen. litt.* III.20.30). Indeed, there is little evidence in these or other works that Augustine considers animals in and of themselves. Even vocabulary is significant: Augustine tends not to use the neutral term *animalia*, which could include humans, but prefers *pecus* (cattle or farm animals: 'herds') and *bestia* or *belua* (wild animals) – that is, those creatures who have, or have not, been successfully tamed for human use (Clark 1998: 68). He professes to steer away from Origen's allegory and the 'moral tales' approach found in Basil and Ambrose. Nevertheless, he still uses animals to understand human nature not vice versa and his approach is perhaps not so different from theirs as one might at first think (*pace* Cizewski 1993: 365–66). Even direct examples of human cruelty to animals are condemned because of their effects on the perpetrators, not the victims; meat-eating is judged according to the well-being of the consumer not his prey (Clark 1998: 78–79, 75). (Augustine had very mixed feelings about vegetarianism because it was encouraged by Manichees as well as many Christian ascetics.) In sum, we might well conclude that 'his conviction of human superiority leads him to argue that even the struggle of animals to survive is both appropriate and edifying' (Clark 1998: 72).

Augustine's use of animal examples is undoubtedly given more 'bite' through his encounter with Manichees. They took the existence of 'pernicious or superfluous' animals ('mice and frogs . . . flies and worms') as evidence that material creation was bad (*Gen. Man.* I.16:25-26). Augustine first seems to argue that God sees an overall beauty and good function to the universe (which is both his masterpiece and his workshop: *Gen. Man.* I.16:25-26). From their limited perspective, humans fail to grasp this – although Augustine himself professes to appreciate the 'harmonious unity' in individual mice and worms.

Augustine never wavers from his conviction that creation is good. But in later works, as he wrestles with the problem of evil at all levels, his response is more nuanced. First, he arguably approaches even animal suffering from a less detached, more compassionate perspective (Cizewski 1993: 370–71). Secondly, although he holds that an ultimate harmony explains apparently bad elements of creation '*purely at the level of the natural world at large*', he is insistent that both humans and animals are part of a created world united by a very complex 'interlocking system of action and passion' (Williams 2000: 109; cf. Williams 1999: 252). Who can say how far the effects of human agency ('moral evil') extend into the natural world? Finally, Augustine, like Gregory, balances a strongly hierarchical explanation of the world with an equally strong emphasis on its interconnectedness: 'things further down the scale that contribute to the good of things higher up, find their *own* good in so doing' (Williams 2000: 114; cf. Behr 1999: 228). As we have seen, however, this interconnectedness cuts both ways. Augustine agrees with Basil and Gregory that other animals have a kind of awareness and even, through rudimentary memory, come close to being rational (Clark 1998: 69, 76–77). But he also thinks it is clear both from experience and by theological definition that humans are more rational than other animals and he shares the cultural assumption of his age that the more rational should rule the less (Clark 1998: 68). Beliefs such as these lead to a very anthropocentric theology.

Conclusions

As with the readings of 'in the beginning', these early Christian interpretations of 'image' and 'dominion' show a degree of variety, but are united in what they rule out (the idea that 'image' meant God had a body) and in their assertion of human dominion – albeit a flawed dominion. Several interpretations show an awareness that there might be more than one possible meaning to Gen. 1.26-28, but all simply assume that humans are superior to animals by definition of being created in the image of God.

These authors share an assumption with their non-Christian contemporaries that humans have dominion over other animals because they are more rational than them. They also share a belief that harmony in creation is dependent on a structural hierarchy which binds different kinds of being together (this is evident in the notion of three kinds of 'soul'). But these Christian writers deny that humans have dominion because they *simply happen* to be more rational than other animals (a 'natural' difference, if you like); rather they claim that God created them as rational beings in his image *in order* that they could exercise dominion over the rest of creation as his regents (a theological difference). Although it is profoundly theological, the understanding of dominion over other animals in terms of the *imago dei* is seen by all the fathers examined here as a literal reading – in contrast with the allegorical reading of dominion as reason's control over passions. Nevertheless, the influence of that allegorical reading continued to be felt: one senses that the fathers thought that the providential ordering of creation with rational humanity at its head was as obviously harmonious and good as the providential ordering of human nature with reason (at least ideally) having dominion over passions.

It is difficult to see how Christians of their era could have moved beyond this anthropocentric theology without a radical reassessment of the belief in humanity's creation in the image of God. Greco-Roman philosophy assumed that being rational (*logikos*, possessing reason/*logos*) was necessary for spiritual awareness – that is, for a conscious relationship with God. Christianity affirmed this idea (Behr 1999: 225–33, 246; Clark 1998: 68). But Christian theology pushed it in an even more anthropocentric direction: first by (usually) connecting the 'image of God' directly with human reason and secondly by connecting it with the doctrine of the incarnation. Once *logikos* meant not only 'word-endowed' but 'Word-endowed' it became even more impossible for Christian theologians to view the world from anything but a thoroughly anthropocentric perspective.

In sum, in these fathers' view of dominion at least three ideas are intertwined: the notion that the harmony of creation is dependent on a hierarchy with reason at its head; the notion that God created humans to have a king-like role over creation which echoed his own lordship; and the notion that humans' special status was confirmed (or restored) by the incarnation of the Word as human. In the modern context, several of these ideas have been challenged, or at least, developed: for example, order and harmony is no longer necessarily connected with hierarchy and many have questioned the clear distinction between human reason and emotions, or between human and other animal forms of reasoning. Furthermore, theologians have thoroughly rethought both the notions of the *imago dei* and of the incarnation.

Nevertheless, there are some ideas found in these fathers which might stimulate fruitful reflection on the relationship between humanity and the rest of creation. As we have seen, several of the writers do acknowledge the continuity between humans and other animals. This recognition of continuity rests not only on the acknowledgement of a variety of forms of rationality in human and other animals, but also – crucially – on the essential materiality of humankind. All of these writers repeatedly stress the goodness of God's material creation and thus the value and beauty of human and other bodies. These emphases chime well with modern ecological ideas of the interconnectedness of the natural world, and serve as a useful corrective to those theologies which have tended to see non-human creation as an 'other' or as a mere instrument. In particular, Gregory of Nyssa's recasting of the idea of the image of God less in terms of reason/soul (which has a tendency to separate humans from other animals) and more in terms of qualities or virtues which enable humans as psychosomatic unities to perform a role *in* creation might be a helpful way to reflect on the notion of the *imago dei* while maintaining an emphasis on the interconnectedness of creation. Because of this interconnectedness, these writers also emphasize the complex effects of human sin, including its disruptive effects on the rest of creation. Thus Chrysostom and Augustine see the untameable brutality of wild animals as evidence of the fall (see pages 146 and 149), and Basil and Gregory of Nyssa think that the mortality of non-human animals was due to the Fall (see page 146 and Gregory *Catechetical Oration* §VIII). Although these ideas depend on rather literal conceptions of Adam and Eve's actions, the general idea that human sinfulness has insidious and destructive effects on the whole of creation is a useful one. Augustine's complex reflections on the relationship between natural and moral evil are an example of how that basic idea might be explored in a more philosophical direction.

References

Primary Texts

Augustine 1998 *Confessions (Conf.)* [397–398] tr. H. Chadwick, *Augustine's Confessions* (Oxford: Oxford University Press).

Augustine 2002 *On Genesis: A Refutation of the Manichees* (*Gen. Man.*) [c.388–389], *Unfinished Literal Commentary on Genesis* (*Gen. imp.*) [393], *The Literal Meaning of Genesis* (*Gen. Litt.*) [401–414] tr. E. Hill, *Saint Augustine on Genesis* (New York: New City Press).
Basil of Caesarea 1894 *Homilies on the Hexameron* (*Hex.*) [370s] tr. B. Jackson, *Nicene and Post-Nicene Fathers*, series 2, vol. 8 (reprinted 1989; Edinburgh: T&T Clark).
Basil of Caesarea 2005 *On the Origin of Humanity I & II* (*De orig.*) [370s] tr. N. Harrison, *St Basil the Great, On the Human Condition* (Crestwood, NY: St Vladimir's Seminary Press).
Gregory of Nyssa 1892 *Catechetical Oration* (*Or. cat.*) [c.386–387] tr. H. A. Wilson, *Nicene and Post-Nicene Fathers*, series 2, vol. 5 (reprinted 1988; Edinburgh: T&T Clark).
Gregory of Nyssa 1892 *On the Making of Humanity* (*De hom. opif.*) [c.379] tr. H.A. Wilson, *Nicene and Post-Nicene Fathers*, series 2, vol. 5 (reprinted 1988; Edinburgh: T&T Clark).
Gregory of Nyssa 1999a *Gregor von Nyssa, Über das Sechstagewerk* [c.379] tr. F. X. Risch (Stuttgart: Hiersemann).
Gregory of Nyssa 1999b *On the Hexameron* (*In Hex.*) [c.379] tr. T. Lecaudey and J. Rousselet, *Grégoire, évêque de Nysse: Les six jours de la Création (*published online October 1999 www.gregoiredenysse.com/?page_id=66)
Origen 1982 *Homilies on Genesis* (*Hom. Gen.*) [c.238–244] tr. R. Heine, *The Fathers of the Church*, vol. 71 (Washington, DC: Catholic University of America Press).
Origen 1998 *Commentary on John Book I* (*Comm. Joh.*) [c.231] tr. J.W. Trigg, *Origen* (London: Routledge).

Secondary Sources

Alexandre, M. 1976 'L'Exégèse de Gen. 1,1-2a dans l'*in Hexaemeron* de Grégoire de Nysse: deux approches de la matière', in H. Dörrie, M. Altenburger and U. Schramm (eds), *Gregor von Nyssa und die Philosophie* (Leiden: Brill): 159–92.
Behr, J. 1999 'The Rational Animal: A Rereading of Gregory of Nyssa's *De hominis opificio*', *JECS* 7: 219–47.
Cizewski, W. 1993 'The Meaning and Purpose of Animals According to Augustine's Genesis Commentaries', in J. Lienhard, E.C. Muller and R.J. Teske (eds), *Augustine: Presbyter Factus Sum* (New York, Berlin: Peter Lang): 363–73.
Clark, G. 1998 'The Fathers and the Animals: The Rule of Reason?', in A. Linzey and D. Yamamoto (eds), *Animals on the Agenda: Questions About Animals for Theology and Ethics* (London: SCM): 67–79.
Corsini, E. 1972 'L'harmonie du monde et l'homme microcosme dans le *De Hominis Opificio*', in J. Fontaine and C. Kannengiesser (eds), *Epektasis. Mélanges patristiques offerts au Cardinal Jean Daniélou* (Paris: Beauchesne).
Courtonne, Y. 1934 *Saint Basile et l'hellénisme, étude sur la rencontre de la pensée chrétienne avec la sagesse antique dans l'Hexaméron de Basile le Grand* (Paris: Firmin-Didot).
Harrison, N. V. 1990 'Male and Female in Cappadocian Theology', *JTS* 41: 441–71.
Henke, R. 2000 *Basilius und Ambrosius über das Sechstagewerk* (Chrēsis vol. VII; Basel: Schwabe).
Ludlow, M. 2000 *Universal Salvation: Eschatology in the Thought of Gregory of Nyssa and Karl Rahner* (Oxford: Oxford University Press).
Reuling, H. 2006 *After Eden: Church Fathers and Rabbis on Genesis 3:16-21* (Leiden: Brill).
Williams, R. 1999 'Creation', in A.D. Fitzgerald (eds), *Augustine Through the Ages: An Encyclopedia* (Grand Rapids, MI: Eerdmans): 251–54.
Williams, R. 2000 'Insubstantial Evil', in R. Dodaro and G. Lawless (eds), *Augustine and His Critics* (London: Routledge): 105–23.

Chapter 11

Thomas Aquinas: Reading the Idea of Dominion in the Light of the Doctrine of Creation[1]

Mark Wynn

The State of the Question

Theological commentators commonly read Aquinas's account of our relations with non-human animals in thoroughly anthropocentric terms. For example, Andrew Linzey remarks that:

> three elements distinguish Aquinas's views of the status of animals. First, animals are irrational, possessing no mind or reason. Second, they exist to serve human ends by virtue of their nature and by divine providence. Third, they therefore have no moral status in themselves save in so far as some human interest is involved, for example, as human property.

And he adds:

> In case it is thought that this might be a caricature or misreading of Aquinas's position, it is worth noting that this view is consistently defended without substantial deviation throughout the whole of his work. (Linzey 1994: 13–14)

In support of this reading, we might recall Aquinas's discussion in the *Summa Theologiae* (*ST*) of Gen 1.26, and the idea that human beings should 'rule over [or have dominion over] the fishes of the sea, and the birds of the sky and the beasts of the earth'. Having cited this text, Aquinas continues: 'the order of divine providence ... always governs lower things by higher. So since man is above the other animals ... other animals are properly subjected to his government' (*ST* 1a 96.1). Here we find the thought that Linzey attributes to Aquinas: the order of providence requires the ends of non-human animals to be subordinated to those of human beings.

A similar assessment of the tendencies of medieval Western thought is offered by the commentator who is perhaps the single most cited source for the view that

---

[1] I would like to thank the Editors and participants in the research seminar of the Department of Theology and Religion, University of Exeter, for their helpful comments on an earlier draft of this essay.

Christian theology has poisoned our relations with non-human creatures. Lynn White suggests that the attitudes that prevailed in the medieval West are to be distinguished from those which obtained in the 'Greek East', and that it is the mentality of the West that lies at the root of our modern disregard of nature (White 1967: 1204). Taking a similar view, Robin Gill remarks: 'More than Augustine, Aquinas articulated a view of non-human life which appears to many today to be thoroughly anthropocentric. Even if Lynn White's critique is somewhat modified, it does suggest that Aquinas, or the culture that he represented, has had an important influence upon Western society' (Gill 2006: 286). On this perspective, Aquinas's views are objectionable in themselves, and bound up with wider intellectual developments which have licensed, and perhaps encouraged, centuries of bad 'environmental' practice.

Given this tradition of reading Aquinas, it is perhaps surprising to find that there are other commentators who have taken his work to provide the basis for a nuanced and 'sympathetic' appreciation of the nature of our responsibilities to the non-human world. These commentators tend to deflect attention away from passages where Aquinas is concerned specifically with our relations to non-human animals – such as the text on 'dominion' that I cited just now – and to concentrate instead on broader themes in his doctrine of creation. For instance, Celia Deane-Drummond writes with reference to Aquinas in particular: 'I suggest that once understood in the context of evolutionary categories, the Chain of Being . . . affirms the continuity of human life with all life forms: we are an integral part of the whole complex chain of creation' (Deane-Drummond 2004: 77). It is not difficult to see how this reading of Aquinas on creation will issue in a rather different interpretation of the bearing of his thought on questions of environmental ethical practice.

In a similarly enthusiastic spirit, Michael Northcott writes that 'natural law ethics as we encounter it in Aquinas . . . provides the strongest conceptual base within the Christian tradition for an ecological ethic'. And this is because: 'It affirms that the natural order is a moral order . . .' (Northcott 1996: 232). Jill LeBlanc has made perhaps the most systematic attempt to relate the broader principles of Aquinas's metaphysics to questions in environmental ethics. She suggests that three such principles are of particular relevance here: 'First, being is good in all its manifestations . . . Second, the world is an organic unity, in which each part plays a role. Third, diversity is itself good . . .' And the implication of these principles, she suggests, is 'a requirement of respect – for being, for life, and for the world order' (LeBlanc 1999: 306). The approach I am going to adopt here will fit most closely with LeBlanc's. But I shall give particular emphasis to the role that is played by the idea of God as subsistent existence – as *ipsum esse per se subsistens* (*ST* 1a 4.2) – in holding together the various strands of Aquinas's thought on these matters.

Attending to the notion of subsistent existence might seem to imply a rather 'philosophical', non-biblically grounded route into Aquinas's thought, but it should be remembered that this notion is in the service of a biblical theme, a theme which Aquinas did not find in his Aristotelian or other philosophical sources – namely, the idea of God as creator. The notion of subsistent existence is Aquinas's answer to the question of what it would take for something to be the source of the existence of things. In the remainder of this paper, I am going to suggest that Aquinas's doctrine of creation provides a way of framing the passages that exercise Linzey and others, and a way of reading his development of the 'dominion' theme in the light of his broader metaphysical commitments.

Aquinas's Teleology of Creation

One well-trodden route into environmental ethical questions is to consider whether non-human creatures or 'systems' can be deemed to have purposes or interests of their own, which might require some sort of practical acknowledgement in our (human) dealings with them. Aquinas's thought can be brought to bear on these matters with relatively little effort – most obviously by considering his development of the view, which he has inherited from Aristotle, that natural things in general, including inanimate things, are goal-directed. So let us begin here.

If we put to Aquinas's text the question: in what sense or senses is the behaviour of creatures goal-directed?, we will find that he has a ready and systematic response. In *ST* 1a 65.2, Aquinas sets out the ends of creatures in these terms:

> Each creature has its proper operation and perfection; secondly, lower creatures serve the higher, as the creatures below man provide for his welfare; thirdly, individual creatures manifest the perfection of the entire universe; and finally, the whole universe and all its parts have God as their goal, in so far as the divine goodness is reflected through them and thus his glory manifested. Over and above this, however, rational creatures have God as their goal in a special way, since they can attain him by their own operations of knowing and loving. Thus it is apparent that the divine goodness is the goal of everything corporeal. (*ST* 1a 65.2)

So if we were to put to Aquinas the question: in what respects are material things goal-directed?, he would give in response this fivefold typology. It is significant that in this passage, Aquinas maintains that the 'lower' creatures properly serve the 'welfare' of human beings, and that this is part of their divinely ordained *telos*. He also supposes here that rational creatures 'have God as their goal in a special way'. These are, of course, the strands in his thought that have struck Linzey and others in their reading of various passages in Aquinas, such as the 'dominion' text that I cited just now. In these passages, Aquinas tends to be concerned not with the first principles of the cosmos's being, but with the specific question of the relationship of human beings to non-human animals. But it is striking that Aquinas here places these anthropocentric-sounding themes within a broader context – and his remarks on the question of human beings' relationship to non-human animals need to be set, I am going to suggest, within this larger frame of reference. Let us consider now the various dimensions of Aquinas's account.

First, Aquinas holds that 'each creature has its proper operation and perfection'. Now someone who favours an unreservedly anthropocentrist reading of Aquinas might say: but perhaps the 'proper operation and perfection' of non-human creatures is nothing but their pliant conformity to human wants and even human whims. But there must be more to 'proper operation' than this. Consider for instance the following celebrated text, where Aquinas is considering the relationship between 'inclinations' (or goal-directed tendencies) in human beings and in other things, and trying thereby to deduce some of the fundamental principles of the 'natural law':

> in man there is first of all an inclination to good in accordance with the nature which he has in common with all substances, inasmuch as every substance seeks the preservation of its own being according to its nature, and by reason of this inclination, whatever is a means of preserving human life and of warding off its obstacles belongs to the natural law. (*ST* 1a2ae 94.2, cited in Baumgarth and Regan 1988: 48)

Of course, this text is likely to provoke various questions to do with the very idea of a 'natural' law in the human context, but let us set those aside – and return to the matter of the teleology of non-human creatures, and the 'perfection' to which they are directed. This passage makes clear that all created things are directed towards their own continued existence. And this suggests that the teleology of non-human creatures cannot simply consist in their service of human beings: we can intelligibly speak of their own good and accordingly of their own ends.

Of course, an anthropocentrist reading of 1a 65.2 is still possible. It might be said: while non-human creatures aim at their own continued existence, this is a strictly subordinate end. The ultimate end of such creatures, to which their other ends should be subordinated in any case of potential conflict, is to be of use to human beings, where being 'of use' may take the form of ceasing to exist for the sake of satisfying some human want or even some human whim. Such a construal of the text is certainly possible. Indeed, we need to allow for the possibility of some such reading where at least some non-animate creatures are concerned. Otherwise, we may find ourselves admitting the propriety of questions about whether using straw to thatch a roof constitutes an unacceptable frustration of the straw's *telos* to sink to the earth! However, two things do seem to be implied by the position that Aquinas takes in *ST* 1a2ae 94.2.

First, it is at least *intelligible* to pose the question of whether our treatment of non-human creatures is morally or otherwise dubious, because these creatures do after all have ends which are not just trivially identical with the end of serving human interests. There are other worldviews on which it would not even be intelligible to suppose that our relations to other creatures might somehow involve a 'violation' of their own purposes or tendencies. To this extent, Aquinas can already be enlisted (along with Aristotle, of course) as potentially an ally in the construction of an 'ecological ethic'.

Secondly, while the idea that non-animate creatures have 'inclinations' or tendencies which need to be respected for their own sake may prove to be dubious, we do not need to suppose that the same must be true of the idea that non-human life forms have such tendencies (cf. Rolston 1988: 97–106.) The passage from 1a2ae 94.2 that I have just cited goes on to note that the 'inclinations' of, for example, animals include those of non-animate things *and more besides* – and it may be that these additional inclinations are to be given weight even in cases where their fulfilment will involve the frustration of some human want or interest. In fact, for what it is worth, I am inclined to think that even the 'inclinations' of some non-animate things can carry this sort of significance – if we strip a mountainside of its smaller stones, as when walkers pass by and pile them up in a cairn, then there is a sense in which we remove the stones from the order in which they have been placed by 'nature', and it is not fanciful or sentimental, I suggest, to read that as a 'disruption' or 'frustration' of their kind-grounded 'inclinations'.

Let us move now, more briefly, to the second point in Aquinas's fivefold teleological scheme. Aquinas notes that 'lower creatures serve the higher, as the creatures below [human beings] provide for their welfare'. This text may seem to support the idea that while non-human creatures may have ends which are not simply identical with the end of serving human beings, any such end will turn out to be, in every case, subordinate to the end of being of service to us. However, it would be rash to suppose that the text has to be assigned this meaning. If we allow that non-human creatures have ends which are not simply identical with the end of being of service to us, then it is possible that ends of this kind (let us call them: non-human-regarding ends) can come into conflict with those ends which consist in the service of human beings. And in such cases it is not clear that these non-human-regarding ends are always to be assigned a subordinate significance. How might we determine when, if at all, these non-human-regarding ends might override those ends which do consist in being of service to human beings?

The next two steps in Aquinas's scheme are, I think, relevant to this issue. Aquinas continues: 'thirdly, individual creatures manifest the perfection of the entire universe; and finally, the whole universe and all its parts have God as their goal, in so far as the divine goodness is reflected through them and thus his glory manifested.' Let us concentrate on the second of these two steps, which subsumes the first. How is it we might ask, that the goodness of the divine nature is reflected in the universe? Aquinas addresses this question in *ST* 1a 47.1, where he poses the question: is the multiplicity and distinction of things from God? I am going to take his answer to this question as a way of expounding the claim of 1a 65.2 that the universe and its parts are directed to God. He writes:

> distinctiveness and plurality of things is because the first agent, who is God, intended them. For he brought things into existence so that his goodness might be communicated to creatures and re-enacted through them. And because one single creature was not enough, he produced many and diverse, so that what was wanting in one expression of his goodness might be supplied by another, for goodness, which in God is single and all together, in creatures is

multiple and scattered. Hence the whole universe less incompletely than one alone shares and represents his goodness. (*ST* 1a 47.1)

To understand the import of this passage, we need to have recourse to the idea of subsistent existence. Because God is subsistent existence – or being itself rather than a particular being – a universe which comprises a diverse set of creaturely types will image the divine nature more fully than will any one creature. This is because each creature, and each creaturely type, bodies forth what it is to be according to its particular limited mode of being – and it is therefore creatures considered in concert which offer the best image of what it is to be unrestrictedly free from the bounds of a particular nature. Here then is a reason for God to create a diverse creation – so that it will succeed more fully in imaging the divine perfection.

It is worth recalling here why Aquinas supposes that the designation 'The One who Is' (drawn of course from Exod. 3.14), which he reads as a biblical warrant for the doctrine of subsistent existence, is 'the most appropriate name for God'. He comments: 'Any other name selects some particular aspect of the being of the thing, but "The One who Is" fixes on no aspect of being but stands open to all and refers to God as to an infinite ocean of being' (*ST* 1a 13.11, cited in Davies and Leftow 2006: 163). A fuller treatment of these matters would require us to distinguish between the different kinds of resemblance which creatures can bear to God, and to note the difference between a 'trace' and an 'image' in Aquinas's terms (see *ST* 1a 93). However, these passages are sufficient to indicate that for Aquinas, all things, just by virtue of being, present a kind of likeness to God, and a created order will present a better likeness to God the more varied its stock of creaturely types.

The passage I have just cited, from *ST* 1a 47.1, together with the doctrine of subsistent existence, in terms of which it is to be understood, can help us to bring the first two points in Aquinas's typology of 'ends' into clearer focus. First, granted these observations, we can now say that the directedness of creatures to their own perfection is also a directedness to God. As Aquinas puts it: 'In desiring its own perfection everything desires God himself, for the perfections of all things somehow resemble divine existence' (*ST* 1a 6.1 ad 2; Davies and Leftow 2006: 64). This is, I think, a significant claim: the natural kind-grounded tendencies of things can be described not only as directed to the perfection of *the thing* (this is already to use a normative language, and therefore potentially to lay down requirements on our behaviour in relation to such things), but also as directed towards *God*. And the perfection of the thing, we may say, involves an admittedly limited and kind-relative but nonetheless real likeness to the divine perfection. This is, potentially, a very rich and normatively weighty vocabulary for thinking about the sense in which creatures are good – because it sees their goodness as bearing a resemblance to the divine goodness, which by assumption is the source and summit of goodness.

Given this assessment of the goodness of creatures, we may well wish to suppose that while non-human animals can properly serve the interests of human beings (following the second point in Aquinas's scheme), there is even so a sense in which our allowing them simply to be, where this involves no significant compromise of our own well-being, will constitute a good: because thereby they will be able to present their own, kind-relative likeness to the divine nature. In other words, we seem to have here the raw materials for a defence of the view that *prima facie* anyway, there is reason to respect the natural inclinations of things. And this case will be stronger for animals than for plants, and for plants than for minerals, if we share Aquinas's sense of the hierarchical arrangement of these creatures, and their varying capacities to resemble the divine nature.

The passage I have cited from *ST* 1a 47.1, together with the doctrine of subsistent existence, points to a further respect in which creatures matter. It is not just that they are directed to God, and to the extent that they flourish as individuals of a particular kind succeed in resembling God. It is also true that creatures image God most fully by virtue of their participation within the wider community of created being, since this community presents a better likeness of God than does any individual thing. Might this view suggest that if our human perfection, like that of other creatures, consists in God-likeness, then we should see our human *telos* as inseparably tied to our assuming our proper place within creation – since the creation in its unity-in-diversity offers a better likeness of God than any we human beings can achieve, when considered simply as individuals or even collectively? (Compare Willis Jenkins's discussion of the role of relationship to creation in the sanctification of human beings [2008: 115–32].)

Aquinas touches on these matters in *ST* 1a 93.2, where he asks: is there an image of God in non-rational creatures? He comments, in the body of the article, that 'it is clear that only intelligent creatures are properly speaking after God's image'. However, he goes on to say that:

> The universe is more perfect than the intelligent creation in extent and diffusion. But in intensity and concentration a better likeness of the divine perfection is to be found in the intelligent creation, which has a capacity for the highest good [of knowing and loving God]. Or else you can say that part should not be compared with whole, but with another part. Thus when it is said that intelligent nature alone is after God's image, this merely excludes other parts of the universe from being after God's image, not the universe as a whole with respect to some of its parts. (*ST* 1a 93.2 ad 3)

So Aquinas allows that there is a sense (connected to the idea of 'extent and diffusion') in which the universe presents a better likeness to God than does 'the intelligent creation'. (So this likeness is superior, in these respects, to any provided by human beings.) And he allows that the universe as a whole can be said to 'image' God. Admittedly, he goes on to say that this is 'with respect to some of its parts', and evidently he means by this 'with respect to its intelligent parts' in particular. But even on this reading, the universe as a whole will depend for its capacity to image God upon the ability of non-rational creatures to realize the perfections that are proper to them, if the order of the whole is to be preserved. The stance that Aquinas adopts here might well lead us to suppose that we human beings are to respect the diversity of creaturely types not only in so far as each type has its own perfection, and resembles God after its own fashion, but also because we ourselves can image God through our participation in the integrated perfection of the universe as a whole, where that perfection depends upon the existence of a diverse range of creaturely types, and upon each type being able to achieve its own perfection. And the sort of resemblance that is presented by the universe as an integrated whole provides, indeed, in at least one sense, a better image of God than can be provided by individual human beings or by the 'intelligent creation' in its entirety.

This appreciation of the goodness of the universe as an integrated totality, and of the significance of individual creatures in so far as they participate in this totality, is apparent again when Aquinas considers the problem of evil. Here he is explicit that the goodness of non-rational creatures cannot be reduced to their usefulness to human beings. For instance, he remarks that:

> Material creatures are by nature good, but not inexhaustibly and universally so, since they are particular and restricted. Thus contrariety is found among them: one is different from another, although each in itself is good. Yet certain thinkers, considering not natures but utility, regard harmful things as completely evil, failing to see that what is harmful to one being under a particular aspect is advantageous for another or even for the same being, when seen under a different aspect. This could never happen if bodies were intrinsically evil and harmful. (*ST* 1a 65.2 ad 2)

Aquinas discusses these matters more fully in questions 48–49, but from this remark it is sufficiently clear that the expression of a creature's nature is of itself good, even if it should make for some frustration of the goals of another creature. And at points, Aquinas seems to extrapolate this thought in the direction of a radically non-anthropocentric account of value. For instance, he describes in these terms the error of those who thought that some sort of ultimate or metaphysical dualism is required to account for the presence in the world of both good and evil:

> they did not consider the universal cause of the whole of being, but only the particular cause of particular effects. On this account, when they discovered that by the strength of its own nature one thing was damaging to another they reckoned that the nature of that thing was evil; for example, that fire's nature was bad for burning down some poor man's home. The goodness, however, of a thing should not be assessed from its reference to another particular thing, but on its own worth according to the universal scheme of things, wherein each . . . most admirably holds an appointed place. (*ST* 1a 49.3)

Here Aquinas's commitment to the goodness of the universe in its variety seems to issue in the thought that it is overall good, sometimes anyway, that human beings should suffer frustration, even if the nature which is hereby fulfilled is that of a non-animate thing such as fire!

So there are a number of considerations in Aquinas's text which might incline us to say not only that non-human creatures, including non-animate creatures, aim at their own perfection, rather than being directed simply to the service of human beings, but also that their goals cannot be deemed merely trivial when they come into conflict with the ends of human beings – or at any rate, with human ends which do not touch on vital human interests. These considerations are: (1) these creatures also aim at God, by resembling God so far as they can, according to the constraints of their particular kind; (2) the universe as a whole, in its unity-in-diversity, which requires the flourishing of the full range of creaturely types, images God better in some respects than does any individual creature; and (3) the fulfilment of the nature of 'lesser' creatures, and even of non-animate creatures, can count as a good, even when this results in a human being suffering some deprivation of good. These themes allow us to fill out the idea set down in Aquinas's fivefold typology that individual creatures and the universe as a whole have God as their end. Although Aquinas does not explicitly do so, I would add that the universe's perfection requires not only the existence of many types of creature, but also the flourishing of many individuals within any one type – since these individuals will realize the potentialities of the type in different ways, and thereby make a distinctive contribution *as individuals* to the unity-in-diversity by virtue of which the creation is able to image the God who simply is.

Of course, in the passage from *ST* 1a 65.2 which we have been considering, Aquinas also says that 'rational creatures have God as their goal in a special way, since they can attain him by their own operations of knowing and loving'. But this addition to the foregoing account does not shake the thought that the flourishing of non-human creatures, especially in their diversity, constitutes a profound good – and one to which we should assign some weight, therefore, in our practical deliberations.

Revisiting the Literature

As we have seen, Andrew Linzey summarizes Aquinas's assessment of the significance of animals in these terms: 'they exist to serve human ends by virtue of their nature and by divine providence . . . they therefore have *no moral status in themselves* save in so far as some human interest is involved' (my emphasis). Our discussion suggests that the 'therefore' here is too quick. It is true that Aquinas supposes that animals 'exist to serve human ends', but he also considers how animals can be assigned various other goals – and these other goals, I have been arguing, seem not to be reducible to, nor are they evidently in all cases subordinate to, the goal of being of service to human beings. Some of these goals (for example, those of resembling God by virtue of their own perfections, or of contributing, collectively, to an image of God which is in some respects better than any which individual human beings can provide) suggest that the flourishing of non-human animals has a deep theological significance independently of their importance for the sustaining of human life – and that their well-being is therefore not to be put at risk for the sake of relatively trivial, or even perhaps for pretty weighty, human purposes. In this connection, it is significant that when expounding his fivefold typology, Aquinas seems to move from localized goals, including the goal which fits the 'dominion' theme most directly (the second goal in his list), to goals which concern the character of creation as a whole – and given his tendency to think of the whole as more perfect than the part (for the reasons we have been considering), this should lead us to suppose that the goals which are listed after the goal of being of service to human beings are indeed of considerable importance.

For the same reasons, Robin Gill's suggestion that Aquinas's views appear to be 'thoroughly anthropocentric' also invites qualification. By thinking of God as the creator, and therefore as subsistent existence, and by placing this conception of God at the centre of his philosophical theology, Aquinas provides, I have been suggesting, a very rich way of articulating the goodness of the material order – and of reflecting upon the sense in which its goodness is not reducible to its serviceability for human purposes. To put the point most simply, if we *begin* not from a conception of God as mind or intelligence, or as non-material, but from a conception of God as being, then immediately we have a way of recognising the God-likeness of all things, in so far as they simply are. Of course, Aristotle also supposed that animals and plants and also non-animate things aim at God by striving for actuality (*The Metaphysics* [*Metaph*.]. 12.7 [373–75]) – but he does not articulate, and does not have the conceptual resources to articulate, the distinctively Thomistic thought that God is imaged by the material order in its unity-in-diversity in so far as God is subsistent existence.

On the other side of the debate, we have seen, are commentators who want to appropriate Aquinas's work for the purpose of defending a non-anthropocentric ethic. Celia Deane-Drummond suggests that the 'Chain of Being ... affirms the continuity of human life with all life forms', and that this is a reason for treating non-human creatures as morally considerable. This is a suggestive thought. But it passes by the thought that the creatures which make up the chain are able to image God because of their diversity. And this latter point should lead us to suppose that creatures which manifestly are *not* closely continuous with ourselves are even so important, in so far as their flourishing is required if the universe is to image God – and if we human beings are to fulfil our *telos* of participating in the universe's unity-in-diversity.

Michael Northcott commends Aquinas's work as a resource for 'ecological ethics' because it represents the creation as a moral order. In light of the themes in Aquinas that we have been exploring, we could say that his approach is significant in this context because it takes the creation to bear a likeness to God. While enthusiastic about the general drift of Aquinas's thought, Northcott takes exception to his 'tendency to discount the significance of natural evil ...' (1996: 231). Aquinas's stance on these matters offers, we have seen, a particularly radical route into a non-anthropocentric ethic. But Northcott finds this route too costly, and he envisages a time when predation, for example, will be at an end. By contrast, Aquinas sees predation as part of the Edenic ordering of things – since the fulfilment of a leonine nature, for example, requires the hunting of other creatures (*ST* 1a 96.1 ad 2). This perspective suggests a very generous assessment of the good of lions' flourishing – an assessment which indicates that, on certain points, Aquinas is far less 'anthropocentric' than are some of his ecologically minded critics.

Finally, I have noted Jill LeBlanc's defence of an 'eco-Thomist' perspective. She is right to say that for Aquinas: 'being is good in all its manifestations', and 'the world is an organic unity, in which each part plays a role'; and 'diversity is itself good, both as an expression of being, and because diversity enables the functioning of the whole'. The central matters which an eco-Thomist must address, I would suggest, are these: to what extent are the goals of non-human creatures conceptually independent of the goal of being useful to human beings? ('Useful' here is to be understood 'narrowly' – that is, useful as a resource for meeting human beings' material wants or whims.) And secondly, in so far as these goals do exhibit such independence, to what extent can they be overridden or set aside if they come into conflict with the fulfilment of various human goals? To my mind, the idea of God as subsistent existence holds the key to answering these questions, since it enables us to see how creatures, including non-rational and even non-animate creatures, may be said to resemble God, and how the created order as a whole may be said to 'image' God even more fully than can an individual human being. When understood in these terms, the goals of non-human creatures have to be assigned a considerable, even if not (given Aquinas's discussion) a fully determinate, weight.

Of course, someone might grant all that I have said here, as a reading of Aquinas, and still think that he has an impoverished conception of animals and other non-human embodied life forms. It might be said for example that Aquinas envisages no place for these creatures in the life of the world to come (*ST Supplement* 3a 91.5). And if that is so, then the good of their flourishing surely cannot be all that fundamental after all. The metaphysical position which I have been attributing to Aquinas might suggest that it would be truer to the spirit of his account, and its accent on the fundamental goodness of diversity, to allow plant and non-human animal life a place in the world to come. But on this point, we would certainly be reading beyond and even against the text – using Aquinas's metaphysics of creation to challenge his own teaching on certain specific issues. For what it is worth, I would say that such a case could be made, by analogy with the case that Aquinas himself makes for the contribution of the human body to the condition of the blessed in the afterlife (see *ST* 1a2ae 4.6). But however that may be, Aquinas has surely given us, at least, the elements for a deeply humane vision of our relations to non-human creatures: these creatures are good in themselves; they are good, and they image God, above all when considered in community; we human beings therefore share with other creatures the project of imaging God; and we are called to recognize and respect difference in creation, while finding in this difference an invitation to a common, God-directed end.

References

Aquinas, T. 1922 *The Summa Theologica*, Third Part (Supplement), QQ 87–99 (tr. Fathers of the English Dominican Province; London: Burns Oates and Washbourne Ltd).
Aquinas, T. 1964–1974 *Summa Theologiae* T. Gilby (ed.) (60 vols; London: Blackfriars).
Aristotle 1998 *The Metaphysics* (ed. H. Lawson-Tancred; London: Penguin Books).
Baumgarth, W.P. and Regan, R.J. (eds) 1988 *Saint Thomas Aquinas: On Law, Morality, and Politics* (Cambridge: Hackett Publishing Company).
Davies, B. and Leftow, B. (eds) 2006 *Thomas Aquinas: Summa Theologiae, Questions on God* (Cambridge: Cambridge University Press).
Deane-Drummond, C. 2004 *The Ethics of Nature* (Oxford: Blackwell).
Gill, R. (ed.) 2006 *A Textbook of Christian Ethics* (third edition; London: T&T Clark).
Jenkins, W. 2008 *Ecologies of Grace: Environmental Ethics and Christian Theology* (Oxford: Oxford University Press).
LeBlanc, J. 1999 'Eco-Thomism', *Environmental Ethics* 21: 293–306.
Linzey, A. 1994 *Animal Theology* (London: SCM).
Northcott, M.S. 1996 *The Environment and Christian Ethics* (Cambridge: Cambridge University Press).
Rolston, H. 1988 *Environmental Ethics: Duties to and Values in the Natural World* (Philadelphia, PA: Temple University Press).
White, L., Jr 1967 'The Historical Roots of Our Ecologic Crisis', *Science* 155: 1203–207.

Chapter 12

Martin Luther, the Word of God and Nature: Reformation Hermeneutics in Context[1]

H. Paul Santmire

'Nature' is not a word that Martin Luther used to refer to what we commonly call the world of stars and planets, mountains and oceans, animals and plants, and humans, too, insofar as humans are products of evolutionary processes and integrally belong to the earth's biosphere. Luther preferred to use the word 'creation' to refer to all such things, humans included. Further, the word 'nature' is often employed in modern scientific and philosophical discourse to refer to a self-enclosed system that, as it were, runs by itself. In contrast, Luther's view of things was profoundly theocentric. For Luther the created world is not self-enclosed. It does not run by itself. So we will hear him speaking of the powerful presence of God in, with and under all creatures, holding all things in being and energizing their becoming.

Why, then, employ the term 'nature' to interpret Luther's thought? The answer is this. It is both theologically possible and situationally necessary to do so. It is theologically possible because the word 'nature' can be defined in a way that resonates with Luther's own theology of creation. Nature can be thought of under the rubric of the idea of creation itself, as 'the biophysical dimension of creation' (Santmire 1985: 11–12). This definition presupposes, moreover, that humans are essentially natural. But for our purposes here, we can bracket the highly complicated and much discussed issue about whether the human creature in some sense transcends nature in some creaturely fashion. Our inquiry will focus on what Luther has to say about the physical and biological dimension of the creation, what the Nicene Creed refers to as 'all things visible' and that dimension includes humans insofar as they are bodily creatures.

It is situationally necessary to use the term 'nature' here, once it has been defined in terms of the creation, because many, if not most treatments of Luther's thought, from his own era to the present, address this theme in his theology only in passing, if at all. Interpreters of Luther's theology of creation have explored Luther's creational ethics, his theology of divine immanence in the creation, especially in connection

---

1   I want to thank three friends, scholars in their own right, who read this essay along the way and made helpful suggestions for clarifications and emendations: Mark Edwards, Clifford Green and Roger Johnson. I, of course, take full responsibility for this essay as it now stands.

with his treatment of the sacraments, his teaching about 'creation out of nothing', his views of human corporeality, his understanding of the eschatological consummation of all things and other related themes. But rarely have they focused on Luther's theology of nature, as the term is being used here.[2] The signs of our times compel us, however, to do precisely that, to inquire whether Luther's theology may have something to teach us about such matters. Conversely, if we do *not* ask about this aspect of Luther's thought, then those critics of the Christian tradition, who have argued that Christianity is ecologically bankrupt, that it has nothing helpful to teach us about world of nature, will have Luther all to themselves, as it were, to set aside as one more allegedly irrelevant and perhaps even dangerously anthropocentric voice.

If we must be cautious about our use of the term 'nature' in interpreting Luther, however, we can be confident that the accent on the Word of God announced by our theme takes us to the heart of his thought. Whatever else Martin Luther may have been, he was fundamentally a theologian of the Word of God (Pelikan 1959: 48–70). Still, we will not have understood Luther's reading of the Scriptures correctly if we do not see these two constructs together, Word *and* nature. However Luther may have interpreted the Scriptures as the Word of God, in different ways at different times, his mature theology, as it came into view in the 1520s and thereafter, was a theology of the Word of God *in nature*. Majestically in nature, we may say.

Thus, in one of his sermons on the Gospel of John, preached in 1537, we hear these words, regarding Jn 1.3:

> God the Father initiated and executed the creation of all things through the Word; and he now continues to preserve His creation through the Word, and that forever and ever . . . Hence, as heaven, earth, sun, moon, stars, man, and all living things were created in the beginning through the Word, so they are wonderfully governed and preserved through that Word. (*Luthers's Works* [LW XXII, 26])

Such thoughts might be read, to be sure, as a kind of faithful recapitulation of traditional trinitarian formulations, and little more. But Luther could not leave it at that, as he might well have done – he was, after all, interpreting the first chapter of John, not the first chapter of Genesis.

Rather, Luther presents us with an exuberantly extended confession of the Word of God in nature, not just of the Word of God in the world of human affairs, and does so vividly, as nature was concretely known to Luther and to his contemporaries:

> How long, do you suppose, would the sun, the moon, the entire firmament keep to the course maintained for so many thousands of years? Or how would the sun rise or set year after year at the same time in the same place if God, its Creator, did not continue to sustain it daily? If

---

2   For two of the few available descriptions of Luther's treatment of nature, see Bornkamm 1965: 177–94 and Gregersen 2005. For an overview of Luther's theology of nature in the context of the unfolding of the Reformation tradition, see Santmire 1985: 121–43.

it were not for the divine power, it would be impossible for mankind to be fruitful and beget children; the beasts could not bring forth their young, each after its own kind, as they do every day; the earth would not be rejuvenated each year, producing a variety of fruit; the ocean would not supply fish . . . If God were to withdraw His hand, this building and everything in it would collapse . . . The sun would not long retain its position and shine in the heavens; no child would be born; no kernel, no blade of grass, nothing at all would grow on the earth or reproduce itself if God did not work forever and ever . . . Daily we can see the birth into this world of new human beings, young children who were nonexistent before; we behold new trees, new animals on the earth, new fish in the water, new birds in the air. And such creation and preservation will continue until the Last Day. (*LW* XXII, 26–27)

In this our ecological era, those who are seeking to recapture long-forgotten traditional theological testimonies to the glory of God in nature and thereby to celebrate God's embrace of the whole creation, not just humankind, will surely want to welcome the kind of theological discourse that we hear in Luther's commentary on John. But if we are theologically to appropriate the promise of Luther's interpretation of the Scriptures for our own purposes, as distinct from merely gathering what may seem to us to be relevant theological quotations, we will have to study the kind of exegetical testimony we meet in Luther's commentary on John in its own context, fraught as that context was with its own complexities and ambiguities.

The necessity of such a contextual approach to Luther's biblical interpretation is already signalled, for those who have eyes to see, by his passing reference above to the whole of creation as 'this building'. By that Luther meant, and he often took this for granted, that the whole earth is constructed and sustained by God to be a home and a blessing *for humans*, as if that were its chief or even only *raison d'être*. As Luther wrote in 1528: 'The Father gives himself to us, with heaven and earth and all the creatures, in order that they may serve us and benefit us' (*LW* XXXVII, 366). This kind of thinking has the ring of a surreptitious but nevertheless ominous anthropocentrism, which could be more counterproductive for our ecological interests today than helpful. Does Luther, then, have a rich understanding of God in nature and yet somehow undercut that understanding by veering in the direction of anthropocentrism? To answer this kind of question, we must probe the varied historical textures and spiritual sensibilities of his thought.

To that end, in turn, it will be necessary for us to follow a somewhat meandering course. We will seek to understand, as carefully as we can in the short compass of an essay, what can be called *the formal and the material elements of Luther's hermeneutic*, with particular attention to his thought about nature, as that term is being used in this essay. We will explore (I) how Luther actually approached the Scriptures and (II) what some of the major theological assumptions were that he brought with him as he formed his judgement about the meanings of biblical texts. These are weighty matters in Luther studies, of course. But we can circumspectly address them in a single essay by depending, wherever possible, on the findings of modern Luther scholarship (see Bayer 2003; Isaac 2001). In a postscript, finally (III), we will consider the challenge of appropriating Luther's formal and material hermeneutic of nature in a contemporary theological context.

I

It is frequently said, in various ways, that Luther was a biblical theologian, not a systematic theologian.³ And there is some truth in that affirmation. As is often noted, Luther never produced a Summa Theologiae nor even an Institutes of the Christian Religion, as Aquinas and Calvin did. Many of Luther's writings, such as his sermons on John, which we have already encountered, were in fact, formally speaking, biblical commentaries, which represented an enormously substantive theological output (Pelikan 1959: 5–31). One noted scholar, indeed, once referred to Luther's commentary on Genesis as Luther's *Summa*.⁴

But the construct 'commentary', as it is understood today, scarcely does justice to what Luther thought he was doing in his interpretations of the Scriptures. Karl Barth's commentary on *Romans*, which precipitated a theological revolution in the first half of the twentieth century, may be the closest example in our era of the kind of biblical interpretation that Luther practised throughout much of his theological career. Luther thought of his work as a commentator as hearing the living voice of God speaking to him, to the church and to the world. In this sense, he can be called an 'existential' interpreter of Scripture, using the language of Otto Pesch (1970). Thus, in interpreting Genesis, as Johannes Schwanke explains, 'Luther interprets primordial history as a history of the present. For Luther, creation is not something past, but something present. Because Luther sees himself in his individuality as created, addressed, and desired by God, the history of creation can be nothing other than present history' (2004: 81).

Of particular significance for his biblical interpretation of the history of creation, moreover, and, in some respects, as we will see presently, for his biblical interpretation of nature in particular, Luther came to believe, with increasing existential pathos during the course of his life, that the end of the world was close at hand. He was, in this respect, a prophet of the Last Days in his preaching and exposition of Scripture and public life in general (Oberman 2001: 193–98).

But we have yet to identify the full concreteness of what can be called Luther's existential interpretation of the Scriptures. Not only did Luther hear the Word of God in the Scriptures addressing the present, even the present eschatologically construed, much more particularly, he was inclined to hear the Word as addressed

---

3   A more sophisticated statement of this kind of distinction has been developed by Otto H. Pesch, who thinks of Luther as an 'existential theologian' and Thomas Aquinas, in comparison, as a 'sapiential theologian' (Pesch 1970). On Luther as a 'biblical theologian' see Pelikan 1959: 46–47.
4   Heiko Oberman, in a lecture at Harvard Divinity School, 1964.

to the individual believer. Thus, Luther distinguished between historical and living faith (*fides historica, fides vera*) (*Werke: Kritische Gesamtausgabe* [*WA*] XXXIX.1, 46.7-8). Even the Devil could believe that Christ died for the sins of the world, Luther would say. But the Devil cannot or will not believe that Christ died *for him*. Call this Luther's existential hermeneutical concentration: my faith, if it is living faith, must be predicated on the conviction that the grace of God is given for me – *pro me*. As Kenneth Hagen has observed, Luther claimed that his biblical work was 'not so much a commentary as a testimony of my faith in Christ' (Hagen 1993: 2). This is not to suggest that Luther's exegesis was some kind of arbitrary testimonial literature. On the contrary, Luther was at home with the best humanistic and monastic scholarship of his day. And he was gifted with an extensive knowledge of the Scriptures, which made it possible for him creatively to view a variety of biblical texts in relationship with many others. Rather, the point here is that, precisely with the benefit of his scholarly approach to Scripture, Luther was personally driven to hear the Word of God speaking to him and his world (Maschke 2001: 181–82).

With Luther's commitment to existential interpretation of the Scripture thus before us, it is possible, and for our purposes necessary, to probe still more deeply into the dynamics of this kind of biblical interpretation. We have seen that Luther's mode of biblical interpretation is fundamentally predicated on the notion of the Word of God *speaking* to the believer. Beneath this, and reinforced by this understanding of the Word of God, is a somewhat more elusive set of interpretative assumptions: Luther's deep commitment to the sensibility of *hearing*, over against the sensibility of seeing.[5] This may seem to be an obvious point at first – for what is speaking without hearing? – but, as we will presently see, it would seem to have profound implications for Luther's understanding of the biblical view of nature.

For Luther, as many observers have noted, and as he himself often stated, 'The ear is the only organ of the Christian' (*LW* XIX.1.1, cited by Miles 1985: 515). This is a typical exegetical comment of the Reformer, regarding the account of Jesus riding into Jerusalem:

> But shut your eyes and open your ears and perceive not how [Christ] rides there so beggarly, but hearken to what is said and preached about this poor king. His wretchedness and poverty are manifest . . . But that he will take from us sin, strangle death, endow us with eternal holiness, eternal bliss, and eternal life, this cannot be seen. Wherefore you must hear and believe. (*WA* XXXVII, 201–202, quoted by Steinmetz 1993: 5)

Since, for Luther, only the Word of God liberates us from sin and reveals to us the purpose of the Creator, '[a] right faith goes right on with its eyes closed; it clings to God's Word; it follows that Word; it believes that Word' (*WA* XLVIII, 48).

---

5   In considering the sensibilities of hearing and seeing, we touch on a highly complex and much discussed subject in Western philosophy and theology; see Blumenberg 1993; Chidester 1992; Levin 1993; Miles 1985.

This emphasis on hearing was no less true of Luther's teaching about the sacraments, where one might have expected, if anywhere, to encounter a shift of sensibility from the moment of hearing to the moment of seeing. But Luther took up, with a passion, the traditional Augustinian view that the sacraments are 'visible Words'. 'You should know', he stated characteristically, 'that the Word of God is the chief thing in the sacrament'. The Word is to the elements, he explained, as the soul is to the body (WA XLVII, 219).

Luther carried through the same agenda architecturally, as well. On occasion, he could speak approvingly of images in the churches, but he generally did so only if those images had an evident pedagogical purpose, only if they communicated the Word (Koerner 2004). Indeed, he liked to think of the church building as a 'mouth-house' (WA X.1.2, 48, cited by Pelikan 1959: 63). It would, therefore, not be an overstatement to characterize the earliest example of a surviving church building designed and built within the Reformation milieu, dedicated by Luther in 1534, the small Schloss Kapelle in Torgau, Germany, precisely in those terms. This was veritably a house for preaching. The elevated pulpit that dominates the plain space dramatically announces that the proclamation of the Word of God is that building's primary purpose. The paintings that are in place, by Luther's friend, the well-known Lucas Cranach, depict Luther preaching, among other images of worship in that space, such as the Lord's Supper. In that chapel space, the sensibility of hearing had triumphed.

We have more of Luther's thought to explore now, as we move from considering his approach to the Scriptures – the formal elements of his hermeneutic – to a review of some of the major theological assumptions he brought with him to his biblical interpretation – the material elements of his hermeneutic. But it will be helpful as we chart this course to make some preliminary observations about the significance of the materials we have just reviewed.

In a chapter entitled 'The Uniqueness of Luther's Theology', the eminent Luther scholar Bernhard Lohse writes:

> What is new [in Luther's theology, compared with earlier theological traditions] is that of all the questions with which theology must deal, the aim and goal in any given instance is the question of salvation. Questions about the doctrine of God, about the sacrament, about ecclesiology, can be dealt with only when this aspect is seen from the outset. (1999: 35)

Whether this focus on salvation is indeed unique to Luther is a question that need not concern us here. That salvation, however, specifically human salvation, is at the heart of Luther's theology is a judgement that illuminates the materials we have reviewed thus far. We have observed Luther's existential approach to the Scriptures and indeed his individualizing, existential hermeneutical concentration: he was wont to hear God addressing him, personally, through the biblical Word, for the sake of his own salvation. That theme we saw is undergirded by his commitment to hearing as the primary sensibility of faith. God speaks, the believer hears in faith and the believer then knows the certainty of his or her salvation. That appears to be the paradigmatic moment of the Christian faith, as far as Luther was concerned.

Missing in all this is any kind of thoroughgoing reference to the larger world of nature. The world of sun and stars and earth, trees and lakes, fish and birds is by no means excluded from Luther's way of approaching the Scriptures. We have already seen an instance, in Luther's commentary on John 1, where that world *is* celebrated by Luther. But what Luther finds himself driven to hear, what he is most fascinated with, is not primarily biblical testimony to the works of God in creation, nor even the consummation of the whole creation (more on this presently). Rather, Luther is driven, passionately, to hear the message of human salvation, and of the individual believer's salvation, in particular. The primacy of the sensibility of hearing in Luther's thinking makes the regular, *de facto* inattention to the greater world of nature as an object of exegetical inquiry almost inevitable, it would seem, at least at the heart of Luther's theology. The Word of God is to be proclaimed to sinful humans, according to Luther's way of thinking, not to beasts of the field or trees and the stars, which have not sinned (*LW* XXII, 29; I, 204–205). The creatures of nature, other than humans, do not have ears to hear the Word. So if the Word is the theological centre, all those creatures will, as a matter of course, if not by intention, be pushed to the periphery, if not out of the picture altogether. This much we can notice at this point in the discussion, on the basis of our consideration of the formal elements of Luther's hermeneutic. Now we turn to consider some of the material elements of his hermeneutic.

II

What are the major theological assumptions that Luther, as a matter of course, brings with him when he seeks to interpret the Scriptures? This is a question that would take a whole volume to answer, but it can be addressed sufficiently here, since most of these elements are so well attested in modern Luther studies. We can conveniently begin by identifying the key distinction that shapes so much of Luther's thinking about the content of theology, at least since the time of his 1518 Heidelberg Dissertation, the difference between a 'theology of glory' and the 'theology of the cross' (McGrath 1985). Luther understands the first to be a kind of speculative theology, which is predicated on theological interpretation of the created world. Had he wished to do so, Luther could have called this, in his own terms, a theology of seeing. For this kind of theology, as Luther understood it, contemplates the created world and moves the mind, by that contemplation, to ascend ultimately to the vision of God. The theology of glory, in Luther's view, also leads inevitably, because of its rationalizing methodology, to a theology of justification by works, in one form or another. The theology of the cross, in contrast, sees only the contradictory, inglorious vision of the Crucified, and knows God hidden and revealed there, by the proclamation of the Word of the cross. That Word mediates the justifying grace of God, according to Luther, which the believer receives by faith alone. From the perspective of the theology of the cross, moreover, the theology of glory, which, in Luther's words, 'sees the invisible things of God in works as perceived by man, is completely puffed up, blinded, and hardened' (*LW* XIX, 52–53, cited by Lohse 1999: 38). Whether this core distinction in Luther's thought allows any sustained contemplation of the larger world of nature seems doubtful. Contemplation of nature would appear to fall under the rejected rubric of the theology of glory.

The distinction between the theology of glory and the theology of the cross is intimately related to another teaching of Luther, just alluded to, perhaps *the* core conviction of his thought, and so recognized by most students of Luther: justification by faith alone, apart from works of the law (Lohse 1999: 74–78). For Luther, 'the article of justification is the master and prince, the lord, the ruler, and the judge over all kinds of doctrines; it preserves and governs all church doctrine . . . Without this article the world is utter death and darkness' (*WA* XXXIX.1, 205). Karl Barth coined the term 'the-anthropology' to describe his own thought, focused as it is on God and humanity. The heart of Luther's theology, as he himself describes it, is the-anthropological in that sense. It focuses on the justifying God and the justified sinner. Luther stated this vividly in a 1532 lecture on Psalm 51:

> Knowledge of God and man is divine wisdom, and in the real sense theological. It is such knowledge of God and man as is related to the justifying God and to sinful man, so that in the real sense the subject of theology is guilty and lost man and the justifying and redeeming God. What is inquired into apart from this question and subject is error and vanity in theology. (*WA* II, 327-28, cited by Lohse 1999: 40)

With this core teaching of Luther in view, as when we considered his distinction between the theology of glory and the theology of the cross, we may wonder what is to become of the larger world of nature in Luther's biblical interpretation, since justification, as Luther understands it, seems to be almost exclusively the-anthropological, a matter of God and humanity alone. The beasts of the fields, for example, do not need to be justified, in Luther's view, even if that were conceivable in his terms, since those creatures have not fallen.

This is not to say that Luther has no significant convictions concerning nature that he brings with him to the interpretation of biblical texts. He does have such convictions, as we have already seen in his commentary on John and as we now must consider in some detail. When we do, we will be able to observe a kind of asymmetrical relationship between the formal and the material elements of Luther's hermeneutic. The two are symmetrical insofar as both are the-anthropocentric. The notion of God speaking to the individual believer, undergirded by the accent on the sensibility of hearing, on the one hand, and the themes of the cross and justification by faith, on the other hand, fit together perfectly, since both these formal and material elements have to do, focally, with God and humanity and since the larger world of nature in this respect is peripheral. But the material elements of Luther's hermeneutic are also more comprehensive than his the-anthropocentrism appears to allow. In a variety of contexts, Luther gives direct attention to, indeed, he tends to be fascinated with, the whole world of nature.

Luther, on occasion, can speak powerfully of the immanence of God in nature, of the Creator's majestic presence 'in, with and under' all the creatures of the natural world. Luther can envision the whole creation as the 'mask of God' (WA XL.1, 94). This means, for Luther, that God is hidden there. But it also means that God is powerfully present there. Luther thinks of the Creator as being 'with all creatures, flowing and pouring into them, filling all things' (WA X, 143). For Luther, therefore, creation is not merely some transcendental event before the beginning of time. The Divine act of creation is also now, as we saw in Luther's commentary on John 1. In this connection, Luther has a rich and sophisticated, albeit paradoxical, understanding of the dynamism of the divine immanence:

> God is substantially present everywhere, in and through all creatures, in all their parts and places, so that the world is full of God and He fills all, but without His being encompassed and surrounded by it. He is at the same time outside and above all creatures. These are all exceedingly incomprehensible matters; yet they are articles of our faith and are attested clearly and mightily in Holy Scripture . . . For how can reason tolerate it that the Divine Majesty is so small that it can be substantially present in a grain, on a grain, through a grain, within and without, and that, although it is a single Majesty, it nevertheless is entirely in each grain separately, no matter how immeasurably numerous these grains may be? . . . And that the same Majesty is so large that neither this world nor a thousand worlds can encompass it and say: 'Behold, there it is!' . . . His own divine essence can be in all creatures collectively and in each one individually more profoundly, more intimately, more present than the creature is in itself, yet it can be encompassed nowhere and by no one. It encompasses all things and dwells in all, but not one thing encompasses it and dwells in it. (WA XXIII, 134.34–136.36, cited by Bornkamm 1965: 189)

How then does Luther think of the individual believer's relationship to the whole world of nature thus charged with the powerful presence of God? He gives a variety of answers to this question.

First, for Luther there is, as it were, no direct line of communion between the believer and the God who is in, with and under the larger world of nature. That God is masked. Indeed, for Luther, that God – 'the Majesty' as we have heard him say – is terrifying. So Luther counsels the believer always to seek God in the Word of the cross, not in nature.

Second, the believer – along with all other humans – will, as a matter of course, encounter the whole world of nature as cursed by God. Twenty-first-century ears may not be attuned to such language, but Luther takes it very seriously. The curse of God is the heritage of the fall of Adam and Eve, as Luther sees it. Especially in his Genesis commentary, Luther can describe sinful humanity's relationship with the world of nature in great and vivid detail.

> [T]he earth, which is innocent and committed no sin, is nevertheless compelled to endure a curse . . . [I]t will be freed from this on the Last Day, for which it is waiting . . . [Under the curse,] in the first place, it does not bring forth the good things it would have produced if man had not fallen. In the second place, it produces many harmful plants, which it would not have produced, such as darnel, wild oats, weeds, nettles, thorns, thistles. Add to these the poisons, the injurious vermin, and whatever else there is of this kind. All these things were brought in through sin (*LW* I, 204).

Further, Luther believed that the curse was made more severe following the time of what he reckoned to have been the flood and, indeed, that the effects of the curse of God on nature were being felt with increasing severity in the days at the end of the world in which Luther believed that he was living: 'The world is deteriorating from day to day' (*LW* I, 206). So Luther concludes: 'The closer the world is to its end, the worse human beings become. For this reason it also happens that harsher punishments are exacted from us' (*LW* I, 216).

Thirdly, and in marked contrast with his ideas of nature as the mask of – the hidden – God and nature as cursed by God because of human sin, Luther from time to time gives voice to paeans of praise for the goodness of God in creation (Gregersen 2005). Luther's well-known words in his explanation of the first article of the Apostles' Creed are typical of many other utterances, especially in his Genesis commentary:

> I believe that God has created me and all that exists; that he has given me and still sustains my body and soul, all my limbs and sense, my reason and all the faculties of my mind, together with goods and clothing, house and home, family and property; that he provides me daily and abundantly with all the necessities of life, protects me from all danger, and preserves me from all evil. All this he does out of his pure, fatherly, and divine goodness and mercy, without any merit or worthiness on my part. (1959 ['Small Catechism']: 345)

In the same vein, Luther sees the creative Word of God providing the grain that sustains human life:

> We are . . . to praise and thank God for making the grain to grow. We are to recognize that it is not our work but His blessing and gift that grain, wine, and all kinds of crops grow, for us to eat and drink and use for our needs, as is shown in the Lord's Prayer when we say: 'Give us this day our daily bread' . . . [W]hen we see a whole field or one grain, we should recognize not only God's goodness but also His power . . . And with [that] great power He protects you [Luther says to the wheat itself]! What dangers have you not survived from the hour when you were sown until you are put on the table! (*LW* XIV, 122)

In this sense, for Luther, the grace of God is experienced in both creation and redemption.

This is the context, then, in which Luther's various references to the creation as a divinely made 'building' for the human creature should be understood. Luther is thinking in such settings of the overflowing goodness of God in nature, rather than some kind of property that is given to human creatures to own for their own purposes. True, Luther does restate a traditional theological view of human dominion over the earth, dependent on the words of Gen. 1.28-30: '. . . you must use the things given and granted to you by God in His kindness. You must rule, work, and strive not to tempt God' (*LW* V, 256). But this kind of statement is never translated by Luther into any kind of mandate for the economic transformation of nature.

As a citizen of the sixteenth century, moreover, Luther obviously did not have a twenty-first-century ecological consciousness nor, with that, was he aware of the radical transformations and, indeed, desecrations of nature that would result from the triumph of the spirit of modern capitalism. Nevertheless, Luther was highly critical of many of the policies of early capitalism, particularly that system's exploitation of the poor. Luther's best ethical counsel, indeed, was that believers should always focus on serving the neighbour, which was an ethical stance that he distinguished from the spirit of profit and the drive to acquire goods (Lindberg 2003). Luther understood human 'dominion', then, primarily in terms of service to the neighbour in need, as he wrote in his Genesis commentary: 'God does not give out his gifts so that we can rule and have power over others or so that we should spurn their opinion and judgement: rather so that we should serve those who are in such a case as to need our counsel and help' (*LW* II, 239).

All this Luther can proclaim under the rubric of the sensibility of hearing. All this is a theological *inference*, as it were, from the believer's originating encounter with the proclaimed Word of God. Directly, for Luther, as we have seen, there is no access of any import to the knowledge of God in the world of nature. That would be to enter the province of the theology of glory, in Luther's view. Indeed, nature in itself does, in fact, mask God. Moreover, it is God's Majesty that is active in nature, in overwhelmingly powerful ways, and no one can see the Majesty of God and live. Still, Luther can celebrate the glorious power of God in, with and under nature, as we have just seen, with a kind of mystical passion, however hidden he believes that presence to be and however cursed nature might be, due to human sin. And Luther can also consistently celebrate the blessings that God pours down on human creatures throughout the world of nature.

Further, and strikingly, there are times when Luther seems to move beyond the sensibility of hearing, which he treasures so much, to a kind of contemplation of nature, which could only be born of the sensibility of seeing. This is no theology of glory, in his terms. It is something else.

First, it has to do with what appears to be, for Luther, the new, sanctified life of the believer, who has been justified by faith and who has then received the gift of the Spirit. Redeemed existence, in this sense, seems to bring with it, as Luther thinks about it, a new and more vital, even a contemplative relationship with the whole world of nature. So Luther writes in his commentary on John:

> Now if I believe in God's Son and bear in mind that He became man, all creatures will appear

a hundred times more beautiful to me than before. Then I will properly appreciate the sun, the moon, the stars, trees, apples, pears, as I reflect that he is Lord over and the center of all things. (*LW* XXII, 496)

By 1544, in a sermon, Luther can even somewhat self-consciously shift his discourse from the sensibility of hearing to the sensibility of seeing, alluding as he does to the traditional theological image of the two books of God, the book of Scripture and the book of nature:

Our home, farm, field, garden, and everything, is full of Bible, where God through his wondrous works not only preaches, but also knocks on our eyes, touches our senses, and somehow enlightens our hearts. (*WA* XLIX, 434, quoted by Gregersen 2005: 28)

In the very last year of his life, remarkably, Luther as a matter of course invokes the sensibility of seeing, as he writes a notation in a volume of Pliny's works: 'All creation is the most beautiful book or Bible; in it God has described and portrayed Himself' (*WA* XLVIII, 201.5-6, quoted by Bornkamm 1965: 179). In this sense, for Luther, the justified sinner who has heard the Word of the cross can begin to see nature with new eyes.

Secondly, from this perspective as a redeemed creature in Christ, Luther also seems to have found a way to see the world as God originally intended it to be, 'before the fall'. Luther at times can present an almost Franciscan vision of that primal human identity in nature, particularly with regard to human corporeality. So in his Genesis commentary, where countless doctors of the church had sung the praises of human rationality, under the rubric of the image of God, Luther states that the fact that Adam and Eve walked about naked was their greatest adornment before God and all creatures. In the same vein, Luther envisions Adam and Eve as enjoying a 'common table' with the animals before the fall (*LW* I, 42).

Thirdly, Luther further envisions the sanctified life of the believer, who has been justified by faith, as standing on the threshold of the eschatologically consummated creation. In the following utterance, the sensibility of seeing has definitely taken over Luther's thinking. And his eschatological consciousness has here been shaped by hope and joy, as distinct from the moods of fear and foreboding which sometimes seem to inform Luther's mind and heart most deeply, especially when he is agonizing about the curse of God on nature:

We are now living in the dawn of the future life; for we are beginning to regain a knowledge of the creation, a knowledge forfeited by the fall of Adam. Now we have a correct view of the creatures, more so, I suppose, than they have in the papacy. Erasmus does not concern himself with this; it interests him little how the fetus is made in the womb . . . But by God's mercy we can begin to recognize His wonderful works and wonders also in flowers when we ponder his might and goodness. Therefore we laud, magnify, and thank him. (*WA* [*Tischreden*]: I, 1160, cited by Bornkamm 1965: 184)

All this Luther sees – the proper word – coming together and majestically transfigured on the Day of the consummation of all things, beyond every hint of Divine judgement:

> Then there will also be a new heaven and a new earth, the light of the moon will be as the light of the sun, and the light of the sun will be sevenfold . . . That will be a broad and beautiful heaven and a joyful earth, much more beautiful and joyful than Paradise was. (*LW* XII, 119, 121)

This vision of the end time articulates and completes Luther's occasionally lavish statements about the sanctified life of the justified sinner in the world of nature.

III

At this point the historical task ends. But it may be helpful to ask, as a postscript, how, if at all, Luther's hermeneutic of nature might be appropriated by theologians today. Some individual themes would probably need to be reconfigured, such as Luther's suggestive but underdeveloped treatment of human dominion on the earth or his passionate, yet, to most moderns (we may imagine), perplexing view of the divine curse of the earth. Other themes, such as Luther's rich theology of divine immanence, would doubtlessly commend themselves for deeper exploration.[6]

But the greatest challenge for theologians who may wish to claim Luther's hermeneutic of nature as their own today would undoubtedly be coming to terms with what might be called the the-anthropocentric axis of his theology. That axis tends to drive Luther's vivid attestations to God in nature and to nature itself to the outer edges of his thought or out of the picture altogether, as a matter of consistent emphasis, if in no other way – a tendency which would become the rule as Luther's thought was appropriated by many of his theological heirs (Santmire 1985: 121–43). This is the legacy of the asymmetrical character of the formal and material elements of his hermeneutic.

This would be the challenge, then: to explore whether the axis of his thought could be construed two-dimensionally. Could it be construed both in terms of God and humanity and in terms of God and nature, that is, both the-anthropocentrically and, to introduce a parallel term, the-cosmocentrically? This, in order to bring Luther's rich affirmations about God and nature and nature itself into the centre of the theological narrative. Which could thereby have the positive effect of allowing the formal and the material elements of Luther's hermeneutic to bond much more symmetrically than the single axis of God and humanity permits. The heart of theological narrative would then be this: the story of God and humanity, on the one hand, and the story of God and the whole world of nature, on the other – all viewed as one unfolding narrative of the divine economy.

---

6 For one attempt to develop Luther's theology of divine immanence systematically in the context of the theology of nature, see Santmire 2008, especially 108–31.

To this end, following some of Luther's own affirmations and perhaps building all the more so on the insights of Calvin (see Dyrness 2004; Zachman 2007), the fundamentally the-anthropocentric sensibility of hearing in Luther's thought could be reconfigured as a sensibility of hearing-and-seeing. This would allow us to envision nature from the vantage point of the justified sinner now being sanctified, to see nature with new eyes. Inspired by the Spirit, we would then be enabled to contemplate nature as Calvin did, as 'the theater of God's glory' (Schreiner 1991), in a way that would disclose its divinely charged beauty and goodness and mystery, but which would steer clear of any kind of theology of glory. This would be a theology of seeing through a glass darkly, but seeing nevertheless, all in the context of hearing-faith. And this would be the vision: the whole of nature at the centre of things, along with humanity.[7]

The new the-cosmocentric dimension of the theological axis could be further secured with the introduction of a theological theme that seems to be totally missing from Luther's thought – and from much of the theological tradition as well – the integrity of nature (Santmire 1985). This is the theme, arguably biblical, that God has purposes for the whole creation, and for all the creatures that dwell therein, purposes which are independent of the divine purposes with humanity alone (Santmire 1970: 133–39). Given with this theme, too, would be the notion of nature's mysterious otherness and, indeed, its virtual incomprehensibility in the larger scheme of things, a thought that could easily be undergirded by drawing on Luther's vision of the hidden God in, with and under the whole world of nature. Human salvation would still be a central theme in this reconfiguration, as it was for Luther, but with this understanding, which Luther himself affirmed exegetically: according to the Pauline image, we would hear and see the whole creation groaning in travail, waiting in hope for the liberation of the human creature and then, finally, for the divine consummation of all things.

References

Bayer, O. 2003 'Luther as an Interpreter of Scripture', in D.K. McKim (ed.), *The Cambridge Companion to Martin Luther* (Cambridge: Cambridge University Press): 73–85.
Blumenberg, H. 1993 'Light as a Metaphor for Truth: At the Preliminary Stage of Philosophical Concept Formation', in D.M. Levin (ed.), *Modernity and the Hegemony of Vision* (Berkeley: University of California): 30–62.
Bornkamm, H. 1965 *Luther's World of Thought* (tr. M. H. Bertram; St. Louis: Concordia).
Chidester, D. 1992 *Word and Light: Seeing, Hearing, and Religious Discourse* (Urbana: University of Chicago Press).

---

7   Obviously, this kind of formulation would have to be explicated in a variety of ways, if it were to be theologically satisfactory. One particularly critical issue would be to address human embodiment in nature and whether, or in what respect, it is possible to talk about the embodied human self as transcending nature, as nature is here understood.

Dyrness, W.A. 2004 *Reformed Theology and Visual Culture: The Protestant Imagination from Calvin to Edwards* (Cambridge: Cambridge University Press).
Gregersen, N.H. 2005 'Grace in Nature and History: Luther's Doctrine of Creation Revisited', *Dialog* 44: 19–29.
Hagen, K. 1993 *Luther's Approach to Scripture as Seen in his 'Commentaries' on Galatians 1519–1538* (Tübingen: Mohr Siebeck).
Isaac, G.L. 2001 'The Changing Image of Luther as Biblical Expositor', in T. Maschke, F. Posset and J. Skocir (eds), Ad Fontes Lutheri: *Toward the Recovery of the Real Luther: Essays in Honor of Kenneth Hagen's Sixty-Fifth Birthday* (Milwaukee: Marquette University Press): 67–85.
Koerner, J. 2004 *The Reformation of the Image* (Chicago: University of Chicago).
Levin, D.M. (ed.) 1993 *Modernity and the Hegemony of Vision* (Berkeley: University of California).
Lindberg, C. 2003 'Luther's Struggle With Social-Ethical Issues', in D.K. McKim (ed.), *The Cambridge Companion to Martin Luther* (Cambridge: Cambridge University Press): 165–78.
Lohse, B. 1999 *Martin Luther's Theology: Its Historical and Systematic Development* (tr. and ed. R.A. Harrisville; Minneapolis: Fortress).
Luther, M. *Luther's Works* [*LW*] (ed.) J. Pelikan and H. Lehman (St Louis/Philadelphia: Concordia/Muhlenberg 1955–1976).
Luther, M. 1959 'Small Catechism', in T.G. Tappert (tr. and ed.), *The Book of Concord* (Philadelphia: Fortress).
Luther, M. *Werke: Kritische Gesamtausgabe* [*WA*] (Weimar 1883–2005).
Maschke, T. 2001 'Contemporaneity: A Hermeneutical Perspective in Martin Luther's Work', in T. Maschke, F. Posset and J. Skocir (eds), Ad Fontes Lutheri: *Toward the Recovery of the Real Luther: Essays in Honor of Kenneth Hagen's Sixty-Fifth Birthday* (Milwaukee: Marquette University Press): 165–82.
McGrath, A.E. 1985 *Luther's Theology of the Cross: Martin Luther's Theological Breakthrough* (Oxford/New York: Basil Blackwell).
Miles, M. 1985 *Image as Insight: Visual Understanding in Western Christianity and Secular Culture* (Boston: Beacon).
Oberman, H. 2001 'Martin Luther Contra Medieval Monasticism: A Friar in the Lion's Den', in T. Maschke, F. Posset and J. Skocir (eds), Ad Fontes Lutheri: *Toward the Recovery of the Real Luther: Essays in Honor of Kenneth Hagen's Sixty-Fifth Birthday* (Milwaukee: Marquette University Press): 183–213.
Pelikan, J. 1959 *Luther the Expositor: Introduction to the Reformer's Exegetical Writings* (St Louis: Concordia). Companion volume to Luther, M., 1959 *Luther's Works*.
Pesch, O.H. 1970 'Existential and Sapiential Theology: The Theological Confrontation Between Luther and Thomas Aquinas', in J. Wicks (ed.), *Catholic Scholars Dialogue with Luther* (Chicago: Loyola University Press): 61–81.
Santmire, H.P. 1970 *Brother Earth: Nature, God, and Ecology in a Time of Crisis* (New York: Thomas Nelson).
Santmire, H.P. 1985 *The Travail of Nature: The Ambiguous Ecological Promise of Christian Theology* (Minneapolis: Fortress).
Santmire, H.P. 2008 *Ritualizing Nature: Renewing Christian Liturgy in a Time of Crisis* (Minneapolis: Fortress).
Schreiner, S.E. 1991 *The Theater of His Glory: Nature and the Natural Order in the Thought of John Calvin* (Grand Rapids: Baker).
Schwanke, J. 2004 'Luther on Creation', in T.J. Wengert (ed.), *Harvesting Martin Luther's Reflections on Theology, Ethics, and the Church*, (Grand Rapids: Eerdmans): 78–98.
Steinmetz, D. 1993 'Luther and Loyola', *Interpretation* 67: 5–14.
Zachman, R.C. 2007 *Image and Word in the Theology of John Calvin* (Notre Dame, IN: University of Notre Dame).

Chapter 13

'REMAINING LOYAL TO THE EARTH': HUMANITY, GOD'S OTHER CREATURES AND THE BIBLE IN KARL BARTH

Geoff Thompson

Introduction

In the opening pages of his anthropology, Karl Barth (1886–1968) offered the following warning in relation to a proper Christian account of the human creature: 'If we forget that he must remain loyal to the earth, we shall never truly understand him'. (*CD* III/2: 4).[1] This statement may seem to offer a surprisingly promising beginning for a chapter on Barth's theology in the present volume. Surprising, because so many of Barth's leading ideas and doctrinal commitments, not least those related to his reading of the Bible, would initially seem to be deeply problematic in any conversation about the Bible, Christian theology and environmental ethics. Critics would point to his sustained polemic against 'natural theology', his designation of creation as the 'external' basis of the covenant (with its *prima facie* suggestion of an instrumentalist posture towards creation), his emphasis on the covenant between God and humanity and his insistence that the biblical witness is centred on Jesus Christ's fulfilment of *that* covenant. In fact, such critics would *not* be surprised to find that in the early pages of his doctrine of creation Barth writes that 'man is and represents the secret of the creature' (*CD* III/1: 18). Indeed, taken on their own, this cluster of views could seem at once to locate him among the proponents of precisely that kind of Christian theology which is said to be culpable for the contemporary environmental crisis (e.g. White 1967). In fact, Barth's theology might well be taken as a prime instance of the 'long anthropocentric, patriarchal, and androcentric approach to reading the text that has devalued the Earth' (Habel 2008: 1).

Yet, even granting certain *prima facie* impressions of Barth's theology, the concerns of Barth and the ecotheologians do overlap at one point: they share a sustained critique of and resistance to anthropocentrism. Of course, their respective motivations for such critique and resistance are as divergent as are their endpoints. Nevertheless it does make for an interesting point of entry for Barth into

---

1 All references to Barth's *Church Dogmatics* will be indicated in parentheses in the main body of the text in the format, either *CD* or *KD* vol/part: page(s). Full bibliographical details are included in the References under Barth 1945, 1956, 1957a, 1958, 1960.

contemporary ecotheological debates. Indeed, both his christological understanding of the Bible and his powerful *Nein* to natural theology – the very moves which might be taken as confirming his place among the 'long anthropocentric reading of the text' – are themselves significantly shaped by his particular critique and rejection of anthropocentrism. Of course, Barth did not respond to anthropocentrism by devaluing the human or by turning his attention to the non-human world. Instead, he exposed the anthropocentric tendencies which had taken hold in some of the basic presuppositions of the prevailing theology, not least in the reading of the Bible, and then proceeded to develop a theology freed from those tendencies. What follows in this chapter will, therefore, be an exploration of Barth's own diagnosis of anthropocentric tendencies in Christian theology and of how his own christocentric theology – which was itself based on a certain way of reading the Bible – led to a particular account of the human person, the natural world and the relationships between them. This will involve going well beyond the *prima facie* impressions of Barth's theology.

Uncovering Anthropocentrism

Introductions to Barth's theology are replete with accounts of his break with the liberal Protestant theology in which he had been formed during his theological education. His epochal commentaries on Romans, his shift from the pastorate to academia and his growing commitment to the task of dogmatics are all well documented.[2] Key developments in this intellectual conversion and its aftermath included his discovery that 'within the Bible there is a strange, new world, the world of God' (Barth 1957b: 33), his 'recognition of what Kierkegaard called the "infinite qualitative distinction" between time and eternity' (Barth 1933: 10) and his unfolding commitment to theology as the science of God rather than of the religious experience of human beings. Indeed, it is this latter point which more than any other crystallizes the central issue at stake and was pithily summed up in one of his frequently quoted statements: 'one cannot speak of God simply by speaking of man in a loud voice' (Barth 1957c: 196).

It is tempting to read these various aspects of Barth's theology as merely episodes in an academically domesticated discussion about theological method. Yet Barth's theological reorientation was set within a much broader cultural horizon. For Barth, anthropocentrism was not simply a methodological foible of certain allegedly misguided Christian theologians – it was the symptom of an entire culture. In fact, on Barth's reading it was something of a compensatory, rearguard reaction precisely to the implied *loss* of human status which accompanied the so-called advances of modern thought, specifically those associated with the newly expanding awareness

---

2   For overviews of the genesis, development and content of Barth's theology see, for example, Busch 2004, Mangina 2004, Webster 2000. For the most comprehensive and authoritative account of the nature of Barth's break with liberalism, see McCormack 1995.

of the scale of the cosmos. Barth notes these developments in the fascinating second and third chapters of his *Protestant Theology in the Nineteenth Century*, the chapters headed 'Man in the Eighteenth Century' and 'The Problem in the Eighteenth Century'. Although not published until 1947, this material had been presented as lectures in 1932 and 1933. Barth acknowledges that the 'eighteenth-century man . . . could no longer remain ignorant of the significance of the fact that Copernicus and Galileo were right, that this vast and rich earth of his, the theatre of his deeds was not the centre of the universe, but a grain of dust amid countless others in the universe' (Barth 2001: 23). Did this lead to more modest accounts of the human, to an 'unprecedented and boundless humiliation of man'? According to Barth, quite the contrary:

> [N]o, man is all the greater for this, man is the centre of all things, in a quite different sense, too, for he was able to discover this revolutionary truth by his own resources and to think it abstractly . . .: clearly now the world was even more and properly so *his* world! It is paradoxical and yet it is a fact that the answer to his humiliation was those philosophical systems of rationalism, empiricism and scepticism which made men even more self-confident. The geocentric picture of the universe was replaced as a matter of course by the anthropocentric. (Barth 2001: 23)

Intriguingly, Barth also notes in the same chapter that this same eighteenth-century 'man' did, in fact, have 'very close ties with nature' and that these ties 'were far from being simply of the kind which lead man to study nature scientifically and exploit it for gain; they could also be felt and enjoyed aesthetically' (Barth 2001: 41). Yet, beyond this apparent ecological harmony Barth detects something less balanced:

> It is, however, . . . a humanized nature, a nature which has been put to rights and formed in accordance with man's sensibility and enjoyment, an idealized, and more preferably a visibly idealized nature . . .; a nature which even after the grooming it has had to endure is really beautiful only when there is a Greek temple, a statue or a bust somewhere about which quite unequivocally serves as a reminder of the lords of creation. (Barth 2001: 41)

Therefore, at least part of the background to Barth's own constructive theology is a keen awareness of the immodesty of modern Western humanity, and its willingness to resist and indeed obscure its modest place in the universe. Of course, neither this immodest humanity nor humanized nature were by themselves the presenting issues in his theology. But the associated and consequent 'attempt . . . to humanize Christianity' (Barth 2001: 110) was. Barth's target was a Christianity tailored to the capacity of the human. 'Christianity', he wrote, 'was affirmed, but men affirmed it with a secret sovereignty which already seemed to make it questionable whether what was being affirmed was still Christianity' (Barth 2001: 91). The willingness of Christians – and Christian theologians – to exercise this 'secret sovereignty' had produced a Christianity – and a Christian theology – in which 'we have measured

God with our own measure, conceived of God with our own conceptions, wished ourselves a God according to our own wishes' (Barth 1957b: 47).

Consequently, Barth's counter to modernity's self-aggrandized human being was neither a renewed geocentrism nor a simple subordination of the 'human' to the 'divine'. Instead, Barth's counter was a more christocentric Christianity – one in which humanity's proper place could be recognized – or, more exactly, was revealed – in the unity of God and humanity in Jesus Christ. But in drawing Christian theology away from what he perceived to be its compromise with modern anthropocentrism Barth targeted two particular elements of the theology which on his reading were symptomatic of its anthropocentric tendencies: its appeal to natural theology and its dependence on the historicism of historical-critical exegesis. And in drawing Christian theology towards what he believed was its true object, namely God revealed in Jesus Christ, he proposed a theology which began not with nature but with the biblical witness and which involved a way of reading that witness which dislodged the interpreter from any position of hermeneutical sovereignty. These two counter proposals – both driven in their own way by Barth's critique of modern anthropocentrism and theology's compromise with it – had significant implications for his engagement with what would become the pivotal resource for his doctrine of creation, i.e. the creation narratives of Genesis. So, before turning to examine Barth's engagement with those texts, it will be important to explore his critique of both natural theology and modern biblical hermeneutics.

Natural Theology

Barth's critique of natural theology is broad-ranging, sustained and uncompromising. Of his early engagements with these issues, the best known is his 1934 provocative and somewhat intemperate rejoinder to Emil Brunner's 'Nature and Grace' (Brunner 2002). Barth gave his rejoinder the simple title: 'No! Answer to Emil Brunner' (Barth 2002b). Another important early occasion for Barth's evaluation and response to natural theology was his 1937/38 Gifford Lectures published in 1938 as *The Knowledge of God and the Service of God According to the Teaching of the Reformation*.[3] For this brief engagement with Barth on natural theology I will refer firstly to the later text, largely because it sets out the issues more systematically, before drawing on the earlier text to make a more specific point.

In the Gifford Lectures, Barth takes up the theme of natural theology in the context of an exposition of the Scots Confession. Here he presents natural theology as an outright alternative to the Reformed faith (see Barth 1938: 1–4). What is of interest for the present discussion, however, is that in his definition of natural theology he relates it to a quite specific human posture towards its object. It consists, he indicates,

---

3   For Barth's developed reflections on natural theology see *CD* II/1: 63–178.

of a knowledge of God and God's connection with the world which 'perhaps requires and is capable of development and cultivation, but is none the less a knowledge which man as man is master of, just as he is of chemical and astronomical knowledge' (Barth 1938: 4). It is a knowledge of God – or at least a claim to the knowledge of God – which 'declares that man himself possesses the capacity and the power to inform himself about God, the world and man' (Barth 1938: 9). Then, in his exposition of the Confession's first article on 'the one God', Barth points out that such a confession, in contrast to the 'mastery' of natural theology, 'means the limiting of human self-assertion' (Barth 1938: 17). Barth notes that while the denial of this confession and the voice of human self-assertion which accompanies it was indeed 'heard and obeyed long before the time of Descartes', nevertheless the 'Cartesian revolution' gave particular licence to this phenomenon. So, employing the same language already developed in his lectures on nineteenth-century theology he writes:

> The modern world has failed to hear the warning of the Reformed confession precisely at this point and has thought fit to exchange the medieval conception of the world as geocentric for the much more naïve conception of the world as anthropocentric. (Barth 1938: 17)

For Barth, therefore, although essentially a spiritual issue which constantly threatens the confession of faith, natural theology comes into particular relief in the modern era. It both reflects and feeds on a human self-assertion which is part of an anthropocentric conception of the world. But for Barth, the theological issues are deeper still. For if the human creature positions itself to stand in judgement on God, can it really be God who is the object of the judgement? This is one of the issues which Barth presses upon Brunner and in doing so makes it clear that it is inseparable from the question of theological method. This concern is reflected in the following definition of natural theology.

> By 'natural theology' I mean every (positive or negative) formulation of a system which claims to be theological, i.e., to interpret divine revelation, whose subject, however, differs fundamentally from the revelation in Jesus Christ and whose *method* therefore differs equally from the exposition of Holy Scripture. (Barth 2002b: 74)

A different method of theology implies a different divine subject.[4] Thus the theological issues at stake in the matter of where theological work begins and how it proceeds could scarcely be higher. And it is exactly this concern which provides the background to Barth's objections to creation *per se* as divine revelation. Such appeals 'differ fundamentally' from the revelation in Jesus Christ, and the attempt so to interpret divine revelation is something which 'differs' from the exposition of Holy Scripture.

---

4   Eberhard Busch captures exactly this line of Barth's thought: 'The result [of natural theology] is that God is not only known via another *way*, but is known as *another* God' (Busch 2004: 177).

This is what Barth believed he encountered in Brunner's suggestion that because God 'leaves the imprint of his nature upon what he does', it follows that 'the creation of the world is at the same time a revelation, a self-revelation of God' (Brunner 2002: 25). Brunner maintained that there are 'two revelations, that in creation and that in Jesus Christ' (Brunner 2002: 26) and that in the first the 'creator is in some way recognisable' (Brunner 2002: 24). In his sharp response to these claims, Barth puts this question to Brunner: '[I]f we really do know the true God from his creation without Christ and without the Holy Spirit . . . how can it be said . . . that in matters of the proclamation of the Church Scripture is the only norm . . .?' (Barth 2002b: 82).

Barth's insistence on looking to scripture instead of creation in order to interpret revelation cannot, therefore, be reduced to merely an instance of a generic or polemical Protestant appeal to the primacy of scripture. It is embedded in a set of concerns about natural theology which in turn reflect wider concerns about 'human self-assertion' and a 'secret human sovereignty' exercised in a particularly strident way in modern Western culture. Yet it turns out that the insistence on the primacy of scripture does not by itself provide immediate relief from the anthropocentrism feeding natural theology. For, on Barth's analysis, the reading of the Bible governed by modern hermeneutics reflected that same human assertion and those same claims to sovereignty.

The Bible and Its Interpretation

Explicit references to anthropocentrism do not feature in Barth's engagement with modern hermeneutics in the way they do in his rejection of natural theology. But the issue of human posture towards God clearly does. In his seminal 1917 lecture, 'The Strange New World within the Bible', Barth suggests that the human question which asks 'What is within the Bible?' has a 'mortifying way of converting itself into the opposing question, "Well what are you looking for, and who are you, pray, who make bold to look?"'(Barth 1957b: 32). The same inversion of the human and divine which was at issue in the discussion of natural theology repeatedly comes to the surface in Barth's various reflections on the Bible and hermeneutics. The inflated humanity which affects the reading of the Bible involves a displacement of the true object of interpretation. Countering this, again to quote the 1917 lecture, Barth has the Bible speak back to the modern interpreter with these words: 'You wanted to be mirrored in me, and now you have really found in me your own reflection. But now I bid you come seek *me* as well' (Barth 1957b: 33).

Of course, as Barth's reflections deepen and develop the stress will fall on the fact that it is God who speaks *through* the Bible. Indeed, it was this conviction that lay behind his early wrestling with historical criticism. It came to the fore in his commentaries on Romans and was the focus of Barth's response to his critics in his preface to the second edition. Barth's point was that the historical critics, by confining themselves to literary, archaeological and philological matters in order to understand Paul, stopped short of the very thing, *die Sache*, which preoccupied Paul and propelled his writing, i.e. God's revelation in Jesus Christ. Of such critics he thus wrote: 'Remaining at this level of the textual engagement they failed to recognize the existence of any real substance at all, of any underlying problem, of any Word in the words' (Barth 1933: 9). Therefore, according to Barth, the 'critical historian needs to be more critical' (Barth 1933: 8).[5] Indeed, Barth notes an absence of any real 'struggling' with the text on the part of modern exegetes.[6] In fact, not to engage this struggle is really to exclude God from the exegetical process. As such, in Bruce McCormack's summary of Barth's critique, 'exegesis ... is made an independent human activity, isolated from the process of knowing God' (McCormack 2002: xx). In contrast to such exegesis, Barth claims that the 'matter contained in the text cannot be released save by a creative straining of the sinews' (Barth 1933: 8). The process of interpretation is thus presented as a 'conversation between the original record and reader [which] moves around the subject matter' (Barth 1933: 7).[7] Yet 'conversation' seems more passive than the overall picture Barth presents of the act of interpretation. In fact, it is more a two-way 'struggle' – as hinted at in the following passage from the preface to the third edition. Here Barth combines in an active, dynamic way his insistence on the given words of the text, the indispensability of interpretation, and the real subject (or 'heart' or 'spirit') of the text:

> Is there any way of penetrating the heart of a document ... except on the assumption that its spirit will speak to our spirit through the actual written words? This does not exclude criticism of the letter by the spirit, which is indeed, unavoidable. It is precisely a strict faithfulness which compels us to expand and abbreviate the text, lest a too rigid attitude to the words should obscure that which is struggling to expression in them and which demands expression. (Barth 1933: 18–19)

Despite their rudimentary nature, in these attempts to distinguish his approach from that of the historical critics many of the contours of Barth's developed understanding of scripture and its interpretation are laid down. The arguments developed in the debate about Romans will be extended to the whole Bible.[8] It is a human word which manifestly requires interpretation, and exactly as this interpretable word it bears

---

5   Barth's point here is crystallized by Bruce McCormack: '[I]f the texts that the exegete confronts are essentially *witness*, proclamation, then a truly "scientific" approach to exegesis will seek methods and strategies in accordance with their true character' (McCormack 2002: xx).
6   See Barth 1933: 7. The reference here is to Adolf Jülicher whom Barth cites as typical of modern exegetes.
7   On this see John Webster's description of Barth's account of the interpretation of scripture as 'an episode in the communicative history of God with us' (Webster 2001: 93).
8   For the extended texts in which this development can be seen, see his discussion of the Reformed scripture principle in Barth 2002a: 38–64 and the account of 'Holy Scripture' in CD I/2: 457–740.

witness to God's revelation.[9] God speaks in sovereign freedom – but not arbitrarily: the canonical witness is the 'sphere' where God has spoken and the 'same sphere' where God 'has thereby promised to speak anew' (Barth 2003: 66).[10] In order to hear this Word of the sovereign God, the interpreter must eschew 'our usual self-assured mastery' (*CD* I/2: 470) of the text and our 'evil domination of the text' (*CD* I/2: 471). Assuming this more modest but still engaged posture towards the text

> there can be no question of our achieving, as we do in others, the confident approach which masters and subdues the matter. It is rather a question of our being gripped by the subject-matter ... so that it is only as those who are mastered by the subject-matter, who are subdued by it, that we can investigate the humanity of the word by which it is told us. (*CD* I/2: 470)

Above all, however, this divine revelation, the 'subject matter' which 'struggles to expression' will be more explicitly defined as the Word of God spoken in Jesus Christ as the fulfilment of the covenant between God and humanity. It is this which – at least from the perspective of biblical scholars, and by extension that of the ecotheologians – is arguably the most problematic aspect of Barth's theology of scripture: Jesus Christ – either in expectation or recollection – is the subject matter of all the texts of scripture. 'Scripture ... is the witness of the Old and New Testaments, the witness of the expectation and recollection, the witness of the preparation and the accomplishment of the revelation achieved in Jesus Christ' (*CD* I/2: 481).

These various convictions about the Bible and the rejection of natural theology have deep and manifold foundations. Nevertheless, their respective features and accents were shaped, in part, by a common, if varying, dependence on Barth's rejection of the anthropocentrism which he detected in modern Western culture and which he believed had been wrongly appropriated by modern Protestant theologians. Eventually, they converge in quite striking ways in the first part of Barth's doctrine of creation, involving as it does detailed exegesis of the Genesis creation narratives. Yet for all the reasons discussed at the outset of this chapter, the very moves which Barth makes to resist anthropocentrism may end up producing his own version of it. To examine this possibility, it is now necessary to turn to the first part of the third volume of the *Church Dogmatics*, and to Barth's doctrine of creation.[11]

---

9   On the 'humanity' of the Bible see especially *CD* I/2: 462–72. For a critical discussion of the theological foundations and hermeneutical consequences of the category of 'witness' see Wood 2007: 137–49.

10   The relationship between God's sovereign freedom and the texts through which God speaks is helpfully summarised by Francis Watson in his reference to the 'Reality' of God's self-revelation 'preceding the text yet articulating itself through the text' (Watson 2002: li).

11   The present discussion is necessarily limited to this single doctrinal locus not only for reasons of space, but also to focus more directly on the links between this text, hermeneutics and Barth's earlier critique of anthropocentrism. For a longer and doctrinally more comprehensive engagement with Barth on issues of environmental ethics see Jenkins 2008.

The Doctrine of Creation

The distinctiveness of Barth's doctrine of creation stems precisely from its christological foundation. For all the reasons he resists natural theology, he resists any secular knowledge of creation which might offer itself as an apologetic foundation for Christian theology. Instead, 'the knowledge of creation, of the Creator, and of the creature, is a knowledge of faith and that here too the Christian doctrine is a doctrine of faith' (*CD* III/1: 28). Fundamentally, 'Jesus Christ is the key to the secret of creation' (*CD* III/1: 28), and for that reason creation has a quite particular *telos*: 'God wills and God creates the creature for the sake of His Son or Word and therefore in harmony with Himself' (*CD* III/1: 59). As with all God's works, creation has 'in view the institution, preservation and execution of the covenant of grace, for partnership in which He has predestined and called man' (*CD* III/1: 43). It 'sets the stage for the story of the covenant of grace' (*CD* III/1: 44).

These broad doctrinal claims prompt at least two critical questions. First, given his commitment to the primacy of scripture, how has Barth actually drawn this christological account of creation from scripture? Secondly, does creation's status as the 'external' basis of, or the 'stage' for, the covenant between humanity and God betray a *de facto* separation of creation from covenant and therefore a separation of humanity from the rest of creation?

Creation and Covenant in the Genesis Narratives

Several factors combine to shape Barth's reading of the Genesis narratives within the framework of the expectation of Jesus Christ. As noted above, that this is the subject matter of the text neither negates the humanity of the word nor prohibits the investigation of that word. Nor does it determine the exegetical outcomes in advance or suggest that Jesus Christ is somehow immediately transparent in these texts. So, respect for the text's divine subject and a commitment to its human word combine in an investigation which involves Barth giving maximal hermeneutical weight to the canonical context, making certain judgements about the genre of the material, and drawing on the source-critical observation of two distinct narratives.

Recognition of the canonical context means first that the reader of the Genesis narratives must not ignore those texts' connection with 'what follows in the Pentateuch and the rest of the Old Testament' (*CD* III/1: 64). In fact the 'decisive commentary on the biblical histories of creation is the rest of the Old Testament' (*CD* III/1: 65). Secondly, that Genesis 1 and 2 speak of the Creator is, for the Christian theologian, to immediately bring them into connection with those New Testament passages (e.g. Col. 1.17; Jn 1.1; 1 Jn 2.13-14; Col. 1.15; Heb. 1.2) which speak of the 'ontological connection between Christ and creation' (*CD* III/1: 51) and in which 'the position, dignity and power of the Creator . . . are unquestionably ascribed to Christ' (*CD* III/1: 51). It is these large-scale canonical-hermeneutical moves which form the basis of his claim that creation and covenant are a particular kind of unity.

Barth designates the genre of these narratives as 'saga' in order to distinguish them from 'myth' and 'history'. This designation itself already reflects the convergence of doctrinal and exegetical considerations, and the theological issues at stake are very significant.[12] In fact, far from being a theologically neutral discussion about literary forms the discussion about saga is a theologically freighted discussion which is not unrelated to Barth's claims about the unity of the Bible's subject matter. It therefore plays a role in Barth's discussion about the unity of creation and covenant. Crucial in all of this is Barth's general claim about the nature of revelation as portrayed across scripture: 'According to Scripture, there are no timeless truths, but all truths according to Scripture are specific acts of God' (*CD* III/1: 60). Therefore, with its emphasis on timeless truths, myth cannot bear witness to the truth of creation (itself an 'historical' event because an act of the God of Scripture). On the other hand, saga bears witness to the historical element of creation without being reduced to the historicist stress on 'that which is accessible to man because it is visible and perceptible' (*CD* III/1: 78). Because it is an *event*, but without human witnesses, creation belongs to that 'history (*Geschichte*) which we cannot see and comprehend' and which 'is not history in the historicist sense' (*keine historische Geschichte*). Rather, it is a '"non-historical" history' (*unhistorische Geschichte*, *CD* III/1: 78; *KD* III/1: 86). It is to such 'history' that saga bears witness. As David Ford notes, Barth's discussion of saga connects the creation narratives 'with the rest of the Bible on the basis of form and content' (Ford 1985: 108).

If Barth has argued for the unity of creation and covenant by appealing to the canonical framework and by the discussion of saga, he draws a distinction between them by building on the observation that there are clearly two distinct creation narratives. The Priestly narration of the history of creation is focused on the Creator's creative work itself, the culmination of which is not the creation of human beings on the sixth day but God's rest on the seventh: 'The goal of creation, and at the same time the beginning of all that follows is the event of God's Sabbath freedom' which is 'His invitation to man to rest with Him' (*CD* III/1: 98). Because oriented to this goal, creation itself, therefore, 'prepares and establishes the sphere in which the institution and history of the covenant take place' (*CD* III/1: 97). On the other hand, the Yahwist's narrative points in a more focused way to the human being and the Creator in relationship. Crucial to Barth's reading of this second narrative is the setting of the human creature in the garden prepared by God. The garden is 'God's sanctuary' (*CD* III/1: 254) and it is here that the human creature is brought into the divine rest – the 'rest of his normal existence in relation to his Creator and to the earth as the creaturely sphere' (*CD* III/1: 251). This (and even more so once the creature is differentiated between male and female) is covenantal life: it is to 'hold fellowship

---

12   The key focus of critical discussion is Barth's insistence *contra* Augustine on the temporality of creation. On this and other critical issues regarding Barth's doctrine of creation see Crisp 2006 and with particular reference to the role of the Genesis narratives see MacDonald 2000: 135–62.

with the Creator . . . in assuming by conscious spontaneous and active assent to His divine decision' (*CD* III/1: 265–66). On Barth's reading, therefore, by being focused on the various works of creation *per se*, the first narrative becomes the basis for describing creation as the external basis of the covenant. The second narrative, by being focused on the relationship between God and the human creature, becomes the basis for describing the covenant as the internal basis of creation.

Humanity and the Rest of Creation

Does Barth's appeal to creation as the 'external' basis of the covenant between God and humanity or his description of creation as a 'stage' for the covenant betray an unwitting return to the very anthropocentrism he resisted at so many points in his theology? There is no doubt that taken on their own, these are problematic images. Reflecting exactly such concerns in relation to Barth's 'stage' metaphor it has recently been claimed that '[c]reation has a God-given integrity and purposefulness and is not simply a stage for the drama between God and human beings' (McIntosh 2009: 27).[13] Does the language of 'externality' and 'stage', however, fully express Barth's understanding of the relationship between creation and covenant, and does it sanction a new anthropocentrism? To answer these questions, our attention will turn to some of the details of Barth's exegesis of the creation narratives.

For the purposes of this present discussion it is very important to note that Barth is explicitly aware of the potential for these texts to be misread anthropocentrically. Moreover, he even differentiates between the tendencies to anthropocentricity of the respective narratives. Perhaps most strikingly of all, he makes this judgement in the course of introductory comments on the *second* narrative – the one that he deems to be focused on the covenant between God and humanity. He points out not only that this second saga 'is not as anthropocentric as it is often made out to be' (*CD* III/1: 235), but also that it is *less* anthropocentric than the first – the one which he deemed to be focused on creation more generally. Barth displays a noticeable sensitivity to the possibility of misusing these texts to magnify the human in relation to both God and the rest of creation. This is most evident in his treatment of the sagas' respective accounts of the creation of the human.

In relation to Gen. 1.26-28 Barth shows no hesitation in affirming that the human being has been given precedence by God not only over the firmament, the earth, the constellations, the creatures of sea and air, but 'also over his immediate but very different fellow-animals within the one dwelling place' (*CD* III/1: 177). Indeed, the human is 'more noble than these creatures' (*CD* III/1: 177). Yet, within this framework Barth makes two anti-anthropocentric exegetical moves. The first

---

13   By too readily accepting the 'stage' metaphor, McIntosh understates the full extent of Barth's evaluation of creation. Nevertheless, he offers an illuminating and important account of human and animal relations in Barth based on Barth's discussion of vegetarianism in *CD* III/4: 351–56.

subverts any passivity or muteness on the part of the non-human creation which might be suggested by the 'stage' metaphor. According to the saga the animals are no less creatures of the will and Word of God than humans and therefore the human is constantly surrounded by 'the spectacle of a submission to this Word which, if it is not free, is in its own way real and complete' (*CD* III/1: 177). In fact, the human creature finds itself addressed by its fellow animals as examples of a certain kind of praise of the Creator and of creaturely limitation.

> The creature precedes man in a self-evident praise of its Creator, in the natural fulfilment of the destiny given to it at its creation, in the actual humble recognition and confirmation of its creatureliness. It also precedes him in the fact that it does not forget but maintains its animal nature, with its dignity and also its limitation, and thus asks man whether and to what extent the same can be said of him. (*CD* III/1: 177)

This suggestion of the collective voice of the non-human animals at the very least stretches the 'stage' metaphor, albeit without completely dislodging it.

The second move of note in relation to Gen. 1.26-28 is one which challenges any crass instrumentalism which might be suggested by the stage metaphor. Although Barth maintains that the human creature is God's representative on earth, he insists that there is no equality between divine and human lordship. This does not depend, however, on any attempt to tone down what he explicitly acknowledges is the strength of *radah* and *kabash* (even acknowledging certain violent overtones to the latter). Instead, this limitation to human lordship is based on the fact that within these verses there is 'no expansion of human lordship beyond the animal kingdom' (*CD* III/1: 205). Precisely because human lordship is limited it does not share in the sovereignty of God's lordship. It was, of course, some such human appropriation of divine sovereignty which was a key target of Barth's critique of modern anthropocentrism. Against this background, these particular observations lead to a sharp rejection of attempts to invoke this text to justify claims for unlimited human lordship over the earth[14] and thereby to use it as a warrant for 'such things as the tunnelling and levelling of mountains, or the drying up or diversion of rivers' (*CD* III/1: 206). Such claims, Barth maintains, are 'foreign to the passage' (*CD* III/1: 205) and he sides with those who have elsewhere described them as blasphemous (see *CD* III/1: 206).

It is in relation to Gen. 2.4b-7 that Barth draws the distinction between the relative anthropocentricity of the two sagas. At issue is their respective accounts of the relationship of the human creature to the world of vegetation. In contrast to the anthropocentric tendency of the Priestly saga where the 'world of vegetation was ordained and created only to be the food of men and animals' (*CD* III/1: 235), the Yahwist narrative presents the human as the servant of the earth and its vegetation. Indeed, Barth suggests that in this narrative, the latter 'is a kind of end

---

14 Barth is here referring to the work of the Jewish commentator, B. Jacob.

in itself' (*CD* III/1: 235). The creation of the human as the farmer and gardener fills the 'gap' between the barren earth and its goal of fruitfulness. The human 'is first introduced only as the being who had to be created for the sake of the earth and to serve it' (*CD* III/1: 235). On the basis of this reading of these verses, Barth offers a commentary which strikes a now-familiar anti-anthropocentric note: 'In view of his complete integration into the totality of the created order there can be no question of a superiority of man supported by appeals to his special dignity, or of forgetfulness not merely of a general but a very definite control of Yahweh-Elohim over man' (*CD* III/1: 235). Notably, this is followed not by an immediate shift to the human creature's corresponding responsibility to the Creator, but its responsibility to the earth: 'In spite of all the particular things that God may plan to do with him, in the first instance man can only serve the earth and will continually have to do so' (*CD* III/1: 235).

So, notwithstanding the relation with the Creator to which the human is summoned, Barth presents the human creature as 'completely integrated' into the 'totality' of creation and as one who is summoned to 'serve the earth'. 'Integration' and 'servanthood' do not undermine the particular uses to which Barth places the language of 'externality' and 'stage', but the former do expose the limitations of the latter as comprehensive summaries of Barth's account of the status of creation.

Finally, the reference to the human as the servant of the earth echoes Barth's comment about 'loyalty' to the earth which was quoted at the outset of this chapter. These themes of 'loyalty' and 'service' are never fully developed as independent, let alone dominant, themes in Barth's doctrine of creation. Nor do they obscure what Barth points out as he turns to the doctrine of the creature *per se* in the second part of his doctrine of creation: the human creature is indeed the 'goal and centre' of the 'gracious plan' for which God created the universe (*CD* III/2: 14). This does not mean, however, that the human can be understood as 'the cosmos *in nuce*' (*CD* III/2: 15). Nor does it mean that 'our attitude to the wider creation [could] be one of blindness, indifference or disparagement' (*CD* III/2: 4). Besides the human, says Barth, 'there are other creatures posited by God and distinct from God, and with their own dignity and right, and enveloped in the secret of their own relation to their Creator' (*CD* III/2: 4). As such, 'loyalty' and 'service' point to the proper mode of the relationship between the human and these other creatures. Not to be loyal, and not to serve, would be symptomatic of the human creature who had forgotten its limits, forgotten to understand itself from the Word of God: 'Man is a creature in the midst of others which were directly created by God and exist independently of man. The Word of God itself sees man in this context and within these appointed limits' (*CD* III/2: 4).

Conclusion

Perhaps because the themes of human 'loyalty' and 'service' to the non-human creation are never fully developed, Karl Barth's theology is unlikely ever to be a major resource for contemporary discussion of environmental ethics. Arguably, however, it is not an insignificant resource for Christian theologians seeking to engage those discussions (cf. further Jenkins 2008). His alertness to the problem and the consequences of anthropocentricity is acute, wide ranging and deeply rooted. He recognizes its pervasiveness: the anthropocentricity which seeks to 'humanize nature' is the same as that which seeks to 'master the text' of scripture. Of course, his own attempts to resist such 'mastery' of the text will remain contested and controversial. Nevertheless, his reading of the Bible as witness to Jesus Christ is multi-layered and – precisely because it *is* a reading centred on Jesus Christ – deeply sensitive to the possibilities of a humanity which refuses and resists its limits. At the very least, Barth's theology is a reminder that even in its classical expressions, far from necessarily legitimating anthropocentrism and its devaluing of the environment, Christianity has its own reasons for both refusing anthropocentrism and for valuing the environment.

References

Barth, K. 1933 *Epistle to the Romans* (6th edn; Oxford: Oxford University Press).
Barth, K. 1938 *The Knowledge of God and the Service of God According to the Teaching of the Reformation* (London: Hodder and Stoughton).
Barth, K. 1945 *Die kirchliche Dogmatik: Band 1: Die Lehre von der Schöpfung: Teil Eins* (Zurich: Evangelischer Verlag).
Barth, K. 1956 *Church Dogmatics: Volume 1: The Doctrine of the Word of God: Part Two* (Edinburgh: T&T Clark).
Barth, K. 1957a *Church Dogmatics: Volume II: The Doctrine of God: Part One* (Edinburgh: T&T Clark).
Barth, K. 1957b 'The Strange New World within the Bible' in *The Word of God and the Word of Man* (New York: Harper and Brothers): 28–50.
Barth, K. 1957c 'The Word of God and the Task of the Ministry' in *The Word of God and the Word of Man* (New York, NY: Harper and Brothers): 183–217.
Barth, K. 1958 *Church Dogmatics: Volume III: The Doctrine of Creation: Part One* (Edinburgh: T&T Clark).
Barth, K. 1960 *Church Dogmatics: Volume III: The Doctrine of Creation: Part Two* (Edinburgh: T&T Clark).
Barth, K. 2001 *Protestant Theology in the Nineteenth Century: Its Background and History* (London: SCM).
Barth, K. 2002a *The Theology of the Reformed Confessions* (Louisville, KY: Westminster John Knox).
Barth, K. 2002b 'No! Answer to Emil Brunner' in E. Brunner and K. Barth, *Natural Theology: Comprising 'Nature and Grace' by Professor Dr. Emil Brunner and the Reply 'No!' by Dr. Karl Barth* (Eugene, OR: Wipf and Stock): 65–128.
Barth, K. 2003 'The Authority and the Significance of the Bible: Twelve Theses' in *God Here and Now* (London: Routledge): 55–74.
Brunner, E. 2002 'Nature and Grace' in E. Brunner and K. Barth, *Natural Theology: Comprising 'Nature and Grace' by Professor Dr. Emil Brunner and the Reply 'No!' by Dr. Karl Barth* (Eugene, OR: Wipf and Stock): 15–64.
Busch, E. 2004 *The Great Passion: An Introduction to Karl Barth's Theology* (Grand Rapids, MI: Eerdmans).

Crisp, O. 2006 'Karl Barth on Creation', in S.W. Chung (ed.), *Karl Barth and Evangelical Theology: Convergences and Divergences* (Grand Rapids, MI: Baker Academic): 77–95.

Ford, D. 1985 *Barth and God's Story: Biblical Narrative and the Theological Method of Karl Barth in the 'Church Dogmatics'* (Studies in the Intercultural History of Christianity, 27; Bern: Peter Lang).

Habel, N. C. 2008 'Introducing Ecological Hermeneutics' in N.C. Habel and P. Trudinger (eds), *Exploring Ecological Hermeneutics* (Atlanta: Society of Biblical Literature): 1–8.

Jenkins, W. 2008 *Ecologies of Grace: Environmental Ethics and Christian Theology* (Oxford: Oxford University Press).

McCormack, B.L. 1995 *Karl Barth's Critically Realistic Dialectical Theology: Its Genesis and Development 1909–1936* (Oxford: Clarendon Press).

McCormack, B.L. 2002 'The Significance of Karl Barth's Theological Exegesis of Philippians' in K. Barth, *Epistle to the Philippians: 40th Anniversary Edition*. (Louisville, KY: Westminster John Knox): v–xxv.

MacDonald, N.B. 2000 *Karl Barth and the Strange New World within the Bible: Barth, Wittgenstein and the Metadilemmas of the Enlightenment* (Paternoster Biblical and Theological Monographs; Carlisle: Paternoster).

McIntosh. A. 2009 'Human and Animal Relations in the Theology of Karl Barth', *Pacifica* 22: 20–35.

Mangina, J.L. 2004 *Karl Barth: Theologian of Christian Witness* (Louisville, KY: Westminster John Knox).

Watson, F. 2002 'Barth's Philippians as Theological Exegesis' in K. Barth, *Epistle to the Philippians: 40th Anniversary Edition*. (Louisville, KY: Westminster John Knox): xxvi–li.

Webster, J. 2000 *Barth* (Outstanding Christian Thinkers; London: Continuum).

Webster, J. 2001 'Reading the Bible: The Example of Barth and Bonhoeffer' in *Word and Church: Essays in Christian Dogmatics* (Edinburgh: T&T Clark): 87–112.

White, L. Jr 1967 'The Historical Roots of Our Ecologic Crisis', *Science* 155: 1203–207.

Wood, D. 2007 *Barth's Theology of Interpretation* (Barth Studies Series; Aldershot: Ashgate).

Chapter 14

HANS URS VON BALTHASAR: BEGINNING WITH BEAUTY

David Moss

If we took [Balthasar] as seriously as he deserves, we would have to change our lives.

(Donoghue 2004: 56)

I. *Situating Balthasar*

To my knowledge Hans Urs von Balthasar, through all his truly prodigious theological output, said little, if anything, about what we have learnt to call, and more experience, as the environmental crisis today. For sure, there may be some sort of biographical apologia for this. Balthasar died on 26 May 1988 and perhaps one could enter the mitigating plea that even by the late 1980s the true challenge of our situation, along with the impact of the environmental movement, still remained out of view to many.[1] After all, the Rio Earth Summit was still four years ahead. However, Balthasar's theological productivity only slightly diminished with his advancing years, and when he came to review the main 'trends of modern theology' in the introduction to *Theo-drama I: Theological Dramatic Theory, Volume I: Prolegomena* in 1983 (Balthasar 1988: 25–50), the manifestly *dramatic* impact that the fate of the environment stands to have on theology's construal of the relationship between creature and Creator is utterly neglected in favour of Balthasar's conviction that the most pressing concern for theological thinking today is to 'build from scratch' a fully theological rendition of the confrontation between 'divine and human freedom' (Balthasar 1988: 50).

Thus, if Balthasar's theology has been adjudged – although not incontestably – 'ahead of its time' in terms of engaging those themes that have so entranced postmodern theoretics, in the case of ecology and the seemingly inexorable fate of

---

1   Although Lynn White's 1967 article 'The Historical Roots of Our Ecological Crisis' has been credited with setting the agenda for Christian environmental theologies (see Jenkins 2008: 10–15), a largely unscientific review of the bibliographies of books and articles concerned with ecotheology tends to suggest that it was not until the late 1980s and early 1990s that the environment became a pressing theme for theological reflection and publication.

the ancient and fragile biosphere we inhabit he can hardly be claimed to be any sort of ecotheologian at all; or even, for that matter, sensitive to its appeal. And even if we are to agree with Francis Watson (Chapter 9 in this volume) that 'From the perspective of Christian faith, the "environment" will be understood as "creation"', this would still appear to offer little encouragement to our endeavour when, as John Riches suggests, 'There is . . . little doubt that [Balthasar] actually spends little time developing his own theology of creation' (Riches 1996: 169).

That this is a rather partial judgement (as Riches is aware), I will have cause to consider below; however, it does resonate with the perception that Balthasar's overwhelming theological focus dwelt elsewhere. Which is to say, not with the testimony of the 'natural sciences' to the irreparable damage we may be inflicting on the planet – for as Balthasar airily remarks: 'The Bible has never shown any interest in so-called natural laws' (Balthasar 1982: 665) – but with the focal encounter of a loving God with sinful men and women. For Balthasar what 'is specifically Christian about Christianity' (Balthasar 2004a: 7) is just this: 'Man's participation in God which, from God's perspective, is actualized as "revelation" (culminating in Christ's Godmanhood) and which, from man's perspective, is actualized as "faith" (culminating in Christ's Godmanhood)' (Balthasar 1982: 125). An exchange, of course, that is theologically dramatized by Balthasar's very Barthian concentration on 'the way of the Son of God into the far country'; although as appropriated – in very *un*-Barthian fashion – through the liturgical and theologically speculative resources of the *Triduum Mortis* (see Balthasar 1993a).

Thus, what to do in pursuit of saying something about Balthasar's ecological credentials; or even more, his provision of resources for generating an ecological hermeneutic? The soil would appear to be very thin indeed.

But is it truly the case that so colossal a thinker has nothing, or almost nothing, to say to our crisis *today*? Is it that a theologian who 'more or less single-handedly heaved up a huge mountain range of theology' (Oakes and Moss 2004: 2) has so quickly become outdated, outmoded and irrelevant? And I raise this suggestion not as a merely idle remark, but as a serious *theological question* – a question that in many ways will dictate the contention of this essay. For if we countenance such a conclusion (and this has surely been reckoned 'necessary' by some for whom the corrosive emergency of our current situation demands the root and branch deconstruction of the Christian tradition[2]), then in the case of Balthasar at least, this can only reinforce

---

2   John Milbank offers a harsh judgement on this theological 'fashion' when he writes, '[Ecotheology] assumes that re-sacralizing nature, and de-throning a super-natural God, must obviously be the key to our sick condition. But this repeats the facile mis-deduction . . . [that] . . . we have been nasty to nature, so let us have more nature, more science even (after all it's about nature, and quantum physics is really Taoism and so forth). Also more creation, more animality, more body . . . and less fall and redemption, less doctrine of sin, less history, less humanity, less spirit. Never mind that "spirit", as the realm of culture, is the only possible source of all our eco-problems, such that their solution demands that this realm be set to rights, not asked to efface itself before an affronted nature' (Milbank 1997: 262).

a sobering hermeneutical realization. For in so far as Balthasar's project was nothing if not the self-conscious attempt to re-present in synoptic repletion the fullness of the catholic Faith, then is it that our *reception* of that Faith today can only be experienced as though a natural resource fast running out – deforested, over-mined or exhausted? Is it that what goes for 'our' natural resources today – in their scarcity and depletion – should also go for any synoptic presentation of the Faith in this 'new paradigm' of environmental crisis? In short, recognition that the tradition is no longer prophetic of 'a new heaven and a new earth' (Rev. 21.1), but is now recognisably toxic by virtue of the ideology of 'dominion' (Gen. 1.26) that it historically released.

No doubt, this is to play rather fast and loose with ecological images of a (polluted?) tradition (see Merchant 1982). Nonetheless, does it not, in some manner, also betoken what is really at stake in any theological step 'towards an ecological hermeneutic'? And if this is really so, then perhaps Balthasar does indeed represent something of a 'test case'. For in eschewing the urgent contemporaneity of a Jürgen Moltmann, the scientific concern of a Wolfhart Pannenberg or even the creaturely sympathies of a Karl Barth, it appears difficult to avoid the conclusion that Balthasar's theology represents anything other than what Moltmann once derided as a now discredited old anthropocentric picture of the world.

Nonetheless, if this view is to merit serious support (while, of course, leaving us to plunder the body parts of the Balthasarian *corpus*), it can only do so in recognition of the fact that Balthasar's entire diagnosis of modern ('anthropocentric') theology – which includes, of course, modern biblical hermeneutics[3] – remained riveted to the ailments afflicting our sense and experience of nature, the natural or creation – all, no doubt, slippery terms – *in light of the supernatural*. For according to Balthasar: '[The] sign imprinted on nature . . . comes to light only when the sign of absolute love appears'. For 'the light of the Cross makes worldly being intelligible, it allows the inchoate forms and ways of love, which otherwise threaten to stray into trackless thickets, to receive a foundation in their true transcendent ground' (Balthasar 2004a: 142).

---

3   The scope of this essay does not allow me to explore Balthasar's distinctive engagement with the Bible. However, what is important to recognize here is that his *Aesthetics* – that we have as the main focus of this essay – remains 'of-a-piece' with his Biblical hermeneutics. Eschewing varieties of either propositional fundamentalism on the one hand, or modernist liberalism on the other (both of which, for Balthasar, spring from the same mistake), he contended that a disregard for beauty has left modern hermeneutics with little resource by which to integrate scriptural sign and referent. Or, in categories that he will deploy in his *Aesthetics*: unable to recognize the true splendour of revelation as mediated through its scriptural form. His approach thus reconnects with aspects of a pre-modern hermeneutic in its claim upon the liturgical context for scriptural interpretation, which remains allegorically directed towards Christ and informed by the Holy Spirit. However, as W.T. Dickens (2003) has argued in an excellent and not uncritical essay, Balthasar's approach also offers profound resources for a genuinely post-critical biblical hermeneutic. To what extent Balthasar's specific exegeses could contribute to a so-called ecological reading of Scripture would be a matter of some interest. However, I would suggest – as above – that the real value in his approach would lie in the manner in which his hermeneutic 'performance' sustained a *dramatic* and genuine openness to the plight of the environment.

Thus, while Balthasar may have spent little time 'developing his own theology of creation', it is nonetheless crucial to recognize that for Balthasar 'nature' is *essentially theophanic*; although theophanic in his precise sense:

> [For] if the cosmos as a whole has been created in the image of God that appears in the First-Born of creation . . . and if this First-Born indwells the world as its head through the Church, then in the last analysis the world is a 'body' of God, who represents and expresses himself in this body, on the basis of the principle not of pantheistic but hypostatic union. (Balthasar 1982: 679)

The key to reading the cosmos, its origin and destiny, lies in no pantheistic (or even panentheistic) narrative, but, according to Balthasar, in the manner through which Christ, through an obedience to the fate of creaturely being in his death and burial, thereby shepherded creation up from nothingness in his rising from 'the lower parts of the earth' (Eph. 4.9). And while technically this will be articulated by Balthasar in terms of linking the Thomistic 'Real Distinction' (that subtends every creaturely being as being both what it is and that it is) to the character of Christological love (see below), what this recognition demands first of all is that we '*See the Form*' of the world in the image of love – the image of the 'First Born of creation'.

Thus, when Rowan Williams urges that Balthasar's analysis, through the meandering volumes of the *Aesthetics*, poses the 'profoundly important question about our understanding of the human *vis-à-vis* the world as a whole, [in] echoing Heidegger's polemic against the technocratic distortion of human relations with the natural order' (Williams 2007: 95), then just perhaps a more nuanced perspective may begin to open up for appropriation and understanding. Such an approach though is by no means easy to fathom; nor is it to be pragmatically, or even theoretically, 'read off' from Balthasar's 'script'.

In the light of this suggestion then, the following essay has the very modest aim of sketching in briefest terms Balthasar's hermeneutics of beauty, of 'seeing the form', which, although coming to a point of maximal intensity in the person of Jesus Christ, crucified and risen – just as in 'an hour-glass', Balthasar explains[4] – reaches up to receive 'from above' the cascading flow of graceful Being, while embracing its sedimentation in the shifting sands of the environment 'here below'.

Thus, in slight adjustment to the suggestion made by John Riches (above), according to Balthasar what is required to bolster contemporary doctrines of creation is

---

4 'We could describe this . . . as a kind of hourglass, where the two contiguous vessels (God and creature) meet only at the narrow passage through the centre: where they both encounter each other in Jesus Christ. The purpose of the image is to show that there is no other point of contact between the two chambers of the hourglass. And just as the sand flows only from top to bottom, so too God's revelation is one-sided, flowing from his gracious decision alone. But of course the sand flows down into the other chamber so that the sand can really *increase*. In other words, there *is* a countermovement in the other chamber but only because of the first movement, the initiative of the first chamber' (Balthasar 1992: 197).

precisely *not* the fabrication of reconstructed theologies that would transcribe, for example, the gaia-like quality of nature as the 'body of God', but the renewal of a 'cultural' wonderment (*thaumazein*) at the theophanic quality of beings through which the light of divine Love itself shines. And what this suggests, to use Willis Jenkins' richly suggestive phrase, is attention to Balthasar's 'ecology of grace' which comprehensively and Christologically indicates *how nature becomes significant for Christian existence* (Jenkins 2008). Consequently, if an ethics is to be discovered here – as assuredly it must – it is not in emergency recoil to the 'state we're in', but as contemplatively dependent upon, although coincident with, a prior receptivity to the world's *beauty* which initiates the drama of the earth as 'always-already' soteriological.[5]

If 'love and gratitude are starting points for determining our ethical obligations' with regard to the environment (Sideris 2003: 254), then moving *towards* an ecological hermeneutic demands, in Balthasarian terms, not the construction of a new theological paradigm, or even raiding of his comprehensive *oeuvre*, but the re-attunement of an ancient and creaturely capacity to perceive *das Ganze im Fragment*: that 'intuition' through which we receive (subjectively), from amidst all the teeming variety and particularity of our environment, a testimony (objectively) to its environing source and sustenance.[6]

But we must surely wonder, does beauty have anything to offer an ecological hermeneutic today – other, that is, than a haunting melancholia, given the urgent straits in which we live?

II. Seeing the Form

Beauty is the word that shall be our first (Balthasar 1982: 18).

I begin a course for undergraduates on Balthasar's theology with a brief section from Dennis Potter's last interview, given to Melvyn Bragg, several weeks before his death from cancer in 1994.[7] The choice is hardly accidental given Balthasar's commitment to the work of the poets and dramatists (see Balthasar 1984; 1986). However, the

---

5   The central merit of Jenkins' valuable book is in re-establishing soteriology at the centre of environmental ethics by way, not of displacing an ecologically attuned sense of creation, but by reminding us of the profound interconnectedness of creation, salvation and sanctification in any truly Christian 'ecology of grace'.

6   *Das Ganze im Fragment* is the title of Balthasar's 1963 study of theological anthropology – translated as *Man in History: A Theological Study* (1972). The German title translates 'the whole in the fragment' and indicates Balthasar's abiding conviction that the metaphysical and religious 'quest' begins not in some sort of pre-apprehension of infinity, but rather through an astonishment at particular and concrete form.

7   Dennis Potter is probably Britain's most acclaimed and creative television dramatist remembered particularly for his innovative and biographically inspired plays including *Pennies for Heaven* (1978) and *The Singing Detective* (1986).

question it poses – and especially for those new to Balthasar's *oeuvre* – is quite simply this: is there anything more to be understood in Potter's testimony than the subjective reflex of a 'poetically' attuned playwright?

Potter records of his current life:

> Below my window in Ross . . . there at this season, the blossom is out in full now . . . it's a plum tree, it looks like apple blossom but it's white, and looking at it instead of saying 'Oh that's nice apple blossom' . . . last week looking at it through the window when I'm writing, I see it as the whitest, frothiest, blossomest blossom that there ever could be, and I can see it. Things are both more trivial than they ever were, and more important than they ever were, and the difference between the trivial and the important doesn't seem to matter. But the nowness of everything is absolutely wondrous, and if people could see that you know. There's no way of telling, you have to experience it, but the glory of it, if you like, the comfort of it, the reassurance . . . not that I'm interested in reassuring people, bugger that. The fact is, if you see the present tense, boy you see it! And boy you can celebrate it. (Potter 1994: 5)

And so I ask: is Potter, in short, saying anything fundamental – anything true or good – about the world, the cosmos, in which we live? And is this moment of being struck by the beauty and *glory* of the blossom in any sense revelatory of the way the world, the cosmos, *is*? Revelatory that is of its truth, goodness and unity through a modality of human intellection and imagination which promises access to the Real beyond the omnivorous grasp of 'promethean' reduction and ecological spoiling? The responses I receive tend to remain – to pick up Balthasar's suggestion from above – rather 'inchoate'. And indeed, as Frederick Ferré comments, in his ecologically inspired *Being and Value: Toward a Constructive Postmodern Metaphysics*:

> Probably the most difficult domain for modern people considering the reality-grounding of value intuitions is that of beauty. We live surrounded by stimuli that give us experiences of aesthetic aversion and attraction but our world view leads us to doubt that there is anything 'out there' that is ugly or beautiful. Our dominant theories assure us that that the hues of the rose in full bloom, the sunset's splendour, or the rainbow's subtle spectrum are not to be reckoned in the world but only in human responses to the world. (Ferré 1996: 14)

Ferré's judgement accords well with Balthasar's conviction, and moreover suggests that what we have to reckon with here is no mere temporary impairment, but the result of a complex historical and cultural story which involves so severe a depletion of our creaturely capacity that:

> the world, formerly penetrated by God's light, now becomes but an appearance and a dream – the Romantic vision – and soon thereafter nothing but music. But where the cloud disperses, naked matter remains as an indigestible symbol of fear and anguish. Since nothing else remains, and yet *something* must be embraced, twentieth-century man is urged to enter this impossible marriage with matter, a union which finally spoils all man's taste for love. But

man cannot bear to live with the object of his impotence, that which remains permanently unmastered. He must either deny or conceal it in the silence of death.s (Balthasar 1982: 18–19)

Where we can no longer read the language of beauty so, for Balthasar, the witness of creation *as created* becomes untrustworthy and open to abuse; and where we cannot embrace creativity, just so love becomes impotent and impossible. Potter's lyrical outburst, in Balthasarian terms, is anything but a frivolous 'subjective' testimony, but rather resonates – if problematically – with the 'intuition' (as Balthasar calls it) that had prevailed in the West up until the late Middle Ages. In short, that those transitory experiences of the truth, goodness and beauty of the cosmos are intelligible only by way of reference to a transcendent order of Being that is absolutely true, good and beautiful. And if such reference secured, as it were, the vision of the *whole* of creation through (and by way of participation in) its fragmentary parts – and which now is, in some sense, evoked by way of allusion to the 'biosphere' – then the *logos* of this reference was established precisely in so far as 'creation's aesthetic values' were attributed '*eminenter* to the creating principle itself' (Balthasar 1982: 38). Perhaps, we could suggest, a kind of 'ecologic hermeneutic' to(wards) which the enrapturing experience of beauty gave *entrée*?

But this is to have travelled too far, too quickly and to have potentially resolved Balthasar's hermeneutic into an altogether different context from that for which it was originally conceived. However, the analogy has been drawn (in returning to Francis Watson's equation of 'creation' and 'environment') – and it is always helpful when setting out upon a journey to have a sense of the place to which one is heading. We now, however, need to retrace our steps and lay out why 'beginning with beauty' may yet give theological and biblical *purchase* to an ecological hermeneutic. For the matter must go beyond (while never abandoning) lyrical testimony to the 'dearest freshness deep down things' – as Hopkins describes the depths of nature as brooded over by the Holy Spirit.

For when we find ourselves caught up by the glory of a particular form in showy presentation, or register in sensuous distress the wanton spoilment of nature, are we to reckon these charismatic interludes as anything other than a mere (and increasingly dulled) 'subjective' response to the environment around us? For if this is all there is to say, then from where will come the motivational basis for ethical action as well as ethical restraint? If we are to follow Balthasar, however, such intimations – of the glorious as well as ugly – have something to *say* to us, just as they leave us with a *mission* to be undertaken.

III. A Hermeneutic of Beauty

A moment of grace lies in all beauty: it shows itself to me far beyond what I have a right to expect, which is why we feel astonishment and admiration. (Balthasar 2004b: 66)

In 1963 Balthasar published a short and programmatic essay which, to all intents and purposes, foreshadowed the colossal amplitude of his great theological triptych. In *Love Alone is Credible* Balthasar offered a genealogy of historically situated approaches to the perennial question: 'What is specifically Christian about Christianity?' (Balthasar 2004a: 9). As he argued, within the overarching framework of any epoch Christian theology has always sought to find 'a *logos* that, however particular it might be, nevertheless had the power to persuade, and indeed to overwhelm, a *logos* that, in breaking out of the sphere of "accidental historical truths" would lend these truths a necessity' (Balthasar 2004a: 9).

For the ancients, Balthasar suggested, this was the 'cosmological reduction'; for the moderns, the 'anthropological'. And while Balthasar was by no means wholly unsympathetic to aspects of these richly orchestrated approaches, he nonetheless concluded that, if the cosmological approach suffered too much the 'limitations of temporal history' following the disenchantment of nature, then the anthropological approach betrayed 'a fundamental flaw' in promoting the dialectics of self-consciousness as the measure of all things, including the divine. For Balthasar then, the framework of God's message in Christ cannot be tied to the world in general, nor to human being in particular. It is, and remains, an act of God on human being; an act (revelation) whose only credibility is that of love – 'God's own love, the manifestation of which is the manifestation of the glory of God' (Balthasar 2004a: 10).

For Balthasar, the radicality of this claim, transgressing any and every historical epoch, consists in the fact that far from being the merely pious grammar of Christian practice, or methodological *discrimens* for disentangling the love of God from our worldly loves, the revelation of this divine love is the revelation of that which holds sway over all the realms of being. Or as St Paul expresses this same truth: 'all things hold together (*sunestēken*) in him' (Col. 1:17) – Jesus the Christ. The light of divine love is the very *logos* of being and thus demands, so Balthasar claims, the need for a genuinely theological aesthetic which opens onto, while continuing to fund, the recognition that created objects derive their value from participation in their transcendent ground.

God has created the natural world in such a way that its depth bears the supernatural stamp of its divine origin and end, and that what is required to read this ontological depth is a hermeneutic which, enraptured by the sensuous signals of beauty, is thus consequently transported towards the reality of this donation – the 'creating principle itself'. Thus, for Balthasar these two approaches of *aesthetics* and *love* coincide in fathoming the intelligibility of revelation. For in so far as 'whatever we love – no matter how profoundly or superficially we may love it – always appears radiant with glory', so 'whatever is objectively perceived as glorious – no matter how profoundly or superficially we experience it – does not penetrate into the onlooker except through the specificity of an eros' (Balthasar 2004a: 54). Altogether then, while this spiralling hermeneutic is firmly rooted in creation – in responding to the full sensuality of nature's touch in all its particularity (thus renewing the sympathies of classical Christianity, and most assuredly Balthasar's own sympathies as well) – it nonetheless renovates modernity's anthropological starting-point by locating this not in the solipsism of self but through the free encounter of an I with a Thou or 'Wholly Other', whether this 'other' be animal, mineral, or spiritual.

This approach, I would suggest, shares something with Lisa Sideris's contention, that while some forms of reconstructive ecotheology can all too easily and paradoxically stray into offering their 'results' as though products of knowledge, what is really required here is that 'we [both] have to turn *inward* – to an understanding of human moral reasoning and moral complexity – and *outward* – to a source of values beyond strictly anthropocentric values'. In other words, we have to turn to what Balthasar called, at a distance, a *meta-anthropology* – 'presupposing not only the cosmological sciences but also the anthropological sciences and surpassing them' (Balthasar 1993b: 115).

But is this all lyrical pretence? For how can something so transcending and spiritual as beauty and love be discovered in the 'givenness' of things – things that constitute our environment? And how can the 'quiddity' of the plum blossom ultimately instigate anything other than poetic lyricism giving way to exhausted aphasia ('There's no way of telling. . .'!)? But then again perhaps we need, at this very juncture, to become more attentive to the intensive reiteration that, albeit fleetingly, signals in Potter's evocation of the *glory* of the 'blossomest blossom'? For in this moment of astonished vision, I want to suggest, a *difference* appears that will, if we will but let it, fuel the (hermeneutic) transcription of the *truth* of creaturely existence amidst the *good* of its social environing ('if you see the present tense, boy you see it. And boy can you celebrate it!') And how so? Balthasar explains with deceptive simplicity (an explanation which dictates the order of his theological triptych) as follows:

> A being *appears*, it has an epiphany: in that it is beautiful and makes us marvel. In appearing it *gives* itself, it delivers itself to us: it is good. And in giving itself up, it *speaks* itself, it unveils itself: it is true (in itself, but in the other to which it reveals itself). (Balthasar 1993b: 116)

For the present though we need to remain with this inaugurating moment which is never to be superseded lest the testimony of things fall silent (into the simply logically correct) or barren (into the merely useful).

'A being *appears* . . .': but how does it appear? As Potter recalls, tautologically, through the blossoming of the blossom. The blossom all-of-a-sudden presents itself ('objectively') to Potter's sight as though through an illumination and depth which, as it were, back-lights its showy and engaging appearance as that which it truly is. We rejoice in the presentation of an object when through the experience of a rich and expressive encounter we feel the object lay itself open to us, and sense that this signals a mysterious *more* to the object's nature than can appear in this or any other single expression. Thus, in appreciating the clear, rich and expressive form of the blossoming *blossom* so we espy radiance – a 'glory' Potter says – breaking forth from the *blossoming* blossom. What asserts itself to Potter, beyond the correct and useful, is a positive delight to his intellect and will, causing him to want to 'celebrate' the apprehension of the blossom. And Balthasar has a vocabulary for precisely this experience: beauty is to be conceived, he explains in the language of scholasticism, through the imbrication of *formae* and *splendor*. Form, not as the objective skeleton of a thing, but as its integrated integrity through which an inexhaustible intelligibility and splendour appears to shine for us.

Moreover, since we can never draw from the object all of its beauty ('you have to experience it . . .'), so we feel ourselves bound to it in expectation of something more, still to arrive. Thus, in so far as I am satisfied by the beautiful, so I am frustratingly so ('and if people could *see* that you know. There's no way of telling you . . .'). I sense that not only does the deepest truth of the object appear in its epiphany, but that in some still more mysterious manner its goodness provides me with a sort of destiny to this encounter.

But can we go further and speak of a still deeper signal betokening that vast ocean of formal fertility which is the mystery of being? The curtailment of Potter's quest at this point – at once breached and then, in somewhat embarrassed recognition, dismissed – is illustrative indeed. And illustrative of the surd element – as a sort of Kantian noumena – that materiality has so much become for modernity. For with the disenchantment of the world, so modern aesthetics in its anthropological turn (which is paradoxically also 'a turn to nature') has abandoned talk about 'being' as empty and convictions about 'beauty' (especially in relation to God) as sentimental. Rather, it has bidden us see the source of all form in the constructive powers of the mind. Consequently the aesthetics of modernity – as mere addendum to our energies for valuing and willing – has focused 'artistically' on the way in which our subjectivity *uses* nature as a medium for self-expression.

Balthasar, however, in a brief and brilliant metaphysical sketch that concludes the fifth volume of the *Aesthetics* (Balthasar 1991: 613–27) refuses this modern ban upon the transport (*ecstasy*) of beauty and recalls us to the fact that the most significant thing in aesthetic experience is not that it is a sort of creation or expression, but rather an exploration and discovery, much like love. Thus, beginning from the startled reflex of wonderment, I recognize through the variety of particular forms an apprehension of participating in the whole of existence. I recognize that the light that shines through *this* blossom, in enabling it to come into its own, while also illuminating all else, is nonetheless never to be discovered apart from the sheer plenitude and accidentality of particular form. The metaphysical and religious quest is ultimately riveted into the sensuous experience of being-in-the-world of things – the environment.

Moreover, in appearing in this manner, so this presentation can hardly be construed as any sort of *function* of the whole, as though creation were some sort of enormous circuit board intermittently switching on and off. Or, as Williams explains: given the characteristic and paradoxical interdependence of splendour and form 'it is impossible to conceive being-as-a-whole in a mechanical, supra-personal mode'. Much rather, have we not to conclude that it is some sort of 'system of contingent and flexible interdependence in which novelty and gratuity are possible – *and in which therefore beauty is intelligible*' (Williams 2007: 93, my italics). But what of this intelligibility?

For Balthasar this is to promote once again the perennial philosophical question:

'Why is there anything at all and not simply nothing?' (Balthasar 1991: 614). For in following Thomas Aquinas, Balthasar will discover in the polarity of form and splendour, erupting in the experience of beauty, *entrée* into the heart of the 'Real Distinction' itself: the difference between what a thing is and that a thing is that runs through every existent thing in creation. Given that in created being the two never coincide such that an apprehension of essence can automatically generate existence, then what of this 'suspension' of created beings? What of this indecipherable symbol that arrests us when we *see the form*?

Balthasar is clear: the 'question remains open regardless of whether one affirms or denies the existence of an absolute being' (Balthasar 2004a: 143). For while on the one hand, construing being as arising out of an abysmal dialectic with 'Nothing' would seem merely to stay the true urgency of the question; so on the other, positing the action of absolute being already sufficient to itself would end up with much the same result. Thus, Balthasar's conclusion:

> Only a philosophy of freedom and love can account for our existence, though not unless it also interprets the essence of finite beings in terms of love. In terms of love – and not, in the final analysis, in terms of consciousness, or spirit, or knowledge, or power, or desire, or usefulness. Rather, all of these must be seen as ways toward and presuppositions for the single fulfilling act that comes to light in a superabundant way in the sign of God.
>
> Thus, beyond existence in general and beyond the composition of essence, a light breaks on the constitution of being itself, insofar as it subsists in no other way than in the 'refusal-to-cling-to-itself', in the emptying of itself into the finite and concrete, while finite entities in turn are able to receive and retain it, as it is in itself, only as that which does not hold onto itself. Finite beings are thus trained by it in giving themselves away in love. One's consciousness, one's self-possession and possession of being, can grow only and precisely to the extent that one breaks out of being in and for oneself in the act of communication, in exchange, and in human and cosmic *sympatheia*. It is only the sign of God that places all the world's values in their true light, because it is only here that the limitations of love and all the objections to it are overcome, all the mysterious depths of self-sacrificing love are preserved and wrested from the grip of unrestrained knowledge.[8] (Balthasar 2004a: 143–44)

---

8   This dense passage makes a key claim that we have already had occasion to mention: the connection Balthasar draws between the Thomistic 'Real Distinction' – between the being and nature of a thing – and the archetypical character of divine love as manifest in Christ's kenosis (Phil. 2.7). The 'metaphysics' of this can be sketched as follows: in that Christ's incarnation reveals the character of divine love, just so is this reflected in the divine liberality of being which in accounting for nature as its formal cause nonetheless depends on it for its instantiation. Christ is thus prototype for the whole relationship by which created being both causes and depends on created nature. As Williams concludes, 'The structure of created being itself thus presupposes a Trinitarian foundation once it is recognized as centering upon the incarnate word' (Williams 2004: 41). To which, we need only add, as the Incarnate Word Christ not only grounds nature but simultaneously presupposes and receives himself from it, so nature's own characteristic interiority is given as no dull and protected hinterland but as, similarly, kenotic and ecstatic. For a scholarly elucidation of this see Healy 2005.

For Balthasar then a hermeneutic of beauty recovers for the environment – the 'whole' of finite being as accessed through particular beings – a quality of 'penultimate' valuation in the indecipherable signal it offers to 'human and cosmic *sympatheia*'. Which is to say, the testimony that finite beings offer to the paradoxical character of their appearing as both replete in being what they are and yet dependent upon receiving this existence in sheerly chance and limited circumstances – as though always and only ever *gift and gifted*. And this, surprisingly enough, remains in touch with Potter's intuition of both the sheer triviality and yet staggering importance of his 'experience': in short, the utterly mundane and yet wondrous quality of things.

Thus far we have travelled with Potter, and thus far, I want to suggest, does Balthasar provide us with – beginning with beauty – an interpretative energy *towards* an ecological hermeneutic.

However, if such a hermeneutic proper pretends towards a reason (*logos*) that understands our 'home' (*oikos*) as this ancient and fragile biosphere, then it will only be (as it always is with *logos*) as ordered about a point or 'explanation' for the dynamics of this teeming environment that we can both enliven and exploit. We may begin with rapture at this theophanic creation (and with, as it were, its 'inexhaustible' fuel of created Being), but its beauties will still, and always, appeal to our laborious 'completion' of the same, by way of cultural construct and fabrication.

And here, of course, Potter and Balthasar – the poet and the theologian – part company. For while the poet's artifice remains absolutely fundamental to understanding our place in the world (on this both Balthasar and Heidegger agree), for Balthasar, this witness – apart from revelation – will always remain constrained within the ever-alluring play of a 'nature that loves to hide'[9] – a game of hide and seek, of gain and, no doubt, loss. The theologian however, beyond so showy, even sublime, an appearance, looks *towards* 'the sign of absolute love' (Balthasar 2004a: 142)

---

9   In his brilliant survey of the idea of nature in the Western tradition, Pierre Hadot reveals how variant interpretations of Heraclitus' cryptic saying *Phusis kruptesthai philei* ('Nature loves to hide') have sustained 'two fundamental attitudes with regard to the secrets of nature: one voluntarist, the other contemplative'. Thus, under the patronage of Prometheus, Hadot describes the first as laying claim very early on to its legitimacy by affirming mankind's right to dominate nature – conferred on man by the God of Genesis – and to submit it, if necessary, to a judicial procedure and even torture, in order to make it hand over its secrets: Francis Bacon's famous metaphor would still be used by Kant and Cuvier. Magic, mechanics and technology take their place within this tradition, and each, moreover, had as its goal, each in its own way, to defend mankind's vital interests. In counterpoint, Hadot invokes the name of Orpheus to stand over a Nature which loves to hide for her secrets are dangerous to humankind. Thus, Hadot writes,

> By intervening technologically in natural processes, man risks discovering them and, what is worse, unleashing unforeseeable consequences. From this perspective, it is the philosophical or aesthetic approach . . . two attitudes that have their end in themselves and presuppose a disinterested approach, that will be the best means of knowing nature. Besides scientific truth, we will also have to allow for an aesthetic truth, which provides an authentic knowledge of nature. (Hadot 2006: 317)

imprinted on nature – for sure, the *Logos* as prototype of everything that is, but the *Logos* as most fully revealed in the Cross and Holy Saturday.

IV. *For the Drama of the Earth*

> [The] formative power of Christ lies in the formlessness of the grain of wheat that dies and wastes away [*verwesen*] in the humus, the grain that rises again, not in its own form but in that of a stalk of wheat (Jn 12:24; 1 Cor. 15:36, 42–44). This movement into the earth (*humilis*) is universally Christian . . .. (Balthasar 2004a: 137)

This essay has done no more than point to the manner in which the deepest *motivuum* of Balthasar's aesthetics may be understood to signal towards an ecological hermeneutic of *creation*.

However, if, following Balthasar, the 'surpassing' of cosmological and anthropological sciences is occasioned by the experience of beauty as both inward ('subjective') reception and outward ('objective') valuation, then this only goes to reinforce the always-already *dramatic* character of our immersion in the environment we inhabit; and, no doubt, dramatic resolution to the indecipherable sign that nature is to us.

For Balthasar there can be no re-establishment of an ascending 'great chain of Being' today – for the time of the cosmological vision has passed and, as is clear from Potter's testimony, no romantically slanted *eros*-nostalgia will ever reclaim it. What then of our crisis today? Is it that in circumstances such as this, the ecstatic quality of created being, stands to reveal its chthonic frailty in a distinctly *apocalyptic* hue – a seeing-through to the exhaustion of its gifted and gifting effluence? Certainly the apocalyptic register of our crisis is everywhere apparent.

But if such is to be reckoned the case, then it is perhaps particularly intriguing for any ecological appropriation of Balthasar's theology 'in-the-round' that nature – as bearing the imprint of sacrificial love – is finally revealed in its greatest Christological foundation and Trinitarian calibration through a decoding of the Book of Revelation (see Balthasar 1994). For Balthasar's 'theo-dramatics' (his 'ethics') is not a 'part-two' of a three-part story – such that we can (should we choose) isolate the transcendentals one by one – but is more properly to be seen as the apocalyptic 'overwriting' of divine theophany. Thus, as Balthasar writes:

> The image that should interpret the mystery of Christ is, in itself as an image of nature, utterly overtaxed, but in so far as it is grounded in Christ as the presupposition of nature, it is allowed to say by grace of the archetype what it cannot say of itself. (Balthasar 1986: 394)

Perhaps then, we can venture one final comment with regard to the 'light' that Balthasar's theology may throw on the project of an ecological hermeneutic. There is much in Balthasar's theology, as I have suggested, that can viably be conscripted, in the words of Lisa Sideris, to the 'imperatives of ecotheologians (particularly, I think of McFague's arguments) that we work harder at seeing the world around us with different eyes, [and] that concepts of knowing and loving become more closely aligned' (Sideris 2003: 259).

However, as Sideris' passing reference to the work of Sallie McFague – and her influential 'body of God' ecotheology – may suggest, the emergency of the moment has as much power to initiate genuinely fresh perspectives on the theological tradition as it does to fabricate passionately conceived simulacra of salvation as, perhaps, *survival*. No doubt serious theological thinking always needs to remind itself that the most apocalyptic 'seeing' stands, in some manner, to be bedazzled by the look-alike; and this precisely because in such a rapture one is brought face-to-face with that desire that has not been satisfied and perhaps may even remain chronically dissatisfied. As Balthasar concludes: 'The "program" of the Lamb, true to the earth by being truly *humilis* (i.e. close to the *humus*), can be popular with neither right nor left. It cannot be built into earthly programs; it does not offer enough for them and it cannot be exploited' (Balthasar 1972: viii).

References

Balthasar, H. Urs von 1972 *Man in History: A Theological Study* (London: Sheed and Ward).
Balthasar, H. Urs von 1982 *The Glory of the Lord, Volume I: Seeing the Form* (Edinburgh: T&T Clark).
Balthasar, H. Urs von 1984 *The Glory of the Lord: A Theological Aesthetics. Volume II, Studies in Theological Style: Clerical Styles* (Edinburgh: T&T Clark).
Balthasar, H. Urs von 1986 *The Glory of the Lord, Volume III: Studies in Theological Style: Lay Styles* (Edinburgh: T&T Clark).
Balthasar, H. Urs von 1988 *Theo-drama: Theological Dramatic Theory, Volume I: Prolegomena* (San Francisco: Ignatius Press).
Balthasar, H. Urs von 1991 *The Glory of the Lord, Volume V: The Realm of Metaphysics in the Modern Age* (Edinburgh: T&T Clark).
Balthasar, H. Urs von 1992 *The Theology of Karl Barth* (San Francisco: Ignatius Press).
Balthasar, H. Urs von 1993a *Mysterium Paschale* (Grand Rapids, MI: Eerdmans).
Balthasar, H. Urs von 1993b *My Work: In Retrospect* (San Francisco, CA: Ignatius Press).
Balthasar, H. Urs von 1994 *Theo-drama: Theological Dramatic Theory, Volume IV: The Action* (San Francisco: Ignatius Press).
Balthasar, H. Urs von 2004a *Love Alone Is Credible* (San Francisco, CA: Ignatius Press).
Balthasar, H. Urs von 2004b *Epilogue* (San Francisco, CA: Ignatius Press).
Dickens, W.T. 2003 *Hans Urs von Balthasar's Theological Aesthetics: A Model for Post-Critical Biblical Interpretation* (Notre Dame, IN: University of Notre Dame Press).
Donoghue, D. 2004 *Speaking of Beauty* (New Haven, CT: Yale University Press).
Ferré, F. 1996 *Being and Value: Toward a Constructive Postmodern Metaphysics* (New York, NY: State University of New York Press).
Hadot, P. 2006 *The Veil of Isis. An Essay on the History of the Idea of Nature* (Cambridge, MA: The Belknapp Press of Harvard University Press).
Healy, N.J. 2005 *The Eschatology of Hans Urs von Balthasar. Being as Communion* (Oxford: Oxford University Press).
Jenkins, W. 2008 *Ecologies of Grace: Environmental Ethics and Christian Theology* (Oxford: Oxford University Press).

Merchant, C. 1982 *The Death of Nature: Women, Ecology and the Scientific Revolution* (London: Wildwood House).
Milbank, J. 1997 *The Word Made Strange. Theology, Language, Culture* (Oxford: Blackwell).
Oakes, E.T. and Moss, D. 2004 *The Cambridge Companion to Hans Urs von Balthasar* (Cambridge: Cambridge University Press).
Potter, D. 1994 *Seeing the Blossom* (London: Faber & Faber).
Riches, J. 1996 'Balthasar's Sacramental Spirituality and Hopkins's Poetry of Nature: The Sacrifice Imprinted upon Nature', in D. Brown and A. Loades (eds), *Christ: The Sacramental Word. Incarnation, Sacrament and Poetry* (London: SPCK): 168–80.
Sideris, L.H. 2003 *Environmental Ethics, Ecological Selection and Natural Selection* (New York, NY: Columbia University Press).
White, L., Jr 1967 'The Historical Roots of Our Ecologic Crisis', *Science* 155: 1203–207.
Williams, R.D. 2004 'Balthasar and the Trinity', in E.T. Oakes and D. Moss (eds), *The Cambridge Companion to Hans Urs von Balthasar* (Cambridge: Cambridge University Press): 37–50.
Williams, R.D. 2007 'Balthasar, Rahner and the Apprehension of Being', in M. Higton (ed.), *Rowan Williams, Wrestling With Angels: Conversations in Modern Theology* (London: SCM): 86–105.

Chapter 15

Between Creation and Transfiguration:
The Environment in the Eastern Orthodox Tradition

Andrew Louth

Every evening – in theory as the sun is setting, and indeed in practice on the Holy Mountain and many other monasteries – Orthodox Christians throughout the world celebrate the service of Vespers. It begins with Psalm 103 (104, in the Hebrew enumeration), a song of creation.

> Bless the Lord, my soul! O Lord my God, you have been greatly magnified. You have clothed yourself with thanksgiving and majesty, wrapping yourself in light as in a cloak, stretching out the heavens like a curtain, roofing his upper chambers with waters, placing clouds as his mount, walking on the wings of the wind, making spirits his Angels and a flame of fire his Ministers, establishing the earth on its sure base; it will not be moved to age on age. The deep, like a cloak, is its mantle; waters will stand upon the mountains . . . How your works have been magnified, O Lord. With wisdom you have made them all, and the earth was filled with your creation . . . All things look to you to give them their food in due season. When you give it them, they will gather it.

Vespers marks the beginning of the liturgical day, following the Hebrew custom of beginning the day in the evening. The day moves from the setting of the sun, through the coming night, to the approaching day: liturgically we move from darkness to light, to welcome the light of the coming day, as a symbol of the *phos anesperon*, the 'light without evening', or the unfading light of the Kingdom. This, it seems to me, lays down the two poles of Eastern Orthodox reflection on the environment, the created order in which we are placed as human beings: creation and the coming revelation of a light that transfigures. This reflects an emphasis characteristic of all Orthodox theology, found, for example, in all the great Orthodox theologians of the last century – Sergii Bulgakov, Georges Florovsky, Vladimir Lossky, Dumitru Stăniloae – whatever other differences they may have had: a sense that the great arc of God's economy moves from creation to transfiguration or deification, and that the lesser arc, that we are all too often obsessed with – from fall to redemption – lies under this great arc, and finds its true meaning only in relation to it. Too often, it has seemed to the Orthodox, Western theology has become so concerned with the movement from fall to redemption that it has lost sight of the fact that all this takes place in the created environment, that rests on God's Word, in contrast with which human sin belongs strictly to the creaturely realm and cannot challenge what God has established through his creative Word, even though Eastern tradition sees human sin as having had cosmic consequences. Metropolitan Philaret has a marvellous image of creation – frequently quoted, or sometimes mis-quoted, by both Lossky and Florensky – in which he says that 'the creative Word is like an adamantine bridge, upon which creatures stand balanced beneath the abyss of divine infinitude, and above that of their own nothingness' (Philaret 2003: 268). We find in the Orthodox tradition a profound sense of the integrity of creation, based on the fact that it is founded on God's created word. Creation . . . and transfiguration. For the purpose of creation is to declare the glory of God, as another psalm of creation has it (Ps. 18.1 LXX [Ps. 19.1]): to declare God's glory by becoming a theophany, a manifestation of God; and the symbol of this is the event in Christ's life known as the Transfiguration.

So, let us explore a little the Orthodox understanding of creation and transfiguration, and then go on to explore two other concepts that underlie this linking of creation and transfiguration: the notion of the *logoi* of God, the divine principles of meaning written deep in the created order and the notion of Sophia, the Divine Wisdom, which became highly controversial in Russian theology in the first third of the last century, and is finding something of a revival nowadays.

It is, I think, impossible to overemphasize the importance for Orthodox theology of the doctrine of the creation of the cosmos out of nothing by God's Word. Creation out of nothing entails, first of all, that there is nothing in the creature that is not created, which means that everything we are we owe to God, there is nothing in us that is independent of God. Being created is, then, first and foremost a privilege, something that calls forth from us a fundamental attitude of thanksgiving. To realize the truth of creation is to realize the beauty and wonder of the created order. Being created is not a handicap or a disadvantage. As Nicolay Berdyaev (1937: 27) remarked, 'There can be no question of the work of a great artist being poor, low and insignificant simply because it is created'. Among created beings, humans have a unique privilege: that of being able to know that they are created, to be conscious of the fact. We can acknowledge that with thanksgiving, or we can resent it, and attempt to endow our own natural view of the world – from our own perspective – with some metaphysical significance, as if the world really turned around us and our priorities, and in this way turn away from the creator. If, however, we turn from the creator, the source of our being, there is nowhere real to turn. And so we turn inwards, to a world centred on ourselves, a world of unreality. This is how St Athanasios (1971: 11) understands it in the early chapters of his *Contra Gentes* (*C. Gent*), and he remarks: 'I call unreality what is evil because what has no real existence has been invented by the conceits of men' (*C. Gent* 4). If we turn away from God, we turn to a realm of unreality, of nothingness. This is what Philaret means by the image already quoted: the creatures on the adamantine bridge of the creative word are poised between the 'abyss of the divine infinitude' – which draws them into being – and that of 'their own nothingness' – that is ultimately threatening.

To acknowledge the creator is fundamentally an act of prayer, so it is no surprise that in *The Way of the Pilgrim*, as the pilgrim learns to pray the Jesus prayer, he finds that

> The prayer of my heart gave me such consolation that I felt there was no happier person on earth than I, and I doubted if there could be greater and fuller happiness in the kingdom of Heaven. Not only did I feel this in my own soul, but the whole outside world also seemed to me full of charm and delight. Everything drew me to love and thank God: people, trees, plants, animals. I saw them all as my kinsfolk, I found on all of them the magic of the Name of Jesus. Sometimes I felt as light as though I had no body and was floating through the air instead of walking. Sometimes when I withdrew into myself I saw clearly all my internal organs, and was filled with wonder at the wisdom with which the human body is made . . . (French 1954: 105–106)

The doctrine of creation, then, means that our created environment is touched by the hand of God, is a place where we can encounter God, and still in some way bears the traces of the paradise of delight that God intended his creation to be. Human sin obscures our perception of this, and encourages an attitude to the created order that ceases to take seriously the fact that it is created, seeing it rather as a resource to be exploited for our own purposes. As we do that, we begin to misconstrue the world around us, our own attitude becomes destructive, we cease to see the world as a gift, and instead begin to compete one with another in fashioning our own worlds, which encroach on one another, so that it becomes a matter of contention whether this is mine or yours, as we forget the reality that it is God's – and so both mine and yours, as a gift to share, or neither mine nor yours, as a possession to grasp and hold.

It is a striking fact of Church history that, as Christianity emerged in Roman society, what was distinctive about it was not just its confession of the crucified Lord as the one who rose from the dead, but also the Christian confession of God as creator. They were seen to be linked together. Salomina, the mother of the Maccabaean martyrs, on whose lips are placed the first explicit confession of creation out of nothing – 'look at heaven and earth . . . and recognize that God did not make them out of things that existed' – assures her last son that 'the Creator of the world, who shaped the beginning of man and devised the origin of all things, will in his mercy give life and breath back to you', through resurrection (*2 Macc.* 7.28, 23). The one who created the world out of nothing could well be believed to raise the dead. Against traditional paganism that took the world of men and gods for granted as an ultimate reality, and against various forms of gnosticism that attributed this world to a God either malevolent or incompetent, but not the true Father of the Lord Jesus Christ, Christians believed that the one who hung on the cross and rose from the dead was the one through whom the created order had come into being. Though the terms have changed, it seems to me that our situation today, in a world of exploitative consumerism and the dream of life as something that can be confected, is not that different from that of our Fathers in the faith in the second century. The doctrine of creation out of nothing by God is a radical doctrine with radical consequences.

There is more, however, to the Patristic – and Orthodox – understanding of creation than creation out of nothing. Much of what we have outlined above is readily to be seen in the Genesis account of creation, especially the so-called 'first' account (Gen. 1.1–2.3): the created order is good, *kalos*, and created by a word, with no suggestion that God has had to impose his will on recalcitrant material. But the Fathers read the Genesis account with what was for them a contemporary understanding of the cosmos, which meant one derived for the most part from Plato's *Timaeus*. Ideas in that dialogue that contravened their understanding of God were discarded: the idea that God imposed his purpose on pre-existent matter that only yielded 'for the most part' to the Creator's intentions, the notion that the cosmos is itself a living being, as are the celestial bodies. But much else they retained – mainly, I think, because it was simply part of current contemporary wisdom. So the idea that the cosmos was made out of the four elements; what we call a 'Ptolemaic' picture of the cosmos, with the earth at the centre, surrounded by the planetary spheres and at its furthest limit the fixed sphere of the stars: these ideas they retained. It was something almost unconscious. A striking example can be found in the first chapter of St Gregory of Nyssa's vastly influential *De hominis opificio* [On the Making of Human kind] (*opif.*). He begins by quoting Gen. 2.4 – 'This is the book of the generation of heaven and earth' – and then continues in the rest of the chapter to give an account of the Ptolemaic system of the universe, with the heavy earth at the centre surrounded by planetary and stellar spheres, the latter revolving at an alarming speed. The transition from quoting the Scriptures to expounding a view of the universe stemming ultimately from Plato's *Timaeus* is unconscious. The most important idea, however, the Christian Fathers took from the *Timaeus* was the notion of the cosmos as modelled on the human, so that the human can be called a 'little cosmos', a *microcosmos*, to use the coinage of the Renaissance, suggesting that there is a profound correlation between the cosmic and the human. They found this idea in the Genesis account of creation by observing that the human came last, and that he was created by God not just with a word, but with deliberation: 'Let us make man', says God, 'after our image and likeness' (Gen. 1.26). The human came last, because the cosmos had been prepared for him, as a kind of 'royal lodging for a future king' (*opif.* 2.1), and it was because the human had been created in the image and likeness of God, that the human was in some sense a mediator between God and the created order, the 'bond of creation'. So the human, for the Fathers and for subsequent Orthodox theology, is a final ornament of creation, but also deeply implicated in its fate. The decay and corruption of the cosmos is due, in some way, to human sin and disobedience to God that has prevented the human from fulfilling its role as the centre point of the cosmos, the bond of creation. The human and cosmic are mutually implicated, the one in the other. The human story is a story with cosmic implications; the cosmic story a human one. It is this mutual correlation that provides what one might call a matrix for the Incarnation. God incarnate as human is not some alien incursion into the cosmos, but rather the presupposition that makes possible the true destiny of humanity – to become God.

All this becomes important when we turn to look at the transfiguration of the cosmos. Creation is the presupposition of our existence; it is where we start from. Our destiny is transfiguration. We can do no better than look at the way in which the Greek Fathers, especially, interpret the Gospel account of the Transfiguration. The key to patristic understanding of the Transfiguration can be seen in the sixth-century apse mosaic at the Monastery of St Catherine on Sinai (then, and for most of the Middle Ages, called the Monastery of the Burning Bush, near to which the monastery is situated). In the centre of the apse Christ appears transfigured, flanked by Moses and Elias, with the three Apostles at the foot of the mountain, overwhelmed and amazed. In two roundels to the side of the apse there is depicted Moses, before the Burning Bush on one side and on Mount Sinai itself, receiving the tablets of the Law. To anyone with any familiarity with Patristic interpretation of Moses' ascent of Sinai, what is suggested by these juxtapositions is obvious. Christians from the time of Clement of Alexandria, inspired by Philo, had interpreted Moses' ascent of Mount Sinai in terms of the soul's ascent to the contemplation of God. The revelation at the Burning Bush, soon interpreted by Christians as a symbol of the perpetual virginity of the Mother of God – the most palpable of all theophanies that did not, however, breach her bodily integrity – followed by the ascent in the dark clouds of Sinai to the 'place where God stood' (Gen. 24.10): all this is interpreted of the mysterious encounter between the soul and God, mysterious because God remains one who is sought but never found. The mosaic of the Transfiguration in the monastic church at Sinai superimposes, as it were, two mountains: Mount Tabor and Mount Sinai, the mount of God's revelation with the mount of the soul's search for God.

So, too, does St Maximos in his several interpretations of the Transfiguration that we find in his early works.[1] The three Apostles represent faith, hope and love, the qualities required of Christian discipleship. Elias, Moses and Christ represent what Evagrios had called the stage of ascetic struggle (*praktiki*), natural contemplation (*physiki*) and *theologia*, contemplation of God Himself – the three stages of the soul's progress towards God. In the account of the Transfiguration, the evangelists draw attention to the radiant face of the Christ and his shining garments. Maximos makes a play on meanings with the word for face, *prosōpon* in Greek, which also means person. The radiant face of Christ, on which the disciples cannot look, is the hidden mystery of the being of the Divine Person that he is: beholding the light that reveals and blinds, the disciples acknowledge the divinity of Christ by apophatic theology, that denies any human access to the being of God himself, revealed in the face. The shining garments of Christ are creation and Scripture: the created order in which the God is revealed through the divine principles, the *logoi* of creation, and the Scriptures in which God is revealed through the verbal *logoi* of the text. This represents cataphatic theology: words, ideas and images which enable us to say something about God. Transfiguration, then, sums up everything that theophany represents: God's self-manifestation in creation, in his communication of himself in revelation,

---

1   Maximos discusses the Transfiguration in the following works: *Centuries on Theology and the Incarnate Dispensation* (*CT*) II. 13–16; *Questions and Answers* 191–92; *Amb.* 10.

and ultimately in the communication of his own personal being in the Incarnation. Not only that, though, but also the capacity to receive, understand and participate in God's self-communication, something made possible only by all the demands of the spiritual life, the renunciation of self-centred snatching at the divine mystery, the ingrained passion to possess, together with the cultivation of a patient waiting on God and his word, a letting-go of the self in the divine mystery. Transfiguration is ultimately nothing less than the return of the creature to God, a return in which the creatures and the whole of creation discover their own deepest meaning. In this transfiguration, the human once again discovers its role at the heart of the created order, the human once again becomes priest of the creation, through his own capacity to think and understand, to pray and to relate. What this means ultimately, indeed what this means penultimately, is far from clear, and teases us out of thought.

I need to pause here, as I have presented a picture that is dense with meaning and full of allusive links. I have done this, not to confuse or impress, but because it seems to me that it is characteristic of the Byzantine imagination – that modern Orthodox theology tries, at best, to emulate – to hold a number of interrelating themes together, so that theology itself becomes almost iconic: something to look at, explore, puzzle over and ultimately to respond to. Transfiguration, as I have presented it, is similarly complex, and it might help if I attempt to list some of its components. First of all, to speak of transfiguration as the goal and purpose of creation is to suggest a genuine transformation, but not a transformation *into something else*, rather it is a transformation that reveals the true reality of what is transfigured. Christ is revealed as how he really is; the creation, that he has assumed in the Incarnation, is similarly revealed as what it truly is, not as a backdrop to the drama of revelation and atonement. One of the leading ideas of St Maximos' theology – equally important in the speculative and ascetic theology of his early period and in the Christological controversies of his later years – is that 'nothing natural can be opposed to God in any way' (*Opuscula theologica et polemica* [*Opusc.*] 3). This is fundamental to his defence of the full humanity of Christ: there is nothing in human nature that is opposed to God, and so nothing that the Word of God does not assume, including a human will. But it is also fundamental to his understanding of our experience of human nature. The ascetic ideal, that he pursued, does not involve any kind of repudiation of human nature. The flight from the world that monasticism entails is a flight from our limited and debased conception of the world: so that we can see the world as it truly is. At every turn, we come back in Maximos' thought to the conviction of the integrity of the natural. But there are two other aspects of the concept of transfiguration I want to underline. First, in the image of the mountain, the cosmos is the place of our encounter with God: this is why, it seems to me, the Greek Fathers, including St Maximos, see the episode of the Transfiguration as an epitome of the spiritual life – reminding us of the virtues of faith, hope and love, or of the way in which we reach contemplation of God, through an ascetic struggle that enables us, first of all, to contemplate the created order itself. I am a little hesitant (unlike some of my Orthodox colleagues) in drawing on William Blake, who made such individual use of the ideas that attracted him, but the expression 'cleansing the doors of perception' seems to me to sum up what is required in our human encounter with the world in which we live. The doors of perception that lead out on to the world have become encrusted with our own concerns to the extent that they can no longer be opened, we can no longer, through our senses, pass to any real encounter with the world of God's creation; what we encounter is what we want to make of it. To see the cosmos as transfigured is to see it as it really is. Secondly, in this encounter with creation transfigured, we encounter Christ himself, Christ as revealed in nature and revelation, which is what is meant by the Byzantine interpretation of the shining garments as nature and Scripture. Christ is clothed, as it were, in the garments of nature and history, the history of God's encounter with the human to which the Scripture bears witness. But the shining garments are shining because of the light that transfigures, a light that shines in its purity from Christ's face, and dazzles, even as it draws us into a face-to-face encounter with Christ.

There are two ways, as I have mentioned, in which the understanding of the cosmos as existing between creation and transfiguration have been drawn out in Orthodox theology: the doctrine of the *logoi* of creation, especially associated with St Maximos the Confessor,[2] and the notion of Sophia, the Divine Wisdom, especially associated with Russian theology at the end of the nineteenth/beginning of the twentieth century.

Let us begin with the doctrine of the *logoi* of creation. The very word *logos* causes problems: it is a very special word in Greek. Theodor Haecker, the lay Austrian Catholic theologian who died at the end of the Second World War, once suggested that in every language there are one or two untranslatable words – he called them *Herzwörter*, heart words – in which is concentrated something of the genius of the language. In Latin, it is *res*, usually translated 'thing'; in German, *Wesen*, 'essence'; in French, *raison*, 'reason'; in English, *sense*. In Greek it is, he suggested, *logos* (Haecker 1958: 131–32). It can be translated, according to context, word, reason, principle, meaning; but this fragments the connotation of the Greek word, which holds all these meanings together. There is a lot that could be said about the history of the word *logos* in Greek thought, but I shall simply dwell on its use in Greek Christian thought. The universe was created by God, through his *Logos*, which is identical with the second person of the Trinity, the Son of the Father. To say that the universe is created by the *Logos* entails that the universe has a meaning, both as a whole and in each of its parts. That 'meaning' is *logos*: everything that exists has its own *logos*, and that *logos* is derived from God the *Logos*. To have meaning, *logos*, is to participate in the *Logos* of God. Behind this lurks a Platonic idea, that everything exists by participating in its form, or idea, which is characterized by its definition; the Greek for definition (in this sense) is, again, *logos*. These Platonic forms, or *logoi*, to call them by what defines them, are eternal. In the period between Plato and St Maximos much water had flowed

---

2   On this topic see Dalmais 1952, Van Rossum 1993, Tollefsen 2008: 64–137.

down the history of ideas, and for Maximos, because the world has been created by God through his *Logos*, it can no longer be regarded as a pale reflection of eternal reality, as with Plato's world. The created world has value, meaning, beauty, in itself: because God is the supreme craftsman, his creation is supremely lovely. The beauty and meaning is found in the *logoi*: so the *logoi*, in one sense at least, are created: they belong to the created order. In another sense they are uncreated, because they are, as it were, God's thoughts, or intentions, or, to use the words Maximos borrows from the early sixth-century Dionysios the Areopagite, 'divine predeterminations and wills'.[3] So the *logos* of a created being means what it is, what defines its nature – Maximos speaks of the *logos tēs phuseōs*, meaning or definition or principle of nature – but this means what God intends it to be, what he wills, what he predetermines. This final point needs to be underlined: the divine *logoi* are expressions of the divine will. Here we find perhaps the most important point at which Maximos, building on his Christian predecessors, advances beyond Plato. For Plato, beings participate in the Forms; for Maximos created beings participate in God through the *logoi*, but these *logoi* must also be seen as expressing God's will and intention, for each created being, and for the cosmos as a whole. There is a dynamism about Maximos' understanding of God's relationship to the cosmos through the *logoi*, that is lacking in Plato; the cosmos itself is moving towards fulfilment, and that fulfilment is ultimately found in union with God, from whom it has received being. This opens out into an aspect of Maximos' thought of which we can only catch glimpses: on the one hand, these *logoi* are inviolable, they may be obscured by the fall, but they cannot be distorted – as we have seen, 'nothing that is natural is opposed to God' (*Opusc.* 7: PG 91.80A). But on the other hand, these *logoi* are not static, certainly not if we take into account the fact that they represent God's will for each creature. Maximos assumes that natures are fixed – all his contemporaries did – but his thought is open to the idea of evolution, say, as a way of expressing God's providence, and certainly in the case of human beings, who possess rational freedom, the meaning of each human *logos* is expressed through what he calls *logoi* of providence and judgement, by which God's providential intention is expressed through a working together with free human actions (*synergeia*).

But to understand Maximos properly, we have to add something else that we have already begun to adumbrate. For if human beings are created in the image of God, and it is the *Logos* of God that communicates the divine nature, that displays God's image, then this means that human beings are fashioned after the *Logos* of God, something manifest in the fact that human beings are *logikos*, the adjective from *logos*, usually translated as 'rational', but really connoting something much broader and deeper. One could say that human beings, as *logikos*, are capable of discerning meaning, maybe even conferring meaning (is that the implication of the story of Adam naming the animals?); it certainly includes freewill, which Maximos designates by the Greek word, *autexousia*, which means fundamentally 'authority over oneself'.

---

3 Cf. Dionysios, *Divine Names* 5.8, quoted by Maximos, *Ambigua* (*Amb.*) 7 (PG 91.1085A).

Because human beings participate in the divine *Logos*, they are *logikos*, and are therefore capable of discerning meaning, that is *logos*: they are capable of discerning the *logoi* of creation, the whole depth of meaning that can be found in creation in all its manifold splendour: this understanding of the cosmos he calls *phusikē theōria*, natural contemplation. But alas, because of the fall, human beings can no longer fulfil this their role as priests and interpreters of creation: they fail to achieve understanding, and the limpid meaning of the cosmos becomes dark obscurity. What is needed is for the *Logos* himself, the Son of God, to assume rational humanity, and to renew the human function as bond of the cosmos from within, so to speak. That is the purpose of the Incarnation: through being born of Mary, the Mother of God, the *Logos* of God lives through human existence from within, renewing it in the course of his life, finally confronting the ultimate meaninglessness of death, and giving it meaning in the resurrection. But that is only part, though the most important part, of the story, for this renewal worked by the Incarnate Word of God has to be appropriated by all those who are baptized into the death and resurrection of Christ, and this appropriation takes place through participation in the sacramental life of the Church and through the ascetic struggle of the Christian life, the overcoming of vices and growing in virtue. This entails that the personal life of struggle against temptation, and growing in virtue, is not simply a personal matter, what Michel Foucault has called '*souci de soi*', care for the self, it is a matter of cosmic significance, for such ascetic struggle restores the human capacity of being priest of nature, interpreter of the cosmos. This is true for Maximos in various ways, but one that is immediately relevant here is that through ascetic struggle the Christian attains a state of serenity, and one of the fruits of that serenity is to be able to discern the *logoi* of creation: to see the cosmos as God intended it, to have our capacity for spiritual sight restored.

Spiritual sight enables us to attain understanding, and this understanding involves more than an expansion of our knowledge (though it does not exclude that): the understanding gained here involves an inner transformation – requiring personal effort, personal asceticism – that opens us up to that which we know (or the One whom we know), so that it is through *participation* that our understanding is deepened. How far such participation can go – Maximos certainly speaks of it in terms of union with God and even deification or *theosis*, 'becoming God' – is a natural question to raise here. For Maximos this participation in God is through the *logoi* (and therefore through the *Logos* himself, for 'the One Logos is many logoi and the many logoi one': PG 91.1081B) remains creaturely participation, and only takes place through grace: however deeply one comes to participate in God, one remains a creature, and that movement of participation, or deification, is only possible in response to God's prior movement towards us in incarnation (in any of its forms).

But the point of mentioning participation in this context is less to raise such questions than to draw attention to the kind of understanding attained through participation in God through the *logoi*. Just as we can only understand Scripture if we let it call in question the smallness of our ideas and the narrowness of our desires; so we can only understand the *logoi* of the cosmos if we renounce any attempt on our part to understand the world as material for human exploitation, and seek to see it as expressive of the *Logos* of God. Maximos' doctrine of the *logoi* of creation is not simply a way of expressing the immanence of the divine will, but also a way of finding a place for human understanding of that will as expressed in creation – a way of human understanding that has its own ascetic demands of patience and objectivity.

The doctrine of the *logoi* reveals a cosmos suffused with divine meaning. It seems to me that it was something similar that the Russians were trying to express with their sophiology, as it came to be called. To simplify, I shall simply discuss Fr Sergii Bulgakov, the one around whom the controversy came to revolve, not that other protagonists – such as Solov'ev and Florensky – are not interesting, but simply for reasons of space. With all of them, we have a sense of an ancient tradition coming to the aid of modern man, who is attracted by the Promethean promise of what humans might now achieve through technology. Bulgakov is, I believe, best approached through his autobiographical reflections; his formal statements on sophiology are heavy with the conceptual weight of nineteenth-century German idealism, especially in the form it took with Schelling. Nowadays, this seems to me to present barriers to understanding him: why should we have to think through the dark weavings of an out-dated philosophical system?

One thing that is striking about Bulgakov's spiritual journey – sharing in this with Solov'ev and Florensky – is the importance of personal experience, in his case of art and nature. First, his account of an experience from the days of his early manhood, attracted by the Marxist vision to see the natural world as a source of economic wealth through the 'industry' of agriculture.

> For a decade I have lived without faith and, after early stormy doubts, a religious emptiness reigned in my soul. One evening we were driving across the southern steppes of Russia, and the strong-scented spring grass was gilded by the rays of a glorious sunset. Far in the distance I saw the blue outlines of the Caucasus. This was my first sight of the mountains. I looked with ecstatic delight at their rising slopes. I drank in the light and the air of the steppes. I listened to the revelation of nature. My soul was accustomed to the dull pain of seeing nature as a lifeless desert and of treating its surface beauty as a deceptive mask. Yet, contrary to my intellectual convictions, I could not be reconciled to nature without God. (Bulgakov 1976: 10)

This marked the beginnings of Bulgakov's return to the faith of his childhood and his ancestors. The revelation of the beauty of nature was something he could not deny, nor, however, could he accept it with his atheistic convictions: he realized that, as he put it, he 'could not be reconciled to nature without God'. The reconciliation took many years. Another step on the way occurred three years later, in Dresden. He says:

> It was a foggy autumn morning. I went to the art gallery in order to do my duty as a tourist. My knowledge of European painting was negligible. I did not know what to expect. The eyes of the Heavenly Queen, the Mother who holds in her arms the Eternal Infant, pierced my soul. I cried joyful and yet bitter tears, and with them the ice melted from my soul, and

some of my psychological knots were loosened. This was an aesthetic emotion, but it was also a new knowledge; it was a miracle. I was then still a Marxist, but I was obliged to call my contemplation of the Madonna by the name of 'prayer'. I went to the Zwinger Gallery early in the mornings in order to pray and weep in front of the Virgin . . . (Bulgakov 1976: 11)

This step involved loosening the strings of his heart – through an aesthetic experience that led him to the experience of prayer, and not just a 'form of words', but tearful prayers from the depths of his heart. The appreciation of nature, the melting of a heart frozen by a purely rationalist way of looking at reality: these led Bulgakov to embrace once again the faith. The person of Christ does not stand obviously at the centre of this experience, rather it is the vulnerable beauty of nature and the tender gaze of the Mother of God. And it is this that lies, I would maintain, at the heart of Bulgakov's notion of the Divine Wisdom, Sophia. His clearest words on this are found in his account of another vision, somewhat later than the ones related. In January 1923, having just been expelled from Russia at Lenin's decree, alongside other non-Marxist intellectuals, he found himself standing in the Great Church of Hagia Sophia in Constantinople, then a mosque.

Human tongue cannot express the lightness, the clarity, the simplicity, the wonderful harmony which completely dispels all sense of heaviness – the heaviness of the cupola and the walls. A sea of light pours from above and dominates all this space, enclosed and yet free. The grace of the columns and the beauty of their marble lace, the royal dignity – not luxury, but regality – of the golden walls and the marvellous ornamentation: it captivates and melts the heart, subdues and convinces. It creates a sense of inner transparency; the weightiness and limitations of the small and suffering self disappear; the self is gone, the soul is healed of it, losing itself in these arches and merging into them. It becomes the world: I am in the world and the world is in me . . . This is indeed Sophia, the real unity of the world in the Logos, the co-inherence of all with all, the world of divine ideas, κόσμος νοητός. It is Plato baptized by the Hellenic genius of Byzantium – it is his world, his lofty realm to which souls ascend for the contemplation of Ideas. The pagan Sophia of Plato beholds herself mirrored in the Christian Sophia, the divine Wisdom. Truly, the church of Hagia Sophia is the artistic, tangible proof and manifestation of Hagia Sophia – of the Sophianic nature of the world and the cosmic nature of Sophia. It is neither heaven nor earth, but the vault of heaven above the earth. We perceive here neither God nor man, but divinity, the divine veil thrown over the world. How true was our ancestors' feeling in this temple, how right they were in saying that they did not know whether they were in heaven or on earth! Indeed they were neither in heaven nor on earth, they were in Hagia Sophia – between the two: this is the μεταξύ of Plato's philosophical intuition. Hagia Sophia is the last silent testimony to the future ages of the Greek genius: a revelation in stone . . . The church of Hagia Sophia is Plato's realm of ideas in stone rising above the chaos of non-being and subduing it through persuasion: the actual *pleroma*, all as a single whole, pan-unity. Here it is manifested and shown to the world. O Lord, how holy, how marvellous, how precious is this manifestation! (Bulgakov 1976: 13–14)

This extraordinary account draws together themes we have already encountered, and expresses the idea of creation as touched by God with his Sophia, as it were, so that nothing that exists can be thought of as alien to God; all that exists feels the presence of Sophia, and manifests God's holiness, revealing his presence.

'The environment in the Eastern Orthodox Tradition': that title may have created the expectation of some direct engagement with environmental problems from a fresh perspective, and readers may by now be feeling disappointed. In my view, the contribution of Eastern Orthodoxy to the pressing questions of the environment is not to be sought in any specific solutions, not thought of by others, but rather in our faithfulness to a sense of the holiness of the created order, and a sense of the holiness of the human being. Such a sense of the holiness of the created undermines any view of the world as pure nature, opposed to God – an idea I would not want to characterize as typical of post-scholastic theology (though some would), but rather the result of the kind of amnesia that a Christianity too focused on minute arguments about grace can so easily succumb to. It is not as merely human (or 'all too human') that we should regard our fallen human condition, for it is already on the brink of transformation – transfiguration – by the One who, as we sing often during Eastertide, has come 'to raise up fallen Adam'.

References

Athanasios 1971 Contra Gentes *and* De Incarnatione (Oxford: Clarendon Press).
Berdyaev, N. 1937 *The Destiny of Man* (London: Geoffrey Bles).
Bulgakov, S. 1976 *A Bulgakov Anthology: Sergius Bulgakov 1871–1944* (J. Pain and N. Zernov [eds]; London: SPCK).
Dalmais, I. H. 1952 'La théorie des "logoi" des creatures chez S. Maxime le Confesseur', *Revue des Sciences Philosophiques et Théologiques* 36: 244–49.
French, R.M. 1954 *The Way of a Pilgrim* (London: SPCK)
Gregory of Nyssa *De hominis opificio (opif.)* (PG 44.124–256).
Haecker, T. 1958 *Hirtengedichte, Vergil: Vater des Abendlandes* (Frankfurt am Main and Hamburg: Fischer Bücherei).
Maximos *Ambigua (Amb.)* 10 (PG 91.1125D–1128D).
Maximos *Centuries on Theology and the Incarnate Dispensation (CT)* II. 13–16 (PG 90.1129C–1132C);
Maximos *Opuscula theologica et polemica (Opusc.)* 3 (PG 90.48D).
Maximos 1982 *Questions and Answers*, in J.H. Declerck (ed.), *Corpus Christianorum, Series Graeca* 10: 132–35, 191–92.
Philaret (Drozdov) of Moscow 2003 *Izbrannye Trudy, Pisma, Vospomunaniya* (Moscow: St Tikhon's Orthodox Theological Institute).
Tollefsen, T. T. 2008 *The Christological Cosmology of St Maximus the Confessor* (Oxford: Oxford University Press).
Van Rossum, J. 1993 'The λόγοι of Creation and the Divine "energies" in Maximus the Confessor and Gregory Palamas', *Studia Patristica* 27: 213–17.

Chapter 16

JÜRGEN MOLTMANN'S ECOLOGICAL HERMENEUTICS

Jeremy Law

The theology of Jürgen Moltmann has always been situated theology. It has been theology forged in the creative pressure between the anvil of the particular account which the Christian faith gives of the history of the Father, the Son and the Holy Spirit, and the hammer of present circumstance. More specifically, it has long been ecological theology. This has been explicitly so since at least 1972 and the publication of *The Crucified God*, the second of Moltmann's first trilogy of major volumes.[1] Here industrial pollution of nature was seen as one of four vicious circles of death arising from a one-sided focus on economic values, profit and progress (CG[2] 329–31). The implicit grounding for a theology that supported ecological concern, however, was already to be found in *Theology of Hope* (1964), Moltmann's first, and, in this author's view, still his greatest major work. This is because the eschatological prospect of the new creation of all things, entailed in Jesus' resurrection, concerns 'the future of the very earth on which his cross stands' (TH 21). Ecological attention has remained a prominent feature of Moltmann's thinking ever since.

The Nature of the Ecological Crisis

What Moltmann terms the 'scientific and technological civilisation' (WJC 63 *et passim*) of the contemporary Western world is responsible for the 'ecological crisis'. Its 'reckless exploitation of natural resources is destroying the natural foundations of life' (CJF 51). The consequences of this project manifest themselves in the physical environment. Extinctions, pollution, desertification, water shortages and climate change are its hallmarks (HTG 71). This physical manifestation of the crisis also

---

1   It is this first trilogy, and the associated smaller publications, which constitute Moltmann's 'early theology'. By 'later theology' is intended his series of 'systematic contributions to theology' (TKG xi) which began with *The Trinity and the Kingdom of God* (1980) and continued formally until *Experiences in Theology* (2000). This series has effectively been prolonged, however, in a succession of later volumes, the most recent of which is his autobiography, *A Broad Place* (2007).
2   Abbreviations are used for the titles of Moltmann's primary texts. The bibliography provides a key to their interpretation.

contains an inevitable social cost: 'The Western standard of living cannot be universalised. It can only be sustained at the expense of others: at the expense of people in the Third World, at the expense of coming generations, and at the expense of the earth' (GSS 93).

For Moltmann, however, the primary location of the 'ecological crisis' is to be found in neither the physical environment nor its social consequences. It is a crisis of values. In fact, it is a religious crisis, a crisis of that in which people in the Western world place their trust (GSS 95). 'The crisis we are experiencing is therefore not just an "ecological crisis", nor can it be solved by purely technical means. A change in convictions and basic values is as necessary as a change in attitudes in life and life-style' (CJF 53). When the 'ravaged earth' is understood not merely as human environment but as creation destined to be God's environment, then such a 'nihilistic destruction of nature' is revealed as 'atheism put into practice' (HTG 75). Again, the unfettered demand of the modern scientific and technological civilization for 'progress' and 'growth' (GinC 28) is nothing less than a death-drive (CG 331; SofL 97):

> Nietzsche's 'will to power' and the growth-orientated 'increase in life' manifests a climber mentality which is contrary to nature, destructive of nature, and suicidal; it aims to tread underfoot anyone who is weaker, or different, or alien, and it digs its own mass grave. The German 'will to power' ended up in two world wars, in Verdun, Stalingrad and Auschwitz. (EinT 149)

Precisely because the 'ecological crisis' is seen to be rooted in a particular human self-interpretation, and so calls for an urgent re-evaluation of values, there is a public role for theology (SW 49). Theology can make its contribution, and this chapter will seek to unfold how Moltmann attempts an ecological hermeneutic of theology to achieve just this. It is an urgent task. Moltmann consistently holds open the question of whether the 'ecological crisis' is reversible. His own personal experience (of the Second World War, and of retirement)[3] has been that 'in every end a new beginning lies hidden' (IEB 35). This is also a profound theological principle. It can be seen in the resurrection of the crucified Christ, the continuing epicentre of Moltmann's theology. Yet when Moltmann examines the 'creeping ecological catastrophe' within the rubric of this pattern (IEB 33–52) there is silence concerning a new beginning. With the 'ecological crisis' human life has entered an 'End-time' condition in which its very future existence is threatened (CJF 72; cf. WJC 45–46; CofG 208; GSS 117).

Anthropological Theology

The 'will to power', that Moltmann diagnoses to be at the root of the 'ecological crisis', also extends to the attitude people display towards their own bodies (GSS 15).

---

3   For details see BP 13–15, 335–63.

We treat our bodies as we do our cars (CJF 75). Our bodies are subjugated to the demands of the will and alienated from their own intrinsic rhythms with disastrous consequences for both our health and our attitude to sickness (GinC 270–77). 'The alienation of the human being from his bodily existence must be viewed as the inner aspect of the external ecological crisis of modern industrial society' (GinC 48). This inner dimension of the 'ecological crisis' is not merely a worthy additional observation, rather it points to the fundamental Cartesian dichotomy between the thinking subject (*res cogitans*) and the rest of the extended world (*res extensa*), including the subject's own body. It was within this bifurcated world that modern, liberal theology sought refuge in the subjective realm of human 'history', leaving the realm of 'nature' to the rapidly advancing exact sciences (GinC 31–32). But this reduction of theology's compass to human existence, this reduction of theology to 'anthropological theology',[4] carries a set of consequences which means that, far from being a source of challenge to the values which have led to the 'ecological crisis', anthropological theology becomes a contributor. It does so because it effectively separates human existence from the rest of creation. Thus, God's presence and revelation are discerned in human history, not in nature. It is the soul which possesses God's Spirit and image, not the body. Consequently, anthropological theology is in danger of producing 'a godless view of nature and a natureless view of God' (CJF 75). Salvation, within this purview, is merely salvation of the soul, and begins to look like a Gnostic myth (CofG 259–60). 'A doctrine of God which leads to a cleavage in reality [between soul and body] is not a doctrine of God the Creator' (SofL 37). An important strand of Moltmann's endeavour is, therefore, the attempt to burst apart this Cartesian prison and bring the language of theology into direct confrontation with the extended world once again.

Biblical Contingence and Universal Relevance

Of programmatic significance for Moltmann's theological method is the following statement from the essay 'Theology as Eschatology' (1970):

> Christian theology speaks of God with respect to the concrete, specific, and contingent history, which is told and witnessed to in the biblical writings . . . as long as the dialectical unity of particular history and special historical mediation with the universally relevant that pertains directly to everyone can be retained, that is, as long as the unity of Jesus with God and of God with Jesus can be retained Christianity is alive. As soon as the dialectical unity between history and absolute is broken, Christianity disintegrates. (TasE 1–2)

---

[4] Moltmann's more common use of 'anthropological' as a qualifier is in relation to Christology (see, for example, WJC 55–63). He does though extend it to theology as such (for example, IEB 161).

Moltmann is determined that the biblical portrayal of Jesus Christ, in all its specific and contingent detail, should come to shape, and not merely illustrate, theology's claim to speak on a level that is universally relevant. He thus rejects what he calls the 'palimpsest' technique which reads the biblical story of Jesus as the answer to an imposed, allegedly universally relevant, question (HP 3–30). For the cosmological theology of the patristic era this was the question: '[H]ow can finite being participate in Being that is infinite . . .?' (WJC 47). For anthropological theology operating in the wake of the 'turn to the subject', and examined above, it was the question of where to discover true human authenticity (cf. WJC 56–57). Thus, respectively, Jesus either becomes the incarnation of the God who has been independently interpreted as the inverse of the world (infinite, eternal, immutable and the rest), or Jesus becomes the projection screen for images of human self-realization sourced from elsewhere (WJC 61). Both of these portrayals find themselves in tension with the identifying biblical details of a Jesus who suffers, and dies godforsaken (WJC 51–53, 61–63).

What Moltmann requires is an interpretative horizon that not only reaches to the universal plane but which is also an *inherent* part of the biblical presentation of Jesus. This he finds in the horizon of eschatological promise,[5] the promise of new creation. The resurrection of the crucified and dead Jesus constitutes the enactment of the promise of new creation in the midst of present creation. It is the incarnation of the transformation of creation, in creation. Moreover, it is the source and ground of this future. What Moltmann terms 'biblical identifiability' (WJC 41) flows from perceiving the resurrection of Jesus as the defining ground of theology. In this way, God is defined as 'the God and Father of our Lord Jesus Christ' (Rom. 15.4), the one who raised him from the dead (Rom. 4.24). Jesus is the Christ in, and not apart from, this eschatological history of God (cf. Rom. 1.4). The Spirit is the power of resurrection (Rom. 8.11). And salvation comes from participating in the death and resurrection of Christ (Rom. 6.3-11). Not surprisingly then, and notwithstanding the broadening interests of Moltmann's theology over time, the cross and resurrection of Jesus stand at its very centre. This is as true of *Theology of Hope* (1964)[6] as it is of *The Coming of God* (1995),[7] Moltmann's return to eschatology thirty years later. Thus Moltmann can affirm that the universal relevance of Christ,[8] and so his relevance to a world under ecological threat, is the eschatological future he projects and will realize (WJC 119).

---

5   One of the jewels of *Theology of Hope* is a seven-part analysis of just such promise (103–105).
6   'For Christian faith lives from the raising of the crucified Christ, and strains after the promises of the universal future of Christ' (TH 16).
7   'Christian eschatology has its foundation in the experience of Christ's death and resurrection' (CofG 261).
8   Müller-Fahrenholz worries that the comprehensiveness of Moltmann's universal vision may contain a 'disguised claim to domination' over against other perspectives (2000: 232). Perhaps significantly, therefore, in relation to the world religions, Moltmann writes: '[they] too must subordinate themselves to the preservation of this world' (GSS 133).

Why Bother with Scripture?

We are now in a position to appreciate Moltmann's interest in, and response to, a fundamental question: why should one bother with the biblical texts at all? And more specifically for our purposes, why turn to the Iron Age texts of Scripture in order to develop a response to the twenty-first-century issue of the 'ecological crisis'? What can they know of carbon footprints and genetic modification? Moltmann shapes his general response quite sharply:

> In modern hermeneutics the question generally asked is *how* texts belonging to the tradition should be interpreted, not *why* we should interpret them at all, or what *compels* us to explain and apply them . . . Only a view of reality in the context of promissory history discloses the need to interpret and apply the subject of the texts to the present day. The historical view of history has no knowledge of this, and existential hermeneutics only that it is possible, not that it is necessary. (EinT 103)

It is the promissory character of Scripture that makes it relevant. The biblical histories of promise and gospel point eccentrically beyond themselves to the new creation, to the coming kingdom of God (EinT 125). They point to an end when 'it is written' becomes 'it has happened' (EinT 127).

It is this future-open character of Scripture which prevents a Biblicist approach to the text. If the 'matter of Scripture' is this promise of new creation, then God's Word cannot be bound to the historical context of its origination. Rather, '[o]nly what goes beyond the times in which the texts were written and points to our future is relevant' (EinT xxii; cf. EH 46). The interpreter is thus afforded a creative liberty over against texts which are subject to their own time, as he or she seeks to follow out the trajectory of promise they trace towards the horizon of the new creation, a task that must inevitably utilize the faculty of imagination (cf. GinC 4, 65; HP vii). This approach also provides a mediating path between what Moltmann terms a 'hermeneutics from above', which, in Barthian fashion, emphasizes the absolute sovereignty of the divine subject in revelation, and a 'hermeneutics from below' which places the emphasis on the role of human subjectivity, seeing the text as a historically, socially and culturally conditioned expression of human faith (EinT 140–42). Mediating the dialectic is Moltmann's 'Trinitarian hermeneutics' (EinT 144) which comprehends Scripture as the root to participation in the forward-moving Trinitarian history of God with the world. It therefore contains both movements 'from above' (God's action) and 'from below' (human response) as it perceives Scripture as the mode of access to integration, through the Spirit, into the eschatological history of Christ, which brings us to the Father (EinT 143–45; cf. TKG 73, 89–90, 122–28; GinC 242–43; SofL 204).

A fascinating insight into the difference between Moltmann's approach to Scripture and that of a New Testament exegete, albeit one highly sympathetic to Moltmann's theology, is afforded by his dialogue with Richard Bauckham in *God*

Will be All in All (1999). Moltmann writes: 'Taking account of exegetical discipline, I can develop my own theological relationship to the biblical texts; for theology is not a commentary on the biblical writings, and commentaries on the biblical writings are not a substitute for theological reflection' (GAA 230). Moltmann has little time for exegetical detail for its own sake, even when Bauckham makes some astute points. Rather, building upon what he takes to be the broad theological concern of the texts, he seeks to build a bridge between exegesis (what the text *meant*) and theological reflection (what the text *means* in the context of today). In explicating this further, Moltmann articulates what amounts to a hermeneutic spiral: (1) read the texts and ask what they are saying: what is their subject and concern?; (2) try to comprehend this subject and concern within the mental categories of today; (3) check this comprehension again against the text. Theology, he assures us, cannot be dictated to by text or by exegete (GAA 230–31)! Clearly, though, Moltmann needs, and desires, to protect himself from the accusation of an arbitrary imposition on the text that would take him back to the 'palimpsest' hermeneutic we have seen him reject.[9]

Return to Origins

In the context of the 'ecological crisis' where anthropological theology appears to have nothing to contribute, or worse, has become a factor in the crisis itself, Moltmann's commitment to the relevance of the biblical text leads him to a re-examination of what the doctrines of creation and redemption might contribute in the light of the biblical sources that originally helped fashion them. The doctrine of creation, he asserts, 'must be exposed to the criticism of the present day, so that it may arrive at its own origins . . . The more clearly the experiences and recognitions, questions and impasses of the present situation are recognized and accepted, the more clearly and unequivocally belief in creation can speak' (GinC 22). The same holds for a re-evaluation of redemption: 'Only in an age of ecological crisis can the promise of a new heaven and a new earth be heard again after the narrow view of anthropological theology which could only consider the realm of human subjectivity. The old images come to life once more' (IEB 161).

What then are the key biblical motifs to which Moltmann turns in an attempt to construct a theology which can speak to the crisis of values which has led to the present ecological impasse? We shall briefly examine five which occupy a recurring place in his thought.

---

9   See GAA 231–32 for Moltmann's attempted rebuttal of Bauckham's specific exegetical criticisms. The reader can judge the success or otherwise of this effort. I judge the debate fairly evenly matched.

A. Genesis 1.26-28.

Moltmann traces one of the root causes of the destructive posture of human beings towards nature to a misinterpretation of what it means to link human beings made in the image of God with the call to dominion over all living creatures. Foundational culprits in this respect are Francis Bacon and René Descartes who, in the words of the latter, saw the natural sciences as the route to restoring human beings to the status of the 'lords and possessors of nature', so imaging the all-powerful God of Renaissance nominalism (GinC 26–27). Moltmann seeks to overturn such an understanding in a number of ways.

First, Moltmann offers a series of exegetical observations. Given that there are two accounts of creation in Genesis, what Gen. 1.28 means by 'subdue' and 'dominion' must be read in the light of Gen. 2.15's 'tilling and keeping' (SW 47). Following Odil Steck (2008 [1978]), Moltmann also suggests that 'subdue the earth' is in fact a dietary command and 'have dominion' a call for humanity to act as justices of the peace in creation (GinC 29–30). Another tack is to emphasize the importance of community, both by seeing the God to be imaged as Trinity (GinC 216, 241) and by noticing that Genesis 1 and 2 point to humanity as one creature within a community of others, on which humanity is irreducibly dependent (GinC 185–88). This dovetails with Moltmann's Christological conditioning of what image means. If Christ is the measure of the image of God, and a model of the exercise of dominion, then what is envisaged is a servanthood aimed at community. Gen. 1.28 then becomes, 'free the earth through community with it' (SW 50; cf. FofC 129; GinC 227–28).

Secondly, and slightly in tension with the first approach, Moltmann seeks to impose an eschatological conditionality on the description of the human role in relation to nature offered in Genesis 1. Given that creation is an open system (FofC 115–30), and so creation-in-the-beginning is but the first stage of a continuing 'process' that points forward, beyond itself, towards the consummation that God will bring: 'fill the earth and subdue it' cannot be the last word on the subject of human destiny (SW 47, cf. FofC 129). Indeed, *God in Creation* (1985) offers an expansion of *imago Dei* into *imago Christi* and finally *Gloria Dei est homo* as what it means to be human unfolds within the eschatological process of God with the world.

Moltmann also traces the misappropriation of Genesis 1 to the medieval distinction between the *image* of God in the reasonable soul and mere *traces* of God in the body and other created things (SofL 36). Picking up on the reference to 'male and female' (Gen. 1.27), Moltmann asserts that God's image does not correspond to the soul detached from the body but to, 'men and women in their wholeness, in their full, sexually specific community with one another' (SofL 94). In other words, the image has to do with bodily existence (CJF 78–79), with a humanity rooted firmly in the world.

B. Genesis 2.1-3

The scriptural motif of the Sabbath is perhaps the most far reaching of those employed by Moltmann. Indeed, he can speak explicitly of his intention to develop a 'sabbath doctrine of creation' (GinC 6). The Sabbath motif becomes a way to de-centre the place of both humanity and work, which have taken centre stage in the traditional Western 'six days' account of creation (GinC 276). It can thus become an effective tool of ecological reform. Key to his interpretation is the recognition that 'it is only the sabbath which completes and crowns creation' for here 'the creative God comes to his goal' (GinC 6; cf. CofG 264). For Moltmann, the Sabbath rest of God constitutes an anticipation of the redemption of the world (GinC 276) because it points to the final indwelling, resting, of God in creation (Rev. 21.3) which forms the inner ground of the world's redemption (GinC 288; cf. CJF 84; TJ 53–54).

Exegetically, Moltmann grounds this understanding in the observation that the Sabbath, in contrast to the other days of creation, has no following night (GinC 276). It thus holds a permanent meaning for all the days of creation. Additionally, there is an anticipatory progression to be discerned that runs from the Sabbath day to the Sabbath year (Lev. 25.1-7), to the Jubilee (Lev. 25.8-17) and on to the messianic end-time (Isa. 61.1-11) (GinC 289–90). To observe the Sabbath rest is thus not about gaining strength for Monday and the demands of work, it is rather a point of orientation that reveals the meaning of existence itself (OC 70–72).

In fact, the Sabbath undercuts the economic valuation of life. Its rhythm of regular restful interruption acts against the relentless economic pressure for 'flexible working' (EinT 315). Moreover, humanity is set free from 'the striving for happiness and from the will for performance and achievement' (GinC 286). In the Sabbath year the land 'is no longer weighed up and assessed according to its utility for human beings', but rather 'comes to itself' and is respected in its dignity as God's creation (SofL 97). In this way the Sabbath becomes a means to distinguish between the world as nature (open to human exploitation) and creation (GinC 276).[10]

By abolishing the distinctions introduced by the world of work (cf. Exod. 20.8-11), the community of creation is restored, for the Sabbath rest is universal; in the Sabbath year it extends to include the earth itself (GinC 285). This lateral extension of the Sabbath rest means that even through it is defined primarily in terms of time, one day in seven, it also reaches out to include space. For Moltmann it thus becomes a way to hold together history (time) and nature (space) (EinT 314), the very things which anthropological theology, following the Cartesian division of the world, let disastrously fall apart.

Space and time are also integrated in Jesus' proclamation and enactment of the kingdom of God, which Moltmann, in the light of Lk. 4.16-21, interprets as the messianic Sabbath (WJC 91, 119). Jesus introduces a different quality of time

---

10 Moltmann's emphasis on creation as a dual world of heaven and earth (GinC 158–84) can also be considered a component of his strategy to distinguish 'creation' from 'nature'.

(GinC 291), the imminent Kingdom of God (cf. Mk. 1.15) which has as its inner content a new experience of space, the unparalleled closeness of God (cf. WJC 97–99). Jesus' messianic peace brings an end to violence, the fundamental force that is inimical to life (WJC 127–30). Thus for Moltmann, to follow Jesus – drawing on the whole set of Sabbath resonances outlined above – is to seek to end the exploitation of the earth by engaging in ecological reform (WJC 121–22).

While Moltmann's ecologically motivated emphasis on rest is to be welcomed, one is left wondering whether the intimation of the (eschatological) end in the beginning, which the Sabbath constitutes, might not short-circuit the value of a creation that becomes and evolves. Must not the value of creation's defining activity be asserted alongside the value of its sheer existence? In other words, might not the six days be more emphatically linked to the seventh?

C. Psalm 104.29-30

This text grounds Moltmann's understanding of the Spirit as the power of creation, in Calvin's phrase the 'wellspring of life' (SofL 35). A creation created *ex nihilo*, in marked contrast to the working assumption of the natural sciences, does not form the basis of its own existence. It is, therefore, constantly threatened by the fate of nothingness and only exists as it is preserved by the 'source of life', the Spirit (HTG 72, 75). More specifically, for Moltmann, creation exists through the 'unceasing inflow of the energies and potentialities of the cosmic Spirit' (GinC 9). The Spirit thus forms the inner continuity of the community of creation, and it does so in such a way as to anticipate God's final eschatological indwelling (GSS 104). Consequently, within this pneumatic frame of reference, the world constitutes a unity that cannot be thought apart from God. The earth cannot so easily, then, be reduced to mere 'raw materials' to serve human economic activity.

D. Proverbs 8.22-36

In a world threatened by the 'ecological crisis' Moltmann can claim that the most urgent task for theology is to rediscover the wisdom of God in nature (CJF 15, cf. GinC xi). As Prov. 8.35-36 has it, 'For whoever finds me finds life . . . but those who miss me injure themselves; all who hate me love death'. As was the case in the reflection of the early Church, so also for Moltmann, this text can be used as a basis for considering both the role of Christ and the Holy Spirit. Focusing on the former, if Christ is taken to be the mystery of the world, the cosmic wisdom through whom all things exist (cf. Col. 1.15-20), then the one who reveres Christ must also revere all things in him (HTG 73, cf. GSS 103). Thinking now about the latter, this text can ground the concept of creation in the Spirit which Moltmann seeks, following Calvin's intimations, to take up and develop more fully (GinC 10–11). In either case this text can be used to justify the immanence of God in the world.

E. Romans 8.19-26

This passage is used extensively by Moltmann, but essentially only to make one fundamental point. Humanity and creation share in a common plight, and hope for a common liberation (CG 335; GinC 189). This community of hope is rooted in the Spirit (GSS 81–82): '[T]he Spirit of God himself represents believers and creation in their sighs for liberty through his "sighs too deep for words" (Rom. 8:26)' (GinC 69). To 'the redemption of our mortal bodies' (v. 23), for which humanity awaits, corresponds the 'hope that creation itself will be set free from its bondage to decay' (v. 21) which Moltmann takes to be the power of transience (HTG 70–72; CofG 276), the irreversibility and mortality of time. This companionship in hope means that redemption cannot be conceived as something which separates and distinguishes between humanity and nature: 'In physical terms, believers are bound together in a common destiny with the whole world and all earthly creatures. So what they experience in their own body applies to all other created things' (GinC 68). Moltmann suggests that this shared destiny should lead theology to an interest in those sciences which reveal nature's irreversible time structure such as biological evolution and cosmology (GSS 82).

Transforming Theology

In unfolding Moltmann's interpretation of these five biblical motifs we have already begun to touch upon the way in which the fundamental themes of theology are transformed to serve an ecological purpose. Within the limits of the space available, the aim now is to offer an elucidation of some central themes which emerge from this process.

(A) Re-conceiving God's Relationship With the World

Over against pantheism in which creation is dissolved in God, and atheism in which God is dissolved in the world, Moltmann seeks to pursue a Trinitarian panentheism (cf. GinC 98). 'An ecological doctrine of creation implies a new kind of thinking about God. The centre of this thinking is no longer the distinction between God and the world. The centre is the recognition of the presence of God *in* the world and the presence of the world *in* God' (GinC 13). A monotheistic conception of God as one who utterly transcends the world had led, in Moltmann's view, to the secularisation and de-sacralization of the world, as being something totally other than God. Clearly such a view does little to restrain the exploitation of the natural world. Moltmann counters this with a Trinitarian view of creation as taking place by God (the Father) through God (the Son) and in God (the Holy Spirit). While maintaining a sense of God's transcendence, this perspective introduces a balancing emphasis on God's immanence in the world (HTG 72–73). It also replaces a notion of God as subjugating subject with 'a God in community, rich in relationships' (GSS 101; cf. GinC 14). For humanity created to reflect the nature of God, this Trinitarian account suggests a way of relating to nature that contrasts strongly with that of economic domination. This interrelationship between the pattern of God's own life and the ideal mode of human interaction with the world is deepened through Moltmann's use of perichoresis, the notion of the mutual indwelling of the Trinitarian persons in one another. Moltmann gains this insight from the increasing interest in Orthodox theology that colours his later work. '[T]he high priestly prayer of John 17.21 ... "that they may all be one, even as thou, Father, art in me and I in thee, that they also may be in us" ... can become the foundational saying for theological ecology' (GSS 101–102).

The conception of Trinitarian persons as 'existing-in-relation' (TKG 172) comes to shape a notion of creation as 'in-existence' (CofG 301). The ecological web of existence, where one creature exists in, with and out of others, is thus rooted in the being of God. More, in the Spirit, this intricate web is interpenetrated by the Creator himself. The Spirit is 'the immanent transcendence in all things' (CJF 58), 'the infinite in the finite, the eternal in the temporal, and the enduring in the transitory' (SofL 35). Moltmann draws on the Greek derivation of 'ecology' (*oikos*) to suggest it can mean 'a doctrine of the house' indicating, in turn, creation's inner secret: the indwelling of God (GinC xii).

In *Science and Wisdom* (2003), Moltmann describes his theological journey from earlier to later work in a subtitle: 'From the God of Hope to the Indwellable God' (SW 111; cf. EinT 313). What this represents, in part, is Moltmann's own ecologically motivated corrective of his earlier labours. He is concerned that the eschatological vision of *Theology of Hope* could be seen to operate within a historical paradigm (albeit significantly chastened) which has proved incapable of holding humanity and nature together:

> It was only slowly, at the beginning of the 1970s, that we became conscious of the simple fact that human history is located within the ecological limits of this planet earth, and that human civilisation can only survive if it respects these limits, and the laws, cycles and rhythms of the earth. If humanity disturbs, and ultimately destroys its environment, it will annihilate itself. As we became aware of the 'limits of growth' ... we found ourselves facing a problem with the all-dominating category of historical time. (EinT 314)

The developing emphasis in Moltmann's theology on the reciprocal indwelling of God and the world can thus be read as a counteracting of this possible unintended outcome of his earlier thinking.

This strategy entails the risk, however, of realized eschatology, of reading the end goal of redemption, which as early as *Religion, Revolution and the Future* (1969) was 'the earthly and visible inhabitation of God in a new creation' (RRF 33), back into present creation where 'we have to speak of the marvel that the infinite God himself should dwell in his finite creation, making it his own environment' (GinC 150).

This is not a risk that is ever fully realized, it must be said, because Moltmann has numerous ways of safeguarding the qualitative difference between the new creation and present existence. Perhaps one of Moltmann's most robust defences of this difference stems from his conviction that the new creation demands a transformation in the transcendental conditions of time to overcome the present problem of transience (CofG 26). Yet, when Moltmann draws on the Kabbalisitc notion of *zimsum*[11] to speak of an initial self-contraction of God to open up space within himself for creation to exist (TKG 108–11; GinC 86–93, 114–17 *et passim*), or when, in his more Hegelian moments, he seems to make the Spirit the determining subject of evolution[12] (GinC 16, 19, 98–100),[13] this risk of realized eschatology becomes more threatening.

(B) Ecological Christology

With the writing of *The Way of Jesus Christ* (1989), Moltmann explicitly aims at 'a post-modern christology which places human history ecologically in the framework of nature' (WJC xvi). This is because, in the context of the 'ecological crisis', Christ, and the salvation he brings, must be presented for 'the whole threatened earth and all individual created beings, in their common peril' (WJC 46, cf. 64). It means asking, '[w]ho really is Christ for dying nature and ourselves today?' (WJC 68). The result is a new emphasis on 'the bodily nature of the Christ who died and rose again' (WJC 247) since the body serves as the meeting point between human history and the natural world (WJC xvi). The perspective from which the Christ-event of cross and resurrection is viewed shifts accordingly. The 'historical-eschatological theology of resurrection' gives way to the 'historical-ecological theology of rebirth' in the Spirit (WJC 247), as the paradigm 'history', from Moltmann's earliest theology, is once again broadened out to explicitly include nature. Strongly contrasting with *Theology of Hope*, where he was at pains to stress the radical dialectic between cross and resurrection (for example, TH 197–98), the emphasis now falls on the continuity of the process of resurrection through use of the category of 'transition' (WJC 248). Resurrection is the process of the completion of creation and less of a radical interruption. Within this process human history can only be consummated in the 'resurrection of nature' (WJC 254–56).

This focus on all-inclusiveness also pertains to Jesus' suffering and death. Jesus dies the death of everything that lives (WJC 169) and his sufferings must be viewed

---

11 For an analysis of Moltmann's highly selective use of Isaac Luria's *zimsum* conception see Deane-Drummond (1997: 202–205). Its fundamental problem however, is that it turns God and creation into ontological rivals for the same space, thus failing to take account of the essential qualitative difference between the two.
12 Deane-Drummond is also concerned about the biological foundation of such statements (1997: 274, cf. 218–21).
13 Moltmann's explicit method here is to project back from the experience of the Holy Spirit in the New Testament Church (which might also be the source of an anticipation of the saving future) to the presence and efficacy of the Spirit in creation generally.

within the perspective of the sufferings of dying nature (WJC 194–95). It is this which makes his resurrection a sign of universal hope (WJC 170).

Moltmann enthusiastically takes up and develops the cosmic Christology of Joseph Sittler (WJC 276–82). Christ is the mediator of creation (1 Cor. 8.6), the one in whom all things are made and hold together (Jn 1.1-3; Col. 1.15, 17; Heb. 1.3). Christ's death effects a universal reconciliation (Eph. 2.16; Col. 1.20; 2 Cor. 5.19). Moltmann adds his own particular nuance, however, by means of a threefold differentiation: Christ is the ground of all things; the 'moving power of evolution';[14] and the redeemer of the whole creation process (WJC 286). Without explanation of how this might be reconcilable, Christ, we are informed, is not only the 'moving power of evolution', but also a victim of evolution among other victims (WJC 296). Additionally, '[i]f Christ is to be thought of in conjunction with evolution, he must become evolution's redeemer' (WJC 297). The attempt to find a Christological reading of evolution is admirable, but the results are somewhat confusing.[15]

(C) The Scope of Redemption

One way of unfolding Moltmann's eschatological doctrine of creation is to ask about the scope of redemption. How inclusive is creation's future? Moltmann's answer is as broad as is imaginable. His hope for the future embraces the universe, extending beyond humanity to 'animals, plants, stones and all cosmic life-systems' (WJC 258). 'If we were to surrender hope for as much as one single creature, for us God would not be God' (CofG 132). 'Nothing that God has created is lost. Everything returns in transfigured form' (HTG 78; cf. WJC 239, 303; CofG 70, 251, 265). *Nulla salus sine terra!* No salvation without the earth! This is Moltmann's cry (CofG 274). Moltmann's theological logic is this: if the Redeemer is none other than the Creator, then God would contradict himself if he did not redeem all that he has made (CofG 259). On the basis of this promised future, '[t]his earth, with its world of the living, is the real and sensorily experienceable promise of *the new* earth' (CofG 279; cf. GinC 56, 60–65, 204). Thus the whole of the concrete, exploitable world has a future on which human activity should not foreclose.[16]

---

14   Nowhere does Moltmann spell out what this means, nor do we learn how Christ's role relates to the Spirit as the determining power of evolution that we have already met.
15   In her very recent *Christ and Evolution* (2009), Celia Deane-Drummond traces Moltmann's difficulty here, in part, to his use of a broadly narrative approach to a theological appropriation of evolution (2009: 44–49). Her alternative turns on a development of Hans Urs von Balthasar's category of theodrama.
16   While the redemption of every last aspect of the created order is a powerful way to underline the value of the world in an age of ecological threat, it raises important theological questions. It is open, for example, to Bauckham's (1995: 210) 'marigold objection': must every last marigold, every last blade of grass find its way to eternal life? Bauckham also points out the way in which the salvation of *everything*, along with Christ's death in the place of *all* living things, makes any form of moral distinction between the claims of living organisms highly problematic (1995: 210–11).

Christologically grounding this comprehensive future is Moltmann's conception of resurrection as re-uniting that which death divides and separates (WJC 263–73). More particularly for our purposes, this must be read as an implicit corrective of anthropological theology's Cartesian deficiencies. Resurrection in the Spirit overcomes the divisions between: (a) body and soul; (b) a person and the stages of their temporal development (diachronic resurrection); (c) person and community, since bodily existence is social existence; (d) the generations, which has important implications for sustainability; and (e) human civilization and nature, founding a partnership on the way to a common goal.

If, however, God is to redeem all things in the end, so that nothing is lost, could this not become a means to justify present inaction? Use nature as you will, abuse her resources as you wish, because ultimately God will make things good.[17] Moltmann is able to counteract this conclusion by means of his understanding of anticipation. The new creation that transcends present creation is, nevertheless, immanently present in God's liberating action in the world through Christ and the Spirit (CPS 189–90; WJC 97–98). It is in this intervening realm of anticipation that the Church exists. While there remains a 'not yet', there is present in Christian existence a 'no longer' (for example, no longer under law) and an 'already' (for example, already forgiven) (CPS 193). Moreover, the future can be said to be present in action which is obedient to God's transforming intention (CPS 191). Thus, '[i]f Christian anticipation is directed towards the resurrection and eternal life, then it will encourage everything in history which ministers to life, and strive against everything that disseminates death' (CPS 196).

Christian anticipation concerns the construction of representations of what is to come (CPS 195), resistance and protest against that which contradicts this future (EinT 26–27; cf. TH 227) and solidarity with those who presently suffer (FofC 54). Human action, though, has definite limits: 'Human beings cannot redeem nature, and nature cannot redeem human beings. The divine redemption must reach them both' (WJC 272; cf. CJF 6).

Conclusions

Moltmann may be short on concrete practical suggestions in the face of the 'ecological crisis'.[18] Yet this does not mean that his ecological hermeneutic of theology is to no avail. Moltmann is after something larger; he wants to change the future.

---

17 A parallel concern with historical inactivity lay behind the criticisms of *Theology of Hope* mounted by Alves (1969: 59–60) and Gutiérrez (1988: 124).

18 He does, however, suggest having a day a week without work and without car use, implementing a system of regular sabbatical years rather than early retirement, and encouraging the use of fallow land in agriculture (CJF 66; cf. GinC 296).

> Through changes in the horizon of expectation of the project 'modernity' we can make changes in its course ... If we do not want the future to become in a few decades nothing but the past, we shall have to introduce our misgivings into the expectations of 'the modern world'. (CofG 290)

If the 'ecological crisis' is essentially a crisis of human values, and here he is surely correct, then theology can become a powerful agent of ecological reform. Moltmann has two key weapons in his armoury. The first is the eschatological orientation of his early theology which is never surrendered. Put boldly, creation, the whole of creation, has a future with God. It cannot, therefore, be treated as disposable. Its future confers upon creation an inalienable (if undifferentiated) dignity. Secondly, this perspective finds reinforcement in the relational emphasis of his later work. The perichoretic life of the Trinity comes to condition Moltmann's conception of the relation of God to the world (GinC 258). It also fashions the ideal form of relationships within creation, inherently grounding humanity, and humanity's future, in, and not apart from, the community of creation. Significantly, both these themes – the future and relationship – find a common root in the doctrine of the Trinity; for the pattern of God's life is the blueprint of creation's future redemption.

What then of the legitimacy of his hermeneutic method? Moltmann will always frustrate exegetes, just as he has been frustrated by them (EinT xxi–ii), because he will always want to go beyond the text, from, as he says, what it *meant* to what it *means* (GAA 230). And here it is not just what the text means in isolation (even taking account of its broader contextual and historical location) that interests him. The text's significance is what it can contribute to an overarching model of God's developing relationship with the world as this impacts upon the questions of the day.[19] In fact, Moltmann's rejection of 'scientific' exegesis, as a substitute for theology, could be seen as paralleling his rejection of the dominating, objectifying modes of knowledge which have served to separate humanity from nature and so contributed to the 'ecological crisis'. In its place, Moltmann wishes to know in order to participate (cf. GinC 2–4). Participation in the web of life and participation in the Trinitarian history of God with the world (the object of biblical hermeneutics) thus become corollaries of each other.

Moltmann's committed stance places his approach close to, but not identical with, Juan Segundo, one of the founding liberation theologians. For Segundo, the hermeneutic circle is 'the continuing change in our interpretation of the Bible which is dictated by the continuing changes in our present day reality' (1998: 8). It is thus the task of theology to 'designate as the Word of God, that *part* of divine revelation which *today*, in the light of our concrete historical situation, is most useful for the liberation to which God summons us' (1998: 33). Moltmann's move from text to

---

19 It thus seems a little unfair of Deane-Drummond (1997: 211) to criticize Moltmann's Christological reading of the Genesis account of creation on the grounds that it prevents the text's authentic voice being heard. Moltmann is about something else for which synthesis is the essence of his method (cf. GinC 53–54).

theology, however, saves him from the danger of distortion through over-selection while losing nothing of the commitment to context. There is no need for a desperate scrabble around in Scripture searching for possibly ecologically relevant texts, as if the text were the thing in itself. Rather, Moltmann's theological approach enables him to focus on the overarching redemptive movement of Scripture which reaches out towards the universal horizon of new creation (Isa. 65.17; 2 Cor. 5.17; Revelation 21–22).

Keeping faith with Scriptural intention in this way means maintaining theological continuity through risking new language. This, Rowan Williams has suggested (1987: 234-37), is one of the lessons of the Council of Nicaea (325 CE). The Church Fathers found it necessary to go beyond Scripture, in the employment of the term *homoousios*, in order to remain true to what they believed Scripture said about Jesus' relation to the Father. In a parallel fashion Moltmann understands that biblical theology will necessarily entail employing theological models that cannot be justified, in every respect, directly from the text. Here the towering example is the doctrine of the Trinity which is so central to Moltmann's ecological hermeneutics. Faithfulness to the text, then, means moving forward within the theological vector that the text projects, reaching out for that which is the cause, ground and hope of Scripture.

References

Alves, R. 1969 *A Theology of Human Hope* (New York: Corpus).
Bauckham R. 1995 *The Theology of Jürgen Moltmann* (Edinburgh: T&T Clark).
Bauckham, R. (ed.) 1999 *God Will be All in All: The Eschatology of Jürgen Moltmann* (Edinburgh: T&T Clark).
Deane-Drummond, C. 1997 *Ecology in Jürgen Moltmann's Theology* (Lampeter: Edwin Mellen).
Deane-Drummond, C. 2009 *Christ and Evolution: Wonder and Wisdom* (London: SCM).
Gutiérrez, G. 1988 [1971] *A Theology of Liberation: History, Politics, and Salvation* (London: SCM).
Moltmann, J. 1967 [1964] *Theology of Hope* [TH] (London: SCM).
Moltmann, J. 1969 *Religion, Revolution and the Future* [RRF] (New York, Charles Scribner's Sons).
Moltmann, J. 1970 'Theology as Eschatology' [TasE] in F. Herzog (ed.), *The Future of Hope: Theology as Eschatology* (New York: Herder & Herder): 1–50.
Moltmann, J. 1971 [1968] *Hope and Planning* [HP] (London: SCM).
Moltmann, J. 1973 [1971] *Theology and Joy* [TJ] (London: SCM).
Moltmann, J. 1974 [1972] *The Crucified God* [CG] (London: SCM).
Moltmann, J. 1975 *The Experiment Hope* [EH] (London: SCM).
Moltmann, J. 1977 [1975] *The Church in the Power of the Spirit* [CPS] (London: SCM).
Moltmann, J. 1978 *The Open Church: Invitation to a Messianic Life-style* [OC] (London: SCM).
Moltmann, J. 1979 [1977] *The Future of Creation* [FofC] (London: SCM).
Moltmann, J. 1981 [1980] *The Trinity and the Kingdom of God: The Doctrine of God* [TKG] (London: SCM).
Moltmann, J. 1985 [1984] *God in Creation: An Ecological Doctrine of Creation* [GinC] (London: SCM).
Moltmann, J. 1989 *Creating a Just Future* [CJF] (London: SCM).
Moltmann, J. 1990 [1989] *The Way of Jesus Christ: Christology in Messianic Dimensions* [WJC] (London: SCM).
Moltmann, J. 1991 *History and the Triune God* [HTG] (London: SCM).
Moltmann, J. 1992 [1991] *The Spirit of Life: A Universal Affirmation* [SofL] (London: SCM).

Moltmann, J. 1996 [1995] *The Coming of God: Christian Eschatology* [CofG] (London: SCM).
Moltmann, J. 1999a [1997] *God for a Secular Society: The Public Relevance of Theology* [GSS] (London: SCM).
Moltmann, J. 1999b 'The Bible, the Exegete and the Theologian', in R. Bauckham (ed.), *God Will be All in All: The Eschatology of Jürgen Moltmann* [GAA] (Edinburgh: T&T Clark): 227-32.
Moltmann, J. 2000 *Experiences in Theology: Ways and Forms of Christian Theology* [EinT] (London: SCM).
Moltmann, J. 2003 *Science and Wisdom* [SW] (ET 2003; London: SCM).
Moltmann, J. 2004 [2003] *In the End – the Beginning* [IEB] (London: SCM).
Moltmann, J. 2007 *A Broad Place: An Autobiography* [BP] (London: SCM).
Müller-Fahrenholz, G. 2000 *The Kingdom and the Power: The Theology of Jürgen Moltmann* (London: SCM).
Segundo, J.L. 1998 [1975] *The Liberation of Theology* (Maryknoll, NY: Orbis).
Steck, O.H. 2008 [1978] *World and Environment* (Eugene: Wipf and Stock).
Williams, R.D. 1987 *Arius: Heresy and Tradition* (London: Darton, Longman & Todd).

Part III

Contemporary Hermeneutical Possibilities

Introduction to Part III

Christopher Southgate

Our consideration of the contemporary scene is informed first and foremost by our perception that theologizing about the environment and humans' place in it – and hence the need to grapple ecotheologically with the range of understandings offered by the scriptures – has come to stay. Ecotheology may remain a sub-discipline of the main theological enterprise; it may continue to lack the influence that it merits; but few now would see its pursuit as spurious or marginal in the way that might have been possible fifty years ago. Thus also the sub-sub-discipline of ecological *hermeneutics* has gained in stature and perceived importance – it has its own Consultation at the annual meeting of the Society of Biblical Literature, owing much to the work of the Earth Bible project; it has spawned collections of essays including this present one.

This final part of the book ends with a wide-ranging and methodologically focused coda from Ernst Conradie. Before this come essays by Harry Maier and Stephen Barton, both engaging with the role of eschatology in the contemporary debate, and a broader reflection on sustainability from Tim Gorringe.

On a colleague's door in the Department of Theology and Religion at Exeter is a cartoon of a man with a placard proclaiming 'The End is Nigh' and underneath 'I'm unable to go into details'. It is a fair charge against much Christian reflection that it has been obsessed with salvation (without drawing adequately on the resources offered by the contemplation of creation) and yet has been unable to offer any great insight as to what that salvation might mean for the creation as a whole. Yet it is the more alarming – at least as viewed from an academic perspective in the UK – to contemplate the various premillennial and postmillennial schemes that do profess to know the detail of the end-times. Maier offers an elegant taxonomy of such schemes as they have worked themselves out in the North American experience, that unique colonial experiment in which settlers were able to appropriate (not without violence) a great 'wilderness' of huge natural resource, all the while reading their activity and vocation very much in biblical, and indeed in eschatological terms. Maier shows how this 'reading' spans a spectrum from postmillennial optimism about the human role in bringing in the eschaton to the premillennial pessimism more characteristic of the late nineteenth century, and that each element of that spectrum has its correlate in contemporary attitudes towards the environment. These range from a deep suspicion of environmentalism as tainted by the New Age, through a call to 'tend the garden', to a sense of the perfectibility of creation in which the 'fallen' wilderness can be transformed by human effort. Particularly interesting – and hopeful, from my own perspective – is Maier's identification of a new shift among younger evangelicals away from 'traditional hot-button [social] issues' to a new agenda of environmental care stemming from a microcanon of key texts, and enabling a re-reading of biblical apocalyptic.

In an essay that also grapples with the issues raised by the New Testament's eschatological material, Barton presses the question: where, in a scriptural and inescapably eschatological faith, can (ecological) wisdom be found? He concludes that there are three distinguishable tasks that inform the search for Christian wisdom – the historical-exegetical, the theological-hermeneutical and the personal-ascetical. In each category he uses an exemplar – Richard Hays, Kathryn Tanner and Richard Bauckham, respectively – to show what can be achieved in that area. This is not so much spectrum drawing as triangulation – by showing the strengths and limitations of Hays and Tanner, in particular, Barton is able to mark out helpful ground for further exploration, insisting that it be ground-based on 'the central affirmation that underlies New Testament apocalyptic: hope in God grounded in the resurrection of Christ now present in the Spirit'. Wisdom, too, must be sought in dialogue with the insights of contemporary science, chilling though those are in terms of the ultimate future of both earth and cosmos. Helpfully, too, Barton shows how the liturgical practice of the Church, in praise and eucharist, can be a source of formation in wisdom, a wisdom that knows both how to mark time and to keep (Sabbath) time.

Gorringe's reflection is 'earthed' very directly in the question as to how humans can with justice continue to feed themselves, to till and to keep the garden. He sees agriculture as 'in biblical perspective, the paradigm of all human work'; only such nourishing work, done in the spirit of the commandments, will offer a future to humanity. Working from the Revised Common Lectionary's texts for Rogation, Gorringe offers a range of biblical perspectives that mark out the healthful from the oppressive, the destructive and the unsustainable. The Bible's 'long rumours of wisdom' include the insistence that the land belongs to the Lord, and therefore should not – must not – be completely commodified or 'cornered'. The essay ends with an interpretation of the word *epieikes* in Phil. 4.5, and an insistence (common to so many efforts to interpret the Bible as a resource in the ecological crisis) that our environmental problems are *spiritual*, not merely a matter of expediencies, or even simply of morality.

That in a sense begs the question the book began with and ends with – how, when the exegetical, theological, personal and political tasks are fused in a Christian response to the ecological crisis, can the Bible function to transform human practice, imagination, spirit, in ways that further authentic peace, authentic hope?

In other writing some of us have characterised the range of hermeneutical approaches in use in ecotheological writing in terms of readings of recovery, and of two types of resistance – resistance to the environmentalists' agenda in the name of the Bible, and of (elements in) the Bible in the cause of what are taken to be ecological virtues. Horrell, Hunt and I have gone on to seek to locate a hermeneutic between the strategies of recovery and resistance (Horrell *et al.* 2010). This resulted in an approach owing much to the insights of Ernst Conradie into the importance of doctrinal/hermeneutical 'keys' or 'constructs' or 'lenses'. So it is fitting that the last word in this volume goes to Conradie and his understanding of the hermeneutical task. His essay sets out a broad analysis of the way in which biblical interpretation operates, and a programme for ecological biblical interpretation.

Strikingly, Conradie prefers to reserve the term 'hermeneutics' for 'a second-order and disciplined reflection on the praxis of interpretation'. His own essay provides an admirable example. A particularly notable emphasis is his sense that biblical texts are not merely read, they move and change lives, they function through worship and preaching and live in the imaginations of those who cannot read. More technically, Conradie explores the ways interpretative strategies overcome the distance between text and context, and it is here that he deploys his concept of what he now prefers to call 'doctrinal constructs' – well-tried conceptual tools, models and metaphors that can shape interpretation. He goes on to show that a cluster of such constructs is likely to be needed to guide the task of Christian ecotheology. Finally, and no less importantly, Conradie insists that ecotheology not content itself with answering a narrow set of questions, but attempt a reformulation of Christian doctrine as a whole.

This is an expansive note on which to end this collection of explorations. We hope the reader will have found much stimulation, and some challenge, within these pages, and we look forward to the continued conversation to which they give rise.

Reference

Horrell, D.G., Hunt, C. and Southgate, C. 2010 *Greening Paul: Rereading the Apostle in an Age of Ecological Crisis* (Waco, TX: Baylor University Press).

Chapter 17

GREEN MILLENNIALISM: AMERICAN EVANGELICALS, ENVIRONMENTALISM AND THE BOOK OF REVELATION[1]

Harry O. Maier

In his now classic essay Lynn White, Jr traced the origins of the contemporary ecological crisis to the beginning of the Bible and its injunction to have dominion over creation (1967: 1205). Christians and Jews have given enormous attention to offering a rejoinder to White's argument, if only to show that it is a fundamental misreading of the Genesis account to interpret it as license for the human exploitation and disregard of the well-being of creation. But it may be that White's attention on the beginning of the biblical narrative as the root of the ecological crisis was misplaced. For as Frank Kermode reminds us, endings are at least as determinative as beginnings in sustaining the actions, motivations and goals of characters and unfolding narratives, and in shaping the dispositions humans bring to make sense of their brief span of years and months and days. 'Apocalypse depends on a concord of imaginatively recorded past and imaginatively predicted future, achieved on behalf of us, who remain "in the middest". Its predictions, though figurative, *can* be taken literally, and as the future moves in on us we may expect it to conform with the figures' (Kermode 1967: 8). If at its beginning the Bible commands the human creature to govern creation, so at its ending it imagines 'a new heaven and a new earth; for the first heaven and the first earth had passed away' (Rev. 21.1). Genesis begins in a garden, but 2 Peter 3 ends creation with fire, promising that the Lord will come like a thief 'and then the heavens will pass away with a loud noise, and the elements will be dissolved' (v. 10) and that 'the heavens will be set ablaze and dissolved, and the elements will melt with fire' (v. 12). Figurative predictions taken literally: are not eschatological expectations determinative of the way Christians view and treat the environment?[2]

1   I would like to acknowledge the contribution of David Horrell, Cherryl Hunt and Christopher Southgate, who offered insightful comments on an earlier draft of this paper during a stay at the University of Exeter. I am grateful to David Taylor for his help in the research of this essay. All biblical references are from the NRSV unless otherwise stated.
2   See especially Finger 1998; Trusdale 1994; Curry-Roper 1990 for a general sketch of the eschatological frameworks most associated with care for and resistance to the natural world. See similarly, Granberg-Michaelson 1984: 105–17. Trusdale, Curry-Roper and Granberg-Michaelson predict an inverse correlation between a literal belief in Jesus' Second Coming as an interruption of history and concern for the environment. As we will see below, the evidence is far more complex than the linear relationship they argue.

Revelation is patient of widely differing versions of the end of history and hence of a present way to make sense of the meantime. On the one hand, there are the texts that represent the destruction of creation: for example, the visions of natural calamity of Revelation 8 and 16, as well as those from elsewhere in the New Testament that promise calamities on earth and in the heavens. On the other hand, there are those texts that reveal God transforming an old creation with the new, for which all physical creation longs and hopes. The Bible's eschatological texts can be read both for continuity and discontinuity between the old world and the new. This invites conflicting senses of an ending. Certainly this is the case among those historical and contemporary Americans this essay will take up, Evangelicals who have lived and continue to live 'in the middest' of a peculiar sense of an apocalyptic ending and the environmental considerations that ending encourages.[3] The Apocalypse has loomed large in shaping the American civic and religious imagination and it is not surprising to discover that it plays a significant role in shaping American attitudes towards the environment. On the one side are those who urge abandonment of environmentalism as a misconceived and misplaced concern. For example, Todd Strandberg argues, 'If environmentalists want to do some lasting good they would be wise to devote their energy to evangelizing lost souls'. Indeed, '[w]ithout the transforming power of Jesus Christ, the environment will be resigned to its determined fate [sic]'.[4] On the other hand, however, are those who link eschatological hope with the transformation of the present creation. Thus, Douglas Moo argues, 'In Rev 21.5, God proclaims, "I am making everything new!" he does not proclaim, "I am making new things." The language here suggests renewal, not destruction and recreation' (2006: 455). In what follows I take up these differing senses of an ending and show how eschatology and theological interpretation of the natural world are intimately interconnected in American Evangelicalism. The Book of Revelation as well as other eschatological texts and themes from the Bible have had a profound influence on the way Americans, and especially Evangelicals, have viewed the environment and how the faithful are to relate to creation. Predictably, many have used Revelation to urge the faithful to abandon creation; intriguingly, however, a large minority of Evangelicals argue that Revelation invites the faithful to the care of creation, even if differing philosophical

---

3   The terms 'Evangelical' and 'Evangelicalism' I use in what follows to describe a broad trans-denominational American religious movement that traces its origins to the religious revivals of the eighteenth and nineteenth centuries, and which subscribes to the statement of belief of the National Association of Evangelicals (http://www.nae.net/index.cfm?FUSEACTION=nae.statement_of_faith; accessed 1 April 2009). This essay explores Evangelicalism's belief 'in [Jesus'] personal return in power and glory' and the way readings of Revelation that sustain that belief affect environmental considerations. In what follows I distinguish Fundamentalism from Evangelicalism; Fundamentalism traces its origins to an anti-Modernist Evangelical revivalism of the late nineteenth and early twentieth century. In contemporary usage, especially in the secular media, 'conservative Evangelicalism', 'the Religious Right', and 'American Fundamentalism' are often erroneously treated as synonyms. For a good overview of the various terms, see Johnston 1991.

4   See T. Strandberg, 'Bible Prophecy and Environmentalism', *Rapture Ready* (www.raptureready.com/rr-environmental.html; accessed 11 March 2009).

and theological convictions lead its members to disagree with one another about the forms such care is to take and the goals it is to achieve. Will the millennium be green? American Evangelicals answer that question differently and in doing so invite an investigation of the uses of apocalyptic and eschatological biblical texts, theological tradition, and contemporary experience in the construction of religious identity and civic engagement.[5]

Revelation in the Wilderness

John's Apocalypse has loomed large in the considerations of the natural world that have accompanied Christians through four centuries of the settlement and development of North America. To assess the place of Revelation and eschatology in contemporary Evangelical reflection on the environment and environmentalism it is necessary first to offer a sketch of the varying and changing attitudes towards the natural world championed first by Puritans and then taken up by successive generations of Evangelicals. Conflicting senses of an ending have shaped the way Americans have viewed and treated the natural world around them. The Puritans who escaped religious persecution in Great Britain located both their exile and their arrival in a new continent with the help of apocalyptic timetables. Cities with names like Salem reflect the way some Puritans interpreted their presence in the wilderness of North America with the help of the Bible's rich wilderness traditions. Surrounded as they were by the hostile, papist French and their Amerindian allies, Puritans like Edward Johnson (1598–1672) found shelter in the view that their residence in America's wilderness was the fulfilment of Rev. 12.14 where the serpent cast down from heaven chases the mother 'into the wilderness . . . where she is nourished for a time and times, and half a time' (Stoll 1997: 26). Guided by apocalyptic theology and Calvinist injunctions to rule creation, Johnson considered North America as a wilderness to till, garden and make ready for God who was to come and inaugurate the thousand-year reign of Christ and erect the New Jerusalem (Stoll 1997: 64–71).[6] This view, which is broadly classed as postmillennial because it expects humans to

---

5   For an excellent review of the history of the debates that have divided American Evangelicals over environmental causes, see Simmons 2009: 50–57; also, Larsen 2001, who traces Evangelical treatment of environmentalism since the publication of Schaeffer's *Pollution and the Death of Man: The Christian View of Ecology* (1970), which he argues inaugurated Evangelical engagement with secular environmentalism. As early as 1971 the National Association of Evangelicals in *Resolution on Environment and Ecology* (www.nae.net/index.cfm?FUSEACTION=editor.page&pageID=199&IDCategory=9; accessed 24 March 2009), endorsed an Evangelical environmentalism. In 1979 Evangelicals founded the Au Sable Institute in Michigan, as a centre of Evangelical scholarship dedicated to Christian environmentalism in Evangelical perspective. See www.earthcareonline.org/creation_care_websites.pdf (accessed 24 March 2009) for Evangelical statements on the environment from the 1970s onward.

6   See also Nash 2001: 24–43, who discusses the link with Calvinism.

establish the conditions for the millennial reign of Christ promised in Rev. 20.4, dominated American eschatological preaching until the second half of the nineteenth century when it was supplanted by a far more pessimistic view of the human capacity to transform wilderness and the social order into a more perfect union. Both Cotton Mather (1663–1728) and Jonathan Edwards (1703–1758) considered the domestication of nature as part of the necessary preparation for establishing the conditions to welcome Jesus' promised millennial reign, even if they interpreted the New Heaven and Earth of Rev. 21.1 as a sweeping away of the old creation to make way for a new. Evangelical revival united with the taming of a seemingly endless wilderness represented the cultivation of the inner and outer world to make ready the coming reign of Christ promised in Revelation (Stoll 1997: 71–76, 79–83).

Earthquakes in New England as well as the military successes of New France led some among the generation after Mather and Edwards to give up the optimistic view that humans could create the conditions for the Second Coming. This view, the premillennialist framework, is opposite to the postmillennial one: Christ's second coming is not assured through human strategizing and planning and steady progress, but is an interruption of history after which Christ inaugurates his millennial reign. While the premillennialist framework would in due course be hostile even to modest attempts to ameliorate the present world order and by the early twentieth century be associated with expectations of extreme and inevitable ecological devastation, in the eighteenth and nineteenth centuries it was still wedded to a profound ecological vision of nature tamed and domesticated as anticipation of what was still to come. Indeed, steady progress in cultivating and taming the American wilderness, together with successes in the Revolutionary War, were taken as outward signs that it was among the Americans that the millennium would be erected (Bloch 1985: 33–50). In the eighteenth century, American revolutionaries formulated a potent union of republican values with the steady exploitation of the seemingly unending abundance of North America's natural resources to reinforce the idea that among the Americans, God's new Israel, God would establish the Jerusalem of Revelation 20.

Post- and premillennialists may have disagreed whether the millennium would come before or after the Second Coming, but they agreed on the notion of a Manifest Destiny that God had given the United States to bring civilization to the rest of the continent and ultimately the world (Tuveson 1968: 91–136). What oriented and steered both pre- and post-millennialists, however differing their eschatological expectations, were the ideals of Baconianism and the Enlightenment convictions of Scottish Common Sense philosophy. The former affirmed the power of nature to teach moral and scientific lessons and bring human progress through empirical observation; the latter affirmed that the starting point for common sense was true for all times, cultures and socio-economic locations (Marsden 1982: 83–84). Even in its most pessimistic periods, the steady progress of converting wilderness to a peaceable garden won through learning nature's lessons and a non-speculative, literal reading of the Bible remained the guiding vision of a divinely established Arcadia planted on American soil. Edward Hicks' painting of 1834 entitled *The Peaceable*

Kingdom, though painted by a Quaker, expresses the realized natural eschatology of an American infused with a particular reading of the Apocalypse and prophecies believed to be fulfilled in the artist's own life. As representation of the ecological vision of harmony depicted in Isaiah 11, it also expresses the ideals voiced by the contemporary interpreters of Revelation: the domesticated animals and children lying alongside and playing among predators in the painting's foreground exegetes the meeting of colonizers and American Indians in the background. Here is a vision of ecological and social wilderness tamed and harnessed for the sake of a colonial civilization in anticipation of a new world to come.[7]

There is not room here to offer a full discussion of the reasons for the profound shift in eschatological beliefs from relative optimism towards deep pessimism among Evangelical Christians in the second half of the nineteenth century. Its transformation included a new negative attitude towards the environment that continues to shape the contemporary Evangelical debate concerning the environment and its care. The violence of the Civil War, social dislocation as a consequence of industrialization and urbanization, economic depression, difficulties in integrating vast numbers of immigrants into American society, economic exploitation of the working class through laissez-faire capitalism, the perceived threat to traditional beliefs by the rise of Darwinian science and the ascendancy of historical critical biblical exegesis and a resulting revision of Christian theology: all these contributed to a profound pessimism among latter-day Evangelicals.[8] They became in due course militantly opposed to the postmillennialist vision of an earlier generation now championed by advocates of the Social Gospel who agitated for social reform and government intervention to overcome social ills. And they became divisive with those premillennialists of an increasingly bygone era of civic theology who expressed their discipleship by working for an improvement of society while time remained. Such efforts these later premillennialists judged deeply flawed and doomed to disappointment. What is remarkable in postbellum American Evangelicalism is the increasing emphasis on the discontinuity of the New Heaven and Earth of Rev. 21.1 with the present ones and the turn towards the salvation of individuals as the only appropriate form of Christian discipleship. Here Baconianism and Common Sense philosophy continued to hold sway, but now, wedding a profound historical pessimism with a futurist premillennialism, Evangelicals sought to exegete from contemporary social chaos, and from the environmental decay and devastation of industrialization around them, evidence of divine wrath for human sinfulness as a harbinger of the Parousia Jesus promised and the New Testament prophesied. Premillennialist preachers sought to convince audiences that the world was ripe for judgement. The signs of its condemnation were well anticipated by the ecological disasters foretold in the cataclysms of the Book of Revelation; the Bible plainly described them and anyone with enough

---

7   For utopian ideals, pastoral visions, and the Book of Revelation in late eighteenth and early nineteenth century American Christianity, see Tuveson 1968: 52–90.
8   For a definitive account see Weber 1979: 82–104.

common sense could see them unfolding all around them. If in earlier generations nature was a book from which to learn lessons for the betterment and progress of humankind, nature now became the mirror God used to reflect human sinfulness back to itself and a divine whip to bring repentance before the inevitable conflagration and annihilation of a tired and used up earth. In doing so, premillennialists played on the values of what Alexis de Tocqueville called 'enlightened self-love' when he visited the continent and overheard the sermons of Evangelical revival in the 1830s. Self-interest he argued bound citizens together in a common democratic cause of liberty (de Tocqueville 2003: 609–13).

John Nelson Darby (1800–1882) and Cyrus Scofield (1843–1921) were leading nineteenth and twentieth century proponents of these apocalyptic points of view and their work transformed an earlier American premillennialism already disposed in that direction into a militant rejection of any human attempt to ameliorate the present world order. Darby divided history into a series of dispensations or different epochs represented in biblical history in which God offered differing means of salvation.[9] The present dispensation – the Age of Grace – will end with the Rapture (the spiriting away from the earth of Christ's true believers), which will inaugurate The Great Tribulation – the persecution of a remnant church – and rule of the Antichrist, ending with the Battle of Armageddon of Rev. 16.16, and the consequent inauguration of Christ's millennium described in Rev. 20.2. Darby indefatigably championed this schematization of the end and in turn won the allegiance of hundreds of revivalist preachers, most notably Dwight L. Moody who in 1886 founded the Moody Bible Institute in Chicago which in due course became the American centre for promoting prophecy belief in the imminent Second Coming and which in turn was instrumental in transforming the face of American Evangelicalism in the decades that followed. In 1909 Cyrus Scofield, converted by revivalist-dispensationalist preaching, published his *Scofield Reference Bible* solidifying premillennialist dispensationalism through mass publication (by 1967, 10 million were in print; between 1967 and 1990 Oxford University Press sold an extra 2.5 million copies [Boyer 1992: 97–98]). The Fundamentalist wing of the American Evangelical movement further spread these ideas with the publication between 1910 and 1915 of 12 tracts collectively titled *The Fundamentals: A Testimony of Truth*, sent to some 3 million Protestant church leaders. The premillennialist dispensationalists of the first half of the twentieth century unleashed jeremiads decrying mistaken notions of human progress, materialism, capitalism and political attempts to stave off an inevitable coming conflagration.

Many dispensationalist preachers from the later nineteenth century onwards have taught that the New Heaven and Earth of Rev. 21.1-2 will be a restored and revived present earth. Scofield envisioned a creation healed from the marring effects of human 'avarice, . . . ruthless use of [nature's] power, [and] unequal distribution of

---

9   See http://www.biblebelievers.com/Dispensation_Chart.html (accessed 29 April 2009) for a chart showing the dispensations.

her benefits'.[10] Like contemporary interpreters, these dispensationalists interpreted the conflagration of 2 Pet. 3.10 not as an annihilation of creation but its purification from the effects of evil and sin. However, as environmentalist issues came to public attention in the post-WWII period, Dispensationalist Evangelicals not only doubted the ability of an already doomed humankind to deal effectively with environmental problems, they wondered whether attempts at international cooperation in the care of the planet was the means of creating the right climate for a one-world government and the rise of the Antichrist, the dictator who will be Satan's vice-regent to rule the earth and persecute a remnant church until his reign is ended by Christ's coming. However much earlier twentieth century Dispensationalists affirmed notions of transformation, suspicions of environmentalist causes have increasingly encouraged a more disjunctive view of the relation between the old and new creations.

On this account environmentalism is deeply suspect as a subterfuge for a hidden agenda. Constance Cumbey connects environmentalism with an international New Age movement from which Christians are to distance themselves, and chastises green Evangelicals for the way their promotion of environmental causes reveals how far they have strayed from saving Christian doctrine (Cumbey 1983: 63, 15, 162–69). Pat Robertson, televangelist Dispensationalist preacher and candidate for the Republican presidential nomination in 1988, linked environmentalism with globalism and the erosion of the nation state in the movement towards a new global order. Indeed, he considers such movements as an attempt on the part of Satan to undermine American economic power and political power to thwart worldwide evangelism (Robertson 1991: 176, 192–97, 267–68; similarly, 1990: 225–27). In fact, Robertson celebrates the New Heaven and Earth of Revelation 21 as a place where free enterprise will flower free from government intervention and regulation under the presidency of Jesus Christ! Other writers think that one of the attractions of the coming Antichrist will be to solve environmental problems as a means of winning support and deceiving the nations.

Ultimately, from this perspective, there can be no hope for environmentalist causes because the Book of Revelation reveals a different picture of the future. Hal Lindsey, the most published popular Dispensationalist in American history, interprets Revelation as predicting 'the death of world ecology' in the visions of ecological devastation in Rev. 8.6-13 (1974: 126–35). Following this theme, others link human afflictions like boils and sores to the depletion of the ozone layer and the effects of radiation from a coming nuclear war. For Lindsey the wages of sin are pollution and environmental death; human fatality and suffering arising from ecological devastation fulfils the prophecy that God (using natural causes) is 'destroying ... the destroyers of the earth' (Rev. 11.18). William Badke (1991: 149), in a rare Dispensationalist apology for Christian environmentalism, contends that creation is the mirror of human sin and that ecological disaster is the sign of humankind's fallen condition. Indeed, 'in

---

10 Cited by Boyer 1992: 335; for discussion of dispensationalist treatment of the environment generally, see 331–39.

seeming contradiction to his purposes . . ., God in certain circumstances attacks his earth' in order to 'call us to repentance and salvation'. Pollution's only real solution is Christian conversion. Only Christians fully understand why humans should work to care for the earth, because they know its creator and the Creator's love for the planet most clearly. So they should not expect very much from labouring among unrepentant sinners for the good of the planet: 'uncreation . . . will consume the earth and lead to a new creation'. This leads some to draw direct links between natural catastrophes and politics: a recent YouTube video for example links weather disasters, like Hurricane Katrina, with American foreign policy decisions that allegedly undermine the national security of the State of Israel.[11] This introduces a decidedly Deuteronomist thematization to America's relation with the environment: even as God used environmental disaster to punish the Israelites and the nations around them for impiety, so in God's providential arrangement of the ascendancy of America to protect Israel, God uses the natural world as means of reward and punishment. This leads to an account of the natural world completely immune to environmental critique or analysis.

Ecological disaster, environmental degradation and pollution are all either the result of human sin, or are God's punishment for it. Either these are harbingers of the Second Coming, revealing human wickedness, or faith in the Second Coming is the only way to escape these disasters. But in traditional Dispensationalist preaching there is no way to stave off sin's disastrous consequences either for humans or planet earth. To attempt to do so is to stand in the way of a divinely appointed end and God's plan for a new heaven and earth. Christians should distrust environmentalism as a distraction. Elver Voth calculates that even with far greater levels of consumption among industrial and developing nations, there are more than enough resources to last until the Second Coming of Christ. The maths shows that Christians should not worry about the environment since the end is so imminent. Rather they should focus on missions and limitless growth:

> Premillennial theology sets proper limits on time projections so that the earth's resources are adequate to complete an assigned task at depletion rates even far greater than current rates. In response to the Great Commission, I say, forget conformity to those elements of environmental advocacy intended as impediments to growth in evangelical missions, and let the missions grow, and grow, and grow. (Voth 1982: 64)

Green Millennium versus Rapture Culture

These ideas with their long historical legacy are the backdrop for a lively debate among contemporary American Evangelicals concerning the environment, environmentalism and the correct way to understand the contribution of eschatology to

---

11   www.youtube.com/watch?v=yNrONw2dopU (accessed 27 March 2009).

considerations of the natural world and its preservation. The debate is especially intense since so many Americans are premillennialist, literal readers of the Book of Revelation. A 2002 *Time*/CNN poll found 36 per cent of Americans believe the Bible should be read literally and 59 per cent believe the events prophesied in the Book of Revelation will happen as described.[12] Another poll conducted by the Pew Research Centre in 1999 found that 44 per cent of Americans believe that Jesus will return in their lifetime.[13] Studies consistently show that the more literally American Christians read the Book of Revelation and expect an imminent Second Coming, the less likely they are to show concern for environmental issues, and the more likely they are to be skeptical or hostile towards environmentalism, especially when it is linked with governmental agencies.[14]

However, in contrast to those points of view just represented, there is a growing number of Evangelicals who resist a premillennialist reading of Revelation that invites Americans to give up on an old creation in eager anticipation of the new one to come. 'So long as evangelicals hold to an eschatology that understands the world to exist under a divinely imposed death sentence', writes Alan Trusdale, 'we should expect no major change in their disposition towards the environment or the environmental movement' (1994: 117). He consequently encourages a complete revision of American eschatological thinking in a way that makes room for environmental concerns. Wesley Granberg-Michaelson criticizes premillennialism for leading to quietism and neglecting the biblical exhortation to 'the task of bringing God's shalom, justice, and peace to the creation . . .' (1984: 109). Instead, he champions amillennialism – the view traditionally associated with the eschatological ideas of Augustine and his Reformation interpreters, Luther and Calvin. For complex reasons Augustine and his successors tended to spiritualize their eschatology, and for this reason Dispensationalism in particular has tended to reject the amillennialist eschatology as not reading Revelation's visions of the end of the world literally enough. Granberg-Michaelson's amillennialism, however, champions the physical creation as worthy in its own right as the place where God's reign is inextricably interwoven, albeit in a hidden way. Revelation in particular and New Testament eschatology in general does not advocate a disjunction between the old creation and the new, but the

12 www.time.com/time/covers/1101020701/story2.html (accessed 20 March 2009).
13 www.religioustolerance.org/end_wrl6.htm (accessed 20 March 2009).
14 Guth *et al.* 1995. Similarly, Guth *et al.* 1993; Shaiko 1987. However, it is not clear from the statistical analysis whether it is the case that political affiliation or religious conviction is more determinative in opposition to environmental causes among Evangelical Christians. Do they resist environmental causes because they belong to political movements that value freedom over government intervention, or do they belong to such movements because of their religious beliefs? For a refusal to assert simple lines of cause and effect, see Kanagy 1995; Eckburg and Blocker 1996; Boyd 1999; Woodrum and Hoban 1994. This is consistent with other studies that find a negative correlation between premillennialism and belief in the efficacy of political participation to solve the world's problems: Wilcox *et al.* 1991. Nevertheless, the consensus is that literalist eschatology is inversely correlated with concern for the environment.

transformation and full revelation of the new world to come already present in the natural world. His amillennialism is not spiritual, but physical and environmentalist.

Granberg-Michaelson is representative of what we might call a green Evangelical environmentalism. It too arises from a long tradition of Evangelicalism on the American continent, one that reaches back in celebration of the natural world as a gift God commands to care for and preserve.[15] In fact, far from retreating from public life and societal concern to await the coming of Jesus, for over forty years a differently minded series of American Evangelicals have been leading voices on behalf of Christian churches promoting environmentalist causes both nationally and in their denominational bodies. Here Revelation's many visions of creation in turmoil and renewed are not read to wed newspaper headlines to biblical texts, nor to demonstrate the inevitability of environmental annihilation and conflagration, but to see how they affirm God's faithfulness to the transformation and reconciliation of a creation once cursed by, with and through human sin (Gen. 3.17) through renewal and salvation. Rather than emphasizing the disjunction of the old creation with the new, traditional among Dispensationalist Evangelicals, they argue for their continuity and the transformation of the old creation into the new.[16] 'What does God's good future look like?' asks Steven Bouma-Prediger. The answer: earthly. 'Heaven and earth are renewed and are one. God dwells with us, at home in creation' (2001: 115–16). Calvin DeWitt, the founder of the Au Sable Institute of Environmental Studies – a centre that occupies the mainstream of American Evangelicalism and is dedicated to the sound application of its principles and theology, and especially its biblical interpretation, to what it describes as 'creation care' – also discovers in Revelation reason to be green: 'All who follow Jesus follow the example of the one who makes all things new, the one who makes all things right again (Revelation 21:5)' (2008: I-31). That observation appears in the recently published *Green Bible* – an NRSV edition of Scripture that marks each 'green' passage of the Bible in green print, in order to disclose the pro-environmental themes of Judaism's and Christianity's foundational texts.

The Evangelical Environmental Network, founded in 1992 to promote a Green Evangelical vision, cites Rev. 21.1-2 as scriptural warrant for its concerns, as well as Rev. 11.18: a time of divine wrath is coming 'for destroying those who destroy the earth'.[17] Such opinions represent a transformation of American Evangelicalism,

---

15 See for example, official denominational statements (accessed 25 March 2009) of premillennialist Dispensationalist churches such as the Seventh Day Adventist Church (http://www.adventist.org/beliefs/statements/main_stat54.html) and of the Assemblies of God (http://ag.org/top/Beliefs/contempissues_02_environment.cfm), both of which insist on the responsible care of creation even as they insist upon end-time scenarios. The Adventists do not share the Assemblies of God's belief in an annihilated old creation replaced with a new, but expect rather the physical world's renewal.

16 Finger (1998: 14–36), insightfully charts the interpretation of biblical texts reflecting the disjunctive and those affirming a more continuous view in various forms of Evangelical eschatological expectation.

17 www.creationcare.org/resources/scripture.php (accessed 26 March 2009).

especially among its younger generation, that signifies a shift away from traditional hot-button issues (abortion, the debate over evolution, prayer in schools, homosexuality, etc.) towards a different set of interests in a socially engaged conservative Christian faith (Rice and Choi 2008). These 'green' Evangelicals weave together a tapestry of New Testament texts to argue for Christian environmentalism. The Evangelical Environmental Network, for example, lists texts often cited by Evangelicals championing the environment: the Colossian 'Christ Hymn' (1.15-20); the description of a groaning creation awaiting salvation in Rom. 8.19-23; 2 Cor. 5.17 (with the critical variant, 'all things are new'); the Parable of the Talents (Mt. 25.14-30; Lk. 19.12-28); the *apokatastasis* of all things (Acts 3.21); commandments to love neighbour and care for the poor (Jn 13.34; Mt. 25.31-46); texts affirming the Son's agency in creation (Jn 1.1-3; Heb. 1.2-3; 1 Cor. 8.6b); statements affirming creation as reflecting God's glory and will (Rom. 1.20-23); and that reconciliation includes all things cosmic, created and human (Eph. 1.10); as well as the release from bondage (Lk. 4.18-19). Additionally it cites Hebrew Bible eschatological portraits – especially from Isaiah (on which Rev. 21.1-4 is based) – of harmony with nature to depict salvation and concord of humans with God and creation (Isa. 5.1-2, 11.1-9, 55.12-13, 65.17-25).[18]

The uses of these texts represent a skilful application of an Evangelical biblical hermeneutics that interprets Scripture with Scripture to recover the plain meaning of biblical revelation. In the absence of a notion of canon within the canon, or tradition as guide to interpretation, foregrounding one set of texts over another here makes room for re-reading an apocalyptic biblical tradition that *prima facie* is less friendly to Christian environmental considerations, such as those more disjunctive visions of ecological disaster found in the Revelation and elsewhere (especially in Revelation 8, 16 and 2 Pet. 3.10). Such foregrounding also strategically counters a heavy emphasis on the Fall, the cursed earth of Gen. 3.17 and notions of depravity favoured especially in the Reformed theological systems out of which Evangelicalism traditionally emerges.

In the revivalist preaching of earlier generations, visions of environmental calamity accompanied jeremiads exposing human wickedness as a means of persuasion to contrast the old life of sin and death – in which creation also participates – with the new one of salvation and life brought through repentance. Cosmic and natural disaster – the typical literary characteristics of apocalyptic – found pride of place in a homiletical tradition that urged listeners to throw off an old order doomed to punishment to embrace a new one. Stephen D. O'Leary has insightfully represented this as the 'tragic frame' in the American millennialist rhetorical tradition designed to win and reinforce consent (1994: 68–69). Green Evangelicals, without renouncing the call to repentance and conversion to a personal relationship with God through faith in Jesus Christ, mine the tradition for a different portrait of the new life in

---

18   See www.creationcare.org/resources/scripture.php (accessed 31 March 2009) for texts; similarly, Zerbe 1991; also, Wise 1991; Ro 1993: 8–11.

Christ. Here the tragic frame gives way to what O'Leary exegetes as the more comic mode of millennial rhetorical persuasion: environmental catastrophe and so on are episodic in the larger narrative of improving not only one's own private condition, but that of society's as well. Conversion and salvation are social and environmental even as they are a vertical restoration of a relationship with God broken through sin. This version – to the degree it is premillennialist – returns adherents full circle to an antebellum premillennialism that considered societal improvement as a necessary component for preparing for Jesus' Second Coming. These Evangelicals note that, notwithstanding his emphasis on humanity's sinful condition, Calvin took a dim view of human exploitation of the natural world, celebrated the creation in his *Institutes* and New Testament commentaries and insisted in his *Commentary on Genesis* that humans so work out their salvation that they leave the world in a better condition for the next generation.[19] Loren Wilkinson, one of the founders of the contemporary Evangelical green movement, criticizes the classic Reformed notion of the stewardship of the earth's natural resources as encouraging a quantitative and mechanistic relationship with creation that falls short of recognizing that humans are not above creation but a part of it. Instead, he prefers the terms 'earthkeeping' and 'stewardship of creation' to describe humankind's divinely commissioned ecological responsibility (1991: x).

This has engendered no small debate among Evangelicals, especially since environmentalism has traditionally been a cause championed by those left of the American political centre.[20] Some on the right have urged their green brothers and sisters to stay out of environmental science and to resist accepting correlations it considers dubious between global warming and greenhouse gas emissions; to keep to missions; the championing of family values; and traditional Evangelical causes like opposition to abortion and homosexuality.[21] The Bible hardly allows a complete dismissal of values of environmental stewardship and accordingly they affirm the importance of wise stewardship but do so in a way they believe consistent with the market capitalism they argue best reinforces conservative religious values and is most likely to help realize God's intentions for the global order, as well as the preservation of the nuclear

---

19   See for example, Peter Bakken in an Au Sable Institute discussion of stewardship (www.clas.ufl.edu/users/bron/PDF--Christianity/Bakken--Stewardship.pdf; accessed 9 July 2009), Michael Sleeth's use of Calvin's *Commentary on Genesis* to support an Evangelical environmentalism (http://www.servegodsavetheplanet.org/?page_id=22; accessed 9 July 2009), and the use of Calvin by the Evangelical Environmental Network in support of Christian environmentalism (www.creationcare.org/responses/faq.php; accessed 30 March 2009).
20   See the excellent survey by Fowler 1995: 45–57.
21   See for example, Colson 1993; Coffman 1994; Burkett 1993: 39–51.

family.²² This Evangelical position links with the 'Wise Use' response to environmental challenges associated preeminently with the work of secular writer Ron Arnold.²³ It affirms the divinely appointed role of humans to exercise dominion over creation in a responsible way. In opposition to the Evangelical Environmental Network's statement promoting the care of creation, proponents of this view have formulated *The Cornwall Declaration on Environmental Stewardship*, a position endorsed by a broad coalition of conservative Jews, Roman Catholics and Christians who champion marrying environmentalism with the values of a free market economy.²⁴

In advancing causes such as this, Wise Use Evangelicals also reach for the New Testament and especially the Book of Revelation. E. Calvin Beisner, co-author of the *Declaration* and national spokesperson for Alliance, has been the leading Evangelical critic of the green Evangelical movement. He discovers in John of Patmos' vision of a heavenly Jerusalem with its tree and river of life in the heart of the city a vision that encourages humans to exercise their appointed role as the lords of creation to engage in a global conversion of wilderness into garden, perfecting the nature God has created through science, technology and progress (Beisner 1997). In this Beisner follows the more traditional Reformed path of viewing Christian responsibility to the world as the stewardship of natural resources. He walks a well-trodden path of the American conservative right's appropriation of Calvinist economic conceptions that promote the pursuit of wealth as part of God's plan for a redeemed humankind to convert a wilderness marred by sin and corruption into a garden of economic productiveness.²⁵ For George Grant, a conservative economist steeped in Calvinist tradition, for example, 'The Bible shows the righteous man starting with a corrupted

---

22   Thus, for example, 'Focus on the Family: A Statement on the Environment' (www.family.org/sharedassets/correspondence/pdfs/PublicPolicy/Environmental_Statement.pdf; accessed 26 March 2009), posted on the website of James Dobson's conservative religious organization, Focus on the Family: 'we tremble to consider the consequences to a nation that spends billions for pure air and water, yet whose land – among other ills – is polluted by the blood of more than 40 million innocent preborn children.' Gary Bauer articulates its point of view in a chapter entitled 'The Green Monsters of Environmental Extremism' (1996: 119–29).

23   See for example, Arnold 1996: 15–26. Perhaps the most famous of Wise Use Evangelicals was James Watt, secretary of the environment in the Republican administration of Ronald Reagan, who wedded economics with management of national parks by endorsing logging of their forests and mining of their resources. Watt forcefully expresses an Evangelical appropriation of Wise Use when he writes, 'being a good steward involves decisions on the *use* of resources as well as the *preservation* of resources' (author's emphasis; Watt 1982: 103). The language of 'resources' is noteworthy in the economic representation of the environment and its uses for human development, and contrasts sharply with the 'creation' language favoured by Wilkinson, DeWitt and others of the Evangelical Environmental Network and its allies.

24   *The Cornwall Declaration on Environmental Stewardship* (www.cornwallalliance.org/articles/read/the-cornwall-declaration-on-environmental-stewardship/; accessed 24 March 2009), published by The Interfaith Council for Environmental Stewardship (ICES) and the Acton Institute, 'an ecumenical think-tank dedicated to the study of free-market economics informed by religious faith and moral absolutes' (www.acton.org/; accessed 24 March 2009). James Dobson for example is one of its signatories, as is Pat Robertson.

25   Nash (2001: 24–43) furnishes a classic account of the role of Calvinism in treatment of the American wilderness; Lienesch 1993: 94–138.

earth: thorns and thistles (Genesis 3:18) . . . [H]e takes it from a wilderness into a garden . . . The Bible is the story of Paradise Restored' (Grant 1986: 122). Similarly, Beisner argues that humans have been appointed by God to rule over creation and express a dominion that will, with God's illumination, improve the natural world. Also Reformed is his critique of writers like Wilkinson and DeWitt, and the authors of the *Evangelical Statement on Creation Care*, for their failure to write of the curse of God upon creation, the effects of the Fall on the natural world and their passing over texts that show God bringing about natural calamity to punish sin and idolatry (Beisner 1997: 19–23, 53–57). The Bible reveals a creation languishing under the curse of sin, incomplete without the human ingenuity that seeks to reverse it as a sign of things to come. Revelation, like the rest of the biblical witness, discloses a creation incomplete without its human and divine improvement and the realization of its full potential (Beisner 1997: 115). Elsewhere, Evangelical signatories to the *Declaration* invoke Francis Bacon – a name historically at the hermeneutical heart of American Evangelical Bible reading – to lend support to humankind's transformation of a sinful wilderness into a sanctified garden. 'Man by the Fall fell at the same time from his state of innocence and from his domination over creation. Both of these losses, however, can even in this life be in some parts repaired; the former by religion and faith, the latter by the arts and sciences.'[26] Disagreeing not so much with green Evangelical ends as means, these Evangelicals nevertheless reject as unsound the view that champions a disposable old creation on the way towards the new one. Theirs, as the quotation from Bacon indicates, centres in the notion of the perfectibility of creation and the indispensable human contribution towards achieving that ending.

While there are predictably shrill voices raised in protest against even this paler green version of an Evangelical environmentalism, support for greening the millennium vision has come even from the premillennialist corner of the American Evangelicalism most usually associated with rejection of environmentalist causes. The Book of Revelation is patient of widely diverging interpretation; while its visions of ecological carnage can be read as emphasizing the disruption of the old creation on the way to the new, it is possible also to emphasize that the new creation remains the *creation* nevertheless. As we have already seen, even Moody and Scofield, who encouraged the most disjunctive interpretations, still anticipated the new creation as a transformation of the old. In the same vein, some contemporary premillennialist Dispensationalists like Billy Graham (1984: 220) actively promoted the environmentalist movement as consistent with God's will for creation and a Christian call to social activism. Many Dispensationalists have opposed anti-environmentalist Evangelical critics by arguing that the new creation inaugurated by Jesus after the coming Tribulation will be a renewal of nature, not a replacement of it. This urges care of the creation as an anticipation of the order to come (for example, Beal 1994). This is consistent in fact with a main emphasis of Dispensationalism – namely the

---

26 Beisner *et al.* 2000: 66, quoting Bacon's *Novum organum scientiarum* (52), a treatise that has been highly influential in Evangelical interpretation of the Bible and the natural world.

working out of God's purposes not only spiritually, but also in physical history.[27]

These considerations are given a direct ecological application especially in 'progressive dispensationalism' where one discovers a formal articulation of creation care (Saucy 1993: 13–35). As the name implies, this Dispensationalism revises earlier models that have traditionally treated the dispensations of grace dividing history into discrete and separable ages. Instead, they argue for a growing transformation of one dispensation into another, with each prior age accumulated and carried forward into the next. On this account, the care of creation now more emphatically than in earlier forms of Dispensationalism anticipates the age to come. On this progressive view, the privileged locus of environmentalism in this world, as indeed for all aspects of advocacy for justice, is the Church, the place where God's will and grace are most directly revealed and manifested.

Already in 1970 Francis Schaeffer, in a book widely acclaimed as inaugurating the Evangelical environmentalist movement, argued that the Church was 'the Pilot Plant' for anticipating God's future redemption of creation that is fully to come (81–93). In a seminal essay, David Turner frames this notion in a progressive Dispensationalist scheme that insists on Christian commitment to the renewal of creation in anticipation of the end of human history (1992: 264–92). This 'even now but not yet' model of Dispensationalist eschatology celebrates the Church as the present revelation of the Kingdom of God. Christian advocacy for creation and for neighbour expresses the healing and justice Jesus will bring with him in the new millennium.[28]

Richard Young agrees with those Dispensationalists who argue that the only solution to the environmental crisis is Christian conversion, but this does not lead him either to speculation as to how newspaper headlines herald the events of the Book of Revelation, nor to a dismissal of environmentalism. Rather, he celebrates a creation slowly healed from sin, greeted by the new creation of humankind in the Church. Predictably, he rejects the biocentric model of secular environmentalism as insufficient from a Christian perspective. More surprising, however, is his critique of premillennialist models of ecological stewardship that link creation care with benefiting humankind and working for its future – the viewpoint championed, for example, by William Badke, as well as Calvin Beisner (though in a not-explicitly Dispensationalist framework) and others like Pat Robertson and James Dobson inclined by their political and economic views to endorse the *Cornwall Declaration* and the Wise Use movement. Their problematic common denominator is a 'theanthropocentrism' – the placement of humankind and its divine redemption and God's plan for human thriving at the centre of creation, if necessary even at the cost of the natural world. As such these models participate in the curse of creation because they still continue to place humankind's, rather than God's, interests at the centre of creation and human existence. In opposition to this, Young champions theocentrism as the true biblical account of humankind and nature: 'Theocentrism

---

27   For an excellent overview and orientation, see Finger 1998: 17–24, with bibliography.
28   See similarly, Blaising and Bock 1993: 232–301.

teaches that God is the center of the universe and that He alone is the Source and Upholder of meaning, purpose, values, and ethics, as well as the unifying principle of the cosmos' (Young 1994: 128).

Young's green millennialism discovers in the story of redemption, and in the realization of God's promise in the full restoration of a creation inaugurated even now in the life of the Church, an invitation to the whole natural order into relationship with God. Like Schaeffer and others, he sees the life of the redeemed gathered in the Church as the revelation of a humankind that, following the *kenosis* of the Son's incarnation, has emptied itself of anthropocentric power and arrogance for the sake of love not only of neighbour but also for all creation (Young 1994: 171). This anticipates the healing of the nations and the planet revealed in Revelation's final vision (22.1-5). A premillennial interruption of history is not an invitation to give up on creation or the world:

> God expects His people to take care of the earth; yet at the same time the Bible predicts that the heavens and earth will be remade. Properly understood, this does not pose a tension between the present and future. God still loves His creation and is not going to destroy it. It is the evil principle God hates and will purge as He remakes heaven and earth. God's eschatological intervention to purge the corrupting elements does not nullify our present responsibility for taking care of His creation. It should rather encourage the opposite. We are to assist in the purging of evil and the reclamation of the earth. The earth is still of value to God, and we are still to be faithful stewards, helping nature be all that God intended in the face of ever-present evil. (Young 1994: 155)

From a green Evangelical perspective, this represents a promising development of a Dispensationalist tradition that has been inclined to give up on an old earth even as it hopes for the promised new one. It creatively deploys O'Leary's comic frame of apocalypse – namely the role of jeremiad in bringing about repentance and reformation (here environmental repentance) – to participate in the happy outcome of creation promised in Revelation's final chapters. However, it has had its critics. As Thomas Finger argues (1998: 27, 32), the ecclesiocentrism of these eschatological applications to ecological issues can lead to restrictions on considering the value of the natural world outside of an anthropocentric soteriological scheme, as well as on involvement with secular environmentalist causes because they do not fit into its timetables and because of pessimism concerning humankind's capacity to solve ecological challenges. It nevertheless represents an intriguing way a movement – best known for retreat from social engagement – discovers in apocalyptic theology a reason for involvement in social causes. This represents a profound transformation of a tradition of Apocalypse interpretation.

In articulating their arguments in this way, progressive Dispensationalism, as well as those versions of Evangelical faith that promote a green world in the light of a future revealed in Revelation, puts its finger on the pulse of an American Evangelical movement inclined towards privatizing belief as a means of coping with seemingly intractable social and political problems, or engaging contemporary challenges with a view to a relatively narrow set of interests and concerns. In a qualitative investigation of Evangelicals who are devotees of Dispensationalist literature, especially the premillennialist Left Behind series, Amy Johnson Frykholm (2004) describes contemporary popular Evangelicalism in America as belonging to a 'Rapture Culture'. Rapture Culture devours apocalyptic as a means of securing a certain future in an uncertain present, and to shore up religious beliefs challenged by secularism. She has discovered that most believers in the imminent return of Jesus think his coming will be either when they are old or just after they die. With a certain future to come, whose signs can be read in environmental disasters and political events even now, these Evangelicals discover an impetus to engage in evangelism and to join the battle against evil secular forces that have legalized abortion, protected the rights of homosexuals, forbidden prayer in school, promoted the teaching of evolution and so on. Indeed, by linking global evangelism with the military and economic security of the United States, Rapture Culture finds an apocalyptic window for its adherents to engage in particular forms of social activism, even as the forces of evil gather to bring the creation to an apocalyptic ending.[29] However, the disjunction of the coming age with the present one leads these Evangelicals towards a social engagement on terms that paradoxically favour freedom from government policies to solve global problems and that advance economic and social policies favouring individualism and self-interest. The powerful allegiance of conservative private values with distrust of the government as often a secular force for evil leads to a deep distrust of environmentalism and those who would preserve an order destined for annihilation.

Those Evangelicals, including green premillennialists, who read the Book of Revelation as transformation rather than replacement of the present creation urge a different mode of political and social engagement upon America's conservative Christians. Creation care, not creation annihilation; justice, not quietism; engagement, not retreat – all in ways that encourage a green Christian faith – invite an American Rapture Culture to a new model of political and religious engagement. The green Evangelicals who read the Book of Revelation for the signs of divine future that includes a creation groaning with birth pangs represent a new chapter in the centuries-long history of American millennialist engagement. They anticipate a green millennium that thoughtful Evangelical environmentalism can even now begin to secure. 'Jesus is coming, so plant a tree!' (Wright 2008: I-79).

References

Arnold, R. 1996 'Overcoming Ideology', in P.D. Brick and R. McGreggor Cawley (eds), *A Wolf in the Garden: The Land Rights Movement and the New Environmental Debate* (Lanham, MD: Rowman & Littlefield): 15–26.

---

29   See also, Lienesch 1993: 157–260; Harding 1994.

Badke, W.B. 1991 *Project Earth: Preserving the World God Created* (Portland, OR: Multnomah).
Bauer, G. 1996 *Our Hope Our Dreams: A Vision for America* (Colorado Springs, CO: Focus on the Family Publishing).
Beal, R.S. 1994 'Can a Premillennialist Consistently Entertain a Concern for the Environment? A Rejoinder to Al Truesdale', *PSCF* 46: 172-77.
Beisner, E.C. 1997 *Where Garden Meets Wilderness: Evangelical Entry into the Environmental Debate* (Grand Rapids, MI: Acton Institute for the Study of Religion and Liberty/Eerdmans).
Beisner, E.C., M. Cromartie, T. Sieger, D. Knippers, P.J. Hill and T. Terrell 2000 'A Biblical Perspective on Environmental Stewardship', in M.B. Barkey (ed.), *Environmental Stewardship in the Judeo-Christian Tradition: Jewish, Catholic, and Protestant Wisdom on the Environment* (Interfaith Council for Environmental Stewardship; Grand Rapids, MI: Acton Institute): 63-124.
Blaising C.A. and D.L. Bock 1993 *Progressive Dispensationalism* (Grand Rapids, MI: Baker).
Bloch, R.H. 1985 *Visionary Republic: Millennial Themes in American Thought, 1756-1800* (Cambridge: Cambridge University Press).
Bouma-Prediger, S. 2001 *For the Beauty of the Earth: A Christian Vision of Creation Care* (Grand Rapids, MI: Baker Academic).
Boyd, H.H. 1999 'Christianity and the Environment in the American Public', *JSSR* 38: 36-44.
Boyer, P. 1992 *When Time Shall be no More: Prophecy Belief in Modern American Culture* (Cambridge, MS: Belknap).
Burkett, L. 1993 *Whatever Happened to the American Dream?* (Chicago, IL: Moody Press).
Coffman, M.S. 1994 *Saviors of the Earth? The Politics and Religion of the Environmental Movement* (Chicago: Northfield Publishing).
Colson, C. 1993 *A Dance with Deception: Revealing the Truth Behind the Headlines* (Dallas, TX: Word).
Cumbey, C. 1983 *The Hidden Dangers of the Rainbow: The New Age Movement and Our Coming Age of Barbarism* (Shreveport, LA: Huntington House).
Curry-Roper, J.M. 1990 'Contemporary Christian Eschatologies and their Relation to Environmental Stewardship', *Professional Geographer* 42: 157-69.
de Tocqueville, A. 2003 *Democracy in America* (trans. G.E. Bevan; London/New York, NY: Penguin).
DeWitt, C.B. 2008 'Reading the Bible through a Green Lens', in *The Green Bible: The New Revised Standard Version* (New York, NY: HarperOne): I-25-I-34.
Eckburg, D.L. and T.J. Blocker 1996 'Christianity, Environmentalism, and the Theoretical Problem of Fundamentalism', *JSSR* 35: 343-55.
Finger, T. 1998 *Evangelicals, Eschatology, and the Environment* (The Scholars Circle Monograph Series 2; Wynnewood, PA: Evangelical Environmental Network).
Fowler, R.B. 1995 *The Greening of Protestant Thought* (Chapel Hill, NC/London: University of North Carolina Press).
Frykholm, A.J. 2004 *Rapture Culture: Left Behind in Evangelical America* (Oxford: Oxford University Press)
Graham, B. 1984 *Approaching Hoofbeats: The Four Horsemen of the Apocalypse* (Waco, TX: Word).
Granberg-Michaelson, W. 1984 *A Worldly Spirituality: The Call to Redeem Life on Earth* (San Francisco, LA: Harper & Row).
Grant, G. 1986 *The Dispossessed: Homelessness in America* (Forth Worth, TX: Dominion Press).
Guth, J.L., J.C. Green, L.A. Kellstedt and C.E. Smidt 1995 'Faith and the Environment: Religious Beliefs and Attitudes on Environmental Policy', *American Journal of Political Science* 39: 364-82.
Guth, J.L., L.A. Kellstedt, C.E. Smidt, and J.C. Green 1993 'Theological Perspectives and Environmentalism Among Religious Activists', *JSSR* 32: 373-82.
Harding, S. 1994 'Imaging the Last Days: The Politics of Apocalyptic Language', in M.E. Marty and R.S. Appleby (eds), *Accounting for Fundamentalisms: The Dynamic Character of Movements* (Chicago, IL: University of Chicago Press): 57-78.

Johnston, R.K. 1991 'American Evangelicalism: An Extended Family', in D.W. Dayton and R.K. Johnston (eds), *The Variety of American Evangelicalism* (Knoxville, TN: University of Tennessee Press): 252–59.

Kanagy, C.L. 1995 'Religion and Environmental Concern: Challenging the Dominant Assumption', *RRR* 37: 33–45.

Kermode, F. 1967 *The Sense of an Ending: Studies in the Theory of Fiction* (Oxford: Oxford University Press).

Larsen, D.K. 2001 'God's Gardeners: American Protestant Evangelicals Confront Environmentalism, 1967–2000' (University of Chicago Ph.D.).

Lienesch, M. 1993 *Redeeming America: Piety & Politics in the New Christian Right* (Chapel Hill, NC: University of North Carolina Press).

Lindsey, H. 1974 *There's a New World Coming; A Prophetic Odyssey* (Santa Clara, CA: Vision House).

Marsden, G.M. 1982 'Everyone One's Own Interpreter? The Bible, Science, and Authority in Mid-Nineteenth-Century America', in N.O. Hatch and M.A. Noll (eds), *The Bible in America: Essays in Cultural History* (Oxford: Oxford University Press): 79–100.

Moo, D.J. 2006 'Nature in the New Creation: New Testament Eschatology and the Environment', *JETS* 49: 449–88.

Nash, R.F. 2001 *Wilderness and the American Mind* (4th edn; New Haven, CT: Yale University Press).

O'Leary, S.D. 1994 *Arguing the Apocalypse: A Theory of Millennial Rhetoric* (Oxford: Oxford University Press).

Rice J. and J. Choi 2008 'The Meaning of "Life": The New Evangelical Voter', *Sojourners* November: 10–27.

Ro, B.R. (ed.) 1993 *Evangelical Christianity and the Environment* (Outreach and Identity: Evangelical Theological Monographs, No. 7; Madison, WI: Au Sable Institute).

Robertson, P. 1990 *The New Millennium: 10 Trends that Will Impact You and Your Family by the Year 2000* (Dallas, TX: Word).

Robertson, P. 1991 *The New World Order* (Dallas, TX: Word).

Saucy, R.L. 1993 *The Case for Progressive Dispensationalism: The Interface Between Dispensational and Non-Dispensational Theology* (Grand Rapids, MI: Zondervan).

Schaeffer, F. 1970 *Pollution and the Death of Man: The Christian View of Ecology* (Wheaton, IL: Tyndale).

Shaiko, R.G. 1987 'Religion, Politics, and Environmental Concern: A Powerful Mix of Passions', *Social Science Quarterly* 68: 244–62.

Simmons, J.A. 2009 'Evangelical Environmentalism: Oxymoron or Opportunity?', *Worldviews: Global Religions, Culture and Ecology* 13: 40–71.

Stoll, M. 1997 *Protestantism, Capitalism, and Nature in America* (Albuquerque, NM: University of New Mexico Press).

Trusdale, A. 1994 'Last Things First: The Impact of Eschatology on Ecology', *PSCF* 46: 116–22.

Turner, D.L. 1992 'The New Jerusalem in Revelation 21:1–22:5: Consummation of a Biblical Continuum', in C.A. Blaising and D.L. Bock (eds), *Dispensationalism, Israel and the Church* (Grand Rapids, MI: Zondervan).

Tuveson, E.L. 1968 *Redeemer Nation: The Idea of America's Millennial Role* (Chicago, IL/London: University of Chicago Press).

Voth, E.H. 1982 'Time in a Christian Environmental Ethic', in E.R. Squiers (ed.), *The Environmental Crisis: The Ethical Dilemma* (Mancelona, MI: The Au Sable Trails Institute of Environmental Studies): 57–66.

Watt, J. 1982 'Ours is the Earth', *Saturday Evening Post* 254, 1: 102–104.

Weber, T.P. 1979 *Living in the Shadow of the Second Coming: American Premillennialism 1875–1925* (Oxford: Oxford University Press).

White, L., Jr 1967 'The Historical Roots of Our Ecologic Crisis', *Science* 155: 1203–207.

Wilcox, C., S. Linzey and T.G. Jelen 1991 'Reluctant Warriors: Premillennialism and Politics in the Moral Majority', *JSSR* 30: 245–58.

Wilkinson, L. (ed.) 1991 *Earthkeeping in the '90s; Stewardship of Creation* (Grand Rapids, MI: Eerdmans)

Wise, D.S. 1991 'Review of Environmental Stewardship Literature and the New Testament', in L. Wilkinson (ed.), *Earthkeeping in the '90s; Stewardship of Creation* (Grand Rapids, MI: Eerdmans): 117–34.

Woodrum, E. and T. Hoban 1994 'Theology and Religiosity Effects on Environmentalism', *RRR* 35: 193–206.

Wright, N.T. 2008 'Jesus is Coming – Plant a Tree!', in *The Green Bible: The New Revised Standard Version* (New York, NY: HarperOne) I-72–I-85.

Young, R.A. 1994 *Healing the Earth: A Theocentric Perspective on Environmental Problems and Their Solutions* (Nashville, TN: Broadman and Tholman).

Zerbe, G. 1991 'The Kingdom of God and the Care of Creation', in C.B. DeWitt (ed.), *The Environment and the Christian: What Can We Learn from the New Testament?* (Grand Rapids, MI: Baker): 73–92.

Chapter 18

NEW TESTAMENT ESCHATOLOGY AND THE ECOLOGICAL CRISIS IN THEOLOGICAL AND ECCLESIAL PERSPECTIVE

Stephen C. Barton

Introduction

This is an essay on the hermeneutical problems and possibilities that arise in attempting to find wisdom from the past in a time of crisis. The crisis is that of global ecology. The potential source of wisdom is Christian Scripture – especially the eschatologically charged texts of the New Testament – interpreted in the light of theology and ecclesial practice.

That there is an ecological crisis needs little elaboration here. As Peter Scott (2000: 89) has put it: 'A set of crises or breaks in human relations with otherkind and non-human nature has come to occupy a central, if rather ill-defined, place in the concerns of Western humanity.' Four *indicators* of the crisis have been identified (Northcott 2001: 209–10): first, the mass extinction of species due to human activity, with the consequent reduction in the biodiversity that sustains the intricate web of life; second, climate change due to global warming caused especially by carbon dioxide emissions from the burning of fossil fuels; third, the pollution of the planet by industrial, post-consumer and chemical wastes, a consequence of which is the thinning of the earth's protective ozone layer; fourth, soil erosion and desertification caused by deforestation, over-intensive industrial farming and overgrazing, and affecting growing areas of the planet.

Speaking of species loss alone, philosopher Stephen Clark (2000: 96, 114) writes as follows:

> [T]he rate of species loss is between a thousand and ten thousand times the usual. We do not know – and probably will not know until it is far too late – if too many key species are being eliminated for the whole to survive in any form hospitable to us. 'One planet, one experiment.' ... Sometime in the next century, we will have pulled so many threads out from life's tapestry that the whole begins to fray.[1]

---

1 The quotation comes in Quash 2004: 305–306.

If they are the indicators of ecological crisis, the list of *causes* – those, at least, for which humankind may be said to be responsible – includes: the rapid increase in the human population (to over six billion); the deleterious consequences of the industrialization of the world's economies; technological advances which enhance the human capacity to adapt and devastate the physical environment; the globalization of production and consumption to unsustainable levels; the instrumentalization of nature to meet human wants and needs; a related, pervasive anthropocentrism that sets human life apart from and over other life forms; and, at an underlying ideological level, the consequences of late modernity, including the capacity of capitalism 'to disembed human life from prior attachments to place, custom and tradition which in the past helped to conserve the environment' (Northcott 2001: 211).

As to *possibilities of survival and change*, suggested strategies have been numerous; but none has gained centre ground (Scott 2000: 90–91). Some seek to apply the liberatory traditions of the Enlightenment to ecological problems. Others seek to de-centre humanity, emphasizing instead the need for what is called a 'relational, total-field image'. Others mount a political exposé of the contradictions of capitalism, caught between accumulation on the one hand and, on the other, the degradation of the environment upon which that accumulation depends. Others advocate a theory of social justice that incorporates the theme of space. Yet others advocate a 'critical ecological feminism' that seeks to overcome patriarchy's domineering mastery both of nature and of women.

It is against this alarming backdrop that we are seeking Christian wisdom from the New Testament. However, it is worth acknowledging, that, at least in general terms, the issues would be the same in consideration of imminent natural or man-made catastrophe *of any kind*, whether ecological or nuclear or military or whatever. The general issue is the relation between the eschatological texts of the New Testament and the moral life. The threats and risks posed by the increasing likelihood of catastrophe may make things more urgent, but they do not change the basic theological issue, which is how to live the moral life in light of the knowledge of the end, above all, the end of all things in God.

In a recent essay on 'Eschatology and Ethics', Kathryn Tanner captures well the bewildering array of feelings and postures generated by Christian beliefs about the 'last things':

> What one believes about the end of things affects how one feels about the world in which one lives and one's attitude towards efforts to make the world a better place. Disgust and appreciation for the life one leads, contentment and discontentment with one's lot, resignation and resistance to the social order, hope and despair of change, eagerness and reluctance to take action, optimism and pessimism about bettering human life, triumphalism and humility about what has been achieved so far, are all associated at one time or another with the theology of the last things. (Tanner 2005: 41)

Given such striking tensions and contradictions, our question as Scripture-reading theologians must be this: can we read New Testament eschatology in a way that undergirds and motivates a positive commitment to environmental care, or does the character of Christian hope inevitably mute such concern? Of course, lying behind this question is the suspicion that New Testament eschatology – in some of its aspects, at least – is fundamentally *pessimistic* about the future of the world; that, if heaven and earth are to pass away (even if to be transformed into something better), a positive theological and psychological commitment to environmental care is undermined.

On the surface of things, this suspicion appears well founded. On the one hand, there is considerable evidence from the New Testament to suggest that early Christians believed that the end of the world – in the sense of the dissolution of the material cosmos – was imminent. In the case of Paul, for example, the imminence of the end justifies an ethic of detachment from mundane ties, since 'the appointed time has grown short . . . [and] the present form of this world is passing away' (1 Cor. 7.29-31). The 'Little Apocalypse' of Mark 13 has Jesus say: 'But in those days, after that suffering, the sun will be darkened, and the moon will not give its light, and the stars will be falling from heaven, and the powers in the heavens will be shaken.' A kindred mentality is expressed in 2 Pet. 3.10-13:

> But the day of the Lord will come like a thief, and then the heavens will pass away with a loud noise, and the elements will be dissolved with fire, and the earth and everything that is done on it will be disclosed. Since all these things are to be dissolved in this way, what sort of persons ought you to be in leading lives of holiness and godliness, waiting for and hastening the coming of the day of God, because of which the heavens will be set ablaze and dissolved, and the elements will melt with fire? But, in accordance with his promise, we wait for new heavens and a new earth, where righteousness is at home.[2]

At the same time, as well as the apocalyptic eschatology of early Christianity, there is plenty of evidence to suggest that Christians down the ages continued to believe in a literal, cataclysmic end of the world and that many (maybe most) still do so today.[3] Even in as utilitarian and technocratic a society as the contemporary United States, there is a pervasive Fundamentalist millenarianism – with roots in seventeenth century Puritanism and growth points in the Great Awakening, the Revolutionary War, the Civil War and subsequent moments of significant social change – that exerts a powerful influence at the highest levels of religious and political life (cf. Jewett 1984). In past decades, this has produced in some circles a certain pessimistic determinism about the likelihood of the end of the world through a nuclear holocaust. Today, anxiety about a nuclear holocaust has been replaced or overlaid by anxiety about ecological catastrophe.

---

2   Other such texts include Heb. 1.10-12, 12.25-28; Rev. 20.11, 21.1. For a thorough treatment, see Adams 2007: 133–251.
3   From a burgeoning literature, see, for example, Bull 1995; McGinn 2000; Thompson 1997. A succinct Christian comment is Bauckham 1999.

For Christian individuals and communities concerned about the environmental crisis and committed to environmental care, this situation invites serious self-examination. By what authority and upon what grounds may Christians engage in action for the good of creation if their scriptures offer little by way of encouragement, let alone command? Is the *anthropocentrism* of the New Testament in particular so strong as to deflect attention away from concern for the environment? Put more strongly, is Christian eschatology so world denying – even *escapist* – as to render Christians *mute* when it comes to the fate of the non-human species and the material world?

If such a conclusion is to be resisted, and if positive Christian warrants for environmental care are to be found, substantial critical work has to be done. As I seek to show, some of this work will be biblical-exegetical, asking: what do these texts mean? Some of the work will be theological-hermeneutical, asking: how might we read these texts reasonably today in ways which accord with and display the Christian gospel? Some of the work will be personal-ascetical, asking: what performances of Scripture do we as Christians need to master, what processes of formation do we need to embrace, that will predispose us towards true discernment and right action for the common good, including the good of creation? In what follows, each of these three dimensions of the task is opened up by means of case studies of recent scholarly contributions that offer fruitful avenues for discussion and reflection.

The Biblical-Exegetical Task

A significant contribution of a biblical-exegetical kind is that offered by leading New Testament scholar Richard Hays (2000) in his essay, 'New Testament Eschatology at the Turn of the Millennium'. Acknowledging with evident embarrassment the 'millennial fever' of millions of his fellow Americans at the turn of the millennium, yet troubled at the same time by the rejection or downplaying of biblical eschatology and the doctrine of the Second Coming that has taken place by way of liberal theological backlash, Hays seeks to shore up an understanding of the Christian gospel for which the apocalyptic dimension – shorn of millenarianism – is and remains absolutely fundamental. Against the liberal backlash, Hays stakes his claim thus:

> [S]uch a reaction [against the New Testament's apocalyptic imagery] is both hasty and self-defeating, for apocalyptic categories are neither peripheral nor dispensable; they stand at the heart of the gospel of Jesus Christ, as proclaimed and interpreted by the New Testament writers. The resurrection itself is an apocalyptic event, and it can be understood as a saving event for the world only within the framework of the New Testament's dialectical already/ not yet eschatology. Thus, Christians who scoff at apocalyptic are sawing off the branch on which they sit – or, to give the metaphor a more biblical turn, tearing out the roots of a tree of which they themselves are the branches. Apocalyptic narrative and apocalyptic expectation are integral to the logic of the gospel. (2000: 116)

However, given (with Ernst Käsemann) that 'apocalyptic is the mother of Christian theology', how, asks Hays, are Christians to respond to the delay of the Parousia and the non-fulfilment of eschatological hope? In responding to this age-old question, Hays begins by identifying three unsatisfactory strategies.

First, there is what he calls, 'the Johannine option: eternal life now'. Here, Hays identifies in John's Gospel an emphatic 'realized' eschatology, itself a reinterpretation of traditional, future eschatology to meet the needs of second-generation believers needing assurance of salvation. But, against Rudolf Bultmann's attribution of remaining elements of future, 'unrealized' eschatology in the Gospel to a conservative 'ecclesiastical redactor', Hays argues, not only that the manuscript evidence offers no warrant for excision, but also that these future-oriented passages, along with future-oriented themes in the First Letter of John, provide 'the temporal framework within which the realized eschatology must be understood: i.e. the eternal life that the believer experiences in the present *points forward to* a final consummation in the resurrection at the last day' (Hays 2000: 119).

Hays's reluctance to allow John's distinctive realized eschatology its full weight has point. He waves the red flag of 'incipient Gnosticism' to warn against reading John as offering 'an unqualified eschatology of eternal life in the present', since then the Gospel would appear as 'unconcerned about the fate of God's created world, the physical body, and the suffering that we will still experience in the present time' (Hays 2000: 119). He also identifies Bultmann's approach in wanting to trim the text of its Jewish apocalyptic eschatology as a kind of Marcionism. Instead, to be interpreted responsibly, the text has to be read in ways that do justice to its elements of future eschatology as well as its more distinctive realized eschatology.

The second strategy for dealing with unfulfilled eschatological hope that Hays deems unsatisfactory is that of driving a wedge between Jesus and the gospels, a strategy he associates particularly with the Jesus Seminar and its 'discovery' of a 'non-eschatological Jesus' (Hays 2000: 120). According to this approach, the original, non-eschatological teaching of Jesus was reinterpreted by his followers in terms of Jewish apocalyptic: but Jesus himself – as evidenced (controversially!) in early Q traditions and the Gospel of Thomas – is to be seen as 'an itinerant sage, a teacher of subversive wisdom and spirituality, more like a Cynic philosopher than an eschatological prophet' (Hays 2000: 121). In this way, the problem of non-fulfilment is dissolved, at least so far as Jesus is concerned. Instead, it is an artificial problem created by the early church.

This second strategy is analogous to the first. Whereas the Bultmannian 'Johannine option' implicitly drives a wedge between John and the Synoptics (or between John and more future-oriented New Testament texts), the 'Jesus Seminar option' drives a wedge between the Synoptics and Jesus. If you like, the wedge is driven in just one stage further back. The criticisms Hays offers are twofold. In historical terms, it is difficult to justify a method which distinguishes a non-apocalyptic Jesus so clearly both from John the Baptist who preceded him and those followers after him who passed on our earliest (apocalypticized) traditions about him. In terms of theology, the elimination of future eschatology undermines the gospel by displacing a conception of God active in the world bringing his salvific purposes to fulfilment. It also erodes the foundation of the church's confession by its devaluation of the canon of Scripture.

The third unsatisfactory strategy Hays identifies is that of N.T. Wright, and is dubbed, 'apocalyptic eschatology historicized' (Hays 2000: 122). In striking contradiction of the 'Jesus Seminar' strategy, this approach prescinds from denying an apocalyptic eschatology to Jesus. On the contrary, it happily accords historical authenticity to all such material, but interprets it as symbolic language for events to come in the immediate historical setting of first-century Israel as a consequence of Jesus' own activity. The problem of non-fulfilment of end-time warnings and hopes is solved, not by denying to Jesus such warnings and hopes, but by claiming that by the time the gospels were written they had, in fact, been fulfilled already in Jesus' death and resurrection and, finally, in the destruction of Jerusalem and the temple in 70 CE. Wright acknowledges, nevertheless, that not all New Testament texts can be historicized in this way: above all, the expectation of a future *return* of Jesus is quite explicit in texts like Acts 1.10-11, and in Paul as well. So for Hays, what is unsatisfactory in Wright's account is that, precisely because it historicizes end-time expectation, it is unable to give an adequate account of what remains unfulfilled and of the persistence of suffering and evil in Christian experience.

It may well be the case, furthermore, that Hays's criticism of Wright does not go far enough. If, as Edward Adams (2007) has argued, the apocalyptic language used by Jesus and the early Christians resists historicization in a socio-political direction and is explained more plausibly as symbolic of literal end-time cosmic catastrophe and dissolution – most likely with a view to radical transformation in a new creation – then the problem of non-fulfilment is greater still.

Instead of these three unsatisfactory strategies, Hays re-asserts his central claim: 'The gospel is intelligible only within a narrative world shaped by biblical apocalyptic hope' (Hays 2000: 125). He then proceeds to lay out seven reasons why the church needs an apocalyptic eschatology: first, to carry Israel's story forward in terms of the historical fate of the Jewish people, and therefore in defence of God's biblically narrated faithfulness to Israel; second, so that the cross of Christ can be understood in a larger context as a saving event for the world through an ultimate, future triumph over evil and death; third, to enable the gospel's political critique of pagan culture and to direct the church away from accommodation with the values of an unjust world; fourth, to help the church keep awake and so resist complacency and triumphalism; fifth, to affirm the body and material creation on the understanding that God will redeem what God has created; sixth, to ground the church's Spirit-empowered mission in a space in time designated 'the last days'; seventh, to enable the church to speak with integrity and truthfulness about suffering and death as both real, but in the light of resurrection hope, not final (Hays 2000: 125–31).

Hays appears to be conscious that, however impressive this list of reasons why the church *needs* apocalyptic eschatology, the question remains: but is it *true*? His responses are the conventional ones. To the objection that literal apocalyptic hope has been disconfirmed by the grinding passing of millennia, Hays offers a straight rebuttal by appeal to the construal of time offered in 2 Pet. 3.8-10 ('with the Lord one day is like a thousand years . . .'). To the objection that scientific cosmology has displaced the mythic cosmology of apocalyptic, he argues (*with* N.T Wright and, before him, George Caird) that apocalyptic language has to be interpreted metaphorically in accordance with the literary conventions of its own time: 'The images refer to real events in the future (i.e. the return of Christ, the resurrection of the dead), but the details of the description are imaginative constructions that should not be pressed literalistically' (Hays 2000: 132).

He then concludes with a powerful plea for the recovery of 'unabashed apocalyptic theology' of an explicitly 'intratextual' kind (i.e. one that involves living within the apocalyptic frame of reference of the New Testament text): 'I would suggest that the New Testament's story leads us to affirm, in a strong literal sense, the ultimate glorification of Jesus Christ as Lord over all creation, the resurrection of the body, God's final judgment of all humanity, and "the life of the world to come" in true justice and peace' (Hays 2000: 133).

Appreciative though I am of Hays's attempt to tread a line between liberals and fundamentalists, certain reservations remain. Briefly, I wonder if it is possible to discriminate reasonably between apocalyptic language that 'should not be pressed literalistically', on the one hand, and an apocalyptic narrative of salvation to be affirmed 'in a strong literal sense', on the other. A better interpretation of biblical apocalyptic as a whole has to be found. Whatever form that takes, this will be one that gives central place to the central affirmation that underlies New Testament apocalyptic: *hope in God grounded in the resurrection of Christ now present in the world as Spirit.*

Second, we are surely at a stage where a contemporary hermeneutic of the New Testament takes the postmodern turn seriously, i.e. takes seriously (if also critically) contemporary suspicions regarding the enclosure of meaning in universal, grand narratives, and is open instead (or in addition) to alternative ways of reading, ways that are more local, plural, performative, even parodic (cf. Adam 1995). Because Hays is still engaged in modernist debates with the likes of the Jesus Seminar, the consequence is that, in refusing the alternatives they offer, he has to defend instead a theology which, with its summons to return to an 'unabashed apocalyptic theology', sounds *pre*-modern, while simultaneously giving room for what he says to be taken hostage by 'back-to-the Bible' fundamentalists, Christian Zionists and the like.

Third, and related, I do not believe that we can make headway in understanding the Christian doctrine of 'the last things' without attending to intellectual developments in the natural sciences. Hays has managed to write an essay on 'New Testament Eschatology at the Turn of the [Third] Millennium' without engaging with those realms of human knowledge and understanding (to do with time, space, matter and energy) which have made such dramatic advances in the last half century. I do not deny that all of this is a tall order. Nor would I begin to claim for myself the necessary competence. But reading Hays has helped clarify for me the kinds of inquiry and engagement that appear to be needed if the eschatological perspectives of the New Testament, the creeds and the liturgy of the Church are to connect in a compelling way with the current crisis.

The Theological-Hermeneutical Task

From Hays's biblical-exegetical approach, I turn to one which is more theological-hermeneutical. It is the work of Kathryn Tanner, already cited, whose own approach from a systematic theological perspective, developed in two recent essays (Tanner 2000; 2005), is well worth our attention, not least for the contrast it offers with that of Hays. Strikingly, both her essays involve a direct theological engagement with the natural sciences. Her point is this. In the face of the scientific consensus 'that death is the end toward which our solar system and the universe as a whole are moving', Christian theologians can respond in basically one of two ways. On the one hand, they can create a kind of *gap* in naturalistic proposals, a gap that leaves room for the action of God. Then the theologian can propose either that God as Creator and Redeemer will overcome the natural forces of cosmic entropy and intervene to avert disaster, or that God will use cosmic self-destruction to bring a new heaven and earth into being. Such responses allow traditional, future-oriented eschatologies to remain unaffected, since they avoid conflict with scientific end-of-the-world scenarios. It is basically a case of future, this-world eschatology either bypassing, or acting to trump, the scientific evolutionary perspective.[4]

The other approach (and the one that Tanner herself here adopts) is to accept the scientific account on its own terms, and to ask 'what a Christian eschatology might be like if scientists are right that the world does not have a future. Is it really the case that such an end is simply incompatible as it stands with Christian hopes for the world?' (Tanner 2000: 224). Her suggestion is that theologians do in relation to endings what they have done in relation to beginnings, i.e. that they do in relation to eschatology what they have done in relation to the doctrine of creation. In the case of creation, and taking fully into account what science and philosophy say about beginnings and the process of origination, they have argued that what needs to be affirmed theologically is that *the world belongs to God and exists in relation to God*. Similarly, in relation to eschatology. What needs to be affirmed theologically is

---

4 In a significant statement, Tanner (2000: 223) elaborates thus: 'The consummation of the world is not brought about by the world. A gap exists between the results of world processes and the world's consummation, a gap to be bridged by a God with the power to reverse those results, the power to bring what is otherwise absolutely unexpected into existence – say, a world that knows neither loss nor suffering. Or, a grace-motored continuity, rather than a continuity of purely natural processes, spans the world as we know it and the world to come: the world moves without any great interruption to its consummation but it does so only in virtue of divine powers not its own.'

neither an end-of-world scenario that contradicts or trumps science, nor a spiritualized eschatology that absolves itself of concerns for this world, but what she calls 'a more comprehensively cosmic eschatology ... comprehensively cosmic in the sense that its preoccupations would not center on the world of the future but on the world as a whole and on an ongoing redemptive (rather than simply creative) relation to God that holds for the world of the past, present, and future' (Tanner 2000: 225).

On this basis, the striking move she makes is away from a narrowly temporalized understanding of Christian eschatology to a *de-temporalized* understanding – to one that is *more spatialized* in conception and practice. Tanner acknowledges the contribution of Jürgen Moltmann's *Theology of Hope* (1967) in returning eschatology to the heart of Christian theology and deepening 'the future orientation of action in modern movements for social change' by setting the historical process in the context of the in-breaking of God's future; and she implies that this temporalized, future-oriented understanding made good sense in the context of modernity, characterized as it was by the rise of historical consciousness and powerful movements for reform and social change (Tanner 2005: 44–45).

In the context of postmodernity, however, what is needed, according to Tanner, is an eschatology more attuned to questions of space than time, more given to geography than temporality, more about making connection in a world of movement and fluidity than of progress towards a new future. Such an eschatology would also be more in tune with the intransigent pessimism which characterizes contemporary life, pessimism which includes the likely inevitability of ecological disaster:

> Naturalism is now associated more with fatalism than with confidence in the powers of human achievement: death, transience, and failure seem simply the irremediable stuff of life. Things will ultimately come to a bad end of cosmic proportions if the physicists are right: dissipation or conflagration is our universe's sorry future. (Tanner 2005: 46)

According to Tanner, a de-temporalized eschatology is better able to accommodate postmodernity's less optimistic worldview. What is more, it can do so without loss of hope in God and without undermining the imperative of progressive social action. What it requires, however, is 'uncoupling the eschaton from hopes for the world's future. We have our hope in God whether or not things are likely to turn out well in the end, whether or not things are likely to turn out badly in the end' (Tanner 2005: 46).

Already in the Old Testament, she points out, there are notions of life and death that relativize the religious significance of the cessation of the biological life of the individual (cf. also Levenson 2006). There is, for example, the notion of life as fruitfulness, longevity and communal flourishing, and death as barrenness, oppression, social fragmentation and isolation. Related to this, there is a conception of life and death as alternative 'ways' or patterns of existence arising out of how one is in relation to God (cf. Deut. 30.19-20). There is also the sense that the life of the individual carries on in the life of the community, in the form of progeny and communal memory. Above all, a number of texts (e.g. Job 1.21; Deut. 32.39; Ps. 139.7-8) affirm that 'the dead are not cut off from God because God is the Lord of both life and death' (Tanner 2000: 228). In sum, the most important senses of 'life' and 'death' have to do with *relation with God*, a relation which is seen, in various ways, to transcend biological death: and this may have implications for reflection beyond the biological death of the individual to reflection on the death of the cosmos.

Crossing over into the New Testament, what Tanner proposes by way of a more relational or spatialized eschatology is one that readers of the New Testament would recognize as close in important ways to the Christ mysticism of the Fourth Gospel in particular, but arguably of Paul as well. The key phrase for Tanner is *'eternal life in God'*, understood as a new level of relationship with God, transcending the relationship with God that creatures enjoy by virtue of their creatureliness. Thus, just as the doctrine of creation 'refers to a relationship of dependence upon God which holds whether or not the world has a beginning, and whatever the worldly mechanism by which it may have come to be', so the eschaton, understood as 'consummation in the good', has to do with 'a new level of relationship with God, the final one surpassing what we are simply as creatures, beyond which there is not other. Eschatology's fundamental interest is in the character of this relationship to God and not in what the world is like or what happens to it considered independently of that relationship – say, at its end'.[5]

Importantly, the model for life so understood is the incarnation: 'Jesus is the one who lives in God, the one who is all that he is as a human being without existing independently of God, the human being whose very existence is God's own' (Tanner 2005: 48). And just as Jesus' life in God was displayed in a life given over to action for the world's good (without concern for success or failure), so also Christians, united with Christ's life by grace through the Spirit, are called and enabled to act in the world in accordance with the gift of eternal life they have received and in which they dwell.

In other words, Tanner rejects the idea that a de-temporalized eschatology has apathy or passivity in the face of evil and injustice as inevitable corollaries:

> One is led to see the way the world currently runs as an insufferable, unacceptable affront, not by the disparity between the present and God's coming future, but by the utter disjunction between patterns of injustice, exclusion, and impoverishment, which make up the realm of death, and the new paradigm of existence empowered by life in God as a force working in the present. In short, complacency is ruled out not by a transcendent future but by a transcendent present – by the present life in God as the source of goods that the world one lives in fails to match. (Tanner 2000: 234; cf. also 2005: 54)

---

5   Tanner 2005: 47–48. Cf. also 49: 'Eternal life is not the endless extension of present existence into an endless future, but a matter of a new quality of life in God, at the ready, even now infiltrating, seeping into the whole. Eternal life is less a matter of duration than a matter of the mode of one's existence in relation to God, as that calibre of relation shows itself in a new pattern for the whole of life.'

Tanner's distinctive 'spatialized' approach to the doctrine of the 'last things' is certainly noteworthy. While not denying completely the temporal aspect, it avoids some of the problems of overly temporalized eschatologies that have been, at best, problematic, at worst, downright dangerous in Christian times past and present. It resonates with the spatial connotations of the biblical idea of 'the kingdom of God' as the universal realm of God's sovereign power. In relation to recent scholarship on eschatological texts, it fits well with that understanding of apocalyptic which brings to the fore the more mystical aspects of its intuitions about earthly reality seen from the perspective of heaven (e.g. Rowland 1982). It is grounded theologically in a well-nuanced notion of 'life in God', reflected already in the Old Testament, fully revealed in the incarnation, and offered unconditionally as gift to the world through union with Christ. It can claim serious warrant in the New Testament in the 'realized' eschatology and Christ mysticism of the Fourth Gospel. It takes the findings of the natural sciences with full seriousness, and is a position worked out in dialogue with them in a way that displays rational credibility. It resonates deeply with the contemporary cultural turn to spatiality and connection characteristic of the postmodern condition, mentioned earlier. Finally, it offers a profound motivation for action for the good in the present – understood as what life *in God* is all about – irrespective of success or failure, irrespective also of the world's prospects.

Nevertheless, as I have reservations about Hays's position, so also I have reservations about Tanner's. Briefly, they are as follows. First, while cognisant of her attempt to engage intelligently with the natural sciences, I wonder if Tanner is wise to spurn theological approaches to naturalistic accounts of beginnings and endings that seek to create space – in her words, a 'gap' – for the action of God. It is one thing laudably to offer a theology that avoids the reductionism implicit in a 'God of the gaps', where the idea of God shrinks every time a 'gap' is filled. It is another to surrender discourse about beginnings and endings *tout court* to the terms offered by scientific naturalism and its accompanying pessimism. Along with the potentially serious moral and motivational consequences for environmental concern and action of such a surrender, this kind of position threatens the hope in God that is at the core of Christian conviction precisely because the naturalistic account is deemed not to be the whole story or the best way of telling the story. To say that '[w]e have our hope in God whether or not things are likely to turn out well in the end, whether or not things are likely to turn out badly in the end', surely departs radically from the central Christian conviction that, *because of Christ crucified, risen and coming again*, all in the end 'shall be well'.

Second, Tanner's concern to 'de-temporalize' Christian eschatology in favour of a more 'spatial' paradigm, while helpful in drawing attention to important aspects of the invitation to 'life in God' characteristic of biblical faith with its climax in the incarnation, overplays the distinction between temporal and spatial paradigms at the expense of the former. Telltale here is what appears to me to be a very significant – *and theologically-speaking, fatal* – omission: particular attention is drawn to the incarnation, but not to the resurrection. Proper attention to the resurrection as the revelation in present space-time reality of the glorious future of a creation redeemed by the Death-defeating death of the Son of God and transformed by the Spirit is the *essential corollary* of the incarnation. Indeed, without the resurrection as its fulfilment, the incarnation – indeed, creation as a whole – is unintelligible, Christianly speaking. Tanner's failure here to engage with eschatological texts as weighty as 1 Thessalonians 4, Romans 8, 1 Corinthians 15 and the book of Revelation, not to mention the strong orientation on the future in the teaching of Jesus, is a serious omission.[6] However, it is not a matter simply of citing Paul or the Seer as having a more 'temporal', future-oriented eschatology over against John as having a more 'spatial', present-oriented eschatology, for in all three of these New Testament witnesses eschatology interpreted in the light of Christ crucified and risen has elements both temporal and spatial.[7]

Third, if Hays can be criticized for allowing his interpretation to become captive to concerns characteristic of modernity, Tanner may be judged to be attempting an alignment with postmodernity the benefit of which is quite ambiguous from a Christian point of view. In so far as an alignment with postmodernity involves downplaying temporality – especially in its past and future aspects – the prospect of repentance for historic ills in time past and of moral action for the future good of creation in anticipation of a greater good still to come, is seriously compromised.

To sum up so far: in focusing – appreciatively but also critically – first on Hays and then on Tanner, I have offered examples of two of the three approaches to the task of discerning wisdom from Christian scripture and tradition in a time of ecological crisis that I identified as important at the outset – the biblical-exegetical and the theological-hermeneutical. It may be inferred, on the basis of what I have said to this point, that significant enrichment comes when the biblical-exegetical and the theological-hermeneutical tasks take place in engagement with each other. With such an engagement, Hays's biblical-exegetical work might escape the rather claustrophobic confines of biblicism in its various (liberal and conservative) forms, and Tanner's theological-hermeneutical work might be less prone to attend one-sidedly to the immanent spatial aspects of existence at the expense of the temporal, less prone also to interpret creation and incarnation without new creation and resurrection.

The Personal-Ascetical Task

But neither the biblical-exegetical nor the theological-hermeneutical is sufficient as an exposition and display of biblical eschatology in its full ecological significance. A third dimension remains to be opened up, that of the personal-ascetical – to do, that is, with the processes of formation and discipline that Christians need to embrace if

---

6   For a recent exegetical examination of eschatological texts in the New Testament in relation to the question of the environment, cf. Moo 2006.
7   For example, on spatial and temporal dimensions in the Apocalypse, see Gilbertson 2003, especially chs 4 and 5.

they are to be predisposed towards true discernment and right action for the common good, including the good of creation, in a time of crisis. To put the issue succinctly and in a way appropriate to matters ecological and environmental set against the horizon of God's grace: *how does one receive the gift?* What patterns of life, ordering of needs, and ways of being in the world (in every sense of 'world') constitute an appropriate response to the gifts of God in creation, Christ and the Spirit? By what practices and performances may the gift of life in God be signified and sustained?[8]

Here I concur with that emphasis in recent Christian ethics that finds a significant (but, of course, not the only) answer – especially at the symbolic and cultural levels – in the practices and performances of the corporate life of the church (cf. Hauerwas and Wells 2004; also, Wannenwetsch 2004). Ordered according to an economy of grace given articulation in a startling biblical narrative of divine self-dispossession (cf. 2 Cor. 8.9), the church itself is *a school for learning those performances of Scripture which issue in the self-dispossession required to receive and live the gift.*

Liturgical Formation 1: Joining Voice with Creation – The Benedicite

One example, related particularly to the deep-rooted problem of anthropocentrism, is that offered by Richard Bauckham in his essay of 2002, entitled, 'Joining Creation's Praise of God'. The answer Bauckham offers to the question of how to receive and live the gift is: to acknowledge the divine Giver by offering an apposite gift in return – the gift of *praise and thanksgiving*. One form this gift takes is the liturgy of the church. In particular, in the words of the canticle known as the Benedicite – taken from the Greek additions to the book of Daniel, and based on Psalm 148 – the church joins with creation, *as part of creation*, to bless God. Striking, for present purposes, is the fact that, in its context in Daniel, the canticle is placed on the lips of the three young Jewish sages as they walk in Nebuchadnezzar's fiery furnace – in other words, in a place of danger and at a time of crisis. Instead of anxiety for their own fate at the hands of a local despot, they display confidence in the God who is sovereign over all creation and invites creation's praise:

> O all ye Works of the Lord, bless ye the Lord: praise him, and magnify him for ever.
> O ye Angels of the Lord, bless ye the Lord: praise him, and magnify him for ever.
> O ye Heavens, bless ye the Lord: praise him, and magnify him for ever.
> O ye Waters that be above the Firmament, bless ye the Lord: praise him, and magnify him for ever.
> O all ye Powers of the Lord, bless ye the Lord: praise him, and magnify him for ever . . .[9]

As Bauckham (2002: 46) points out, of the thirty verses, each summoning one category of God's creatures to praise God, only the last seven are addressed to humans:

---

8   Important on the idea of (what I have called) 'practices and performances' is Adam 2006.
9   The language is that of *The Book of Common Prayer* (1662) of the Church of England.

'all the others [are addressed] to non-human creatures from the angels, through the heavenly bodies, the elements of the weather, the mountains, the plants, the waters, to all the living creatures of water, air and earth.' There is, in other words, a strong recognition of 'fellow-creatureliness', with humans joining in the whole creation's praise of God: 'In this common attribution of glory to the one Creator there is no hierarchy or anthropocentricity. Here all creatures . . . are simply fellow-creatures expressing the theocentricity of the created world, each in [their] own created way, differently but in complementarity' (Bauckham 2002: 48). Thus, in the practice of sharing in creation's praise of God, a practice shaped by liturgy and modelled – played out, performed – in the lives of saints like Francis of Assisi, the possibility opens up of responding to the gift of life in ways that, instead of destroying the gift, offer it back, in all its distinctiveness and diversity, to the Giver. Of course, such 'offering back' will not be confined to the symbolic actions of the liturgy: rather, it will flow over from the liturgy of the gathered community to the liturgy of everyday life.

Liturgical Formation 2: Bringing Creation's Gifts to the Giver – The Offertory

A second example is the liturgy of the Eucharist – in particular, the Offertory, that point in the service (in the Church of England, at least) when the bread and wine are brought to the altar. The words spoken over the bread and wine by the president evoke the economy of divine grace which makes life possible;[10] and the words of the people express the appropriate response.[11] In a helpful commentary which draws attention to how the liturgy is a schooling in the economy and ecology of grace, Ben Quash says this:

> In these liturgical exchanges the congregation learns to think about the whole creation (in connection with these specific gifts of the creation) as belonging to God ('Lord of all creation'). It learns in appropriate humility . . . to acknowledge that it 'has' these gifts only because of life-giving forces wholly in excess of its own control ('through your goodness'; 'which earth has given') . . . Perhaps more than anywhere in Christian liturgy, this moment of the 'presentation of the gifts' highlights the wondrous possibilities latent in material things – the things of the earth, God's non-human creatures. They are themselves to be the vehicles of 'life' and 'salvation.' They are treated with reverence (carried in procession, no less) and placed on the altar. And the overriding emphasis is that they are not our servants, they are God's blessings, and it is by his relation to them (not our manipulation of them) that they bring life. (2004: 311–12)

10 'Blessed are you, Lord God of all creation; through your goodness we have this bread to offer; which earth has given and human hands have made. It will become for us the bread of life. // Blessed are you, Lord God of all creation; through your goodness we have this wine to offer; fruit of the vine and the work of human hands. It will become for us the cup of salvation.'
11 'Blessed be God forever.'

What is so profound about the liturgy, as exemplified in an example such as this, is the sheer *intensity* with which it displays the ordering and connectedness of creation in the economy and ecology of divine grace in space and time. What is so striking also is the way Scripture and theology find their place – indeed, are transposed into a new key – as they are embodied and performed in the gathering of the people to join with creation *as part of creation* to voice creation's praise. It is this intensity and this transposition that generate the moods and motivations necessary for morally responsible living as God's creatures in God's creation.

Liturgical Formation 3: In Time with Creation and Redemption – Sabbath/Sunday

As a third and final example of the personal-ascetical task – of what scripturally rooted practices and performances shape Christians in ways appropriate to the giftedness of created life – I draw brief attention to one more dimension of ecclesial life: sabbath observance and its Christian eschatological extension or transposition, Sunday (cf. Heschel 1951; Moltmann 1984). Both sabbath and Sunday are about the discipline of life in time, *making space in time* – above all, about the ordering of human time in harmony with God's time. Both are *eschatological*, linking beginnings and endings. The sabbath roots the life of a community in the divine gift of creation, in imitation of the God who rests after the work of creation (cf. Gen. 2.2-3; Exod. 20.8-11). Sunday, 'the Lord's day', the day of resurrection, roots the life of a community in the divine gift of *new* creation. Both speak also of *liberation*. Sabbath liberates the human and non-human community from incessant toil, for the purpose of rest and renewal (cf. Deut. 5.12-15). Sunday speaks of the liberation of humanity and all creation from sin and death for participation as the 'new creation' in eschatological rest, which is life in the Spirit. Jürgen Moltmann articulates the sabbath's all-embracing significance well:

> The peace of the sabbath is peace with God first of all. But this divine peace encompasses not merely the soul but the body too; not merely individuals but family and people; not only human beings but animals as well; not living things alone, but also, as the creation story tells us, the whole creation of heaven and earth. That is why the sabbath peace is also the beginning of that peace with nature which many people are seeking today, in the face of the growing destruction of the environment. But there will never be peace with nature without the experience and celebration of God's sabbath. (1984: 277)

What Moltmann says reinforces my point. The fundamental ecclesial practice of *marking* time and *keeping* time, this locating of our action through time in God's acts of creation and liberation, is a profound pedagogy in how to receive the gift of time in ways that are life-giving and life-sustaining – that is to say, in ways that accord with the character of the divine gift-giver as the source of all life.

Conclusion

My aim has been to address hermeneutical questions arising from the attempt to engage with New Testament eschatology as a source of wisdom for responding to the ecological crisis that faces us today. In making the attempt, I have posited that at least three overlapping and inter-related tasks are necessary – what I have called the biblical-exegetical, the theological-hermeneutical and the personal-ascetical. Each one has been explored through engagement with recent, exemplary work in the field.

The biblical-exegetical, in critical interaction with views that attempt either to 'over-spiritualize' or 'over-literalize' biblical eschatology, confirms the dominant influence of resurrection faith and end-time hope on the first Christian writers' interpretations of the significance of Jesus for the life of the world and the fate of the cosmos. The theological-hermeneutical, engaged with contemporary cultural sensibilities and with conceptions of the fate of the cosmos according to the natural sciences, seeks to offer a way of mitigating the often world-denying orientation of Christian hope by developing a more profound notion of 'eternal life in God'. The personal-ascetical opens up some of the ways in which the habits and disciplines formed in the worship and common life of the church – informing and informed by scripture interpretation and theological insight – make appropriate response to the ecological crisis possible. If the preceding exploration has any merit, it is perhaps in the identification and critical elaboration of these three tasks in the demanding business of seeking Christian wisdom at this critical time.

References

Adam, A.K.M. 1995 *What is Postmodern Biblical Criticism?* (Minneapolis, MN: Fortress).
Adam, A.K.M. 2006 'Poaching on Zion: Biblical Theology as Signifying Practice', in A.K.M. Adam, S.E. Fowl, K.J. Vanhoozer and F. Watson, *Reading Scripture with the Church. Toward a Hermeneutic for Theological Interpretation* (Grand Rapids, MI: Baker Academic): 17–34.
Adams, E. 2007 *The Stars will Fall From Heaven: Cosmic Catastrophe in the New Testament and Its World* (LNTS 347; London: T&T Clark).
Bauckham, R. 1999 'Approaching the Millennium', *Anvil* 16/4: 255–67.
Bauckham, R. 2002 'Joining Creation's Praise of God', *Ecotheology* 7/1: 45–59.
Bull, M. (ed.) 1995 *Apocalypse Theory and the End of the World* (Oxford: Blackwell).
Clark, S.R.L. 2000 *Biology and Christian Ethics* (Cambridge: Cambridge University Press).
Gilbertson, M. 2003 *God and History in the Book of Revelation. New Testament Studies in Dialogue with Pannenberg and Moltmann* (Cambridge: Cambridge University Press).
Hauerwas, S. and S. Wells (eds) 2004 *The Blackwell Companion to Christian Ethics* (Oxford: Blackwell).
Hays, R.B. 2000 '"Why Do You Stand Looking Up Toward Heaven?" New Testament Eschatology at the Turn of the Millennium', *Modern Theology* 16/1: 115–35.
Heschel, A. 1951 *The Sabbath. Its Meaning for Modern Man* (New York, NY: Noonday).
Jewett, R. 1984 'Coming to Terms with the Doom Boom', *Quarterly Review* 4: 9–22.
Levenson, J.D. 2006 *Resurrection and the Restoration of Israel. The Ultimate Victory of the God of Life* (New Haven, CN/London: Yale University Press).

McGinn, B. 2000, J.J. Collins and S.J. Stein (eds) *Encyclopedia of Apocalypticism* (New York, NY: Continuum).

Moltmann, J. 1967 *Theology of Hope. On the Ground and the Implications of a Christian Eschatology* (London: SCM).

Moltmann, J. 1984 *God in Creation. An Ecological Doctrine of Creation* (ET; London: SCM).

Moo, D.J. 2006 'Nature in the New Creation: New Testament Eschatology and the Environment', *JETS* 49: 449–88.

Northcott, M. 2001 'Ecology and Christian Ethics', in R. Gill (ed.), *The Cambridge Companion to Christian Ethics* (Cambridge: Cambridge University Press): 209–27.

Quash, B. 2004 'Offering: Treasuring the Creation', in S. Hauerwas and S. Wells (eds), *The Blackwell Companion to Christian Ethics* (Oxford: Blackwell): 305–18.

Rowland, C. 1982 *The Open Heaven. A Study of Apocalyptic in Judaism and Early Christianity* (London: SPCK).

Scott, P. 2000 'The Future of Creation. Ecology and Eschatology', in D. Fergusson and M. Sarot (eds), *The Future as God's Gift. Explorations in Christian Eschatology* (Edinburgh: T&T Clark): 89–114.

Tanner, K. 2000 'Eschatology Without A Future?', in J. Polkinghorne and M. Welker (eds), *The End of the World and the Ends of God. Science and Theology on Eschatology* (Harrisburg, PA: Trinity Press International): 222–37.

Tanner, K. 2005 'Eschatology and Ethics', in G. Meilander and W. Werpehowski (eds), *Oxford Handbook of Theological Ethics* (Oxford: Oxford University Press): 41–56.

Thompson, D. 1997 *The End of Time. Faith and Fear in the Shadow of the Millennium* (London: Minerva).

Wannenwetsch, B. 2004 *Political Worship. Ethics for Christian Citizens* (Oxford: Oxford University Press).

Chapter 19

KEEPING THE COMMANDMENTS: THE MEANING OF SUSTAINABLE COUNTRYSIDE

Tim Gorringe

In the beginning was the Word. As a Jew that was a very obvious place for John to begin because from the start Israel's existence was defined by the telling of stories. This story telling constitutes what David Ford (1992) has called 'a long rumour of wisdom', a sense of being engaged by the Lord of history, the origin and end of all things, and of responding to that engagement. To be Jewish or Christian today is to share, to dwell within, that long rumour of wisdom. The church witnesses to and acts out of this long rumour of wisdom and in so doing contributes to the conversation of the human race about where we are going and how we are going to get there, a conversation we know as ethics. This conversation includes doctrines, philosophies, ideologies, but it is primarily a matter of stories because the *Logos* of Jn 1.1 is not so much rationality as imagination, the creative imagining of all things into being, and of God's engagement with the world. In the beginning was the imagination, the story telling, of God, which is why, in the Christian Scriptures, we have a book of stories, and why when Christians meet together, we tell a story: 'On the night in which he was betrayed . . .'.

Israel's story tellers knew nothing about the division between sacred and secular, of what today we call 'the separation of powers'. They were not philosophers, interested in penetrating beyond appearances to eternal verities. They believed God engaged them in the minutiae of daily life: this is the substance of what we call 'the law', *Torah*. For Israel, and for Jesus, God is concerned with the ordering of every aspect of human life – agriculture, economics, politics, community, criminal justice, sexuality, house building, the lot. But no blueprints for any of these things were revealed. In Scripture we already listen in to a debate. When we say, 'God reveals Godself', we do not mean that God speaks through a megaphone of enormous dimensions, or even through a whisper into the ears of specially religiously gifted souls. We are talking about a long process of discernment, of argument and theological struggle, of constantly testing the long rumour of wisdom. 'Two Jews, three opinions' is already true in the Hebrew Bible.

All this remains true in the Messianic writings, those writings which witness to Jesus Messiah. Our earliest writings tell of fierce conflict between Peter and Paul about the way in which things ought to go (Gal. 2.11-14). A little later four gospels emerged, the product of four different communities with different worries and different emphases. In the documents we find in the Messianic writings there are strongly different theologies though all agree that, as Hebrews puts it, 'in these last days God has spoken to us by a Son, whom he appointed heir of all things, through whom also he created the ages' (Heb. 1.2), which I take as a rhetorical way of speaking of the significance of Jesus in the history of salvation rather than as an early statement about 'pre-existence'. The struggle to understand that fact led to the emergence of what we know as 'the doctrine of the Trinity', which is, for Christians, the grammar of God's engagement with all that is not God. The doctrine, or as it is called in Greek, the symbol, is a koan which represents the faith that God creates all things, reconciles all things and redeems all things. Put differently, what 'I am who I will be' means is that the being and end of all things, 'God', is encountered in the bringing of order out of chaos, in the reconciliation of persons and communities, and in hope that God's glory will finally irradiate all things and that everything that we do should be shaped by that hope.

It follows that 'Christian ethics' is an imaginative engagement with the stories and ruminations which give distinctiveness to this particular community. In regard to any issue Christians will interrogate contemporary sciences of every kind with these stories, and interrogate the stories with the sciences. The interrogation goes both ways but the interrogation from the side of Scripture has a twofold priority. First, it is part and parcel of the identity of the community called 'Church'. Second, the Church associates revelation with Scripture. Revelation is 'what we cannot tell ourselves' (Barth). This applies primarily to the story of the cross, but also to the rest of Scripture as that is read through the cross.

The somewhat counterintuitive assumption behind this process is that wisdom, by which is meant the things which make for life, is to be found in the stories. 'Counterintuitive' because the Christian story can be read as a history of exclusion and oppression – witch burnings, burnings of heretics, *odium theologicum*, mission riding on the back of colonialism and so forth. The pathos of enlightenment derived from precisely this fact. Here and there, there are genuine marks of progress which derive from the Church – the founding of hospitals, provision of education, care for the homeless and for prisoners, but the balance is more in the red than the black. If we persist in attaching significance to this story telling it is on the cumulative grounds summarized by phrases such as 'grace rather than law', 'justice, mercy and truth', 'the image of God', the priority of forgiveness, the foolishness of God, the resurrection of the body. Such phrases sketch out a vision of life in freedom that transcends the bigotry of Christian history and they suggest that freedom is only attainable in relation to the origin and end of all things that is not part of the created order.

The interrogation of human life by Scripture and of Scripture by human life takes many forms. It has a scholarly form, though this is not primary. The primary form is the exposition of Scripture in the Sunday or Sabbath 'sermon', a feature of Christian practice inherited from the Church's Jewish roots. Very often this will involve teasing out a single verse or phrase of Scripture and trying to understand its significance for the lives of the hearers. This procedure differs from proof texting in that the verse or phrase concerned is read in the context of the ongoing *lectio divina*, the reading of the whole of Scripture by the community. It is part of an ongoing rumination in which the entire text is consulted. Preaching week in, week out on the whole canon, in a lectionary which brings together Hebrew Bible, epistles and gospels, means that the part is read by the whole and the whole by the part, that there is a continuing interrogation of the whole text. One does not lift out a particular verse in order to prove a point but, in the context of ongoing rumination one seeks to learn from Scripture what resources there might be for reflecting on any given issue. It is in this sense that I wish to consult familiar texts to interrogate the idea of sustainable countryside. I do this in a context where 80 million more human beings are added to global population each year, where the amount of fertile land shrinks through desertification and urbanization, where the number of areas seriously water-stressed grows each year and where climate change will almost certainly threaten food production in some of the world's currently fertile areas. If ethics is intergenerational then the question about how grandchildren and their children will be fed, whether a decent quality of life will be open to them, is urgent. This is the question of sustainable countryside. The question of feeding people has always been a priority, as general famines occurred five or six times a century, and the Church used Rogation Sundays to think about these issues. From the texts used for these days I begin with Gen. 2.15.

I

God put human beings in the garden to till and keep it.

The word 'garden' (*gan*) here is, of course, a metaphor for the whole earth but this vision of the earth is as a garden. From the sixteenth century on, with the rise of the industrial city, this came to be visualized as countryside. The most perfect vision of countryside, in fact, comes from Rubens, around about 1620.[1] In the nineteenth century, so Raymond Williams (1976: 81) tells us, the word 'countryside', originally borrowed from Scots to describe a specific locality, became applied to the whole rural life and economy. But countryside also became a place to go for a walk. We are told – I don't know how they arrive at the statistics – that in Britain at least a third of the population go for walks in 'the country' on summer weekends. This practice has its origins in the Romantic retreat to the country from the choked and filthy city. It must have to do with the pace of industrialization and Britain's smallness of scale. John de Gruchy records the astonishment of rural Africans at the idea that anyone should choose simply to 'go for a walk'![2] If you have to walk ten or twelve miles for water every day the need for a little exercise is not so self-evident. In the past fifteen

---

1 'Summer', in the Queen's Gallery in Edinburgh.
2 In personal conversation.

years it has evolved still further. The 'countryside' is where stressed-out city slickers can go to refresh themselves before going back to sweat at the stock exchange; it is the place where quality-of-lifers live, and threaten to sue if your cockerels wake them up in the morning, or your cows make the roads dirty. Now the garden of Genesis 2 is clearly a place of pleasure and refreshment: in Revelation it is described as 'paradise' (Rev. 2.7), a Persian loan word most perfectly instantiated in the Mughal gardens of Kashmir, places of exquisite beauty created for the erotic delight of a handful of rulers. But the idea of a walled garden or a park captured the Western imagination to such an extent that very humble inner city areas still have their 'pleasure gardens'.[3] To the extent that we can identify the garden of Genesis 2 with the paradise of Revelation these elite understandings of the countryside are justified.

However, the dominant way of speaking of the land in Scripture, '*erets*, refers not to a pleasure garden but to the fundamental means of production, the foundation of all human economy. This has been forgotten since the late eighteenth century when heavy industry overtook the importance of farming in Britain and then in the rest of Europe and North America. The conceit grew that farming was secondary, a minor part of the economy. This was possible because food production was pushed out of sight by the invention of refrigerated shipping in 1873. Food was now produced by colonial labourers on the other side of the world. All of a sudden, however, as demand for grain has exceeded grain stocks for the past five years, and as the world's most populous nation, China, has lost the capacity to feed itself, food security has moved back to centre stage. The benefits of financial speculation, or of service industries, are doubtless beyond praise but even the fattest city cat quickly becomes a dead city cat if he or she can't eat. That possibility is concentrating minds. It takes us back to Gen. 2.15.

Human beings were put into the garden to till and to keep it. The verb translated 'till' here is the verb *'abad*, a key word in the Hebrew Bible. It means to work, serve or worship. It is not only human beings who do this, but God as well. 'I have not made you serve', says God in Isaiah, 'but you have made me serve with your sins' (Isa. 43.23-24; author's translation). The noun from it is *'ebed*, servant, fundamental for the theology of second Isaiah and taken up by Jesus in Mark: 'the Son of Man came not to be served but to serve' (Mk 10.45). Serving, in Scripture, is key to understanding what it means to be human, and farming, serving the earth, serving the whole human community, has always been a paradigmatic expression of that.

The verb 'to keep', *shamar*, is likewise fundamental. It is the word invariably used for keeping God's commandments. It is the root of the word Cain uses in reply to the divine question: 'Am I my brother's keeper?' (Gen. 4.9). To keep in this sense likewise goes to the very heart of human identity. To be truly human is to keep my neighbour; it is to keep the commandments and thus to keep the gift, God's earth. Keeping the earth, in fact, is the practical application of keeping the commandments.

Since the Neolithic revolution most humans have been engaged in growing food,

---

3   For example, the 'pleasure gardens' in Heavitree and St Thomas, Exeter.

and this was true beyond the middle of the twentieth century. Only in the past 50 years has the balance tipped towards urbanization and industrialization. Still, worldwide, two and a half billion people work in agriculture, so it is still the world's largest single source of work and, from a biblical perspective, the paradigm of all human work. This has been forgotten in the cheap energy economy in which we have been living for the past two centuries. We are governed by people who think food comes from supermarkets, or is provided by posh restaurants. The real work, they think, is done in the city, which is the source of 'wealth creation' – by which is meant betting on what is going to happen to currencies or to commodities in a month or year from now. But this is not work, in the biblical sense, and it is not true wealth creation either. In fact it is condemned in Scripture as the service of mammon. What is praised is work which serves the human good, which serves the human community. Growing food, farming, is the paradigm of that work. Proverbs has a good deal to say about lazy and careless farmers, but its advice is directed at producing good farmers. A good farmer is one who cares for his or her land, crops and stock, who serves them. You cannot be a good farmer and dominate. The good farmer cares for and nurtures his or her land and stock: s/he husbands them. Good husbandry is the heart of all farming. Alternatively put, the good farmer keeps the land by keeping the commandments, which establish practices of justice and respect. There are practices of domination in farming, and they are the road to ruin. Those who argue that they are the true path of the future are siren voices we must not listen to. Only the ancient practice of service, of nourishing work, of keeping the commandments, will give us a future. In this respect the foolish byword of recent years, 'farming is a business like any other', needs to be dropped. It is not a business like any other. Rather, it is an example of what business ought to be and to look like, or at least, it is when it is done properly.

From an engagement with Gen. 2.15, then, we derive quite considerable grist for the sustainable mill. A sustainable countryside, the wisdom of the text suggests, is a well-husbanded countryside, and one where an understanding of the fundamentals of all human flourishing has priority. You could object that an agnostic like Colin Tudge, in *So Shall We Reap* (2003) reaches similar conclusions without recourse to Scripture, but as the title of his book suggests, even agnostics have sensibilities shaped by our texts.

II

The Revised Common Lectionary sets Deut. 8.1-18 for Rogation Days and Deut. 28.1-14 for Harvest. Both of these texts make the contrast, fundamental to Deuteronomy, between a way of life and a way of death. The curses in 28.15-16 read:

> If you do not obey the LORD your God and do not carefully follow all his commands and decrees I am giving you today, all these curses will come upon you and overtake you: You will

be cursed in the city and cursed in the country. Your basket and your kneading trough will be cursed. The fruit of your womb will be cursed, and the crops of your land, and the calves of your herds and the lambs of your flocks. You will be cursed when you come in and cursed when you go out.

To make this more precise I turn to what I take to be a younger text, Lev. 18.3-5, which reads,

> You shall not do as they do in the land of Egypt, where you lived, and you shall not do as they do in the land of Canaan, to which I am bringing you. You shall not follow their statutes. My ordinances you shall observe and my statutes you shall keep, following them: I am the LORD your God. You shall keep my statutes and my ordinances; by doing so one shall live: I am the LORD.

Genesis, Deuteronomy and Leviticus all form part of *Torah*, that is, 'teaching' or 'instruction'. This instruction, which has a narrative frame, is concerned with what makes for life and what destroys it. This means, inevitably, that it is concerned with economics. Do not do as they do in Egypt, which relied on a slave economy. Do not do as they do in Canaan, an economy of city kings dependent on trade. You shall observe my statutes – for example in keeping the Jubilee year which deconstructs debt and makes sure that families never permanently get alienated from land, the means of production. What might this mean in relation to a sustainable countryside?

First, Egypt and Canaan can be read as metaphors for oppressive structures, in this case, oppressive structures of trade and production. What would this mean in our world? The fate of farming over the past 30 years gives us a good idea. It is part of the overall way in which the market works, or rather doesn't work. The reason that 800 million in the world today are starving is not due to poor distribution, but to tariffs, balance of payments, the ability to pay, and so forth. The world overseen by the World Trade Organization (WTO) is the world which cannot address poverty because to do so breaks the dogma of free trade. The crisis of farming, in which millions of farmers all over the world have been driven out of business over the past 30 years, is part of this whole insane economy. Do not do as they do in Egypt: this was about then, and is about now, a specific way of organizing economy. For example, what we call globalization is a system where giant corporations acquire assets transnationally with a view to making profit. These assets include food and water. The issue of the economy is a fundamental question about who controls the means of production, and primarily food, and for what reason. Six corporations handle 85 per cent of world trade in grain. Brewster Kneen, Canadian beef farmer and food campaigner, writes:

> If five or six corporations have control over every seed of all major commercial crops planted anywhere on earth, this is totalitarian. Add to seeds control over the genetics of all major lines of commercial animals and it will be somewhat more totalitarian. Then engineer all the

genetics – plant or animal – to be hybrids, sterile or both, and the achievement will be without question totalitarian. It will amount to the occupation of the land – the earth itself – by foreign troops and their local mercenaries.

At the other end of the chain there is a growing occupation of the land by a handful of global supermarket chains, and an occupation of the supermarkets themselves by transgenic foods and food products, unlabelled, so that the public cannot identify the invaders and thus avoid and reject them. (Kneen 1999: 179–80)

Food and water, the foundations of life, become part of an economy which is a form of competitive power game. One of the main reasons for the huge fall in the number of farmers worldwide is that farmers have been unable to make a living. Farmers have been put on the rack by having to sell their product at less than the cost of production. The regulations in Deuteronomy 15 and Leviticus 25 were put in place to regulate production and consumption, to see that producers and consumers received a fair wage and paid a just price. This was *Torah*. To swap *Torah* for the gospel of the market is to sell our birthright for a mess of pottage.

Secondly, the question about a sustainable countryside is a question about the most efficient form of farming, and this is an ethical issue, an issue of life and death. For sixty years now all the arguments have been in favour of industrialized (oil-driven) farming. It has delivered a great deal in terms of cheap food. Those in favour of small-scale farming or permaculture have been marginalized. But in a post-carbon world the question of whether small mixed-use farms are more efficient than big monocultural units is moot. To suggest this is not to forget the terrible drudgery involved in much traditional farming. It is a realistic question about how the world is going to be fed. It is not identical with the argument over the virtues of organic farming either. It is going back to Leviticus and suggesting that good husbandry is the key to human flourishing. Jules Pretty (2002) has documented the growth of community food systems and rural partnerships around the world which both develop more vibrant local communities and are involved in real increases in agricultural productivity using locally adapted and sustainable technologies.

From my second text I have taken a word about the kind of economy to avoid, and the kind to look for, if we wish to flourish. I am making analogies between ancient oppressive economies and contemporary ones. The ground for this might be, as commentators such as Lewis Mumford or Walter Wink suggest, that the psychic structures behind oppression remain more or less the same. To appeal to *Torah*, then, is to situate oneself within a tradition of resistance to such structures, to find resources for doing so there.

III

I turn now to Leviticus 25, a text which has shot to prominence because of the theme of the Jubilee Year but which has a great deal to tell us about sustainable countryside.

Verses 18-22 read:

> You shall observe my statutes and faithfully keep my ordinances, so that you may live on the land securely. The land will yield its fruit, and you will eat your fill and live on it securely. Should you ask, 'What shall we eat in the seventh year, if we may not sow or gather in our crop?' I will order my blessing for you in the sixth year, so that it will yield a crop for three years. When you sow in the eighth year, you will be eating from the old crop; until the ninth year, when its produce comes in, you shall eat the old.

It has been pointed out that this could not make sense agriculturally so it is suggested that it refers to a year when labour was pooled to clear waste land in order to increase the amount of land available for farming. This is a pragmatic reading and, as Ton Veerkamp notes, the provisions of this text will hardly convince pragmatic people either then or now. But the sense of the text is rather a challenge to the logic of production as something self-standing, as serving its own purposes. It is an expression of the 'principle of hope' and warns that if human beings think that they can manage land and resources on arbitrary principles which they themselves devise they will end up in the house of slavery. The point of the sabbath year is to cut through the self-evident logic of production (Veerkamp 1993: 98). Never has this text been more relevant than it is today. The tremendous growth in population, in technological capacity and in food resources has all ridden on the back of cheap energy. Very early on it was a clergyman, Thomas Malthus, who raised the question of finitude. The warning that for everyone to live at the level of today's North Americans we need three planets is an updated version of Malthus' gloomy predictions. His warning was not heeded; instead people behaved, and continue to behave, as if cheap energy were infinite: there is no end to the party. No, say the authors of Leviticus, that is not the case. You cannot take resources for granted. For two centuries, in destroying the ecological basis of productivity we have been sawing off the branch on which we sit. The logic of production is not self-evident. The need to respect our ecological basis is what is given to us in the text.

> The land shall not be sold in perpetuity, for the land is mine; with me you are but aliens and tenants. (Lev. 25.23)

Veerkamp calls this perhaps the most important verse in Scripture (1993: 98). The denial of absolute possession of the land, on the ground that 'the land is mine', means that there are no absolute property rights, and that therefore no class structure is other than provisional. 'In every society there is a God, that is, that which finally undergirds everything, the ground order, and at the same time the limiting instance of the right to property' (Veerkamp 1993: 101). The term *naḥalāh*, which is crucial to the Naboth story, is used in relation to the share of land of the family (Mic. 2.2; Ruth 4.5), of the clan (1 Kgs 21.3-4; Lev. 25.10), of the tribe (Josh. 13.8) and of the whole people of Israel (Deut. 32.8-9). It understands the land as gift and trust. Land, for the biblical writers, is not a form of private property with its exclusive character and absolute right of use and abuse. Israel did not have this right, at least according to the authors of Leviticus. Bas Wielenga comments:

> The land is the aim of YHWH's ways with Israel. It is and remains his gift, and the fruits of its soil are his blessing. It is meant to be the basis of a new society, of fellowship in freedom and equality. Such a gift is necessarily demanding. The fellowship in freedom is threatened by the development of inequality and class contradictions in society. When landlordism and slavery take hold of society freedom gets lost. The gift of freedom-in-the-land requires therefore obedience to YHWH's Torah which instructs the people to restrict the strong and strengthen the weak through proper institutions and a practice of solidarity. (1981: 125)

Such institutions were the remission of debt provisions and the limitation of domestic service. The remission codes are based on faith in YHWH, the God who frees from Egypt. That YHWH is God means that the gods of possession are not absolute. This continues to apply to land, as Hernando de Soto's *The Mystery of Capital* (2000) makes clear, but it goes beyond land. Where Leviticus speaks of land we must understand the basic means of production. 'The land is mine' means that the fundamental means of production cannot be alienated. Of course, 'the land is mine' does not stop at common ownership of the means of production. It implies, more fundamentally, an attitude of respect and gratitude, precisely what is intended by the command in Gen. 2.15 to serve and keep the earth. But it also implies common ownership of the means of production.

> Throughout the land that you hold, you shall provide for the redemption of the land. (Lev. 25.24)

The idea of redemption here refers to the *go'el* relationship, according to which it is the task of a kinsman to restore a family's fortunes, as we see in Ruth. In what Veerkamp calls the *ge'ullāh* ordering of society it is the task of every member of society to act as if each were his next of kin. This was essential if, due to debt, people had become oppressed. The text links redemption to land, a point important for Christians in countering a millennium at least of spiritualizing accounts and making clear how redemption applies in the real world. It means two things: (1) freedom from debt, where debt means loss of any stake in the means of production and (2) freedom for a share in the productive process. In a situation where the means of production ('land') are cornered, owned by the few, used for the profit of the few, then 'the land' is unredeemed, not part of the common treasury which is there for the maintenance of life for all people. To corner it, to have it unredeemed, is both to subject life to capital, and therefore a form of idolatry, but also to invite complete social collapse as it makes the mistake of all 'big' owners in failing to understand the mutual indebtedness of the whole of society, without which we simply collapse. No society built on expropriation is ultimately sustainable.

IV

From *Torah* I turn now to Wisdom, and Prov. 8.1-5:

> Does not wisdom call,
> and does not understanding raise her voice?
> On the heights, beside the way,
> at the crossroads she takes her stand;
> beside the gates in front of the town,
> at the entrance of the portals she cries out:
> 'To you, O people, I call,
> and my cry is to all that live.
> O simple ones, learn prudence;
> acquire understanding, you who lack it.

Wisdom here is fear of the Lord, it is obedience to *Torah*. It is quite different to knowledge or technique. In verse 5 the verb is *bin*, to cause to understand. The priority of the search for understanding suggests to us that the assumption that technique, for example the introduction of genetically modified (GM) crops, is what is going to save us is questionable. Let us consider this in relation to GM technology. This involves the insertion of an alien gene into a plant to give it a certain trait, for example vitamin enrichment and drought tolerance. It bypasses conventional breeding and brings about combinations of genes that would not occur naturally. No one knows the upshot of this technology. It is not necessarily a guarantee of better yields: conventional soya is still outperforming GM varieties and GM technology is likely to lead to monocropping and the loss of plant genetic diversity. The main problem, however, is that it puts too much power over food into too few hands. Control is the central issue. Because of corporate control over the food chain GM technology could worsen rather than improve prospects for hungry people. The director of Novartis – one of the world's biggest biotech companies – said: 'If anyone tells you that GM is going to feed the world tell them that it is not . . . To feed the world takes financial and political will – it's not about production but about distribution'.[4] There is an issue here about what constitutes true wisdom. This does not involve the denial of science, but it does involve learning wisdom and in the Hebrew view this would always preclude corporate control of the food chain. The shrill voices which tell us that to obstruct GM technology is equivalent to genocide are actually voices which want more control and bigger profits on world markets. They are the voices of 'the nations' whose ways have to be shunned.

Here I suggest that sustainability involves wisdom and that this in turn warns us against totalitarian control.

---

4   Cited in Madeley (2002: 64). The remark was made at a public meeting in Norfolk in 2000.

V

I turn finally to a text from the Messianic writings, Phil. 4.5: 'Let your *epieikes* be known to all'. *Epieikes* is today translated 'gentleness', which is possible, but the older 'moderation' seems better. It belongs to a group of words 'opposed to unbridled anger, harshness, brutality and self expression' and represents 'the wise man who remains meek in the face of insults, the judge who is lenient in judgement, and the king who is kind in his rule' (Bauder 1980: 256). In the *Nicomachean Ethics* Aristotle uses it for 'equity'. It seems proper to me, therefore, to extend its use beyond human relationships to our relationship to what we call 'the planet' in general. As such it raises the question of lifestyle, and more particularly of the need to recognize limits. What would *epieikes* mean in a world of vast inequity? We can ask who decides who can enjoy what, and at what cost? Since huge numbers mean huge impacts, addressing inequalities in global consumption is essential if ecological damage is to be contained. As has been repeatedly said over the past 20 years, if we all lived like the average Canadian or American, we would need at least three such planets to live as we do. Facing up to that fact is profoundly difficult because the quest for more constitutes the spiritual centre of the capitalist world. A meeting of economists in 1987 rejected the very idea of limits which could not be taken care of by capital. To accept the reality of physical limits (the carrying capacity of the earth) is to accept the need to limit greed and acquisition in favour of economic justice and sufficiency.

The problem breaks down into a number of sectors. First, the astronomic rise of world population, from something like 800 million in (say) 1750 to 6.5 billion today has ridden on the back of cheap energy – first coal, and then oil and gas. It is cheap energy which has enabled us to feed these growing numbers. Modern agriculture is dependent on oil. It has been calculated that if the whole world farmed like the West then, quite apart from cheap flights, two- and three-car families, and all the other things we take for granted, oil reserves would be exhausted in 30 years (Jones 2001: 2). So effective has mechanized agriculture been that we have had butter mountains and wine lakes set aside and farmers as park keepers. The struggle for survival which was still obvious in the 1880s (just see Flora Thompson in *Larkrise to Candleford*) has been entirely forgotten. The supermarket society, only just over 30 years old, has accustomed us to think that shelves overflowing with the food of the whole earth, at bargain basement prices, will be with us forever.

However, as previously noted, population increase is accompanied by a decrease in the amount of fertile land. One response to this dilemma is to say that human beings will come up with something. It's the Micawber principle: something will turn up. Such confidence overlooks the fact that whole civilizations have disappeared because they outgrew their basic resource potential. It seems, for example, that this was part and parcel of the decline of the Roman empire. Something may turn up: let's hope it does. Let's put far more effort and investment into renewable energy than we are doing at present. But banking on it? This is not the Micawber principle: it's the ostrich principle.

The question is about *epieikes* understood not simply as a moral but as a spiritual problem. 'No order can save us which simply limits the excesses of our greed' wrote Rudolf Bahro. 'Only spiritual mastery of the greed itself can help us. It is perhaps only the Prophets and Buddhas, whether or not their answers were perfect, who have at least put the question radically enough' (1989: 25). Schumacher already recognized this in *Small is Beautiful*. 'The cultivation of needs', he wrote, 'is the antithesis of wisdom. It is also the antithesis of freedom and peace. Every increase of needs tends to increase one's dependence on outside forces over which one cannot have control, and therefore increases existential fear' (1974: 23). 'Does not wisdom call, and does not understanding raise her voice? . . . For whoever finds me finds life and obtains favour from the Lord; but those who miss me injure themselves; all who hate me love death' (Prov. 8.1, 35-36). Can we respond to wisdom, to instruction, to *Torah*, or are we condemned, as some think, to a new dark ages? The decisions we make with regard to agriculture and the countryside will be among the most crucial of the next thirty years. Those who take their ethical guidelines from Scripture will not make those decisions but they have something to contribute to them, and in the emerging new world perhaps faith communities with roots to the earth, which understand about serving the earth, are once again going to have a crucial role to play.

References

Bahro, R. 1989 *Overcoming Social and Ecological Disaster* (Bath: Gateway).
Bauder, W. 1980 'Humility, Meekness', in C. Brown (ed.), *Dictionary of New Testament Theology* (vol 2; Exeter: Paternoster): 256.
de Soto, H. 2000 *The Mystery of Capital* (New York: Basic Books)
Ford, D. 1992 *A Long Rumour of Wisdom* (Cambridge: Cambridge University Press).
Jones, A. 2001 *Eating Oil: Food Supply in a Changing Climate* (Sustain/Elm Farm Research Centre).
Kneen, B. 1999 *Farmageddon* (Gabriola: New Society).
Madeley, J. 2002 *Food for All* (London: Zed).
Pretty, J. 2002 *Agri-Culture* (London: Earthscan).
Schumacher, E. 1974 *Small is Beautiful* (London: Sphere).
Tudge, C. 2003 *So Shall We Reap* (Harmondsworth: Penguin).
Veerkamp, T. 1993 *Autonomie und Egalität: Ökonomie, Politik, Ideologie in der Schrift* (Berlin: Alektor).
Wielenga, B. 1981 *It's A Long Road to Freedom* (Madurai: TTS Press).
Williams, R. 1976 *Keywords: A Vocabulary of Culture and Society* (London: Fontana).

Chapter 20

What on Earth is an Ecological Hermeneutics? Some broad parameters[1]

Ernst M. Conradie

Is the Bible 'Filled to the Brim' with Ecological Wisdom?

Ecological theology from within a Christian context may be understood as an attempt to retrieve the ecological wisdom embedded in the Christian tradition as a response to environmental threats and injustices (see Conradie 2006a). At the same time, it is an attempt to reinvestigate, rediscover and renew the Christian tradition in the light of the challenges posed by the environmental crisis. As a result, every single theological sub-discipline has been subjected to scrutiny with newly found ecological sensitivities.

Until recently, most contributions to ecological theology from within the field of biblical studies were shaped by two related factors. First, they were aimed at defending Christianity against the accusations of Lynn White (1967) and other secular critics that Christianity is irredeemably anthropocentric and bears 'a huge burden of guilt' for the ecological crisis. Secondly, they tried to retrieve some ecological wisdom from the biblical texts. The assumption was that the Bible can indeed offer profound ecological wisdom but that this has all too often remained hidden or implicit. Accordingly, the task of exegesis is to uncover such ecological wisdom.

Such studies have typically focused on a few favourite texts such as Genesis 1–2; the theme of the covenant (e.g. Gen. 6–9); the Sabbatical laws (e.g. Lev. 25); Job 37–39; some of the Psalms (8, 19, 24, 98, 104); some prophetic texts such as Isa. 9–11, 40, 65, Ezek. 36, Joel, Amos; some of the sayings of Jesus (e.g. in Mt. 6.28-30, 10.29-31); Rom. 8.18-23, Col. 1; and Rev. 21–22. The selection of these texts is quite understandable since they deal explicitly with nature or with a theology of creation.

The insights on ecological wisdom emerging from these contributions cannot be discussed here. Some comments regarding the hermeneutical approach that is followed in this regard are important though:

a. The selection of some favourite texts may unintentionally reinforce the perception that

---

[1] This essay draws on a number of earlier contributions on the subject of an ecological biblical hermeneutics. See Conradie 2004; 2006b; 2009.

ecology is indeed a marginal concern in the Bible. The focus may be far too narrow. It only relates to an aspect of creation theology or, more specifically, to the relationship between human beings and nature. Accordingly, an environmental concern is one aspect of a Christian ethos, but it does not touch the heart of the Christian gospel. By contrast, a retrieval of the ecological wisdom in the Biblical traditions has to be doctrinally comprehensive. This implies that texts dealing with creation, providence, humanity, sin, redemption, the church, the sacraments and eschatological consummation have to be retrieved from an ecological perspective.
b. Another way of broadening the scope of such a retrieval of ecological wisdom is to trace the Bible for references to the earth, mountains, hills, air, waters, rivers, soil, trees, animals, birds, insects, etc. (as highlighted in the *The Green Bible*, recently published by HarperCollins [2008]). It is important to read the whole Bible through ecological lenses. This soon leads to the discovery that the Bible, from Genesis to Revelation, is indeed 'filled to the brim' with ecological overtones. The earth and all its creatures are intimately interwoven with God's loving care for humanity.
c. As we will see below, such a retrieval of the ecological wisdom in the Bible has to consider the suspicion that the biblical texts do not necessarily support an ecological ethos. This calls for a more critical hermeneutics in which it is *not* presupposed that the Bible must be 'rescued' against its critics.

What on earth, then, would constitute a relatively more adequate form of ecological hermeneutics? Over the last decade a corpus of literature responding to this question has become available. These include a few early contributions (see Van den Brom 1998), the various volumes of the Earth Bible project (edited by Norman Habel), some responses to that (see Conradie 2004; 2006b), publications emerging from the seminar on ecological hermeneutics hosted by the Society for Biblical Literature (see Habel and Trudinger 2008) and now the Exeter project on 'Uses of the Bible in Environmental Ethics'. In this contribution I will explore one crucial aspect of such an ecological hermeneutics, namely the role of interpretative strategies.

Why Hermeneutics?

Hermeneutics is best understood as a systematic and disciplined form of second-order reflection on the praxis of interpretation. This is done in a number of academic disciplines which reflect on various forms of interpretation – for example in the context of philosophy, literary criticism, law, biblical studies and theology. Likewise, ethics is a discipline that reflects on moral judgements (on ethos), while linguistics reflects on language and semiotics on the meaning of signs.

Without this distinction the word 'hermeneutics' is used in a myriad of ways, merely contributing to the confusion around what interpretation entails. Following insights from liberation theology, this distinction is based on the difference between acting and reflecting, between the concrete and the relatively abstract, albeit that reflecting is itself a form of acting. While interpretation is something practical, hermeneutics is more theoretical. This suggests that interpretation is of primary and hermeneutics of secondary importance.

Hermeneutical reflection typically arises when the meaning of something becomes obscure. The emergence of an ecological hermeneutics is a sign that biblical interpretation (in church, society and the academy) has been subject to 'systematically distorted forms of communication' (Habermas). Such distortions remain largely subconscious. Ecological hermeneutics therefore follows upon the insights of the 'masters of suspicion', namely Marx, Nietzsche and Freud, who have identified such systematic distortions with respect to economic oppression, power relations and the subconscious.

In the case of ecological hermeneutics such distortions have been described in various ways. Following Lynn White's famous critique, some have seen the problem in terms of the *anthropocentrism* that pervades the Christian tradition. Others have focused on the deep sense of *alienation* between humankind and otherkind. Larry Rasmussen (1996: 75–89), for example, speaks of the 'apartheid habits' that humans in industrialized societies have adopted, seeing ourselves as an ecologically segregated species. Yet others have focused on various forms of *domination* in the name of differences of gender, race, class, culture, education and species. Ecofeminists have analysed what is termed a set of 'interlocking dualisms' which are based on such differences and which reinforce one another in multiple ways. On this basis Christian theologians have called for an ecological reinterpretation of the doctrine of sin (see Conradie 2005a) – which may be understood as a radicalized version of such secular reflections on systematically distorted forms of communication.

Calls for an ecological hermeneutics that can overcome anthropocentrism (for example) have posed a serious problem for biblical scholars. The problem is that the biblical texts themselves are by no means free of such anthropocentrism. They were written by human beings and reflect various human interests.

Liberation theologians used to argue that the Bible is 'on their side' in the struggle for liberation amidst oppression. They could draw on numerous biblical texts in support of their cause, dealing with issues of poverty, economic inequality, injustice and oppression. However, black theologians such as Itumeleng Mosala (1989) have realized that this is not necessarily the case. All too often the biblical texts not only address class interests but reflect them as well. They were written from the perspective of the ruling class and often legitimize their interests. Accordingly, the Bible is called a 'site of struggle' where contemporary interpretations come into conflict with each other.

This insight was radicalized by feminist theologians. They too could draw upon some favourite texts to support the cause of the liberation of women. However, many could not escape the conclusion that the biblical texts were written within a patriarchal context and more often than not reflect patriarchal interests. The Bible consists of a corpus of books written predominantly by men, reflecting a male-chauvinist perspective and serving primarily male interests. Thus the Bible can be used as a weapon *against* women's struggle for liberation. In the words of Elisabeth Schüssler Fiorenza (1986: 35): 'the source of our power is also the source of our oppression.' This prompted a two-pronged hermeneutics, including both a hermeneutics of suspicion and of reconstruction (see Eaton 1996; 2000).

The form of ecological hermeneutics adopted in the Earth Bible series may be regarded as a radicalized form of such a hermeneutics of suspicion. This was prompted by what Norman Habel describes as exegetical 'cherry picking', namely biblical interpretation that draws upon some favourite texts in support of environmental causes. The problem is that this invites a shallow reading of the texts on the prior assumption that there is ecological wisdom embedded in the text. The anthropocentric orientation of these texts is thus underestimated.

The suspicion articulated in the Earth Bible project is that 'biblical texts, written by humans to meet human circumstances, will reflect human interests at the expense of the non-human Earth community' (Earth Bible Team 2002: 1). It suspects that biblical texts show a preoccupation with human well-being and that the interests of other creatures are as a result marginalized. It therefore seeks to ascertain whether the voice of 'Earth' is silenced or liberated in the production, transmission and interpretation of particular biblical texts. Here the earth is not so much a topic in the text but a voice or (often marginalized) presence in the text that has to be listened to. In this way, earth becomes a subject (with a voice in its own right) and not so much a theme (*topos*) in the biblical texts. This calls for a reflecting *with* earth and not so much *about* the earth, in the same way that feminist biblical scholars would want to read the Bible in solidarity *with* oppressed women and not *for* them (Habel 2000a: 34).

The Task of Hermeneutical Analysis

Hermeneutical analysis is called forth when interpretation has gone awry – in the same way that a doctor is asked for a diagnosis only when the patient becomes ill. Admittedly, while ecological hermeneutics (as an academic discipline) is prompted by such distortions, it is not necessarily free of such distortions. Hermeneutics can come to the aid of interpretation gone awry, but it cannot replace the primary need for interpretation.

How, then, should the act of interpretation be understood? In my view, interpretation is a form of praxis, a way of continuously re-appropriating and responding to the significance of signs in everyday life. Interpretation is therefore, like jurisprudence, a practical skill.

This is of vital importance for biblical interpretation, given the rhetorical thrust of these texts. They are misunderstood if they are merely studied at a distance. They not only teach (*docere*); they also move (*movere*): they change people's lives, for better or for worse. biblical interpretation cannot be reduced to deliberate and explicit acts of reading and studying the Bible. Instead, it takes place in countless other ways as well – including the liturgy, doxologies, sermons, confessions, sacraments, hymns, prayers, catechism, testimonies, various ministries and missions (within Christian communities) and parenting, moral decision-making, stewardship, economic activities, media reports, films, public speeches, etc. It takes place in the academy and in faith communities, but also in civil society, wherever people live and work. In this sense the Bible is also 'read' through the imagination of the illiterate. The point is that the Bible is not only interpreted when it is read; its meaning is appropriated through many more indirect but highly influential ways, whether it is actually read or not, consciously or subconsciously, in word and in deed, in what is done and left undone, for better but often also for worse. This insight is indeed crucial in order to assess the *uses* of the Bible from an environmental perspective.

Hermeneutical reflection entails an ever more detailed analysis of the factors that may influence interpretation. Following the work of several South African colleagues I have proposed a conceptual map where the following seven groups of factors which shape biblical and theological interpretation are identified (Conradie 2008: ch. 4). On this basis one may also identify seven sets of criteria for relative adequacy in biblical interpretation (see Conradie and Jonker 2001):

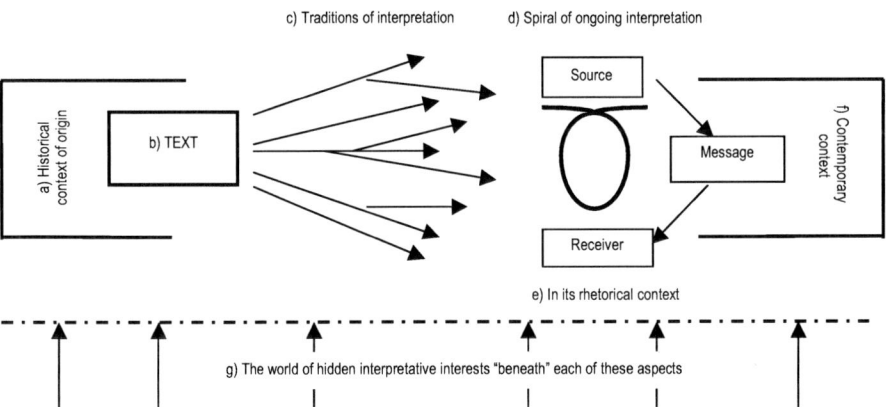

a. The world-behind-the-text (the complex history of the production of the text and the socio historical and the rhetorical contexts within which that took place).
b. The world-of-the-text (various literary features of a text, its co-text and its rhetorical thrust as reflected in the text itself).
c. The world-in-front-of-the-text (traditions of interpretation created by the text, including the confessional traditions, their liturgies, creeds, confessions and practices).
d. The act of interpretation and re-appropriation itself.
e. The rhetorical thrust of the act of interpretation and appropriation (within contemporary interpretative communities, an interpretative culture).
f. The contemporary context (societal challenges, changing circumstances).
g. The world 'below' interpretation (interpretative interests and sub-conscious ideological distortions that influence each of the other aspects).

Interpretative Strategies

In order to reflect on a responsible way of using the Bible in environmental discourse, it will be necessary to investigate one crucial dimension of biblical interpretation in more detail, namely the act of re-appropriation. In the Exeter project with its focus on the uses of the Bible in environmental ethics it was recognized that such re-appropriation may be subject to moral judgement (see further Horrell *et al.* 2008). Here I will investigate the interpretative strategies that are typically employed in the act of re-appropriation.

The notion of interpretative strategies should not be confused with exegetical methods or with the wide range of approaches to biblical interpretation (see Jonker and Lawrie 2005). Interpretative strategies refer to the ways in which readers establish a link between some aspects in the biblical text and some aspects of their context. The notion of interpretative strategies should therefore be understood in a technical sense: it refers to the 'techniques' used by readers to overcome the (historical) distance between the text and a contemporary context. The question is *how* this appropriation takes place.

Indeed, one of the most intriguing aspects of theological interpretation is the very possibility of relating biblical texts in all their plurality and ambiguity to an equally complex contemporary context. It is quite remarkable that one would even dare to do this. Yet, that is precisely the task at hand, for example, in any sermon, in Christian education and in moral instruction somehow derived from the Bible.

David Tracy has suggested that this is *de facto* possible through the power of what he calls an analogical imagination. Interpretation can only take place when some analogies, that is, similarities-amidst-differences, are identified, in the case of Christian interpretation between the biblical texts, the Christian tradition and a contemporary context. Tracy (with Paul Ricoeur) refers to the classic axiom of Aristotle in this regard: 'To spot the similar in the dissimilar is the mark of poetic genius' (Tracy 1981: 410). The ability to identify these similarities, and to express them in an accessible form (image), is based on the power of the imagination.[2]

Although the notion of reading or interpretative strategies is often used in literature on biblical hermeneutics, specific 'strategies' to spot such similarities (to link text and context) are very seldom described or analysed in any detail. Following various contributions in recent South African literature, I suggest that one may identify especially three interpretative strategies popularly employed to establish a bridge between text and context. In each case some form of similarity between text and context is constructed.

One such strategy is to identify something of abiding value in the text that may still be relevant today. Here one may look for 'eternal truths' or 'moral principles' that are uncovered (or demythologized) in the text and appropriated more or less directly in one's contemporary context. For example: 'Unlike Jonah, one should always obey God's commands.'

---

2   For an in-depth analysis of the notion of an 'analogical imagination', emphasizing the identification *and* imaginative expression of analogies, see Conradie 1992.

Another strategy is to identify analogies between the type of situation described in the biblical narratives and experiences in our own context. Thus: 'Jonah was asleep in the boat amidst a fierce storm. Likewise, we also experience many storms in life.' Since few would want to follow Jonah's example of asking to be thrown overboard exactly, this allows ample room for almost any moral to be deducted from the similarities in the stories.

A third strategy identifies certain promises in the text and anticipates the fulfilment of God's promises anew in our context. 'If God was willing to spare the people of Nineveh and their animals, could we not hope that God would spare us too, especially in the context of a loss of biodiversity?' One may observe that this third strategy allows for a more dynamic reading of the text, taking historical changes into account.

The Pervasive Influence of Doctrinal Constructs

Although such strategies are widely used, they can easily become distorted, often yielding rather crude appropriations. However, the identification of such similarities does not take place in a coincidental way. They are discovered through long-standing theological traditions that have developed the necessary conceptual tools that may help Christians in interpreting the Bible. One may argue that such crude appropriations have prompted theologians throughout the history of Christianity to construct conceptual models to facilitate this process.

Such models are typically based on the dominant beliefs, doctrines, values, customs, and habits of ecclesial traditions and communities. They are not derived directly from the biblical texts or from the contemporary world, but are precisely the product of previous attempts to construct a relationship between text, tradition and context. Since such models are typically shaped by the dominant theological motifs within a particular tradition, it may be helpful to refer to them as *doctrinal constructs*.

Such doctrinal constructs play a crucial role in interpretation. They have a triple function: they provide a strategy to identify *both* the meaning of the contemporary context *and* of the biblical texts. They therefore (and simultaneously) enable an interpreter also to establish a *link* between text and contemporary context. Doctrinal constructs are not only employed to *find* similarities but to *construct* similarities, to *make* things similar (*idem-facere*), if necessary.[3] The scope of such doctrinal constructs is often quite comprehensive: they purport to provide a clue to the core

---

3   According to Ricoeur (1978: 148), the creation of metaphorical meaning does not only involve the identification of existing similarities. It also involves an association of semantic fields that have hitherto been considered as quite different from one another. It is thus necessary to *make* these semantic fields similar: 'But we miss entirely its semantic role if we interpret it in terms of the old association by resemblance ... The assimilation consists precisely in *making* similar, that is, semantically proximate, the terms that the metaphorical utterance brings together.'

meaning of the contemporary context *as a whole* and the biblical text *as a whole*. The dangers of simplification and a far-reaching harmonizing of differences in an analysis of both the Bible and the contemporary context are quite apparent. However, this may be inescapable since any act of interpretation requires the identification of some form of *similarity*-in-difference.

Such doctrinal constructs typically have a soteriological focus and an ethical thrust. As is widely recognized in ecumenical hermeneutics, there is a conflicting diversity of such doctrinal constructs that cannot be easily reconciled. In a report on the Fourth World Conference on Faith and Order (Montreal 1963) this was clearly articulated:

> In some confessional traditions the accepted hermeneutical principle has been that any portion of Scripture is to be interpreted in the light of Scripture as a whole. In others the key has been sought in what is considered to be the centre of Holy Scripture, and the emphasis has been primarily on the Atonement and Redemption, or on the justification by faith, or again on the message of the nearness of the kingdom of God, or on the ethical teachings of Jesus. In yet others, all emphasis is laid upon what Scripture says to the individual conscience, under the guidance of the Holy Spirit. In the Orthodox Church the hermeneutical key is found in the mind of the Church, especially as expressed in the Fathers and in the Ecumenical Councils. In the Roman Catholic Church the key is found in the deposit of faith, of which the Church's *magisterium* is the guardian. In other traditions again the creeds, complemented by confessional documents or by the definitions of Ecumenical Councils and the witness of the Fathers, are considered to give the right key to the understanding of Scripture. In none of these cases where the principle of interpretation is found elsewhere than in Scripture is the authority thought to be alien to the central concept of Scripture. On the contrary, it is considered as providing just a key to the understanding of what is said in Scripture. (WCC 1998: 15)

There are indeed numerous examples of such doctrinal constructs that facilitate biblical interpretation. In my view one may identify especially three such constructs that have been extremely influential in the history of Christianity. All three of these examples focus on the Christian message of salvation – which is crucial in any attempt to link text with context. In the paragraphs below I draw on but also adapt the famous analysis of three types of atonement by Gustaf Aulén (1931/2002).

First, many have interpreted the message of salvation in terms of victory over the forces of evil, destruction and death. Here a number of metaphors are employed to indicate how a particular threat is overcome: liberation from political or economic oppression, release from captivity (being held ransom), overcoming a military threat, healing from life-threatening diseases, feeding in a context of famine, exorcism from evil spirits and ultimately victory over death itself. All these concepts suggest the need for victory over some or other threat, typically based on the resurrection hope. In each case such victory may retrospectively be attributed to God.

Secondly, the message of salvation may be understood in terms of the healing of various broken relationships. The root of such alienation may be attributed to a distorted relationship with God. Here another cluster of concepts is used to indicate how such healing is possible, including 'satisfaction' and 'penal substitution', but also sacrifices, confession of guilt, forgiveness and reconciliation. The focus is typically on the cost of reconciliation and therefore on the symbol of the cross.

Thirdly, one may mention various concepts focusing on the moral influence of the biblical narrative. They provide us with the inspiration, the energy to do good, to transform society through appropriate policies towards some or other moral vision, perhaps towards 'justice, peace and the integrity of creation'. Several biblical symbols may play roles here, including God's Law, the teachings of Jesus, his incarnation, life and ministry and the instructions in the Pauline corpus of letters.

One may easily expand the list of such doctrinal concepts on the basis of theological movements emerging over the past 50 years. In each contemporary theological school there is some or other key concept that helps its adherents to connect text, tradition and context: liberation from oppression, relationships based on mutuality and reciprocity, ecological wholeness and so forth. For example, the notion of 'liberation' may help one to see the emancipatory thrust of the text, the liberating and oppressive sides of a theological tradition and current forms of oppression in church and society. The vision of liberation helps one to see such oppression for what it is.

One implication of this analysis is that it is simply not possible to 'jump' from a biblical text to a specific problem in the contemporary context without the use of such doctrinal constructs. Doctrine plays a crucial integrative role in shaping a tradition of interpretation through various practices of repetition and habituation. It also plays a crucial role in the act of appropriation, in the fusion of horizons (see also Thiselton 2006: 723–24).

While biblical scholars, quite rightly, have been dismayed by the way the Bible has been used and abused in systematic theology (by reading support for various doctrines into biblical texts), there has been an unhelpful tendency among some to pretend that faith convictions (and Christian doctrines reflecting on such convictions) do not play an inevitable, necessary and crucial role in interpreting and appropriating biblical texts.[4] While some may prefer to avoid or even to resist traditional doctrinal distinctions at all costs, newly constructed doctrines surface in emerging theological traditions through the persistent use of interpretative strategies. This indicates that it is facile to suggest that Christian hermeneutics is value-laden while secular pluralism, or a retreating from making theological judgements, is somehow value-free. The hegemonic control over biblical interpretation by ecclesial institutions may have been merely replaced by the similarly hegemonic control of secular academic institutions (Thiselton 2006: 13). This confirms the pervasive, if often highly ambiguous influence of Christian doctrine and ethical categories in biblical interpretation. What is required here is not denial but discernment – to recognize the role of such doctrinal constructs and to exercise (moral) judgement where these constructs distort text,

---

4   Despite such a denial, biblical scholars themselves often employ doctrinal categories that they find more to their liking. One example of this is West's consistent use of the soteriological category of 'liberation' in the 'liberation hermeneutics' that he promotes (see West 1991).

tradition and context and where they are abused to legitimize domination.

A few further comments on the role of such doctrinal constructs are important here:

a. The identification of the role of these doctrinal constructs may clarify the rather diffuse use of the word 'hermeneutics'. It is often employed to describe the results of a particular interpretation of the Bible – instead of a theory of interpretation (i.e. at a meta-level). It has, for example, become customary to talk about a feminist hermeneutics, a black hermeneutics of liberation, an ecological hermeneutics or even a reformed, Pentecostal, African or a Lutheran hermeneutics. Technically, these uses of the concept hermeneutics do not indicate a new or a different theory of interpretation but refer to the use of specific doctrinal constructs.

b. These examples make it clear that doctrinal constructs have both a constructive and an ideology-critical function. They enable interpreters to identify and construct the meaning of the text (and the context) but they also provide a tool to evaluate the available evidence and to unmask distortions in any of the seven factors involved in the process of interpretation.

c. The choice of doctrinal constructs will necessarily lead to a distortion of both text and context. Such distortions may well be ideological in the pejorative sense of the word. A hermeneutics of suspicion towards such constructs is therefore much needed. However, this is hampered since such doctrinal constructs also influence the selection of ideology-critical tools. They prescribe to their users what they should be suspicious about.

d. Another danger of such doctrinal constructs is that they could lead to fixation, to a certain rigidity in the tradition of interpretation. Then they regulate the interpretation of the Bible according to the so-called 'rule of faith' as determined by ecclesial or academic authorities. Any re-reading of the texts would then merely confirm what one knew would be there in any case. The text itself can yield no surprises, no challenges, no shock or amazement, no revelation; God's Word can no longer be heard anew.

Especially in the Reformed tradition it was therefore maintained that the living Word of God cannot be captured in any single formula, a system of dogmatic truths, an underlying rule of faith, a canon within the canon (not even justification through faith), a Scriptural centre, confessions, catechisms, beloved themes or key concepts. Although Scripture should be read as a whole and in terms of its central focus, to capture this centre in any way would tend to replace the actual reading of the biblical texts (see Smit 2007).

To conclude, such doctrinal constructs inevitably play a crucial role in the contemporary re-appropriation of biblical texts. This also applies to secular interpretations where traditional beliefs have merely been replaced by a different set of convictions. If so, it becomes important to recognize the role that they do, in fact, play and to reflect on the relative adequacy of such constructs.

Doctrinal Constructs and an Ecological Hermeneutics

In times of social stability there are usually 'plausibility structures' (Peter Berger) in place that suggest the relative adequacy of doctrinal constructs to their users. In times of rapid social change there emerge uncertainties around the validity of such constructs. This does not imply that they are no longer used, only that their meaning is no longer self-evident. Users then begin to emphasize the dissimilarities between text and context and themes that are neglected. Such a doctrinal construct can no longer aid biblical interpreters to connect text, tradition and context. Such times call for hermeneutical reflection.

The looming threat of environmental disaster may be regarded as one such challenge that is calling the use of our dominant doctrinal constructs into question. Whenever such a new challenge appears on the horizon, biblical interpreters typically draw on the cluster of symbols that they are familiar with in order to respond to such a challenge. In discourse on ecotheology one may identify especially three dominant doctrinal constructs that are widely employed (see Conradie 2006a: 119–38):

First, some would emphasize a sense of human responsibility. The gravity of the environmental crisis requires an appropriate response. This may be understood in purely secular terms as a responsibility *towards*, but may also be described as a response *to* God's call. A number of biblical metaphors may be used to express such a responsibility, for example: the call to obedience to a divine command; human dominion correlated with a strong emphasis on human uniqueness; a more humble sense of stewardship for possessions that are not our own (which assumes positions of considerable power and authority); human priesthood understood as a way of mediating between God and creation; a sense of vocation; and an ecclesial covenant with God with responsibilities and blessings that would flow from that.

The controversial term 'stewardship' illustrates the use of such doctrinal constructs to help interpreters to see a way of connecting text (Gen. 1.27-28) with context. The word stewardship does not appear in the text itself. Nevertheless, it has become a common key used to interpret the meaning of the Hebrew words *kabash* ('subdue') and *radah* ('rule'). At the same time it captures the need to address economic injustices and ecological degradation in the contemporary context. It establishes a link in this regard on the basis of the sense of responsibility implied in the metaphor of stewardship.

Many criticisms have been raised against such a notion of stewardship, for example that it is too hierarchical, too managerial, too androcentric, aimed at those in positions of power, not visionary enough and that it portrays God as either a patriarch or an absentee landlord (see Conradie 2005b). Such criticisms again suggest that all doctrinal constructs have to be subjected to a hermeneutics of suspicion, albeit that such suspicion is often derived from a particular doctrinal construct. In essays discussing Gen. 1.26-28, Norman Habel (2000a: 31, also 2000b; 2008: 5–8) adamantly concludes that the claim that the mandate in this passage has been misunderstood, suggesting that it can best be interpreted in terms of a benign model of stewardship, is untenable.[5] It also remains to be seen whether such a sense of responsibility will be powerful enough to encourage people to address a challenge such as climate change. Covenantal promises are all too often broken.

Secondly, some would emphasize a sense of the sacred. They would typically suggest that the earth itself is a sacred gift from God that we are called to treasure and keep. For many the gift itself is holy. It provokes a sense of awe, mystery and distance (even fear and trembling). It is untouchable and should therefore not be exploited or ruined for selfish gain. Others would emphasize the holiness of the Giver, namely God. One may also explore the ecological significance of the category of sanctification. Accordingly, the Holy Spirit does not only sanctify the lives of individuals and Christian communities, but indeed the whole earth. Such an approach is often characterised as 'sacramental' in order to suggest that water, bread and wine can become carriers of God's presence. They symbolize the kind of respect which humans should show to everything on earth. This approach often draws on patristic and medieval mysticism to speak to the heart, to inspire a vision of the sacred and to express an ecstatic experience of communion. Again, the sense of the holy plays a heuristic role since it helps biblical interpreters to contrast the sense of the sacred with acts of environmental sacrilege. This sense of the sacred may also help to explore commonalities with other religious traditions, including various forms of indigenous or pre-Christian spiritualities. Again, one may wonder whether a retrieval of the sacred will be powerful enough to resist the forces of industrialization. Throughout the centuries, societies in which nature was regarded as sacred have nonetheless destroyed their natural habitation whenever economic incentives to do so emerged. A sacramental approach can also be somewhat naive and perhaps too romantic in calling for a return to a bygone era.

Thirdly, some would focus on the need for an appropriate vision for the future (cf. the third interpretative strategy identified above). This is quite understandable since environmental concerns (such as climate change) are often future orientated. This may be correlated with biblical motifs that also speak about the future. A crude form of such an approach is where 'predictions' identified in the Bible (often in apocalyptic texts) are regarded as being 'fulfilled' in contemporary or imminent events. A more sophisticated approach would be to focus on God's promises (not predictions) in the text and to explore the social impact of Christian hope arising from such promises. Either way, on this basis one may articulate an appropriate vision for the future, derived from the biblical texts and appropriated for the current context. Examples would include discourse on economic growth, the eradication of poverty, the UN's millennium goals, sustainable development, cultural evolution (including technological progress), ecojustice and so forth. Although such visions are in conflict with each other, the strategy employed for reading the Bible in each case is similar.

In each of these cases some or other form of similarity is identified in the tension

---

5   By contrast, the fifth principle of the Earth Bible project proposes a sense of *mutual* custodianship, albeit that some of the criticisms raised against stewardship may apply to the notion of custodianship too.

between text and context. The relative adequacy of each of these constructs may be tested in terms of their ability to do justice to the biblical text, the contemporary context and the ecclesial tradition.

Doctrinal Constructs Employed in the Earth Bible Project

As noted above, the ecological hermeneutics employed within the context of the Earth Bible project may be described as being predominantly a hermeneutics of suspicion and retrieval.[6] It investigates whether there is a concern for earth community in the text or whether earth is being treated unjustly in the text. It also offers an incipient 'hermeneutic of retrieval' by seeking to discern and retrieve alternative traditions about earth or the earth community that have been unnoticed, suppressed or hidden and that may help the earth community to flourish again (Earth Bible Team 2002: 1). It facilitates a retrieval of alternative traditions that hear the voice of the earth and that value the earth as more than a human instrument. In this way it seeks to allow the often marginalized voices of Earth to be heard again (Habel 2000a: 35).

The Earth Bible project thus explores the biblical texts from the perspective of earth. In order to clarify this perspective, the Earth Bible team identified the following six guiding ecojustice principles for biblical interpretation:[7]

a. *The principle of intrinsic worth*: the universe, earth and all its components have intrinsic worth/value.
b. *The principle of interconnectedness*: earth is a community of interconnected living things that are mutually dependent on each other for life and survival.
c. *The principle of voice*: earth is a subject capable of raising its voice in celebration and against injustice.
d. *The principle of purpose*: the universe, earth and all its components, are part of a dynamic cosmic design within which each piece has a place in the overall goal of that design.
e. *The principle of mutual custodianship*: earth is a balanced and diverse domain where responsible custodians can function as partners, rather than rulers, to sustain a balanced and diverse earth community.
f. *The principle of resistance*: earth and its components not only suffer from injustices at the hands of humans, but actively resist them in the struggle for justice.

In my view these six ecojustice principles have a similar heuristic function as the doctrinal constructs discussed above. Together, they provide a creative and constructive key to read and appropriate the biblical texts within a context of economic injustices

---

6   Habel (2008: 4-5) adds 'identification' as a second step between suspicion and retrieval. This refers to the possibility of human readers identifying (sympathetically or antipathetically) with their non-human kin as portrayed in the text.
7   See Habel (ed.) 2000: 42-53 and Eaton (2000) for a detailed discussion of these principles.

and environmental destruction. Note that a certain normative priority is attributed to the set of ecojustice principles. They are employed to judge both the validity of the text and contemporary culture. Eaton (2000: 63) notes that this priority of the principles over the texts is indeed appropriate. Likewise, the emancipatory interests of women have priority over both misogynist texts and power structures.

One could even argue that these six ecojustice principles provide nothing less than a 'small dogmatics'. The first two principles on the intrinsic worth (instead of the utilitarian value)[8] of all matter and on interconnectedness form an incipient doctrine of creation. The emphasis on the earth community and kinship between all creatures could also be read as a revised and more inclusive ecclesiology (see Earth Bible Team 2000: 44–46). The third principle on voice (a vital aspect of human personhood) could be read as an anthropology where the voices of humans are situated among (and therefore not necessarily privileged[9]) the varied modes of self-expression or silent communication of others in the earth community and beyond (Ps. 19). The fourth principle on design, purpose and an orientation towards an implicit goal is an (immanent) eschatology in the making. It describes the inherent tendency of matter towards life and of life towards increasing diversity, complexity and symbiosis (Earth Bible Team 2002: 5–6). The fifth principle on mutual custodianship and partnership challenges earlier anthropologies based on dominion and stewardship and constructs a doctrine of providence and an ecological ethics upon a recognition of the ways in which earth as the 'immediate agent of sustenance, support and creative energy' has sustained humanity and other forms of life (Earth Bible Team 2002: 10). The sixth principle on resistance acknowledges the impact of evil and injustices, suggests the focus of an alternative doctrine of sin accordingly (on the distortion of the human ability to see God's glory in creation, see also Habel 1998: 119), and locates the sources of redemption from such injustices in the ability of earth to offer resistance. As the Earth Bible Team (2000: 53) notes, ecosystems are not necessarily fragile, but have a limited yet 'remarkable capacity to survive, to regenerate and adapt to changing physical circumstances in spite of human exploitation and short-sighted greed'.

The vision articulated in these six ecojustice principles is bold, audacious, uncompromising and attractive in many respects. A number of striking features of this 'small dogmatics' may be identified. First, there is no reference to 'creation' or creatures, precisely in order to avoid any reference to or assumption of a Creator. This is indeed a radically this-worldly 'theology' (if it could be called that) with no reference to divine presence (immanence) in the world, not to mention a recognition of the possibility of divine transcendence. As may be expected, any categories reminiscent of the particularity of Christianity (except the focus on the Bible itself) are avoided in order

---

8 See the discussion by Earth Bible Team (2002: 8–10) on the distinction between intrinsic worth, utilitarian value and the notion of 'added value'.
9 The privileging of some voices above others calls for the supplementary principle on ecojustice – precisely because of the conflicting agendas among those humans who wish to function as the mediating voice of the 'voiceless' earth in human decision-making processes. See Eaton 2000: 67.

to allow for a more universal (?) appeal of such an ecological hermeneutics, especially in a secular context and in conversation with other faith traditions.[10] On this basis there can be no suggestion of references to God the Father (or Mother), Jesus Christ or the Holy Spirit, not to mention theological constructs such as trinity, incarnation, cross, resurrection, justification, sanctification, ecclesiology, sacraments or eternal life. The contrast between the 'small dogmatics' of the Earth Bible project and the Nicene Creed could scarcely be starker.

I have no intention of testing the orthodoxy of the Earth Bible's 'small dogmatics' or to supplement the six principles with doctrinal allusions or to legitimate its principles by planting a cross on its fertile soil or to baptize them in the name of the Father, Son and Spirit. That would not only be cheap, but would also be a form of colonization and conquest and would not recognize the resistance against what is perceived as doctrinal meddling in biblical exegesis (which, if my argument holds, is more or less inevitable). It would also fail to see the quite deliberate attempt to appeal to a wider readership. However, in the hope to find a wider appeal, it curiously abandons the attempt to be persuasive within the traditions that have kept the reading of these texts alive. At the same time, the emergence of such a 'small dogmatics' raises one's curiosity precisely because it illustrates the inescapability of such doctrinal constructs very well. It also invites further critical reflection. Clearly the six ecojustice principles cannot be regarded as sacrosanct or in a Platonic way as eternally abiding *principia*. If biblical scholars feel the need to construct their own 'dogmatics' because the doctrinal constructs provided by constructive theologies are no longer plausible, this calls urgently for cooperative efforts and inter-disciplinary work.

In Search of Relatively More Adequate Doctrinal Constructs

What, then, could an ecological biblical hermeneutics entail? Given the argument on the use of doctrinal constructs above, it seems to me that we need to search for relatively adequate constructs in order to do justice both to the rich plurality within the biblical texts and the contemporary demands of ecojustice and sustainability. There are several attempts in contemporary ecotheology to identify or construct concepts that can fulfil such a function.

One such example is the notion of the 'liberation of creation' – as used for example by the Latin American theologian Leonardo Boff (1995). One may develop this into a fairly comprehensive notion that would address the tensions between God's good creation, the suffering of the vulnerable in creation due to (human) oppression, prophetic critiques of such oppression and the hope for the liberation of creation. In addition, one may seek to clarify the Christological and pneumatological content of this notion. The strength of this construct is its ability to confront the socio-economic

---

10 See Habel 2000a: 38 and Habel 2004: 8, where this motivation is explicitly mentioned.

forces that lie at the roots of the current environmental crisis. Its weakness is related to its fairly narrow soteriological focus – for example not bringing into play the role of forgiveness and reconciliation.

Another example is the emphasis on wisdom that is prominent in the work of Celia Deane-Drummond (2006) and several others. Here the cardinal virtue of wisdom is portrayed as a key to Christian earthkeeping, confronting an attitude of mastery and control over nature. In feminist discourse this is often contrasted with notions of male dominance. There are, of course, numerous references to the significance of wisdom in the biblical texts. Moreover, if one takes the personification of wisdom in the book of Proverbs and John 1 into account, it may be developed Christologically. One may also refer to the strange wisdom of the cross, the wisdom of the Father's providence and the work of the Spirit to lead us into wisdom. On this basis the notion of wisdom can be developed into a fairly comprehensive construct that can do justice to text, tradition and the need for responsible decision making amidst environmental challenges.

A third example is the metaphor of 'the whole household of God' that has emerged in ecumenical literature over the last decade or two (see Conradie 2007). The power of this metaphor lies in its ability to integrate especially three core ecumenical themes on the basis of the Greek word *oikos* (household) – which forms the etymological root of the quests for *eco*nomic justice (amidst the inequalities and multiple injustices in the current neo-liberal economic order), *eco*logical sustainability (amidst the degradation of ecosystems) and *ecu*menical fellowship (amidst the many divisions that characterise Christianity worldwide). This construct also helps to integrate several concerns on the social agenda of the church. Such ecumenical discourse on the whole household of God is best understood within the context of the whole work of God (creation, providence, redemption, re-creation) which has traditionally been described as the 'economy of God', from which the term 'economic trinity' has also been derived. On this basis, it may serve as a theological root metaphor to explore a wide variety of other themes – an ecological doctrine of creation based on the indwelling of God's Spirit in creation; an anthropology of stewardship (the *oikonomos*) or one of being 'at-home-on earth'; an ecclesiology focusing on being members of the 'household of God' (Eph. 2.19-22); or, alternatively, an ecclesiology based on the notion of being sojourners (*paroikoi*) who are precisely *not* at home (yet); an understanding of the Eucharist as the table fellowship of the household gathered together, the need for God's Word spoken *at* the table; and an eschatology expressing the hope that the house which we as humans inhabit (the earth) will indeed become God's home. It has also been used for a pastoral theology towards the edification of the household (*oikodomē*) (see Müller-Fahrenholz 1995), and an ethics of ecojustice, inhabitation, homemaking, hospitality and sufficient nourishment.

Conclusion

It is unlikely that any one doctrinal construct will ever be satisfactory. What is required here is perhaps not a single category but a cluster of such constructs, a box full of tools that may be used wherever helpful. What we need is a reconstituted 'horizon' that will enable us to relate with each other a) the biblical roots of Christianity, b) the subsequent history of the Christian tradition (in its rich complexity and its distortions), c) the content and significance of the Christian faith, d) a set of ethical categories and e) the increasingly dramatic challenges of environmental degradation.

This hermeneutical 'horizon' would be constituted by a complex set of convictions, visions, values, virtues, stories, priorities and practices, which are shaped by the Scriptures and which themselves shape the interpretation of Scripture, which may well be in tension with each other, vying for a certain priority, but which together would constitute where ecumenical Christianity stands. For Christian communities, as 'people of the book', this hermeneutical horizon will be shaped in multiple ways by the whole corpus of biblical texts and themes – not so much as a fixed moral deposit but as a precious record of what it meant in previous times and places and under varied conditions to be a 'people of the way' (see Birch and Rasmussen 1989: 32). This sense of orientation, if taken literally, would direct the interpreting community to the Orient, to Jerusalem, to Calvary.

This suggests that an ecological biblical hermeneutics should go hand in hand with an ecological reformulation of Christian doctrine. This cannot be narrowly focused on a revisiting of creation theology but calls for a review of all aspects of the Christian faith. In my view, there are especially four crucial areas where Christian piety has often inhibited an environmental ethos, spirituality and praxis, namely a worldless notion of God's transcendence, a dualist anthropology, a personalist reduction of the cosmic scope of redemption and an escapist eschatology.[11] Any ecological theology will remain shallow unless an adequate response to these four problems can be provided.

This task is taken up in many contributions to ecological theology focusing on the content and significance of the Christian faith. It is also the task of an international collaborative research project entitled Christian Faith and the Earth which is currently underway and which will culminate at an envisaged conference to be held in Cape Town in August 2012. This project offers some hope for such a thorough ecological transformation of the content and significance of the Christian faith. Such a task will indeed be crucial also for an ecological biblical hermeneutics.

---

11 See Conradie 2005b and 2006a for an outline of this agenda for ecological theology.

References

Aulén, G. (1931/2002) *Christus Victor: An Historical Study of the Three Main Types of the Idea of Atonement* (Eugene, OR: Wipf & Stock).

Birch, B.C. and L.L. Rasmussen 1989 *Bible and Ethics in the Christian Life* (Minneapolis: Augsburg).

Boff, L. 1995 *Ecology and Liberation* (Maryknoll, NY: Orbis Books).

Conradie, E.M. 1992 'What is an Analogical Imagination?', *The South African Journal of Philosophy* 11(4): 103–12.

Conradie, E.M. 2004 'Towards an Ecological Biblical Hermeneutics: A Review Essay on the Earth Bible Project', *Scriptura* 85: 123–35.

Conradie, E.M. 2005a 'Towards an Ecological Reformulation of the Christian Doctrine of Sin', *Journal of Theology for Southern Africa* 122: 4–22.

Conradie, E.M. 2005b *An Ecological Christian Anthropology: At Home on Earth?* (Aldershot: Ashgate).

Conradie, E.M. 2006a *Christianity and Ecological Theology: Resources for Further Research* (Study Guides in Religion and Theology 11; Stellenbosch: SUN Press).

Conradie, E.M. 2006b 'The Road Towards an Ecological Biblical and Theological Hermeneutics', *Scriptura* 93: 305–14.

Conradie, E.M. 2007 'The Whole Household of God (*oikos*): Some Ecclesiological Perspectives: Part 1 & 2', *Scriptura* 94: 1–28.

Conradie, E.M. 2008 *Angling for Interpretation: A First Guide to Biblical Theological and Contextual Hermeneutics* (Study Guides in Religion and Theology 13; Stellenbosch: SUN Press).

Conradie, E.M. 2009 'Interpreting the Bible Amidst Ecological Degradation', *Theology* 112: 199–207.

Conradie, E.M. and L.C. Jonker 2001 'Determining Relative Adequacy in Biblical Interpretation', *Scriptura* 78: 442, 448–56.

Deane-Drummond, C.E. 2006 *Wonder and Wisdom: Conversations in Science, Spirituality, and Theology* (Philadelphia, PA: Templeton Foundation Press).

Earth Bible Team 2000 'Guiding Ecojustice Principles', in N.C. Habel (ed.), *Readings from the Perspective of Earth* (The Earth Bible, 1. Sheffield/Cleveland, OH: Sheffield Academic Press/Pilgrim Press): 38–53.

Earth Bible Team 2002 'Ecojustice Hermeneutics: Reflections and Challenges', in N.C. Habel and V. Balabanski (eds), *The Earth Story in the New Testament*, (The Earth Bible, 5. London and New York/Cleveland, OH: Sheffield Academic Press/Pilgrim Press): 1–14.

Eaton, H. 1996 'Ecological-feminist Theology', in D.T. Hessel (ed.), *Theology for Earth Community: A Field Guide* (Maryknoll, NY: Orbis Books): 77–92.

Eaton, H. 2000 'Ecofeminist Contributions to an Ecojustice Hermeneutics', in N.C. Habel (ed.), *Readings from the Perspective of Earth* (The Earth Bible, 1. Sheffield/Cleveland, OH: Sheffield Academic Press/Pilgrim Press): 54–71.

Habel, N.C. 1998 'Key Ecojustice Principles: A *theologia crucis* Perspective', *Ecotheology* 5–6: 114–25.

Habel, N.C. 2000a 'Introducing the Earth Bible', in N.C. Habel (ed.), *Readings from the Perspective of Earth* (The Earth Bible, 1. Sheffield/Cleveland, OH: Sheffield Academic Press/Pilgrim Press): 25–37.

Habel, N.C. 2000b 'Geophany: The Earth Story in Genesis 1', in N.C. Habel and S. Wurst (eds), *The Earth Story in Genesis* (The Earth Bible, 2. Sheffield/Cleveland, OH: Sheffield Academic Press/ Pilgrim Press): 34–48.

Habel, N.C. 2004 'The origins and challenges of an ecojustice hermeneutics', in T.J. Sandoval and C. Mandolft, *Relating to the Text: Interdisciplinary and Form-Critical Insights on the Bible* (New York: Continuum).

Habel, N.C. 2008 'Introducing Ecological Hermeneutics', in N.C. Habel and P. Trudinger (eds), *Exploring Ecological Hermeneutics* (SBLSS 46. Atlanta, GA: SBL): 1–8.

Habel, N.C. and P. Trudinger (eds) 2008 *Exploring Ecological Hermeneutics* (SBLSS 46. Atlanta, GA: SBL).
Horrell, D.G., C. Hunt and C. Southgate 2008 'Appeals to the Bible in Ecotheology and Environmental Ethics: A Typology of Hermeneutical Stances', *SCE* 21: 219–38.
Jonker, L.C. and D.G. Lawrie (eds) 2005 *Fishing for Jonah (Anew): Various Approaches to Biblical Interpretation* (Stellenbosch: SUN Press).
Mosala, I.J. 1989 *Biblical Hermeneutics and Black Theology in South Africa* (Grand Rapids, MI: Eerdmans).
Müller-Fahrenholz, G. 1995 *God's Spirit Transforming a World in Crisis* (New York, NY: Continuum).
Rasmussen, L.L. 1996 *Earth Community, Earth Ethics* (Maryknoll, NY: Orbis).
Ricoeur, P. 1978 *The Rule of Metaphor* (London: Routledge and Kegan Paul).
Schüssler Fiorenza, E. 1986 *In Memory of Her* (New York, NY: Crossroad).
Smit, D.J. 2007 'Rhetoric and Ethic? A Reformed Perspective on the Politics of Reading the Bible', in W. Alston and M. Welker (eds), *Reformed Theology: Identity and Ecumenicity II* (Grand Rapids, MI: Eerdmans): 233–53.
Thiselton, A.C. 2006 *Thiselton on Hermeneutics: Collected Works with New Essays* (Aldershot: Ashgate).
Tracy, D.W. 1981 *The Analogical Imagination: Christian Theology and the Culture of Pluralism* (London: SCM).
Van den Brom, L.J. 1998 'Ecological Hermeneutics', in A. König and S. Maimela (eds), *Initiation into Theology: The Rich Variety of Theology and Hermeneutics* (Pretoria: Van Schaik): 433–50.
West, G.O. 1991 *Biblical Hermeneutics of Liberation. Modes of Reading the Bible in the South African Context* (Pietermaritzburg: Cluster Publications).
White, L., Jr 1967 'The Historical Roots of our Ecological Crisis', *Science* 155: 1203–207.
WWC (World Council of Churches) 1998 *A Treasure in Earthen Vessels: An Instrument for an Ecumenical Reflection on Hermeneutics* (Faith and Order Paper No. 182; Geneva. WCC).

Index of Biblical References

Entries in bold indicate substantial discussions

OLD TESTAMENT (including Apocrypha)

Genesis
1–11	16, 34, 42n. 17
1–9	15, 23, 25–7
1–3	18, 138
1–2	129, 295
1	6, 21, 23–30, 35–6, 51, 59, 62, 116, 137, **140–53**, 167, 189, 229
1.1-2.4a	34, 36
1.1-2.3	214
1.1-2	124, 140–1, 143
1.1	78, 141–3
1.2	142–3
1.4	116
1.10	116
1.12	116
1.20-6	144
1.20-1	147
1.22	76
1.24	147
1.26-8	2–4, 6, 88, 118, 143, 147, 151, 191–2, **229**, 305
1.26	124, 135, 138, 140, 146, 154, 198, 214
1.27-30	26
1.27-8	305
1.27	22, 144, 229
1.28-30	23, 34–6, 176
1.28	4, 22–3, 25–6, 30, 34, 76, 229
1.29-30	26
1.29	22–4, 26–7
1.30	23, 26, 147
2	137, 189, 229, 286
2.1-3	**230–1**
2.1	78
2.2-3	280
2.4b–3.24	88
2.4b-7	192
2.4	78, 214
2.5	137n. 13
2.7	136, 137
2.15	4, 229, 285–7, 291
2.16-17	90
3	129, 130, 138
3.6	90
3.17-19	88, 89, 90
3.17	255, 256
3.18	259
3.21	34n. 4
4.4	24
4.9	286
6–9	111, 295
6.11-13	36
7.23	80
8.1	80
8.17	80
8.22	116
9	27, 35, 37, 40
9.1-7	26, 35
9.1-4	29
9.2	23, 26, 79
9.3	23–5, 36
9.4	37
9.8-17	37
9.9-17	5
9.12	80
24.10	215
49.10-11	80n. 12

Exodus
1.7	22
3.14	159
20.8-11	230, 280
23.9-12	29–30

Leviticus 16, 33, 37
1.2	38
1.3	42
1.4	41

1.10	42	26.21-5	37
3.1	42		
3.2	41	**Deuteronomy**	
3.6	42	5.12-15	280
3.8	41	7.12	76
3.13	41	8.1-18	287
4	39	15	289
4.3	42	20.19-20	30
4.4	41	22	30
4.15	41	26.15	76
4.23	42	27.17	47
4.24	41	28.1-14	287
4.28	42	28.4-5	76
4.29	41	28.15-16	287–8
4.32	42	30.19-20	274
4.33	41	32.8-9	290
5.15	42	32.39	275
5.18	42		
6.6	42	**Joshua**	
8.14-15	39	13.8	290
8.14	41	18.1	22
8.18	41		
8.22	41	**Ruth**	
9.2	42	4.5	290
9.3	42		
12	39	**1 Kings**	
14.1-7	41	1.33	81
14.10	42	21	47
14.48-53	41	21.3-4	290
15	39		
15.31	39	**2 Kings**	
16	39	5.10	71
16.1-22	41		
16.15-19	39	**Job**	**17**
18.3-5	288	1.10	64
18.24-8	38	1.21	275
22.19	42	3.1-10	61
22.21-5	42	4.8	61
22.21	42	6.5	60
23.12	42	9.25-6	61
23.18	42	12.7-10	56
25	**289–91**, 295	12.7-8	56, 64
25.1-7	230	12.10	76
25.8-17	230	26.12	80
25.10	290	28	63–4, 65, 67
25.18-22	289–90	28.24	63n. 18
25.23	38, 290	37–39	295
25.24	291	38–39	57n. 5, 64–5
26	38	38	**64–5**
26.4	76	38.7	64
26.6	37, 79	38.8	64
26.11-12	38	38.25-30	59n. 13
26.19-33	38	38.28-30	65

38.31-3	65	146.10	77
38.34-8	65	147.8	76
38.39	65	147.9	76
38.41	5, 76	148	77, 278
39.14-15	65		
40–41	66	**Proverbs**	**17**
		1.1	58n. 9
Psalms		6.6	60
8	295	8	64, 66–7
11.4	77	8.1-5	**292**
18	5	8.1	294
19	295, 308	8.5	292
19.1	212	8.22-36	**231**
19.4-6	76	8.22-31	135
24	295	8.22	67
29	59	8.31	67
36.6	76	8.35-36	231, 294
51	173	10.1	58n. 9
65.9-11	76	11.28	60
67.6	76	15.17	60
72	54	15.19	60
72.12-14	54	16.20	62–3
72.16	54	17.27-8	66
78.15-16	78	25.14	60
78.23-5	78	25.23	60
90.4	110	30	58n. 11
93	77	30.15-33	61–2
95.5	135		
96.3	77	**Ecclesiastes**	**17**
96.10	77	1.1	58n. 9
96.11-13	77	1.4-9	61, 62
97.1	77	1.5-7	65
98	295	1.12	58n. 9
98.7-8	77	3.18-21	64
98.9	77	3.21	64
102.25-7	116	7.6	61
103.19-22	77, 78	10.1	61
103.19	77		
104	5, 59, 211, 295	**Isaiah**	
104.7	80	1.3	46
104.13	76	5	47
104.21	51	5.1-2	256
104.27-8	76	5.8-10	47
104.29-30	76, **231**	9–11	295
107.38	76	9.6-7	117
139.7-8	275	11	51, 250
145	77	11.1-9	26, 256
145.5	78	11.6-9	79, 88
145.9	76	11.7-8	26
145.10-12	77	11.9	26
145.10-11	78	21-26	112
145.13	77, 78	24	54
145.15-16	76	24.1-13	49

27.1	80	**Hosea**	
30.27	113	2.18	51, 79, 88
32.15-20	117	2.21-2	51
33	54		
33.9	54	**Joel**	54, 295
33.14-16	54	1.15	2
35.1	79		
35.6-7	79	**Amos**	295
40–66	77	1.7	64
40	295	1.10	64
40.4	66	1.12	64
41.14	46	1.14	64
41.18-19	79	2.5	64
43.19-21	88	5.18-20	2
43.23-4	286	8.8	64
51.3	79		
51.6	116	**Micah**	
52.7	117	1.2-4	109n. 8
55.12-13	88, 256	2.1-2	47
60.17-22	117	2.2	290
61.1-11	230	2.4	47
64.1-3	109	2.5	47
65	295		
65.17-25	26, 256	**Nahum**	
65.17	110, 238	1.3-5	109n. 8
65.25	26		
66.2	110	**Habakkuk**	
66.15-18	109	2.4	84
		3.3-15	109n. 8
Jeremiah			
4	54	**Zephaniah**	
4.23-6	50	1.18	113
8.7	46, 78	3.8	113
40.4	113		
		Haggai	
Ezekiel		1.9-11	50
8.6	38n. 7	2.15-19	50
8.12	38n. 7		
9.9	38n. 7	**Zechariah**	
10.18-20	38n. 7	3.10	47
11.9-12	38n. 7	8.12	88
12.1-6	38n. 7	9.9-10	80–1
12.17-20	38n. 7	14.1-5	109
15.7	38n. 7	14.4-5	109n. 8
20.38	38n. 7		
22.15	38n. 7	**Malachi**	
34.25-31	88	1–4	112
34.25	79	3.1-4	109
34.26-39	79		
34.28	79	**2 Maccabees**	
36	295	7.23	213
39.23	38n. 7	7.28	213

Index

4 Ezra
7.11-12	88
8.51-54	88
9.19-20	88

NEW TESTAMENT

Matthew
1.18	137
1.20	137
5.35	133
5.45	76
6.9-10	77–8
6.26	76
6.28-30	76, 295
7.6	73
8.20	73
10.29-31	76, 295
11.6	79n. 10
11.25	75
11.27	133
19.9	75
21.5	80–1
21.18-21	81
23.30	109n. 4
23.32	109n. 4
24.43	110
25.14-30	256
25.31-46	256

Mark
1.13	79, 80n. 11
1.15	231
3.14	80
4.3-8	76
4.26-32	76
4.35-41	80
4.36	80
4.39	80
5.10-13	81
5.18	80
10.6	75
10.45	286
11.1-10	80
11.12-14	81
11.20-1	81
12.30	148
13	268
13.8	3
13.24-7	110
13.24-5	3
13.30	109
13.31	116
14.67	80

Luke
1	134n. 8, 137
1.35	137
1.55	109n. 4
1.72	109n. 4
2.40	72
2.52	72
4.16-21	230
4.18-19	256
7.22	79n. 10
10.21	75
12.6-7	76
12.24	76
12.27-8	76
12.39	110
19.12-28	256
21.20	72

John
1.1-14	133–5
1.1-3	235, 256
1.1	189, 283
1.3	133, 134, 167
1.10	134
1.11	134
1.12	134
1.13	134, 137n. 16
1.14	104n. 11, 133
1.15-18	134
1.18	133
1.19-34	134
4.20	109n. 4
6.31	109n. 4
9.7	71
12.24	208
17.21	233
13.34	256

Acts
1.10-11	271
3.13	109n. 4
3.21	256
3.25	109n. 4

Romans
1.2	85
1.4	226
1.16-17	84, 92
1.18-32	85
1.18	84
1.20-3	256

1.21	89	8.14-16	90
1.24	89	8.15-16	88
3.21-6	85, 92	8.17	85
3.28	92	8.18-30	90
4.1-23	85	8.18-25	111, 115
4.21-5	92	8.18-23	295
4.24	226	8.18	85, 88
4.25	85	8:19-26	**232**
5–8	85, 88, 92	8.19-23	5, 256
5.1-11	85	8.19-22	18, **83–93**
5.1-4	88	8.19	88, 90
5.1	92	8.20-1	88, 90, 116n. 17
5.3-5	90	8.20	89
5.6-11	92	8.21	89, 232
5.6-10	85	8.22	88, 90
5.9-10	84	8.23-5	88
5.9	84, 91	8.23	86–8, 90, 92, 232
5.10	91	8.26-7	88
5.12–8.4	91	8.26	90, 232
5.12-21	85, 91	8.28-30	88
5.12	86, 137n. 13	8.29	87, 136
5.14	136	8.31-9	85
5.15-21	92	8.31-2	92
5.15-17	86	8.32	85
5.15	91, 92	9.5	109n. 4
5.17	91, 92	10.5-13	92
5.19	92, 137n. 13	10.9-13	84
5.20	91	11.36	100
6.1–7.6	92	12.1-15.13	87
6.1-23	86	12.1	87
6.3-11	226	12.2	87
6.4	92	12.5	105
6.6	86	15.1-3	92
6.11	92	15.3	92
6.12	86, 92	15.4	226
6.13	92, 93	16.22	87
7.5	86		
7.14-25	86	**1 Corinthians**	
7.14	86	3.6	76
7.18	86	7.29-31	268
7.24	86	8.6	235, 256
7.25	86	10.16	105
8	277	12.27	105
8.1-4	86	15	84, 87, 277
8.3-9	86	15.22	136, 137n. 15
8.3-4	91	15.23-8	100
8.3	87	15.36	208
8.4	92	15.42-4	208
8.6-8	86	15.45	86, 91, 92, 137n. 13
8.10	86, 87	15.46	137n. 15
8.11	86, 226		
8.12-13	86–7	**2 Corinthians**	
8.13	86	3.6	142

Index

4.4	135
4.16	144
5.17	92, 238, 256
5.18	92
5.19	235
5.21	93
8.9	278
12.7	86

Galatians
2.11-14	283
3.26-8	88
4.3-10	100
4.14	86
6.15	92

Ephesians
1.10	256
2.16	235
2.19-22	310
4.9	199
4.17	89

Philippians
2.6-8	92
2.7	206n. 8
2.8	92
4.5	244, **293–4**

Colossians
	18–19
1	295
1.1	95
1.4	98
1.5	102n. 8
1.7-8	95
1.9	98, 100
1.15-20	5, 231, 256
1.15	135, 140, 189, 235
1.16	103
1.17	105, 189, 203, 235
1.18	105
1.20	103–4, 106, 235
1.26-7	102n. 8
2.1	95, 99
2.2	100
2.10	104n. 10
2.12	102n. 8
2.16	98
2.18	98
2.21	98
2.23	98
3.1	102n. 8
3.3-4	102n. 8
3.6	102n. 8
3.10	100, 136
3.24-5	102n. 8
4.12-13	95
4.18	95

1 Thessalonians
1.10	84
4	277
4.16-17	3
5.2	2, 110
5.4	110
5.23	148

1 Timothy
4.10	140

Hebrews
1.2-3	256
1.2	189, 284
1.3	235
1.10-12	116, 268n. 2
12.25-8	268n. 2

2 Peter
1.4	110, 116n. 17
1.20-1	109
2.1	108
3	4–5, 111n. 10, 112
3.3	109, 118
3.4-13	**108–12**
3.4-10	112
3.4	109
3.5-13	19, **108–20**
3.5-9	109
3.5-6	116
3.5	113
3.7	108, 113–15
3.8-10	272
3,8-9	110
3.8	118
3.10-13	268
3.10-12	113–14
3.10	4, 110, 112, 114–15, 246, 252, 256
3.11-13	110
3.11-12	117
3.11	112, 114
3.12-13	118
3.12	108, 112, 114, 246
3.13	108, 114–15
3.14	117–18

1 John		16.16	251
2.13-14	189	20	249
		20.2	251
Revelation	3, 208, 246–64, 277, 296	20.4	248
		20.11	268n. 2
2.7	286	21-22	5, 110, 238, 295
3.3	110	21	252
4.7	132	21.1-4	256
8	247, 256	21.1-2	251, 255
8.6-13	252	21.1	80, 116, 198, 246, 249, 250, 268n. 2
11.18	252, 255		
12.14	248	21.3	230
16	247, 256	21.5	247, 255
16.15	110	22.1-5	261

INDEX OF NAMES

Entries in bold indicate substantial discussions

Abel, 24, 36
Abraham 41n. 15, 48, 85, 133
Adam, Adamic 34n. 4, 36, 83, 84, 86, 88–92, 136–8, 152, 174, 177, 218, 222
Adam, A. K. M. 139, 272, 278n. 8, 281
Adams, E. 4, 6, 9, 11, 19, 96, 106, 108–9, 113, 114, 116, 118–19, 268n. 2, 271, 281
Ahab 47, 48
Albertz, R. 29, 31
Alexandre, M. 142, 153,
Allison, D. C. 81n. 14, 82
Alves, R. 236n. 17, 238
Ambrose 142, 150
Amery, C. 22, 31
Anderson, B. W. 4, 11, 36n. 6, 44, 59, 68
Aquinas, T. 10, 124, **154–65**, 169, 180, 206
Aristotle 97, 99, 156–7, 163, 165, 293, 300
Arnold, R. 258, 262
Athanasios 212, 222
Attfield, R. 64, 68
Augustine, Augustinian 23–4, 140, 142–3, 149–50, 152, 153, 155, 171, 190n. 12, 254
Aulén, G. 302, 312

Bacon, F., Baconianism 159, 207n. 9, 229, 249–50, 259
Badke, W. B. 252, 260, 263
Bahro, R. 294
Bakken , P. 257n. 19
Balabanski, V. 7, 9, 11–12, 18, 19, 82, 94, 95, 96, 106–7, 119, 312
Balthasar, H. Urs von 10, 125, 138n. 18, 139, 196–210, 235n. 15
Baranzke, H. 2n. 2, 11
Barr, J. 2, 4, 11, 53n. 3, 55, 57, 68
Barth, K., Barthian(ism) 10, 52, 125, 138n. 17, 169, 173, **181–95**, 197, 198, 209, 227, 284
Barton, J. 9, 16–17, 46
Barton, S. 10, 243, 244, 266

Baruch, *Second Apocalypse of* 88
Basil of Caesarea 140–2, 145–50, 152, 153
Bauckham, R. 9, 18, 70, 76n. 9, 80n. 11, 81–2, 104, 107, 109n. 5, 113, 114, 117n. 18, 119, 227–8, 235n. 16, 238–9, 244, 268n. 3, 278–9, 281
Bauder, W. 293, 294
Bauer, G. 258n. 22, 263
Baumgarth, W. P. 157, 165
Bayer, O. 168, 179
Beal, R. S. 259, 263
Beauchamp, P. 26, 31
Beck, H. 117n. 20, 119
Behr, J. 147, 148–9, 150, 151, 153
Beisner, E. C. 3, 11, 258–9, 260, 263
Berdyaev, N. 212, 222
Berry, R. J. 6n. 8, 11, 12, 69
Bigg, C. 109n. 7, 119
Birch, B. C. 312
Bird, M. 110n. 9, 119
Bishop, E. F. F. 81n. 13, 82
Blaising C. A. 260n. 28, 263, 264
Blake, W. 216
Blenkinsopp, J. 2n. 2, 11
Bloch, R. H. 249, 263
Blocker, T. J. 254n. 14, 263
Blumenberg, H. 170n. 5, 179
Bock, D. L. 260n. 28, 263, 264
Boersema, J. J. 96, 107
Boff, L. 309, 312
Bornkamm, H. 167n. 2, 174, 177, 179
Bouma-Prediger, S. 5, 11, 108n. 1, 111n. 11, 112, 119, 255, 263
Boyd, H. H. 254n. 14, 263
Boyer, P. 251, 252n. 10, 263
Bragg, M. 200
Brague, R. 95, 96, 107
Briggs, C. A. 31
Bright, J. 57n. 3, 68
Brown, C. 117n. 20, 119, 294
Brown, F. 25, 31

Brown, W. P. 57, 66, 68
Brunner, E. 184–6, 194
Bulgakov, S. 125, 211, 220–1, 222
Bull, M. 268n. 3, 281
Burkett, L. 257n. 21, 263
Bury, R. G. 95n. 2, 107
Busch, E. 182n. 2, 185n. 4, 194
Byrne, B. 9, 18, 83–5, 86, 88–93

Cain 36, 286
Caird, G. 5, 272
Calvin, J. 169, 179, 254, 257
Carson, R. 1
Charles, N. J. 49n. 2, 55
Chidester, D. 170n. 5, 179
Chilton, B. 77, 82
Choi, J, 256, 264
Chrysippus 101, 113, 116
Chrysostom, J. 146, 149, 152
Cicero 102
Cizewski, W. 150, 153
Clark, G. 150–1, 153
Clark, S. R. L. 266, 281
Clarke, A. 25, 31
Cleanthes 113
Coffman, M. S. 257n. 21, 263
Collins, J. J. 102, 107, 282
Colson, C. 257n. 21, 263
Conradie, E. M. 6, 7, 8n. 12, 10, 11, 243, 245, 295, 296, 297, 299, 300n. 2, 305, 310, 311n. 11, 312
Cooper, J. W. 105n. 12, 107
Copernicus, N. 183
Corsini, E. 148, 153
Courtonne, Y. 141, 153
Cranach, L. 171
Cranfield, C. E. B. 88–9, 93
Crisp, O. 190n. 12, 194
Cumbey, C. 252, 263
Curry-Roper, J. M. 246n. 2, 263

Dalmais, I. H. 217n. 2, 222
Darby, J. N. 251
Darwin, C., Darwinian 21, 63n. 18, 250
David (King), Davidic 48, 58n. 9, 80
Davids, P. H. 109n. 3, 119
Davies, B. 159, 165
Davies, D. 42, 44
Davies, W. D. 81n. 14, 82
De Gruchy, J. 285
De Soto, H. 291, 294
De Tocqueville, A. 251
De Vos, P. 4, 11

Deane-Drummond, C. 57, 62, 63n. 18, 68, 155, 163, 165, 234nn. 11–12, 235n. 15, 237n. 19, 238, 310, 312
Delitzsch, F. 25, 31
Dell, K. J. 9, 17, 56, 56n. 1, 58, 60n. 14, 62–4, 68
Dennis, J. 113n. 12, 119
Descartes, R., Cartesian 23–4, 126 185, 225, 229–30, 236
Devall, B. 56, 68
DeWitt, C. B. 6, 255, 258n. 23, 259, 263, 265
Dickens, W. T. 198n. 3, 209
Dionysios the Areopagite 218
Dobson, J. 258nn. 22 & 24, 260
Dodd, C. H. 74, 82
Donoghue, D. 209
Douglas, M. 40n. 12. 44
Driver, S. R. 31
Dunn, J. D. G. 85, 89
Dyer, K. 3, 11, 108,
Dyrness, W. A. 65n. 22, 68, 179, 180

Earth Bible Team (as authors) *see* Index of Subjects
Eaton, H. 298, 307n. 7, 308, 312
Echlin, E. P. 72, 75, 82
Eckburg, D. L. 254n. 14, 263
Edwards, J. 249
Elijah 47
Enoch, first book of 88, 112
Epaphras 95
Epictetus 113
Epicurus 95
Erasmus, D. 177
Evagrios 215
Evans, J. 98, 100, 107
Eve 34n. 4, 36, 138, 152, 174, 177

Faricy, R. 70, 82
Farrow, D. 136n. 10, 138n. 17, 139
Ferré, F. 201, 209
Finger, T. 5, 11, 108n. 1, 111–12, 114, 119, 246n. 2, 255n. 16, 260n. 27, 261, 263
Fitzmyer, J. A. 89, 93
Florensky, P. 212, 220
Florovsky, G. 211
Ford, D, 107, 190, 194, 283, 294
Foucault, M. 219
Fowler, R. B. 257n. 20, 263
France, R. T. 110n. 9, 119
Francis of Assisi, Franciscan 2, 177, 279
French, R. M. 213, 222
Fretheim, T. E. 63n. 17, 65n. 21, 66n. 23, 67n. 24, 68
Freud, S. 297

Freyne, S. 70–5, 82
Frykholm, A. J. 262, 263

Galileo 183
Gieniusz, C. R. 85, 93
Gilbertson, M. 277n. 7, 281
Gilders, W. K. 39n. 10, 44
Gill, R. 155, 163, 165, 282
Gorringe, T. 10, 243, 244, 283
Grabbe, L. 39n. 10, 44
Graham, B. 259, 263
Granberg-Michaelson, W. 4, 11, 68, 246n. 2, 254–5, 263
Grant, G. 258–9, 263
Gregersen, N. H. 167n. 2, 175, 177, 180
Gregory of Nyssa 140, 142, 145, 147–50, 152, 153, 214, 222
Guth, J. L. 254n. 14, 263
Gutiérrez, G. 236n. 17, 238

Habel, N. C. 7, 8, 11–12, 55, 57, 63n. 18, 68, 82, 93, 94, 95, 104n. 11, 106–7, 119, 181, 195, 296, 298, 305, 307, 308, 309n. 10, 312–13
Habermas, J. 297
Habito, R. L. F. 106n. 14
Hadot, P. 207n. 9, 209
Haecker, T. 217, 222
Hagen, K. 170, 180
Hahne, H. 83, 88, 90, 93
Hall, D. J. 4, 12
Harding, S. 262n. 29, 263
Harrison, N. V. 145, 146, 149, 153
Hatina, T. R. 110n. 9, 119
Hauerwas, S. 278, 281, 282
Haydn, J. 46
Hays, R. B. 244, 269–73, 276–7, 281
Healy, N. J. 206n. 8, 209
Hedrick, C. W. 74n. 7, 82
Hegel, G. W. F., Hegelian 234
Heide, G. Z. 108n. 1, 111, 112, 119
Heidegger, M. 199, 207
Henke, R. 141, 153
Herder, J. G. 24
Hermisson, H-J. 58, 68
Heschel, A. 280, 281
Hicks, E. 249
Hoban, T. 254n. 14, 265
Holsinger-Friesen, T. 136n. 12, 139
Hooker, M. 99n. 4, 107
Hopkins, G. M. 202
Horrell, D. G. 1, 3n. 4, 5n. 6, 8, 12, 109n. 5, 113, 114, 119, 245, 300, 313

Houston, W. 36n. 6, 44–5
Hunt, C. 6n. 9, 8, 10, 12, 123, 245, 313

Irenaeus 10, 115, 123, 127–39
Isaac 41
Isaac, G. L. 168, 180

Jacob, B. 190n. 14
Jelen, T. G. 265
Jenkins, W. 160, 165, 188n. 11, 194, 195, 196n. 1, 200, 209
Jenson, P. P. 39n. 10, 45
Jewett, R. 83, 93, 268, 281
Job 56, 57n. 5, 64, 66
John the Baptist 270
Johnson, E. 248
Johnston, R. K. 57, 68, 247n. 3, 264
Jonah 300–1
Jones, A. 293, 294
Jones, J. 70, 82,
Jonker, L. C. 299–300, 312–13

Kanagy, C. L. 254n. 14, 264
Kant, I., Kantian 205, 207n. 9
Käsemann, E. 270
Kelly, J. N. D. 110, 112
Kermode, F. 246, 264
Kierkegaard, S. 182
Kinzelbach, R. 27–31
Kiuchi, N. 39n. 10, 41, 45
Kneen, B. 288–9, 294
Koerner, J. 171, 180
Kraftchick, S. J. 109n. 5, 114n. 14, 119

Lamberty-Zielinski, H. 2n. 2, 11
Lang, B. 67n. 24, 68
Lapidge, M. 101–2, 107, 114, 119
Larsen, D. K. 248n. 5, 264
Law, J. 10, 126, 223
Lawrie, D. G. 300, 313
LeBlanc, J. 155, 164, 165
Leftow, B. 159, 165
Lenin, V. 221
Leske, A. M. 70, 82
Levenson, J. D. 274, 281
Levin, D. M. 170n. 5, 179–80
Levison, J. R. 84, 93
Lienesch, M. 258n. 25, 262n. 29, 264
Lindberg, C. 176, 180
Lindsey, H. 252, 264
Linzey, A. 45, 82, 153, 154, 156, 162, 165
Linzey, S. 265
Loader, W. 70, 82

Locke, J. 24
Logan, A. H. B.130n. 1, 130n. 2, 139
Lohfink, N. 4, 12, 22–3, 25, 31
Lohse, B. 171, 173, 180
Long, A. A. 113n. 13, 117, 119
Lossky, V. 211–12
Louth, A. 10, 125–6, 211
Lovelock, J. 101n. 6
Loyola, I. 72
Lucas, E. 4–5, 12, 108n. 1, 111n. 11, 112, 119
Ludlow, M. 10, 124, 140, 147, 153
Luria, I. 234n. 11,
Luther, M., Lutheran 10, 124, **166–80**, 254, 304

McCalla, A. 21, 31
McClymond, K. 41n. 14, 45
McCormack, B. L. 182n. 2, 187, 195
MacDonald, M. Y. 105n. 13, 107
Macdonald, N. 34, 35n. 5, 45
MacDonald, N. B. 190n. 12, 195
McFague, S. 105, 107, 209
McGinn, B. 268n. 3, 282
McGrath, A. E. 172, 180
McIntosh, A. 191, 195
McKibben, B. 5, 12, 57, 62n. 16, 67, 68
MacRae, G. 117, 119
Madeley, J. 292n. 4, 294
Maier, H. O. 3, 10, 104, 107, 243–4, 246
Malthus, T. R. 290
Mangina, J. L. 182n. 2, 194
Marcion, Marcionism, Marcionites 130, 132, 135, 270
Marcus, J. 80n. 11, 82
Marlow, H. 58n. 7, 68
Marsden G. M. 249, 264
Marx, K., Marxist 128, 220–1, 297
Mary, Mother of God 134, 137–8, 215, 219–21
Maschke, T. 170, 180
Mason, S. 37, 45
Mather, C. 249
Maximos 125, 215–18, 219–20, 222
May, G. 59n. 12, 68
Meier, J. P. 77, 82
Merchant, C. 198, 210
Metzger, B. M. 134n. 6, 139
Mikhalkov, N. 32
Milbank, J. 197n. 2, 210
Miles, M. 170, 180
Milgrom, J. 39, 44, 45
Min, Y-J 62n. 15, 68
Minns, D. 131n. 4, 139

Moltmann, J. 10, 125–6, 198, 223–39, 274, 280, 281–2
Moo, D. J. 4, 12, 108n. 1, 111–12, 119, 247, 264, 277n. 6, 282
Moody, D. L. 251, 259
Mora, V. 73, 82
Morgan, J. 9, 16, 17, 32, 38n. 8
Mosala, I. J. 297, 313
Moses 48, 50, 58n. 9, 133, 142, 215
Moss, D. 10, 125, 196, 197, 210
Müller-Fahrenholz, G. 226n. 8, 239, 310, 313
Mumford, L. 289
Murray, R. 48–51, 53–4, 55, 70, 79, 82

Naboth 47, 48, 290
Nash, R. F. 248n. 6, 258n. 25, 264
Neumann-Gorsolke, U. 25n. 1, 26n. 2, 31
Neyrey, J. H. 109, 114n. 14, 117n. 19, 119
Nietzsche, F. 224, 297
Noah 16, 35–7, 79, 80, 109
Northcott, M. S. 70, 81, 82, 155, 163, 165, 266–7, 282

O'Leary, S. D. 256–7, 261, 264
Oakes, E. T. 197, 210
Oberman, H. 169, 180
Origen 140–1, 144–7, 149–50, 153
Orpheus 207n. 9
Orr, D. 3, 12
Otto, E. 30, 31
Overstreet, R. L. 111n. 11, 119

Palmer, C. 6, 12, 65n. 20, 68–9
Panaetius of Rhodes 99
Pannenberg, W. 198
Patrick, D. 5, 12
Peacocke, A. 65n. 19, 69
Pelikan, J. 167, 169n. 3, 171, 180
Pesch, O. 169, 180
Peter 108n. 2, 132, 283
Philaret, (Metropolitan) D. 212, 222
Philo 19, 95, 99, 103, 109, 113, 115, 116, 215
Plato, Platonic, Platonism 19, 23, 95, 98–104, 106, 109, 135, 214, 217–18, 221, 309
Plutarch 116
Poole, M. 24, 25, 27, 31
Posidonius of Apamea 99–100
Potter, D. 200–2, 204–5, 207, 208, 210
Pretty, J. 289, 294
Purdue, L. 58, 63n. 18, 66, 69

Quash, B. 266n. 1, 279, 282

Rasmussen, L. L. 297, 311–13
Reagan, R. 258n. 23
Regan, R. J. 157, 165
Renan, E. 72n. 3, 72n. 5, 82
Reuling, H. 146, 153
Rice J. 256, 264
Riches, J. 197, 199, 210
Ricoeur, P. 300, 301n. 3, 313
Ro, B. R. 256n. 18, 264
Robertson, P. 252, 258n. 24, 260, 264
Robinson, J. A. T. 104, 107
Rogerson, J. 4, 6, 9, 15, 16, 17, 21, 36n. 6, 39n. 11, 40n. 12, 42n. 16, 45
Rolston, H. 158, 165
Rowland, C. 276, 282
Rubens, P. 285
Runia, D. T. 95, 99, 103, 107
Russell, D. M. 4, 12
Russell, J. S. 111n. 10, 119

Salomina 213
Santmire, H. P. 10, 21, 31, 66, 69, 124, 166, 167n. 2, 178, 179, 180
Satan, Devil 79, 138, 170, 252
Saucy, R. L. 260, 264
Schaeffer, F. 248n. 5, 260–1, 264
Schmid, H. H. 58n. 10, 68
Schreiner, S. E. 179, 180
Schumacher, E. 294
Schüssler Fiorenza, E. 298, 313
Schwanke, J. 169, 180
Scofield, C. 251–2, 259
Scott, P. 266–7, 282
Scroggs, R. 84, 93
Segundo, J. L. 237, 239
Seneca 113
Sessions, G. 56, 68
Shaiko, R. G. 254n. 14, 264
Shillington, V. G. 72n. 4, 82
Sidcris, L. H. 200, 204, 208–9, 210
Simmons, J. A. 248n. 5, 264
Sittler, J. 235
Sleeth, M. 257n. 19
Smit, D. J. 304, 313
Solomon (King) 58n. 9, 72, 76
Solov'ev, V. 220
Sophia, 131, 212, 217, 221–2
Southgate, C. 6nn. 8–9, 8, 10, 12, 243, 245, 313
Stăniloae, D. 211
Stavrakopoulou, F. 9, 15
Stead, G. C. 103n. 9, 107
Steck, O. H. 229, 239

Steinmetz, D. 170, 180
Still, T. D. 102n. 8, 107
Stoll, M. 248–9, 264
Stordalen, T. 34n. 3, 45
Strandberg, T. 247
Stuckenbruck, L. T. 98, 107

Talmon, S. 43n. 17, 45
Tanner, K. 244, 267, 273–7, 282
Taylor, C. 23–4, 31
Tertullian 115
Thiselton, A. C. 303, 313
Thompson, D. 268n. 3, 282
Thompson, F. 293
Thompson, G. 10, 125, 181
Tollefsen, T. T. 217n. 2, 222
Tracy, D. W. 300, 313
Trudinger, P. 7n. 10, 8, 12, 107, 195, 296, 312–13
Trusdale, A. 246n. 2, 254, 264
Tudge , T. 287, 294
Turner, D. L. 260, 264
Tuveson, E. L. 249, 250n. 7, 264

Valentinus, Valentinian 115, 123, 130–3, 135, 138
Van den Brom, L. J. 296, 313
Van der Horst, P. W. 113, 116, 119
van Kooten, G. H. 95–6, 100, 104n. 10, 107
Van Rossum, J. 217n. 2, 222
Veerkamp, T. 290–1, 294
Vergil/Virgil 83, 102
von Arnim, H. 107
Von Rad, G. 21, 57n. 6, 58, 60, 69
Voth, V. H. 253, 264

Wannenwetsch, B. 278, 282
Watson, F. 10, 123, 127, 132n. 5, 136n. 11, 139, 188n. 10, 195, 197, 202, 281
Watt, J. 258n. 23, 264
Weber, T. P. 250n. 8, 264
Webster, J. 182n. 2, 187n. 7, 195
Wells, S. 278, 281, 282
Wenham, G. J. 34n. 3, 41n. 15, 45
West, G. O. 303n. 4, 313
Westermann, C. 74, 82
White, L. Jr 1, 2, 3, 6, 11, 12, 21, 25, 31, 53, 55, 57, 69, 123, 155, 165, 181, 195, 196n. 1, 210, 246, 264, 295, 297, 313
White, R. S. 82
Wielenga, B. 291, 294
Wilcox, C. 254n. 14, 265
Wilkinson, L. 11, 257, 258n. 23, 259, 265

Williams, R. 285, 294
Williams, R. D. 150, 153, 199, 205, 206n. 8, 210, 238, 239
Willis, T. M. 39n. 10, 45
Wink, W. 289
Wise, D. S. 256n. 18, 265
Wittenberg, G. H. 48n. 1, 55
Wood, D. 188n. 9, 195
Woodrum, E. 254n. 14, 265
Wordsworth, W. 24
Wright, G. E. 21
Wright, N. T. 99n. 4, 110n. 9, 111, 116, 119–20, 262, 265, 271–2
Wurst, S. 7n. 10, 11–12, 57, 68, 312
Wynn, M. 10, 124, 154

Young, R. A. 260–1, 265

Zachman, R. C. 179, 180
Zeno of Cittium 101–3, 106, 113
Zerbe, G. 256n. 18, 265
Zimmerli, W. 58, 69

INDEX OF SUBJECTS
(excluding names)

Entries in bold indicate substantial discussions

air 3, 22, 27, 34, 35, 50, 51, 56, 62n. 15, 76, 114, 143, 168, 191, 213, 220, 258n. 22, 279, 296
allegory, allegorical 74, 124, 133, **140–6, 149–51**, 198n. 3,
amillennialism 254–5
androcentricity 181, 305
angels 79–80, 98–9, 129, 130, 211, 278–9
animal(s)/beasts 4–5, 16, 23–7, 29, 30, 32–7, 40–1, 46, 51–2, 56, 59n. 13, **60–6**, 72–5, 78–81, 111, 124–5, 128, 140, 143–52, 154–6, 158–60, 162–4, 166, 168, 172–3, 177, 191–2, 204, 213, 218, 235, 250, 280, 288, 296, 300;
    in the service of humans, 157–8, 162–3
    sacrifice 16, 24, **32–45**
anthropocentrism 7, 15, 17, 20, 56, 125, 128–9, 168, 174, 181–4, 186, 188, 191–4, 260, 267, 269, 278, 297
anthropology, anthropological 58, 66, 86, 105n. 12, 126, 136n. 10, 173, 181, 200n. 6, 203–5, 208, 224–6, 228, 230, 236, 308, 310–11
anthropomonism 123, **129–30**
Anti-Christ 251–2
apocalypse 102, **246–8**, 250, 261, 268, 277n. 7
apokatastasis 256
ascetics, asceticism 146, 150, 215–16, 219–20, 244, 269, 277–8, 280–1
atheism 224, 232
atonement 216, 302
Au Sable Institute 248n. 5, 255, 257n. 19,
authority 7, 15, 146, 148–9, 218, 269, 302, 305

beasts *see* animals
beauty 66, 125, 141, 145, 147, 149–50, 152, 179, **196–210**, 212, 218, 220–1, 286
biodiversity 63n. 18, 266, 301

birds 18, 22, 30, 32, 34, 50–1, 56, 73–4, 76, 143–4, 154, 168, 172, 296
blood 24, 32, 35–7, 39, 41, 54, 61, 66, 104, 134, 258n. 22

capitalism 176, 250, 251, 257, 267
carbon 227, 266, 289
Catholic, Roman 198, 217, 258, 302
chain of Being 155, 163, 208
chaos 42, 49–50, 58–9, 64–6, 71, 79–80, 97, 221, 250, 284
Christology 17, 19, 96, 100, 103–6, 125, 134, 136–7, 141–3, 149, 182, 189, 199–200, 208, 216, 225n. 4, 229, 234, 236, 237n. 19, 309–10
    cosmic 19, 96, **103–6**, 126, 235
    ecological 234–5
climate change 127, 223, 266, 285, 306
commandment(s) 37, 244, 256, 283, **286–7**
Cornwall Declaration 258, 260
cosmology, Christological *see* Christology, cosmic
countryside 283–94
covenant 5, 17, 42, 57, 85, 125, 181, **188–91**, 295, 305–6
    cosmic 17, **48–55**
    Noahic *see* Noah *in* Index of Names
creation
    doctrine of 59n. 12, **155–6**, 181, 184, 188, **189**, 190n. 12, 193, 199, 212–13, 228, 230, 232, 235, 273, 275, 308, 310
    ex nihilo, out of nothing 59, 111n. 11, 115, 117, 212–13, 231
    new 5, 92, 110, 111n. 11, 115, 117, 126, 223, 226–7, 233–4, 236, 238, 252–3, 259–60, 271, 277, 289
crucifixion 86, 104, 131, 134, 172, 199, 213, 223–4, 226, 276–7

day of the Lord 2, 108, 110, 118, 268
deep ecology 56
deification 211
Devil *see* Satan *in* Index of Names
diet 24, 36, 51, 98, 229
dispensationalism **251–62**
doctrinal constructs 10, 245, **301–11**
dominion 2–4, 6, 22, 25, 33–4, 57, 65n. 20, 80, 124–5, 128, **140–53, 154–6**, 163, 176, 178, 198, **229**, 246, 258–9, 305, 308 *see also radah*
dualism/dualistic 1–2, 101, 105n. 12, 116, 161, 297, 311

Earth Bible (as project) 6–8, 11–12, 55, 68, 82, 93–5, 106–7, 119, 243, 296, 298, 306n. 5, **307–9**, 312
  Team (as authors) 7, 8, 11, 94n. 1, 298, 307, 308, 312
ecclesiology 105, 171, 308–10
ecojustice 8, 94n. 1, 95, 127, 306, 309–10
  hermeneutic 7–8
  principles 7–8, **307–9**
ecological/environmental crisis 2, 21, 24–5, 27, 29, 31, 57n. 5, 123, 125–6, 127, 181, 196–8, 223–5, 227–8, 231, 234, 236–7, 244, 246, 260, 266–7, 269, 277–8, 281, 295, 305, 310
economics 22, 27–8, 42, 73, 176, 220, 223, 230, 213, 233, 249–50, 252, 258, 260, 262, 283, 288, 293, 297, 299, 302, 305–7, 309–10
ecosystems 27, 33, 59n. 13, 67n. 25, 94, 101n. 6, 308, 310
ecotheology, ecotheologians 2, 7, 10–11, 20, 35, 44, 105, 123–6, 127, 181–2, 188, 196n. 1, 197, 204, 208–9, 243–5, 305, 309
ecotopia 79
Eden(ic) 32, 34n. 3, 36, 163
ekpurōsis 102, 113, **115–16**
elements (of cosmos) 4, 39, 80, 104n. 10, 108, 110, **114–15**, 150, 171, 214, 246, 261, 268, 279
ends (*teloi*) 2, 24, 145, **154, 156–9, 162**, 259 *see also* teleology, *telos*
environmental ethic(s) 6, 16, 18–19, 47, 55, 116, 155–6, 181, 188n. 11, 194, 200n. 5, 296, 299
eschatology, eschaton 18–19, 77, 81, 83–5, 102, 104, 108–9, 112, 117–18, 167, 169, 177, 223, 225–7, 229, 231, 233–5, 237, 243–4, 246–50, **253–65, 266–82**, 296, 308, 310, 311

Evangelical Environmental Network 255–6, 257n. 19, 258
evangelicals, evangelicalism 3–4, 8, 104, 244, **247–62**
Evangelicals, National Association of **247n. 3**, 248n. 5
evolution(ary) 65n. 19, 126, 155, 166, 218, 232, 234–5, 256, 262, 273, 306
extinction 27, 223, 266

Fall 89–90, 116n. 17, 123, 125, 129–32, 135, 138, 144, 146–9, 152, 173–5, 177, 197n. 2, 211, 218–19, 256, 259
fall/redemption model 129, 132, 138
farm, farmer, farming 40, 47–8, 73–4, 81, 146, 150, 177, 193, 266, **286–90**, 293
Father (God) 75–7, 99, 106, 133, 136–7, 149, 167–8, 213, 217, 223, 226–7, 232–3, 238, 309–10
Fathers, Church 10, 104, 115, 124, 140, 143, 151–2, 213–16, 238 *see also* patristics
feminism, feminist 128, 267, 297–8, 304, 310
fig tree 47, 50, 72–3, 81
fire 4, 19, 54, 61, 64, 98, 102, **108–15**, 127, 161, 211, 246, 268
Fundamentalism, fundamentalist 3, 193n. 3, **247n. 3**, 251, 268, 272
futility 88–90

Gaia 101n. 6, 200
Galilee **70–4**, 80
genetic modification 277, 292
global warming 1, 127, 257, 266
glory, theology of 124, 172–3, 176, 179
GM *see* genetic modification
Gnosticism 87, 104n. 10, 115, 117, 130, 136n. 10, 213, 225, 270
God, doctrine of 171, 225
gospel(s) 18, **70–82**, 83–5, 93, 95, 99, 100, 104, 123, 129–30, 132–4, 138, 140–1, 167, 215, 227, 250, 269–71, 275–6, 283, 285, 289, 296
grace 5, 83–4, **91–3**, 129, 170, 172, 175, 184, 189, 200, 202, 208, 219, 221, 222, 251, 260, 273n. 4, 275, 278–9, 280, 284
  ecology of 200, 279
grass 32, 60, 65n. 20, 76, 145, 168, 220, 235n. 16
Green Bible, The **5–6**, 8, 12, 255, 263, 265, 296
groaning of creation 18, 83, **88–90**, 179, 256, 262

Hellenism, Hellenistic 19, 59n. 12, 85n. 1, 94–107
hermeneutic of retrieval 307
hermeneutics of suspicion 298, 304–5, 307
household 40, 310
human nature 28–30, 35, 144–6, 149–51, 216, 266

image of God/divine 2, 22, 124, 135–6, 138, 140, **143–52**, 160–2, 177, 199, 218, 229, 284
immanence of God/divine 59, 101, 102n. 7, 124, 166, 174, 178, 220, 231–3, 236, 308
impurity *see* purity
Incarnation, 124, 125, 134–8, 151–2, 206n. 8, 214, 216, 219, 226, 261, **275–7**, 303, 309
injustice 48, 275, 295, 297, 305, 307–8, 310
interconnectedness (of creation) 7, 18–19, 95, 102n. 7, 106, 124–5, 150, 152, 200n. 5, 247, 307–8
instrumentalism 23, 89, 181, 192, 251, 267
intrinsic worth/value of non-human creation 7, 19, 28, 307–8
Israelite(s) 16, 22, 29, 33, 35, 38–40, 43, 49, 58n. 8, 59, 80, 253

Jerusalem 78, 80, 110, 111n. 10, 133, 170, 271, 311
    New 248–9, 258
Jesus Seminar 270–2
Jubilee 230, 288, **289–91**
justice 8, 37, 48, 52, 54–5, 67, 135, 169, 229, 244, 254, 260, 262, 267, 270, 272, 275, 283, 284, 287, 293, 303, 307, 310 *see also* ecojustice
justification 83, 85, 92, 172–3, 176–9, 302, 304, 309

kabash 22, **25–6**, 28, 30, 192, 305 *see also* subdue
keep (as in *shamar*) 229, 244, 257, 285–7, 290–1, 306
Kingdom of God/Heaven 18, 70, **74–81**, 211, 213, 223n. 1, 227, 230–1, 260, 276, 302 *see also* peaceable kingdom

land 16, 22, 27, 29–30, 38, 40, 42, 43n. 17, 47–8, 50, 54, 58, 63, 65, 72, 75, 135, 144, 150, 230, 236n. 18, 244, 258n. 22, **285–91**, 293
Last Day(s) 168, 169, 175
Left Behind series 262

liberation 20, 85–7, 90, 111, 136n. 10, 170, 179, 232, 236, 237, 267, 280, 296–8, 302–4, 309
likeness (of God/the divine) 90, 131, 135, 137, 143–4, 146–7, 149–50, 159–60, 163, 214
liturgy, liturgical 54, 141, 197, 198n. 3, 211, 244, 273, **278–80**, 299
logos, logoi 101n. 6, 102n. 7, 103, 105, 133–5, 151, 202–3, 207–8, 212, 215, 217–20
Lord's prayer 77–8, 95, 175, 213

Manichees 142–3, 150
Manifest Destiny 249
meat 16, 23–6, 34, 36–7, 146, 150
Messiah 48, 80–1, 283
miracles 18, 75, 78, 221
mountain(s) 26, 50, 54, 65, 75, 111, 158, 166, 192, 197, 211, 215–16, 220, 279, 293, 296
multiply 22, 34–7, 43n. 17, 143
mutual custodianship, principle of 7, 306n. 5, 307–8

Nag Hammadi 155
narrative, biblical 129, 135, 246, 278, 301, 303
    creation 6, 21, 25, 123, 130, 184, 188, **190–1**
    Genesis 135, **189–91**
natural theology 125, 181–2, **184–6**, 188–9
naturalism 274, 276
new age 3, 85, 244, 252
new earth, new heaven 5, 19, 104, 108, 110, 112, 114, 117, 178, 198, 228, 235, 246, **249–53**, 268, 273

ocean(s) 59n. 13, 80, 159, 166, 168, 205 *see also* sea(s)
oikos 1n. 1, 105, 207, 233, 310
organic farming/husbandry 75, 289
Orthodoxy (Eastern) **211–22**

panentheism 126, 199, 232
pantheism 105, 199, 232
parables 71–2, 74–6, 78, 256
paradise, paradisal 79, 80n. 12, 81, 149, 213, 286
parousia 109–10, 111n. 10, 250, 270 *see also* Second Coming
patriarchy 99, 181, 267, 297, 305
patristics 103n. 9, 124, **140–53**, 213–15, 226, 306 *see also* Fathers, Church
peaceable kingdom 18, 51, 79–80, 249

perichoresis 126, 233, 237
personification 18, 57n. 4, 61, 86, 310
pets 40
pigs 73, 81
plant(s) 23, 27, 34–6, 56, 60–1, 73–4, 76, 78, 145, 147, 160, 163, 164, 166, 175, 213, 235, 262, 279, 288–9, 292 *see also* trees
politics 253, 283
pollution 29, 39, 44, 48–9, 198, 223, 248n. 5, 252–3, 258n. 22, 266
population 27, 267, 285, 290, 293 *see also* multiply
postmillennialism 243, 248–9
predation 26, 36, 163, 250
premillennialism 243, **249–51, 253–5, 257, 259–62**
priest, priestly 33–44, 49, 55, 148, 190, 192, 233
    of creation/nature, humanity as 125, 148–9, 216, 219, 305
progress 21, 215, 223, 224, 249, 251, 258, 274, 284, 306
Protestant 24, 104, 125, 129, 182, 183, 186, 188, 251
providence 76, 100, 116, 145, 154, 162, 218, 296, 308, 310
Puritans 24, 248, 268
purity/impurity 37–41, 96, 98, 117, 147

radah 22, **25–6**, 28, 30, 192, 305 *see also* dominion
Rapture 247n. 4, 251, 253, 262
reconciliation 117, 284, 303, 310
    of humanity with non-human creation/nature 27–8, 79 220
    of people to God 78, 106
    of whole creation with God 5, 19, 100, 103–4, 235, 255–6, 284
recycling 118, 127
redemption 18, 70, 83, 87, 90, 92, 123, 125, 129–30, 132, 135, 138, 175, 197, 211, 228, 230, 232–3, 235–7, 260–1, 280, 291, 296, 302, 308, 310–11
Religious Right 247n. 3
renewal, of the earth/present creation 5, 19, 75–9, 112, 117, 247, 255, 259–60 *see also* transformation
resurrection 90, 92, 130, 213, 219, 223, 276–7, 280–1, 284, 302, 309
righteousness 54, 84–6, 92–3, 110, 112, 116, 136, 268
Rio Earth Summit 196
river(s) 62n. 15, 192, 258, 296

Sabbath 30, 96, 98, 190, 230–1, 244, 280, 284, 290
Sabbath year 29, 230, 236n. 18, 290
sacraments 105–6, 167, 171, 219, 296, 298, 306, 309
sacred 44, 283, **306**
sacrifice *see* animal sacrifice
sanctuary 38–42, 44, 190
Satan *see* Index of Names
science/scientific 1, 2, 8, 21, 27, 31, 57–8, 63, 97, 101n. 6, 106, 115, 166, 182, 183, 187n. 5, 196n. 1, 197, 198, 204, 207n. 9, 208, 223–5, 229, 231, 232, 233, 237, 244, 249–50, 257–9, 272, 273–4, 276, 281, 284, 292
sea(s) 3, 22, 34–5, 51, 56, 61–4, 65n. 21, 71, 80, 135, 142, 143, 145, 154, 191, 221 *see also* ocean(s)
Second Coming 246n. 2, 249, 251, 253–4, 257, 269 *see also* parousia
secularization 24, 52, 60n. 14, 129, 189, 232, 247n. 3, 248n. 5, 258, 260–2, 283, 295, 297, 303–5, 309
servants, humans as servants of the rest of creation 125, 192–3, 229, 286
shalom 5, **53**, 117, 254
Sinai 48–9, 52, 85n. 2, 215
slave, slavery, enslavement 29–30, 78, 86–7, 91, 288, 290–1
social gospel 250
Son (of God) 85–6, 110, 132–6, 143, 149, 176, 189, 197, 217, 219, 223, 232, 277, 284, 286, 309
Sophia *see* wisdom *and* Index of Names
soul 98, 100, 103, 131, 146–9, 151–2, 171, 175, 211, 213, 215, 220–1, 225, 229, 236, 247, 280, 283
Spirit, cosmic 221, 231
    Holy 135, 142–3, 186, 198n. 3, 202, 223, 231–2, 234n. 13, 302, 306, 309
    in relation to creation 92, 135, 137, 142–3, 179, 202, 231–6, 272, 280, 306, 310
stage, creation as 123, 125, 129–30, 132, 189, **191–3**,
stars 64, 65, 98–9, 110, 114, 166, 167, 172, 177, 214, 268
stewards, stewardship 3–4, 6, 10, 15, 65n. 20, 111, 118, 257–8, 260–1, 299, 305–6, 308, 310
stoicheia 4, 114 *see also* elements
Stoicism 19, 95–6, **99–106**, 113–17

subdue, subduer 2, 22, 25, 34, 89, 143, 188, 229, 305 *see also kabash*
subjection of creation/animals (to futility) 88–90, 154
sun 62, 72, 75–6, 110, 114, 167–8, 172, 177, 178, 211, 268
supernatural 198, 203

technology 2, 21–3, 32, 57, 207n. 9, 220, 223–4, 258, 267, 289–90, 292, 306
teleology of creation 156–62
telos 156–7, 160, 163, 189 *see also* ends
temple in Jerusalem 17, 34n. 3, 37–40, 50, 53, 78, 81, 271
theophany, creation/nature as 125, 199–200, 207–8, 212, 215
till ('*abad*) 244, 248, **285–6**
Torah 96, 283, 288–9, 291–2, 294
transcendence 24, 59, 105, 125, 131, 174, 198, 202–3, 208, 232–4, 275, 308, 311
transfiguration 211–12, 215–16
transformation, of the earth/present creation 4–5, 19, 66, 79n. 10, 88, 92, 108, **110–15**, 116, 118, 176, 216, 226, 234, 247, 252, 255, 259, 262, 271 *see also* renewal

tree(s) 23, 30, 34, 47, 49–50, 62n. 16, 72–4, 78, 81, 168, 172, 177, 201, 213, 258, 262, 269, 296
Trinity 103n. 9, 105, 126, 143, 149, 167, 206n. 8, 208, 217, 223n. 1, 227, 229, **232–3**, **237–8**, 284, 309, 310

universalism, of God's promise to Abraham 85
urbanism, urbanization 48, 250, 285, 287

vegetarianism 23–8, 34, 41, 51, 146, 150, 191n. 13
voice, of non-human creation/earth/animals 7, 62, 192, 280, 298, 307–8
  principle of 7, **307–8**

web of life 17, 67, 94, 104n. 11, 237, 266
wilderness 3, 18, 59n. 13, 65, 67, 78–80, 243–4, 248–50, 258–9
wisdom 17, 55, **56–69**, 73, 75, 97–100, 135, 145, 147, 173, 211–14, 217, 221, 231, 233, 244, 266–7, 270, 281, 283–4, 292, 294, 295–6, 298, 310
Wise Use 258, 260
World Council of Churches 48, 313